Catholic Modern

Catholic Modern

THE CHALLENGE OF TOTALITARIANISM
AND THE REMAKING OF THE CHURCH

James Chappel

Harvard University Press

Cambridge, Massachusetts
London, England
2018

Library of Congress Cataloging-in-Publication Data
Names: Chappel, James, 1983– author.
Title: Catholic modern : the challenge of totalitarianism and the remaking of
the Church / James Chappel.
Description: Cambridge, Massachusetts : Harvard University Press, 2018. |
Includes bibliographical references and index.
Identifiers: LCCN 2017036660 | ISBN 9780674972100 (hardcover : alk. paper)
Subjects: LCSH: Catholic Church—Political activity—Europe. | Catholic
Church—History—20th century. | Church and social problems—Catholic Church. |
Church and social problems—Europe.
Classification: LCC BX1396 .C47 2018 | DDC 261.7088 /282—dc23
LC record available at https://lccn.loc.gov/2017036660

Contents

Catholic Modern

INTRODUCTION

The Catholic Church is the largest and most powerful religious organization in the world—indeed, one of the largest and most powerful organizations of any sort. For hundreds of millions of people, the Church provides guidance on the most intimate questions of sex and marriage, and the most public questions of political and economic order. In a twenty-first-century world of climate change, refugee flows, and bioethical controversy, it seems likely that it will remain as relevant as ever. The Church, after all, is not just a Sunday morning ritual, and it does not wield moral authority alone. It is an archipelago of institutions, from hospitals to shelters to schools, all of which are laboring to theorize and confront the endless challenges offered by a fallen world.

Whatever we might think of the Church's activism on these fronts, one thing at least is clear: it has embraced modernity. With few exceptions, Catholic thinkers and leaders take for granted that they are living in a religiously plural world, and that their task is to collaborate with others in the name of the common good. They no longer call for church-state fusion or the revocation of religious freedom. They invoke, instead, human rights. They are more likely, too, to agitate for civil rights and pursue Christian-Jewish dialogue than they are to revive the Church's long history of anti-Semitism.

Catholics have their own idea of what a just modernity should look like, of course. This often places them in tension with others over key issues such as confessional schools, abortion, and same-sex marriage. And yet even here, Catholics fight for those causes with modern means of electioneering, street activism, or government appointment. They do not, in other words, call for an overturning of the secular order and a reinstatement of the Church as the sole guardian of public and private morality. These aspects of Catholic engagement are so familiar to us that we can sometimes forget how recent they are. A devout Catholic in 1900, anywhere in the world, would have been shocked to learn that the Church would one day support values like these. Sometime between 1900 and the present, the Church became modern. This book is an attempt to explain how that happened.

This is not a story of gentle progress and humanist enlightenment, in which the Church slowly discovered the virtues of tolerance and cooperation. The process was faster, and darker, than that. This is a story of fascism, Communism, violence, and war. The Catholic transition to modernity was less a stately procession than a harried scramble, and a desperate bid for relevance in a Europe that was coming apart. An understanding of that process helps us to understand the nature, purpose, and trajectory of the Catholic Church. And it sheds new light on how religious communities grapple with that complex of institutions and practices that we call modern.

In order to avoid moralizing or simplification, it is necessary to be clear about how that much-abused word "modern" is to be defined. Any reasonable definition of modernity has multiple facets, and a mountain of scholarship in recent years has explored the Catholic engagement with many of them. Catholics participated in the birth of individualism, consumer culture, mass media, scientific rationality, nationalism, and many other phenomena that we might call modern. Catholics performed experiments, rode railroads, voted in parliamentary elections, and fought in mechanized wars, normally without sensing any contradiction between their actions and their faith.[1] This scholarship has done much to upset the familiar notion that the Church was a historical deadweight, blindly standing against progress. Historically speaking, it was just as frequently a source of innovation and transformation.

And yet historians have not explained how Catholics came to accept one of the most important features of modernity: the split between the public sphere of politics and the private sphere of religion. For most of its history, the Catholic Church held that the state and the economy should be governed according to religious principles. Of course, Catholics always recognized some kind of distinction between the realm of God and that of Caesar. All the same, they did want Catholicism to become the official religion of state, competing religions to be discriminated against or repressed, and Catholic moral teachings to pervade political affairs, economic relationships, and popular culture. This was accepted Catholic dogma for most of the history of the Church.[2] For many centuries there was nothing unusual about it.

Around the world, cosmological belief and structures of authority were tightly entwined, and while some imperial structures may have tolerated religious difference, there was little sense of a secular public sphere. Since the eighteenth century, this has started to change. As societies modernized, religious institutions supposedly disentangled themselves from political and economic ones. This is sometimes called "functional differentiation," or, in American parlance, the "separation of church and state." It is now a widely (though not universally) accepted principle of global governance that certain kinds of communities and discursive structures are coded as religious, that the state and economy should be distinguished from that field, and that the state should protect freedom of religion to ensure that citizens can pursue whichever religious identity they choose.

How did Catholics become modern in *this* sense? How, in other words, did they come to embrace religious pluralism, human rights, and the secular state as positive goods—and not only as brute facts to be grudgingly accepted? It is tempting to view the encounter between religion and modernity as a simple story in which religious people and institutions, perhaps through confrontation with the horrors of war or the wonders of science, come to realize the inherent goodness and virtue of church-state separation and tolerance. At this point, the story goes, faith becomes privatized, allowing the public sphere to emerge as a space of religious neutrality.[3] This account presumes what the philosopher Charles Taylor calls a "subtraction story" of modernity.[4] Once religious traditions vacate the public square, the modern condition of liberal tolerance and secular politics is supposedly left behind.

While there is something intuitive about this narrative, it has been widely criticized by scholars in recent years. It turns out that secular modernity is shot through with religiosity in all sorts of ways, and the religiously neutral public square seems to be a chimera. Any concrete form of secularity ends up privileging certain religious traditions, deemed sufficiently "modern," over others. Minority traditions, in turn, are often discriminated against, racialized, or both. In France, to take the classic example, public schools have banned the headscarves worn by many Muslim women, deeming them to be an intrusion of religion into a public space. Secularism, like the modern state that it heralds, empowers some communities while disenfranchising others. This does not mean that the principle is bankrupt, but it does mean that, like every other element of the modern condition, it is contested.[5]

Instead of studying secular modernity as a singular phenomenon, therefore, scholars have begun studying *varieties* of secularism, interrogating the different ways in which the divide between religion and politics can be conceptualized and administered. Many studies have focused on the modern state itself, whose claims to religious neutrality yield, paradoxically, an increasing embroilment with religion as the state finds itself called on to make legal decisions about what constitutes "religion" in the first place and how it should be regulated.[6] These works have tended to focus on the law—an approach that is often revealing but can be limiting, too, given that secular modernity is not a creation of constitutions and courtrooms alone.

This book will study secular modernity from the perspective of Catholics themselves, asking how believers reframe their teachings, aspirations, and institutions in the gothic space of the secular modern. It is far from the first to study modernity from the perspective of a religious tradition. Studies of European Muslims and Jews, for instance, have started to consider not only how Islam and Judaism are regulated by the state but also how Islamic and Jewish communities understand and negotiate the secular condition, in dialogue with partners across the continent and, indeed, the world. Studies of Christianity, too, have begun to move beyond the tired notion of church-state conflict and investigate the ways in which Christian communities have shaped the modern condition in their own image.[7] This scholarship seldom tracks abstract and explicit discussions of "modernity," often more interesting to scholars than to the faithful. It involves, instead, a focus on concrete political, economic, racial, and familial affairs to understand how religious communities generate novel forms of moral and political economy that are compatible with a modern framework.

In this spirit, *Catholic Modern* explores how, when, and why Catholics ceased fighting to overturn modernity and began agitating for Catholic forms *of* modernity—as they do today, and as they have historically done with tremendous consequences. Since the origin of the Church, Catholics have been divided over how to interpret their faith, and this is no less true in the age of modern Catholicism. In lieu of a singular and happy story of Church modernization, this book will track instead the emergence and historical agency of different forms of Catholic *modernism*. By modernism, I am not referring to the aesthetic tradition or to the specific theological crisis that rocked the Church in the early years of the twentieth century. I am referring instead to what historian Peter Fritzsche calls "the different ways that people and institutions have tinkered to make themselves secure in the dangerous zones of a constantly changing world."[8] If secular modernity is a state-sanctioned condition of religious freedom, religious modernism can be understood as the set of tactics that religious communities use to conceptualize, mobilize within, and shape that modern settlement. In other words, the "privatization" of religion in a modern setting seldom leads to depoliticization but rather leads toward new forms of public intervention that can be legitimated in the name of that sacred private sphere.

"Modern" is just one half of the book's title. The "Catholic" half requires clarification, too. The Catholic Church is a challenging object of study. It is almost impossible to write a general history of the Church, an unspeakably complex and profoundly global institution. Any account by necessity must highlight certain regions, ideas, and protagonists at the expense of others. *Catholic Modern* will pursue a transnational intellectual history of the Catholic laity from the 1920s to the 1960s, focusing on France, Germany, and Austria. Each element of this methodology requires a defense, and although each is rooted in an ongoing trend in Catholic scholarship, each comes with costs as well.

The first problem for the student of Catholicism is a distressingly basic one. What is our object of analysis? What is the Church? Catholics themselves differ on this issue, which doctrinally has evolved over time. The historian, thankfully, can sidestep the theological question and focus on the Church as it exists and clamors for power in this vale of tears. Historical studies of the Church have tended to focus on the leadership: bishops, the pope, and the dense network of personal ties and power struggles that crisscross the marbled halls of the Vatican. Thanks largely to the opening of new archives, there has been an outpouring of new research on these figures.[9] And yet there has been, perhaps, an overemphasis on them. Popes and bishops provide convenient ciphers for the Church as a whole but do not necessarily provide the best means of understanding it, any more than presidents and senators provide the royal road to an understanding of American politics. The power of popes, like that of presidents, evolves over time. And the power of popes, like that of presidents, is seldom as great as it seems. Papal teachings often did not even reach the laity, and before John Paul II's reign (1978–2005), the pope was nothing like the media icon that we know today. The clergy are not the key to Catholic modernism, either. While they took on important social and political roles in the nineteenth century, historians have shown that they became less important guides over the course of the twentieth century as they assumed more pastoral roles and left the dangerous work of politics to others.[10]

In lieu of a tight focus on Church leadership, I will focus, as many scholars have done in recent years, on the Catholic laity: Catholic believers who are not part of the Church's formal hierarchy. To a surprising degree, and one that increased over the course of the twentieth century, lay Catholics in different national and regional contexts defined for themselves what it would mean to be Catholic—and, specifically, how the faith would translate into social and political life. They founded their own newspapers, journals, and institutions. They often required the consent of the hierarchy, and the Vatican retained the ability to shut down experiments that seemed to go too far (as it did several times). But beyond that blunt tool, Rome had surprisingly little ability to shape the evolution of Catholic modernism on the ground. While the interventions of official Church leadership will be discussed, of course, the focus will be on their impact on Catholic culture writ large, not on their status as official representatives of the Church. Papal encyclicals, for instance, will be read not simply as evidence of the "Church's" position on an issue but as contested documents that were received in different ways at different times by the laity.

The second problem is methodological: *how* should one study the Church? *Catholic Modern* will use the tools of intellectual history, reading texts carefully to understand how the dominant conception of the faith evolved in response to external events. Intellectual history is uniquely suited to tracking the formation and evolution of Catholic modernism. The Catholic Church, after all, fundamentally exercises power through the circulation of ideas (hence its insistent focus on schooling). Many of those ideas concern the nature of God or the universe, of course, but those strictly theological ideas are not the only, or even most important, subject of Catholic intellectual history.[11] Catholic modernism was often in dialogue with high theology, but the two should not be confused. For one thing, the former involved concrete issues such as social welfare policy that were often quite distinct from the epistemological and metaphysical concerns of leading theologians. For another, Catholic modernism did not fundamentally evolve, as theology did, through argument and counterargument. Intellectual change at any scale does not happen with the publication of one book, or the crafting of an elegant argument, but through the sheer force of repetition as certain concepts or ideas gain traction in multiple venues over time. There are fewer titanic or indispensable figures in the development of Catholic modernism than in the development of Catholic theology. It can best be tracked, therefore, by collecting the widest possible source base: books, magazines, and newspapers, above all, but also private correspondence and the internal records of Catholic trade unions, family organizations, and political parties. I will focus on about fifteen important figures because this lends coherence and stability to the narrative, and also because a biographical approach allows us to see in detail how certain new concepts or strategies emerged as plausible responses in a particular context. The trajectories of these individuals, though, will always be rooted in a broader universe of print culture. They were chosen less because they were of special personal significance, although some were, than because their life and work crystallize a wider transformation in the Catholic public sphere.

The capaciousness of the source base forestalls some familiar objections to intellectual history as a method. Many critics have pointed out that intellectual history fundamentally concerns elites. It is undeniable that the subjects of this book were well-educated elites, in some sense, but they appear in this book as representatives and shapers of broader Catholic publics rather than as lonely geniuses. Like the Church itself, therefore, the protagonists of our story are diverse, including women, converted Jews, and African poets.[12] Intellectual historians are sometimes faulted, too, for neglecting issues of gender and the family, which are often not leading concerns of the canonical (male) thinkers. In this case, precisely the opposite is true. The extant literature on twentieth-century Catholicism has paid surprisingly little attention to gender, *despite* the fact that Catholic writers were transparently obsessed with the theme.[13] Many scholars have simply assumed that Catholics cared about the family because that is something that Catholics do. Intellectual history allows us to see that the truth is far more complex. Interest in the family, and conceptualizations of it, evolves over time, in ways that are utterly central to the different forms of Catholic modernism this book will unpack.

The third problem for the scholar of Catholicism is scope. How wide a net should the historian cast? Catholicism lives in the inner torments of the individual soul, and historians have used individual lives in highly illuminating ways. It lives, too, in ocean-spanning networks of exchange, and others have been just as insightful in using the tools of imperial or global history.[14] Threading the needle between the two, this book will follow the lead of historians who have suggested that Catholic intellectual history is best investigated transnationally—that is, by focusing on several countries together.[15] Texts and people flowed freely across borders, creating not a placeless sphere of "global" thinking but a set of interconnected, transnational networks of Catholic thought.

This book will focus on Europe, which until quite recently was the demographic and intellectual heartland of the Church (in 1910, two-thirds of all Catholics lived there). Within Europe, the book will dwell on France, Germany, and Austria, as well as the émigrés who left their borders but were shaped by—and continued to shape—their Catholic thought. Other samples, of course, would yield a different account. A focus on Italy, Spain, and Portugal would portray a rather different and more conservative Church, while an analysis that extended to Eastern Europe, Latin America, or Africa would differ dramatically from this one, too. While this should be kept in mind, it does not undercut the importance of the chosen sample. For one thing, evidence about other Catholic countries—which will be cited as appropriate—indicates that the general story traced in *Catholic Modern* was replicated elsewhere, even if it did not happen in just the same way or at the same time. For another, the ideas birthed in France, Germany, and Austria are the ones that ended up becoming dominant in the Church. Until the 1960s, intellectual innovation in the Church tended to come from Europe, and especially from these three countries. American Catholics, for instance, were more invested in the network traced here than in its Mediterranean counterpart. The Vatican itself tended to draw on experts from these three countries to prepare its own social and political doctrine, helping it to spread to the global Church.[16]

By covering such a large territory, local nuances will inevitably be downplayed. The analysis will respect the major differences between the three countries, and it is rooted in the capacious specialist literature on each of them. Each chapter except the first will focus on one figure from each country, in some detail, in order to firmly place intellectual developments into their local contexts. The purpose of these local stories is not to create three separate stories for three different countries, because one of the most significant findings of this book is that the development of Catholic modernism did not take place in national spaces. Instead, the point is to elucidate the ways in which intellectual transformation emerged from a specific constellation of problems and possibilities, some of which were more regional or local than they were national. And however parochial the concerns of our protagonists might have been, their response to them both drew from and contributed to the transnational spaces of intellectual exchange in which Catholic modernism was mainly forged. To take one example from Chapter 2: when a German Catholic economist named Theodor Brauer sought Catholic solutions to the Great Depression, he looked to Catholic texts and concepts from across Europe, which involved both reading and physical travel. Even though his concerns, as an individual agent, were primarily German, his evolving theories drew on an emerging European consensus among Catholic economists. His texts and political activities, in turn, contributed to that consensus. He lectured about his new ideas in three languages across Europe, one of his disciples played an important role in developing the Austrian constitution, and Brauer eventually brought his ideas to an American audience once he emigrated.

Given this understanding of Catholicism, and this understanding of the modern, the question posed by this book can now be posed more specifically: how and when did Catholic intellectuals in France, Germany, and Austria abandon their opposition to modernity and what kinds of modernist strategies did they forge in its place? The test of any methodological apparatus, and any research question, is whether it allows us to see something that we could not before. My contention is that this approach shows us something quite remarkable and should lead us to question accepted narratives about what happened to the Church over the course of the twentieth century.

To understand the revision this book suggests, it helps to review the accepted story. This is far from the first book to notice a major shift in European Catholic history between, roughly speaking, 1890 and 1970, nor is it the first one to try and unpack the Church's encounter with modernity. Paying more attention to institutions and elites than to texts and concepts, a number of social and political historians have arrived at a consensus narrative that looks something like the following. Beginning in the late nineteenth century, Catholics began to engage with the modern world by founding Catholic parliamentary parties, trade unions, farmers' movements, and more. Together, these institutions pursued a social Catholic vision that promised a third way between socialism and free-market capitalism. While they may have been theoretically opposed to modernity, in practice they led Catholics toward reformist engagement with the non-Catholic world. These modernizing trends seemed to be triumphing around 1900, but they soon encountered a great deal of resistance from reactionary, medievalist opponents—a conflict that reached a head in the 1930s, when the conservative branch of the Church led the flock into a series of disastrous alliances with fascist leaders. The more modernizing strands of the faith survived these dark years in exile and in the resistance. After World War II, antimodern Catholicism was no longer an option. Even if the occupying armies would have allowed it, the close-knit Catholic milieu in which such ideals had flourished quickly fell prey to the dislocations of war and the onset of mass consumer society. This allowed the long-gestating modernizing trends in Catholic thought and practice to emerge triumphant at the heart of Christian Democratic parties, whose "third way" approach to economic and social questions derive directly from the long Catholic social tradition. At the Second Vatican Council (Vatican II; 1962–1965), these modernist trends finally made their way into official Catholic dogma.[17]

This argument has much to recommend it, and the scholars pursuing it have done a great service by reintegrating the Church into modern European history. For all of its proponents' penetrating analyses of particular institutions or national trajectories, however, there is something unsatisfying about the narrative as a whole. The biggest clue is that it cannot easily account for the experience of the 1930s, when so many Catholics plumped for some variant of authoritarianism or fascism. Most books on the history of the Church between 1890 and 1970 spend only a few pages on the 1930s, which survive as an ironic or tragic tale but not one analytically central to the transformation of the Church. Meanwhile, studies of the Catholic 1930s, of which there are many, tend to be more interested in questions of collaboration or guilt than in the evolution of the Church over a longer term. This is problematic, because the extant scholarship on the Catholic 1930s, like that on the 1930s more generally, indicates that the era was utterly transformative. Scholars of theology proper certainly pay attention to the period, when the great innovations of *nouvelle théologie* were made, novel forms of Catholic antiracism were pioneered, and the groundwork for Vatican II was laid. Scholars of the Vatican, too, recognize that the institution evolved dramatically in those years. Vatican City as a legal entity was founded in 1929, while the urban infrastructure that we know today largely date from the 1930s. As one historian of the papacy has argued, in that decade "the Vatican's grappling with totalitarian regimes, consisting as it did of moments of convergence and others of conflict, ultimately modified in a profound way the theological and pastoral apparatus of the Church; it would never be the same again."[18]

While scholars in many specific areas of Church history have amply documented the transformative impact of the 1930s, these threads have not been gathered together. The major contention of the first half of this book is that the experience of that decade—the real and imagined encounter between Catholicism and totalitarianism—heralded the Church's decisive conceptual transition to modernity. In the 1930s, in short, the Church transitioned from an *antimodern* institution into an *antitotalitarian* one. The two stances had a great deal in common, to be sure. Many doctrines, sensibilities, and strategies remained essentially intact. And yet many did not, and those that did were articulated and framed in a new way. In the antimodern years, Catholics sought to overturn the church-state separation introduced by the French Revolution. In the antitotalitarian years, in contrast, Catholics gave up on contesting the modern settlement and began to adopt the various modernist strategies that they would pursue for the remainder of the century. Faced with totalitarianism of the right (fascism) and totalitarianism of the left (Stalinism), Catholics across Europe engaged in a robust rethinking of what it meant to be Catholic and what role the Church should play in the world. They did so not because they learned humanist lessons from violence but because they imagined that European history had taken a decisive turn and that Europe's Church would have to take one, too. Through a confrontation with totalitarianism, the Church became modern.

To put that experience into relief, Chapter 1 will explore the 1920s in order to contest the reigning presumption that the period was one of Catholic modernization, rudely interrupted by the horrors of the 1930s. To be sure, 1920s Catholics pragmatically and sporadically worked with non-Catholics toward social or cultural goals, as they had for decades (and even centuries). This collaboration was always shaky, however, because it was not based in any theoretical or conceptual conversion to Catholic modernism. It was based, instead, on pragmatism, which is not the same thing and which proved far less effective at mobilizing Catholic support for modern politics. Catholics in the 1920s, that is, still had no particular reason to lend their support to modern politics because they dwelt in a Catholic public sphere that was almost entirely committed to uprooting the modern order altogether. Intellectuals, journalists, and Church leaders in the 1920s tended to reprise the most antimodern elements of Catholic social teaching as it had been formed in the nineteenth century: a vision in which the good life was structured by a dense web of Catholic institutions, supplanting the secular modern state and the secular modern economy. The more "modern" voices, already on the defensive after the vicious modernist controversies of the early twentieth century, were marginalized even further by the horror of World War I—a war that, from the Catholic perspective, proved once again that modern and secular states were turning God's continent into a slaughterhouse.

In the 1920s, Catholic antimodernism had an air of plausibility about it, even if there was disagreement as to its proper shape. Given the chaotic politics of the era, it was far from clear that the secular nation-state was the only horizon of political possibility. In the 1930s, this changed. The two great problems of the era, from the Catholic perspective, were the Great Depression and the threat of international Communism. Neither of these could be met by dreaming of vanished Catholic empires, which clearly had no place in an era of furious state building and rearmament.

In the 1930s, therefore, the framing of Catholic debate shifted from "How can we overcome the secular state?" to "How can we shape secular modernity to our specifications?" This new question was answered in various ways, but the general transition from antimodernism to modernism can be tracked by the emergence of a new set of keywords: antitotalitarianism, dignity, religious freedom, and human rights. This discourse presumed the disentanglement of religion and politics, and of the private sphere from the public. That is, each keyword presumed the demarcation of a sacred private sphere, which should remain autonomous from state institutions. Catholics had been reticent to use terms like these in the past, because they seemed related to the creeping individualism that struck them as the core problem of modernity. In the 1930s, though, Catholics were less worried about individualism than they were about totalitarianism—a political system that threatened total control over the individual. In this new conceptual space, doctrines of individual rights emerged as a potential solution.

The importance of totalitarianism in Catholic intellectual history is that it was interpreted by Catholics at the time as a pathological form of modernity—but not the only one. As Catholics sought an effective alternative to totalitarianism, they came to believe modernist arrangements were the only avenue for Catholic survival. Historians are now rather skeptical that there is such a thing as "totalitarianism," a theory that in its most prominent guise argues that Nazism and Bolshevism were genetically similar in that both sought and largely achieved total domination of their subjects. Nonetheless, the *idea* of totalitarianism was of central importance to 1930s Catholics, who played a signal role in crafting the theory in the first place.[19]

The history of the Church is always polyvalent, and in the crucial decade of the 1930s Catholics forged two fundamentally opposed modernist and antitotalitarian strategies (though it is important to keep in mind that we are investigating conceptual frameworks, and that in reality many believers could and did tack between the two or combine them in some way). The Catholic take on the European 1930s was that liberal democracy was probably dead, and that therefore the Church would have to make common cause with either some variant of fascist authoritarianism or some variant of Marxist socialism. They were under no illusions that either fascism or Communism was inspired by Catholic teachings, and therefore they tended to avoid uncritical celebration of either. The more pressing debate was over which one posed the greater danger, and which one might plausibly be reformed in a Church-friendly direction. The two forms of Catholic modernism, therefore, were not fascist and Communist but *antifascist* and *anti-Communist*. These might sound like negative, limp ideologies, but they were not: over the course of the twentieth century, each of them has been remarkably generative in its own right.

To trace this debate, Chapters 2 and 3 will lay out the anti-Communist and antifascist forms of Catholic modernism, respectively. The strategy I'll adopt to do so is straightforward. If the central fact of any religious modernism is that it accepts a relegation of religion to the private sphere, the analysis of that religious modernism can begin by exploring how that sphere is defined. How, in other words, did the faithful conceptualize the "private" zone to which religion is supposedly relegated? While some scholars have tracked the various ways in which religion *deprivatizes* and enters the public sphere, this book will ask instead about the various ways in which religion *privatizes*, and the various forms of public intervention that this can authorize. As scholars from multiple disciplines have argued in recent decades, the very notion of the "private sphere" is heavily contested, and the ways in which the faithful define it can have enormous repercussions for the sorts of politics they pursue.[20]

Most Catholics in the 1930s pursued a strategy that I'll call "paternal Catholic modernism," which was linked with the soaring importance of anti-Communism in Catholic circles (Chapter 2). In this view, the private sphere of religious jurisdiction was constituted primarily by the reproductive family (by "paternal," I'm referring to both the gendered and the hierarchical components of this particular family conception). Catholics had, of course, always been invested in family ethics, but only in the 1930s did the protection of the private sphere of family life become the central focus of Catholic social thinking. Like many other religious communities grappling with modernity, they came to reason that society could not veer too far off course if the family remained under religious control.[21] This focus on the family counseled Catholics not to give up their claims on the economy or the state but rather to reframe them around the reproductive family, defined as a unit made up of a working father and a caring mother who had multiple children and followed clerical guidance in their sexual lives. While previous Catholic economic and political theories had counseled sweeping revolution, paternal Catholic modernism did nothing of the sort. It tended to privilege private property rights, economic corporatism, family welfare programs, conservative family legislation, and a preference for order and stability. Most importantly, paternal Catholic modernism allowed Catholics to accept the legitimacy and authority of the secular state, something that had previously been controversial in Catholic circles.

Paternal Catholic modernism was certainly not a form of fascism, and in many cases it even legitimated critiques of fascist regimes when they usurped Catholic control over education, youth movements, marriage legislation, or divorce. It seldom, however, legitimated a principled antifascism, and it was far more committed to anti-Communism. As such, it served as an important intellectual rationale for Catholic collaboration with fascist or authoritarian regimes (in our sample, Nazi Germany, authoritarian Austria, and Vichy France). After all, even if they uprooted many Catholic institutions, they also promised to defend the family against Communist enemies. Catholic family ethics were more compatible with nationalism than any other element of the tradition (both Catholic ethicists and nationalists prioritized high birthrates, if for different reasons). A focus on the family also helped Catholics to legitimate modern forms of anti-Semitism, which coded the Jews as Communist-allied enemies of the Catholic family. Indeed, paternal Catholics increasingly claimed that their allegiance was to a cultural and legal community known as "the West," which included authoritarian and fascist regimes in a broad alliance against Communism—and often Judaism, too (Catholics often linked the two).

While this form of Catholic modernism was the mainstream in the 1930s, it was contested, too. Catholic antifascism also existed, and it emerged from a different conceptual formation altogether that I'll call "fraternal Catholic modernism" (Chapter 3). Whereas mainstream Catholics conceptualized the private sphere as a space for reproductive and patriarchal families, the antifascist minority saw it as a site of cooperation and activism, symbolized less by paternal authority than by brotherly solidarity. They began with an alternative conception of the family unit itself, reminding their peers that the marriage, not the multigenerational family, is the only sacramental community that Catholics encounter outside of the Church. And the marriage, they insisted, was structured not by law and obedience but by love, solidarity, and sexuality. Childbirth was the natural goal of marriage, but not its only or even primary purpose. This decentering of sexual ethics and reproduction allowed for an alternative conception of the private sphere as a whole—less a site for law and obedience, more one for nonhierarchical collaboration and solidarity among equals of different faiths. Fraternal Catholics therefore imagined a private sphere made up of a robust civil society, including most notably trade unions, youth movements, and a vibrant press. The fraternal understanding of the private sphere led also to novel accounts of the public sphere that emphasized the role of trade union activism in the economy, and interfaith civic activism in the pluralist public sphere.

This understanding of Catholic social ethics was in some ways closer than its mainstream competitor to the antistatist and anticapitalist elements of the nineteenth-century Catholic tradition. Most importantly, fraternal modernists were unwilling to place their faith in the nation-state as the guardian of social virtue. Instead of looking to a sacral state, as their forebears might have done, they looked to a robust civil society—a sensibility that brought them close, in some ways, to contemporary socialists. Fraternal modernists were certainly not committed Communists, and they almost uniformly repeated the mainstream condemnations of Marxist metaphysics and Marxist accounts of class struggle. Nonetheless, just as paternal modernists sought ways to work with and reform various fascist traditions, their fraternal antagonists did the same with socialist ones. Socialism, they hoped, could mean something other than doctrinaire Stalinism. Intellectually, they engaged with the recently discovered writings of the young Karl Marx, which they saw as more "humanist" and less anticlerical. Politically, they were less enthused by the Soviet Union than by the Popular Front, which promised to gather together antifascist forces under one socialist, revolutionary, but not totalitarian banner. This novel evaluation of the socialist tradition counseled an influential school of Catholic antiracism. Fraternal modernists were not concerned with the putatively

"Jewish" roots of socialism, which they preferred to see as a school of thought inflamed by misdirected Christian virtues. And even while they still hoped that the Jews would eventually convert, they did not believe that the clumsy tools of the secular state should intervene in the fundamentally mysterious and theological Jewish question.

To recap: the first half of the book (Chapters 1–3), covers the roughly twenty-five-year period between the end of World War I and the end of World War II. It argues that the encounter with totalitarianism, as ideology and reality, pushed Catholics to develop two basic forms of Catholic modernism. Each was designed to forge Catholic forms of modernity rather than overcome it altogether. The modernization of the Church, therefore, should not be understood as a simple process of conversion toward tolerance or humanist norms in response to the horrors of war. It should, instead, be understood as a fractured process in which various elements of the tradition were updated for a new context, in response to new kinds of challenges that rendered the old antimodernism implausible.

If the first half of the book is about the forging of Catholic modernism, the second half is about its survival, impact, and transformation in the twenty-five years after World War II came to a close. In many ways, World War II was a caesura in European history—but not when it came to the intellectual history of the Church (a fact that is often missed because so many studies of the Church take 1945 as either a starting point or an endpoint). The basic strategies that were forged in the 1930s survived across the chasm of the war years. Their skirmishes and their alliances helped the Church to make peace with, and even shape, the democratic and consumerist form of modernity that emerged from the war. These chapters show that the modernization of a religious tradition is not a one-time phenomenon but rather an ongoing and continuously contested process—and one that can have tremendous consequences for both those inside and those outside that tradition.

In the late 1940s (Chapter 4), Catholics emerged with considerable strength. The Church was one of the few institutions to survive the war with its basic structure and moral standing relatively intact (this latter feat required a significant public relations effort to convince believers and nonbelievers alike that the Church had been a beacon of antifascist resistance). Christian Democratic parties, founded and led primarily by Catholics, began to emerge across Europe and began to amass considerable authority, winning almost every election held between 1945 and 1950 in Central or

Western Europe. At the heart of those new parties, and elsewhere too, Catholics vigorously debated the strategies they should pursue. In the process, the old debates between paternal and fraternal modernism reemerged. There was surprisingly little conceptual or strategic novelty in these years. No major new concepts or political thinkers emerged in Catholic circles, and Christian Democratic leaders too tended to be geriatric veterans of Catholic thought and action. Almost everywhere in Europe, Catholics had participated happily in parliamentary life for decades, so that was not new. The specific keywords of Christian Democratic political discourse were all relics of the 1930s (antitotalitarianism, human rights, and dignity). Even interconfessionalism was a holdover from that era, although it had normally been put to authoritarian ends (the National Socialist Party, not the Christian Democratic Union, was the first party in German history to garner mass support from both Catholics and Protestants).

The war, somewhat surprisingly, did not effectively alter the balance of power between the two forms of Catholic modernism. After a series of dramatic clashes, the mainstream anti-Communism of paternal modernism reasserted its prominence over the marginal antifascism of its opponents. Antifascists gamely tried to convince postwar Catholics to confront their anti-Semitic legacy while reviving the anticapitalist and antistatist elements of the tradition. Generally speaking, they failed, falling prey to their own long-standing marginality, the hostility of the Vatican, and the unfriendly climes of the early Cold War. By 1950, Christian Democratic parties and mainstream Catholic culture had firmly committed themselves to anti-Communism, family values, the "Defense of the West," and the reconstituted nation-state as central values. This is an important point, one that has seldom been recognized before, and one with possible resonance outside Catholic history. It has long been presumed that Christian Democracy involved the final victory of the modernizing, antifascist currents in the Church. The evidence for this position is slim. In the late 1940s, when Christian Democratic parties were born, it was the mainstream, anti-Communist elements of the tradition that predominated—the same ones that had, just a few years previously, legitimated collaboration with authoritarianism.

Over the course of the long 1950s (roughly speaking, 1949–1965), however, something surprising happened, and something almost without precedent in Catholic history: Catholics reached a rough working agreement about the role that their faith should play in the world (Chapter 5). The conditions were ripe for such a consensus. The threat of totalitarianism was in abeyance, while the sexual revolution that would throw the Church into such disarray had not yet arrived. Economic growth, often a spur to social harmony, was stratospheric, while socialist parties were becoming less anticlerical. The memory of the war was still fresh, and Europeans were clamoring for ideologies of compromise and stability. In these propitious conditions, Christian Democratic modernism was born.

In the 1950s, Christian Democratic parties drew on a novel articulation of Catholic modernism that rocketed through the intertwined circles of Christian Democratic politics and Catholic popular culture (while Catholics never made Christian Democracy alone, they took the leading role in every case). Normally, Christian Democracy is viewed either as the fruit of a long-term process of Catholic modernization or as the contingent result of major shifts in the political and intellectual context of postwar Europe. Chapter 5 makes a novel but commonsense argument: the Catholic modernism of the 1950s, and therefore the leading component of Christian Democracy, developed organically from its predecessors in the 1930s and 1940s. In the 1930s, Catholics had developed new forms of Catholic modernism, while in the 1940s the paternal form secured its dominance over the still-marginal fraternal one. The Christian Democracy of the long 1950s was a logical next step. It drew on both the paternal and the fraternal strategies of the past, creating a consensus form of Catholic modernism that, while still hewing closer to the former than the latter, made space for them both. The genius of the new strategy was twofold. First, it brought together the two wings of the Church. While accounts of Christian Democracy tend to emphasize its success at drawing together Catholics and Protestants, its success at drawing together different sorts of Catholics was in some ways more important and unprecedented. Second, it helped Catholics to legitimate, accept, and reform the consumer revolution that was sweeping the continent.

Christian Democratic modernism essentially adopted the "family values" framework of the paternal modernists, but it did so with an evolved understanding of what the private sphere of the family represented. In lieu of a traditional account that emphasized procreation, Christian Democrats understood the family to be a space of consumption, love, and even sexual satisfaction. This account of the "consuming family" allowed Catholics to square their long-standing suspicion of consumer culture and economic growth with the realities of life in the consumerist 1950s. They remained as critical as ever of consumerism or materialism, understood as the hedonist individual's pursuit of her own pleasure at the expense of her community. But by imagining the agent of consumption to be the happy family instead of the depraved individual, Catholics were able to legitimate the new Europe of prosperity, consumption, and economic growth.

This novel figure of the consuming family in the private sphere legitimated novel Christian Democratic accounts of the public sphere, too. Much of the Christian Democratic agenda was familiar from the 1930s, and even earlier: Catholics wanted to use the tools of the state to protect the consuming family from such supposed vices as licentious media, divorce, homosexuality, and contraception. Christian Democrat modernists were as rigid as ever when it came to those issues, about which fraternal and paternal modernists generally agreed (even if they disagreed about the proper emphasis to place on them). But when it came to other questions of economic and political governance, Christian Democratic modernists pioneered new compromise solutions in the name of the happy and prosperous family. The family needed social welfare, especially to recover from the war, so Christian Democrats labored to create the family-friendly welfare states for which Europe became famous (one that incentivized women to stay at home but was significantly less punitive and natalist than its 1930s predecessor). The family also needed some way to protect the dignity of workers and to ensure that families had enough money to benefit from economic growth. To that end, Christian Democrats supported free trade unionism and various forms of workers' management that promised to provide some measure of social justice and equality without recourse to class struggle or aggressive state management (of the sort that some Catholics had championed in the 1930s). Above all, the family required economic growth. In Catholic circles, as outside them, growth became a litmus test of political legitimacy for the first time, and from the mid-1950s onward, Christian Democrats put organized and regulated growth at the center of their political agenda.

By 1960, Catholic intellectuals had more or less agreed on a particular social vision that was centered on family-friendly economic development, sexual conservatism, a generous welfare state, and free trade union activity. This vision animated the Christian Democratic parties that played such a crucial role in European reconstruction and that shored up the right wing of the new democracies. This was more of a consensus than Catholics had reached since the French Revolution, and its impact was felt in the global Church, too. The 1960s saw a sea change in official doctrine about social and economic affairs, and in broad outlines the new teachings followed the principles of Christian Democratic modernism. The encyclicals of the 1960s (notably, *Mater et magistra* [1961] and *Humanae vitae* [1968]) and the many new teachings announced by Vatican II reproduced several of its central elements, notably its commitment to conservative family values and economic development.

This comity, predicated on a favorable sociopolitical climate and a particularly chastened reading of the Catholic social tradition, proved short lived. In the late 1960s, the culture of consensus and concord that nourished Christian Democracy began to fray. The movement survived, of course, although it entered a relatively weak period and was reborn with a program relying more on fiscal and cultural conservatism than on a novel articulation of Catholic modernism. The collapse of Christian Democratic modernism led to the revival of the old conflicts of the 1930s and 1940s, as fraternal and paternal modernism emerged once again. Paternal modernism gained new life thanks to the sexual revolution of the late 1960s, and especially the threat of legalized abortion. As the broad consensus on these matters fell apart, Catholics organized with great success around family matters, reasoning that the healthy family is the primary building block of the healthy society. The sphere of family and reproduction, they insist, falls under religious jurisdiction, and Church officials have in many countries been able to exercise direct influence over policies on abortion, contraception, and stem cell research.[22] This is the paradigmatic approach of paternal modernism, one shared by Pope John Paul II, and one that has enormously shaped the political intervention of the Church since the late 1960s.

Since the revival of paternal modernism is so well known, I will forgo a direct analysis of it and instead conclude with an analysis of its fraternal antagonist (Chapter 6). Just as the fraternal modernists of the 1930s tried to forge a Catholic form of antifascism, their successors did the same with the various countercultural and emancipatory movements that rocked European societies in the 1960s. The two were integrally related. For one thing, many of the leading lights of the 1960s were veterans of 1930s antifascism. For another, much of the antiauthoritarian energy in the 1960s Church stemmed from historical revelations about Catholic complicity with fascism and the Holocaust. Most importantly, the fraternal modernists of the two periods shared an intellectual framework and a desire to update the antistatism and anticapitalism of the tradition for a modern world.

Catholic radicals of the 1960s critiqued the mainstream account of the private sphere through their resistance to *Humanae vitae,* which announced the Church's total opposition to contraception and led to the most explosive mobilization of the Catholic laity against the official Church in modern history. As in the 1930s, this rejection of mainstream family ideology paved the way for a more robust account of the private sphere, focusing on trade unions and student activist groups rather than reproductive ethics. And, as in the 1930s, this more capacious understanding of the private sphere led to more revolutionary accounts of the public sphere, too. Firmly rejecting the Christian Democratic consensus, a new generation of Catholic intellectuals and activists pioneered searching forms of Catholic socialism and revived forms of political theology that refused to enshrine economic development or family ethics at their core. In place of a Catholicism for the home, they theorized a Catholicism for the streets.

Both of these strategies, which continued to do battle and to forge compromise in the decades after 1970, drew from distinctly Catholic responses to modernity. This is not to say that a history of Catholic thought in three countries over about fifty years reveals the essential nature of the Catholic Church as a whole. And yet an understanding of these crucial countries, in these crucial years, does help us to see what kinds of resources the Catholic tradition has for political and social action, and how they have been mobilized in the past. Even and especially for non-Catholics, this story is an important one. The Church is poised to play just as pivotal a role in the twenty-first century as it did in the twentieth. The shape of Catholic engagement will matter, and if the history in this book teaches anything, it is that this shape is malleable. Whatever stories the Church might tell about itself, it is in reality a socially embedded institution, responsive to overtures from non-Catholics, to social transformations, and to pressures from the laity. It has, in short, a history—and one that will inform its future.

‎‎1‎

CATHOLIC ANTIMODERN,

1920–1929

> But our homeland is in heaven.
> —PHILIPPIANS 3:20

Hugo Ball, a pioneer of Dadaism, was horrified by the carnage of World War I, which left millions dead and punctured the myth of a civilized Europe. The anarchic art he made in response was far ahead of its time. And yet his ultramodernity always had a bit of the premodern about it. Ball was raised a devout Catholic, and elements of scripture and theology made their way into his art—sometimes surreptitiously, as when a string of apparent nonsense symbols reprised Christ's lament, or sometimes conspicuously, as when he dressed up in an avant-garde "magic bishop" costume made of cardboard tubes. After the war, this Catholic element predominated. Ball fled to a monastery, rediscovered the faith of his youth, and called Europe back to Christ.

For Ball, the time was out of joint. His restless invocation of simultaneously premodern and ultramodern tropes was shared by Catholic intellectuals across the continent, who experienced what one historian has called the "mood of messianic expectation and world repudiation" that swept European intellectual life in the shadow of the war.[1] Just as French soldiers had visions of the Virgin Mary on the mechanized killing fields, medieval and Byzantine art informed the most modern aesthetic experiments in its aftermath. Jacques Maritain, a French Catholic philosopher, defined himself as both "antimodern" and "ultramodern." Joseph Eberle, a Viennese Catholic journalist, likewise scrambled temporality in his claim that "the path to a more beautiful future is that of the Crusader." Max Scheler, perhaps Catholic Germany's leading intellectual, hoped that the revolutionary spirit of Marx might combine with the most ancient forms of spiritual leadership, galvanizing Europe with what he called "prophetic socialism."[2]

This sense of temporal dislocation points to the central fact of Catholic intellectual life in the 1920s: a sweeping rejection of the modern world of church-state separation, capitalist economies, liberal democracy, and the nation-state. While there was precedent in Catholic thought for acceptance of all of these, there was even more precedent for a radical rejection of them. Catholics were simply unwilling to restrict their faith to a "private sphere" so that politics and the market could swing free of Church oversight. They were unwilling, therefore, to conceptualize a modern form of the faith.

In practice, many Catholics had learned to live with secular states, Protestant populations, and capitalist economies.[3] In the 1920s, they continued to do so. They were not, however, "modern" in the sense that they could articulate a novel Catholic approach to secular modernity and secular statehood. They were, instead, pragmatists, working in a modern setting *without* a conceptual apparatus to legitimate their behavior (beyond the various defenses of cautious pragmatism that had emerged since the 1860s). Even the most apparently liberal Catholics—those who supported some kind of Christian Democracy—did not have a coherent and widely espoused language to defend and legitimate interconfessional societies and secular politics.[4] While some pioneering souls were working on the problem, they were an embattled minority. The famed "modernist crisis" of the early twentieth century ended with a serious defeat for them, as the 1907 encyclical *Pascendi* reasserted antimodern principles and once again called for some kind of church-state fusion.[5]

Decades later, after World War II, Europe's Catholics would collaborate with Protestants and liberals in the name of a shared vision: a nation-state that defended human rights, religious freedom, European federalism, family values, and a social market economy. This conception of a Catholic modernity, which legitimated all sorts of alliances between Catholics and others, was based not on pragmatism but on a genuine commitment to a particular form of secular modernity. That commitment was simply not available in the wake of World War I. After all, the central argument of Catholic antimodernists had always been that the removal of political and economic affairs from the purview of the Church would lead to horrific bloodshed and social catastrophe. The war, and the wave of revolutionary movements in its wake, seemed to prove them right.[6]

The revived anticlericalism of the 1920s was a stumbling block for Catholic modernism, too. "Is the religious war," one nervous French Catholic wrote in 1924, "beginning again?"[7] Communism threatened the Catholic strongholds of Eastern Europe, while various forms of socialism and republicanism fueled Catholic fears in Central and Western Europe, too. Adolph Hoffmann, an Independent Socialist minister in Prussia, terrified German Catholics when he forbade compulsory attendance at religious services or classes in school, abolished school prayer, and eventually ordered children to give up on confessional schools entirely and attend secular community schools. In Austria, the Socialist Party's 1926 program asserted that religion was a "private affair" of individual "feelings," and the party vowed to struggle "against Churches and religious communities" that seek to influence public affairs. In France, the fractured Left was able to rally behind the old anticlerical cause from 1924 to 1926, when a coalition government came to power with a manifesto that singled out the Church as a counterrevolutionary agent.[8]

Given the circumstances, it is not surprising that 1920s Catholics did not turn en masse toward a celebration of political and economic modernity, or collaboration with others in its name. And it is not surprising, either, that this had dramatic consequences for the broader history of the period. Even if it sometimes conflicted with the lived realities of the faithful, Catholic social thought provided moral and political guidance to millions in an age when the most basic norms of citizenship and progress were up for debate. It circulated in an enormous variety of venues, from Catholic civil society organizations, to trade unions, to newspapers, to sermons. The fact that these networks were used in the 1920s to perpetuate antimodern ideals helps to explain the chaotic role played by Catholics in European politics. Though Catholics after World War II would provide electoral ballast and leadership to parliamentary regimes, after World War I they did nothing of the sort. Truly innovative Catholic parties did exist in France, Italy, and Spain, but they either remained small or fell apart. Mainstream Catholic parties, meanwhile, tended to abandon their commitment to democracy altogether. Germany's Center Party, which ended its long and successful history by throwing its support to Adolf Hitler in 1933, is the most famous example but not the only one.

This is not to say that the 1920s Church was intellectually moribund. On the contrary, Catholic intellectuals—no less than their Marxist opponents— viciously debated with one another about the proper response to a changing Europe. As observers at the time noted, there were two basic forms of Catholic thought and action available in the 1920s, each of which coursed through its own reasonably distinct, transnational network of journals, institutions, and political movements.[9] That debate did not principally pit modernist Catholics against antimodern opponents, and attempts to use this model to understand the period often end up granting unwarranted power and influence to the small groups of Catholic modernists. The debate concerned, instead, the proper Catholic alternative to modernity. Some cherished medievalist premodernity, longing for monarchist and imperial restoration, while others looked toward a prophetic ultramodernity in which the spirit of industry and democracy would inflame some kind of new Christendom. Ball's career shows how, at the level of the individual, these two tendencies could bleed into and inform one another. At the social level, however, they congealed around different geographical centers, journals, and political projects.

The Catholic debate centered less on modernity in the abstract than on the institution that best represented its principles: Weimar Germany, the democratic nation-state that was founded in 1919 as a successor to the German Empire. The Weimar Republic was, as a matter of constitutional principle, secular. It derived its power from the will of the people and not from God. While the constitution promised freedom of conscience, it was reasonably kind to Church interests and was certainly not an anticlerical manifesto (especially for a majority-Protestant state). Culturally, Weimar played host to a rebellious urban life and an avant-garde intellectual and aesthetic scene. Socially, Weimar offered a highly advanced welfare state. Economically, Weimar represented a form of advanced capitalism that, at least in theory, gave significant power to workers.

Weimar, in short, represented the brightest hopes of secular modernity in the wake of a disastrous war. While Catholics participated happily and pragmatically in the Weimar experiment for some years, in the end many of them turned on it—a process that was crucial in the collapse of Weimar and the rise of Hitler. Since the stakes were so high, and the consequences so dramatic, the debates over Weimar provide a useful pathway into the two forms of Catholic antimodernity. Catholics across Europe were obsessed with Weimar as the epitome of secular modernity, and vanishingly few of them found resources in the Catholic tradition for a full-throated defense of it. The larger debate concerned what, precisely, was wrong with it and what should take its place.

To trace the intersecting debates about Weimar and about modernity, this chapter will follow two dynamic, border-crossing young intellectuals, exploring the ways in which they were swept up in transnational intellectual currents. The first, Georg Moenius, was a peripatetic Bavarian priest who spoke for the many Catholics who desired a return to the Middle Ages, or to something very much like them. The second, Waldemar Gurian, was a Russian-Jewish convert who, perhaps because of his own background, had little nostalgia for medieval Europe and argued instead for a path forward, beyond modernity and toward a theological-political settlement not yet seen. The two shared a great deal: a robust interest in French Catholicism, an early hatred of National Socialism, and above all a refusal to allow Catholicism to be sequestered in any sort of private sphere. They traveled, however, in distinct transnational networks. Their writings and careers show us the poles of Catholic debate that were available in the 1920s: one premodern, one ultramodern, and neither of them espousing much hope in the secular modernity that, they would have been sad to learn, was there to stay.

Georg Moenius and Neomedievalism

The 1920s, despite or because of the wreckage of war, were a time of faith in the future. It could, after all, hardly be worse than the past, and the rush of new technologies and aesthetic experimentation captured imaginations across the continent. The title of the most widely circulating Catholic periodical in Central Europe—*More Beautiful Future (Schönere Zukunft)*—encapsulated this spirit. And yet there was a great deal of contestation over which "future" Europe had in store, and the vision in the journal bore little resemblance to the Americanized Europe of consumption and jazz music that was convulsing many of Europe's cities. For these Catholic medievalists, the beautiful future would resemble the beautiful and distant past. As the journal's editor put it, "It cannot be denied that in the Middle Ages, and through Christianity, the relatively best and most successful political and social organization was reached."[10] Europe, he hoped, was striding out of the desert of modernity and into the peaceful, just reign of the Church.

This beautiful future would be a revolution in the truest sense of the word: a return to what had been lost.

The medievalist point was a simple one. The world of industrial capitalism and centralized nation-states was not very old, and the wars it unleashed had brought the world incalculable misery and suffering. Why not simply revive or update the solid forms of hierarchy, obedience, and faith that had kept Europe in relative peace for so many centuries? If capitalism and the nation-state had caused such catastrophe, in other words, why not just forget the whole modern experiment and return to an economic and political order grounded in the eternal values of the Church? The medievalism of the 1920s had little to do with genuine historical inquiry into the Middle Ages. It mobilized, instead, an imagined version of it that allowed for a conceptually rich response to the questions posed by the new age. However fanciful an idea of the past this may have been, it gained significant traction in the 1920s, dovetailing with a Church that paraded its Latin heritage and a culture of war remembrance that tended more toward nostalgia than novelty.[11]

The Catholic medievalists of the 1920s are often viewed as ultranationalists, antidemocrats, or protofascists, representing in embryonic form the movements that would sweep to power in the 1930s.[12] This narrative is misleading, and too quick to read the 1920s through the lens of what was to come later. The Catholic medievalism of the 1920s was primarily a reassertion of its nineteenth-century antecedent, in which figures such as Jaime Balmes, François-René de la Tour du Pin, and Karl von Vogelsang had idealized the Middle Ages as an era of political and economic virtue. As mobilized in the 1920s, it was not inherently antidemocratic, nor was it essentially nationalist. As the editor of *More Beautiful Future* explained, the Catholic faith was technically agnostic on the question of democracy, and the long Catholic intellectual tradition tended to favor some kind of mixture of the democratic and aristocratic principles.[13] Catholics, even the most conservative of them, generally had no problem accepting the kind of parliamentary rule that coexisted with imperial sovereignty, as in the recently departed and much mourned Austro-Hungarian empire. As for nationalism, medievalist Catholics were well aware that the nation-state principle was a novelty on the European scene, more associated with Woodrow Wilson than with Thomas Aquinas. *More Beautiful Future* was self-consciously international, boasting of ties with fifteen other European Catholic journals and publishing contributions by dozens of French,

English, and Belgian Catholics in addition to its regular stock of German, Austrian, Hungarian, and Czech authors.[14] Like the contemporary Muslims who dreamed of the restoration of the caliphate, they hoped that some form of holy empire would return to save Europe from its sad fate as host to dozens of squabbling nation-states.[15]

In lieu of a synoptic summary, it is more illuminating to follow the intellectual and personal journey of one person to understand why Catholic medievalism seemed so plausible, and what sorts of transnational networks it utilized. Born into a working-class Bavarian family in 1890, the young Georg Moenius imbibed a rural, conservative form of Catholic identity, celebrating the authority of the clergy and popular forms of devotion and festival. He spent his childhood, that is, in a region that still had some of the features he would later celebrate as medieval and antimodern. The Bavaria of his youth retained its own monarch and considerable autonomy within the German state, and he surely heard stories about the world before 1871, when Bavaria had still been an independent kingdom, the papacy retained sovereign control over much of central Italy, and the nation-state had not yet reared its head in Central Europe.[16] This experience primed him, as it did many Bavarian Catholics, to loathe the German national project, which was dominated by Protestants in faraway Prussia and which Moenius blamed for starting World War I. He was not alone. Another Munich-based theologian named Dietrich von Hildebrand had the audacity to criticize German war crimes at a 1921 congress—held in Paris, no less. This was not a matter for intellectuals alone. "I'm not going to risk life and limb," one Catholic soldier despaired, "for the damned Prussians and big capitalists any more."[17] This hatred of the German nation-state, amplified by horror at the carnage of the war, led Moenius to craft a form of Catholic antimodernism that would, he hoped, lead Europe back to peace.

Moenius became a priest, but since he saw little distinction between faith and politics, this did not stop him from emerging as one of Catholic Germany's most prominent political thinkers. The German question, specifically, had both geopolitical and spiritual significance for him. Like many other Central European Catholics, Moenius viewed the German state as the epitome of secular modernity, and he despaired in his private journal that its apologists, Catholic and non-Catholic alike, had "betrayed Christendom to the pagan state."[18] For this reason, he was angered by the Versailles settlement and the creation of the Weimar Republic. While John Maynard Keynes famously lambasted the "economic consequences of the peace," another line of criticism, launched by historian Jacques Bainville and popular in Catholic circles, focused instead on what Bainville called the "political consequences of the peace."[19] From this perspective, the tragedy of Versailles was not that it created a weak Germany but that it created a Germany at all. The great peace settlements of the seventeenth and nineteenth centuries had both presumed that a divided Germany was central to a stable Europe (which would be true again after 1945). If a united Germany was the cause of the war, how could it also be the solution to the peace? Prussia, one German Catholic wrote in 1923, "attracts war like the oak tree attracts lightning"—and the peacemakers had botched the opportunity to cut down the tree.[20]

Moenius did not accept that the nation-state should be the guiding principle of postwar politics.[21] In the Middle Ages, he believed, a stable and pious political order had existed and there was no reason why it might not do so again. The beauty of the medieval past was not that popes or clergymen held political power directly. It was instead that the Church had provided a universally accepted vision of human nature, human society, and the good life. This vision suffused the great chain of being that linked together the family, the village, the profession, the Church, and the monarch. All of these communities were legitimate, each had its own sphere of authority, and none of them overstepped their bounds. If the nation-state tended to centralize authority in the name of absolute sovereignty, the medieval polity, in this vision at least, remained loose and federal, lacking both the power and the will to mobilize society in the name of total war. This idealized portrait of the Middle Ages had been nourished by many Catholic writers since the French Revolution. In the 1920s, it was revived; the idea of a common, antinationalist identity linking France and Germany under the sign of the Church answered the intellectual demands of the time. As Moenius's close friend Friedrich Wilhelm Förster argued, "Only the Universal Church has the latent power to check the complete dissolution of Europe." Moenius agreed. "Catholics," he argued, "have the right to secure the Roman Catholic values of order, tradition, continuity, and hierarchy in the political sphere."[22]

Catholic medievalists had more in common with contemporary secular pluralists like Harold Laski than they did with the National Socialists. Hitler did enjoy a significant amount of Catholic support in the early years of his political career. It did not come, however, from medievalists like Moenius. The Nazis' usage of medieval iconography masked a drive for centralization and sovereign power as antidotes to racial degeneration. Moenius saw this with admirable clarity, and together with his Bavarian colleagues he emerged as a prominent opponent of National Socialism. The *Universal Review,* an important Bavarian journal that Moenius eventually bought and edited, contained some of the earliest anti-Nazi Catholic writing anywhere in Europe. As early as 1923, its authors were critiquing the Nazis for their materialist, secular, and nationalist ideals. Hitler was, in Moenius's words, "the last offshoot of the political thought of Hegel and Bismarck," meaning that he pursued "voracious centralization." Eventually, when the party returned to the national spotlight at the end of the decade, the *Review* became one of the most prominent anti-Nazi voices in the country.[23]

Like Laski and other pluralists, Moenius derived anticapitalist consequences from his theory as well. The economy and the state were hardly separate questions, given the expansion of state intervention during the war (Moenius was especially attuned to the needs of the Bavarian Catholic peasantry, who were furious about price controls levied by the state).[24] They were also tied together in the Catholic tradition, insofar as nineteenth-century icons such as Karl von Vogelsang had tried to show that the modern capitalist economy rested on the destruction of medieval guilds by the centralizing state. This fear of centralization distinguished medievalist anticapitalism from its contemporary socialist variant. Moenius looked backward to the Middle Ages, not forward to the workers' paradise—a paradise that, to many German socialists at the time, required just the kind of centralized planning that had marked the war experience. The virtue of that medieval era was not equality but rather a rigidly stratified inequality in which everyone knew their place and treated one another with dignity and respect. Moenius's political economy, that is, was inextricable from the moral economy of the faith. Like many Catholic economic thinkers, he was nostalgic for medieval guilds, which supposedly brought together workers and employers in a spirit of charity. Economic welfare, in turn, came not from the state but from paternalist businessmen looking out for the needs of their pious workers. This moral economy had been, Moenius believed, demolished by the onset of capitalism. "Did we have to cross the Red Sea of Revolution," Moenius despaired, "only to find the promised land of capitalism on the other side? In the strong and pious soil of the Middle Ages, saints and heroes were allowed to emerge as representative powers. In our time businessmen have taken their place."[25]

However much Moenius might have shared with Laski or other secular critics of centralization, it should not be forgotten that his ideas were uniquely Catholic, and rooted in the Catholic antimodernism of the nineteenth century. This is evident above all in the persistence of anti-Semitism in medievalist texts, which had been a central component of mainstream social Catholic thought for decades.[26] Moenius was concerned with a pluralism of powers, not of beliefs. The unquestioned public role of the Catholic Church, he thought, had been central to the peace and virtue of the Middle Ages. By elevating Jews to equal citizenship, the argument went, the state had separated citizenship from religion and therefore signaled an abandonment of any commitment to the public role of faith. Moenius, for his part, tended to blame Protestantism more than Judaism, and he did not indulge in the more paranoid fantasies of all-powerful "world Jewry." All the same, he shared the anti-Semitic prejudices of his milieu. He was convinced that "the Jewish Lodge and Jewish finance" were enemies to be confronted, and studies of the Weimar Catholic press have demonstrated how common ideas like these were. Articles in the *Universal Review*, for instance, took the existence of a "Jewish problem" for granted. One author even provided an anti-Semitic form of anti-Nazism, arguing in 1923 that the Nazis shared much with "emancipated Jews" in that they both hoped to disentangle religion from national citizenship.[27]

Moenius's general anxieties about the Republic, his nostalgia for older forms of political economy, and even his anti-Semitism were widely shared in Catholic Germany. He was a great admirer of Munich's Cardinal Michael von Faulhaber, who had famously decried Weimar as "branded with the mark of Cain" (Moenius even served as the cardinal's personal assistant for a time).[28] The cautious Faulhaber only spoke that way because he knew many agreed with him. The Center Party, which generally supported the Weimar experiment, never gained more than about half of the Catholic vote, and even inside the party many leaders bemoaned the secular republic. In Bavaria, the newly founded Bavarian People's Party (BVP) was incensed at Berlin's usurpation of Bavaria's traditional rights (the BVP was the considerably more conservative version of the national Center Party). Like Moenius, its leaders saw a federation between Bavaria and Austria as a way to dilute the influence of Protestant Prussia and pursue a more Catholic form of German politics and culture.[29] Benedikt Schmittmann, a professor of social science at the University of Cologne, sought to gather German Catholics behind this vision. His economic texts tried to show

how monopoly capitalism and the centralized state fed off of one another, and in his political activism he tried to unravel them both. He cofounded the Imperial and Homeland League of German Catholics (*Reichs- und Heimatbund deutscher Katholiken*), which gave voice to Moenius's federalist ideals. "We do not want to stay here," announced a manifesto in the movement's journal, the *Imperial and Homeland Gazette*. "We do not recognize either Bismarck's *Reich* or the Weimar Constitution as the final form of the German essence."[30] Even Martin Spahn, champion of the right-wing Catholics who gathered into the Protestant-dominated German National People's Party (DNVP), was a pronounced medievalist. In his view, Bismarck had been a devoted federalist whose plans had been derailed by centralizing liberals and Kaiser Wilhelm II.[31]

Moenius inhabited an imagined community that extended far beyond Germany—after all, he was reluctant to grant that such a geopolitical entity as "Germany" had a right to exist in the first place. He was especially fascinated by Vienna, writing that it was "the city that had saved its culture from Turks and Protestants."[32] Moenius lived in Vienna for a period in the late 1920s, traversing the porous border between Bavaria and Austria. Bavarian and Austrian Catholics socialized in many venues, sharing an imagined memory and political project that would reverse the Protestant-dominated German national project. They belonged to the same alpine societies and shooting groups, nourishing the shared German-Catholic heritage that was celebrated at the famous Salzburg Festival, which began in 1920. At the festival, Salzburg's mayor and archbishop alike reached out to the many Bavarian Catholics in attendance. "We are brothers," the archbishop declared to his Bavarian neighbors. "We share our ancestry, our language, our holy Catholic belief, even our emergency and our anguish."[33]

In Vienna, Moenius found himself at the center of a medievalist Catholic renaissance. The city was a beautiful monument to Catholic empire: since the fifteenth century, the Habsburgs had made it their home. When that dynasty collapsed in the wake of World War I, Vienna became a city designed for imperial rule of Central Europe but tasked with being the capital of a tiny, secular, and modern state called Austria. This dissonance, coupled with the constant crises in the new state and the persistence of a long tradition of antimodern thinking, made Vienna a hotbed of Catholic medievalism.

Its primary site was the journal *More Beautiful Future*, at which Moenius assumed an editorial position (the journal shared a healthy stock of authors with both *Universal Review* and the *Imperial and Homeland Gazette*). Its authors agreed with Moenius's critique of modernity, which is no accident because it was rooted in many of the same nineteenth-century sources. The editor's introduction to the journal argued that there were "two great lines of development" in contemporary Europe: one was Catholic, imperial, and international; the other was Protestant, centralizing, and national. "In Austria," another writer opined, "the Holy Roman Empire of the German nation is not entirely dead." Many German authors contributed scathing articles about Prussian hegemony and the shameful collaboration of the Center Party.[34]

The anticapitalist elements of Catholic medievalism found wide expression in Austria, too. Anton Orel and Sándor Horváth both drew on medieval Catholic economic theory to argue that the institutions of usury and private property, central to modern capitalism, were clearly forbidden by Catholic ethics. Austria's bishops printed at least fifty thousand copies of a pamphlet called *Teachings and Directives of the Austrian Bishops on Social Questions of the Present,* in which they gave anticapitalism the force of dogma. "In no time and in no place," they reminded parishioners, "has the Church permitted or promoted capitalism."[35] And, as in Germany, Catholic anticapitalism was part and parcel of Catholic anti-Semitism. The Linz Program of Austria's Christian Workers (1924) rejected "today's economic order" wholesale and sought a world in which "the corrosive influence of Judaism on the economic and spiritual life of the German nation would be overcome." This was apparent even in the social-scientific work of Eugen Kogon and Ernst Karl Winter, both of whom associated with Moenius (Moenius and Kogon worked together on the editorial board of *More Beautiful Future,* while Moenius provided Winter with one of his few German publishing outlets). Kogon's anti-Semitism is surprising, given that he had a Jewish background. Nonetheless, he argued that one would have to be a "sleepwalker" not to understand how the Jews were powerful agents of social atomization and financial capital. Winter, not restrained by any biographical qualms, was more hysterically anti-Semitic. He worried that Germany had "indirectly served the Jewish plans for world domination." "The modern or hypermodern republic of the Judeocracy," he thundered, "stands in the same irreconcilable opposition to Catholic monarchy as monogamy does to promiscuity."[36]

Moenius's medievalist vision extended beyond Central Europe. Following Swiss Catholic Gonzague de Reynold's notion of "Romanitas," he was convinced that Europe's Roman heritage still bound Catholic Europeans to one another and to certain forms of law and authority. "In the thirteenth century," he dreamed, "Frenchmen, Italians, the English, and the Germans were in the first instance citizens of a universal culture." Moenius's travel itinerary traces the outline of this imagined cultural space. While he found his closest comrades in Vienna, that was not actually his first travel destination. As he explained in a 1924 volume based on his trip, the dynamism of Mussolini's Italy, and its rootedness in the Roman imperial past, pointed the way forward for God's continent. He saw Mussolini and Hitler as very different kinds of political leaders, and with some justification (at least in the 1920s). Mussolini was technically subordinate to the king, for instance, and he was willing to declare Catholicism the official state religion. Mussolini, Moenius wrote, "looks to the *Imperium Romanum* and lives from the power of the first Rome of antiquity." Otto Kunze, Moenius's friend and predecessor as editor of *Universal Review,* agreed. While some saw Mussolini's movement as a form of pagan nationalism, Kunze differed. "Fascism," he insisted, "has deeper roots than that. All the spiritual powers ground down by materialist socialism rise up in it," including a pious love for "homeland" and "community."[37]

Pius XI and Mussolini in some ways demonstrated the sort of church-state alliance that Moenius craved. They developed a healthy working relationship in the 1920s, culminating in the 1929 Lateran Accords that created today's Vatican City. Moenius saw Pius XI, too, as an ally in the antimodernist struggle. The latter was entirely uninterested in dialogue with either Jews or Protestants, shutting down experimental efforts to that end, and he refused to remove the reference to the "perfidious Jews" from the standard Good Friday liturgy.[38] At the same time, he worked hard to ban Protestant proselytization in Italy, indicating a conception of state that rejected freedom of religion.[39] Pius XI's rejection of the secular state found expression in the encyclicals *Ubi arcano Dei* and *Quas primas,* both of which emphasized the need for public recognition of God's rule.

Pleased with the turn of events in Italy, Moenius was more concerned about France, both because it represented another Catholic nation gone astray and because Franco-German relations held the key to Europe's past and future alike. In his personal cartography, Paris represented the principles of Catholic political authority as surely as Berlin represented Protestant hubris. "Paris and Berlin," Moenius believed, "remain polar opposites."[40] For Moenius, this was high praise, and he moved to Paris to better understand its Catholic milieu. He was most interested in the intellectual and cultural vitality around the Action française (French Action), a monarchist movement led by Charles Maurras. Moenius became friends with Maurras and his circle of Catholic monarchists, one of whom praised his *Universal Review* as "the most important German Catholic review" (for years after his visit, Moenius kept a signed portrait of Maurras in his bedroom). Moenius himself was Maurras's most prominent German-speaking champion, and probably the only one to publish in two of the movement's allied journals.[41] He was not the only one, though. As a German author in the *Imperial and Homeland Gazette* put it, Maurras's program "does not lose its meaning when applied to Germany." In Austria, Ernst Karl Winter even founded a movement called "Austrian Action" partly in honor of its French counterpart (in its manifesto, he praised Maurras for "reinvigorating the principle of legitimacy in France").[42]

French Catholic medievalism grew, as in Central Europe, from a rich culture of Catholic historical consciousness and rejection of the secular nation-state. If anything, French Catholics considered themselves to be even more under siege than their German counterparts. Bismarck's Germany and its Weimar successor allowed considerable leeway to the churches, granting them public financing and adopting flexible policies toward religious education in public schools. The French form of secularism, known as *laïcité,* was more rigorous in its attempt to scrub the public sphere of religious influence, and in 1905 church and state were officially separated. This led, in turn, to more rigorous assaults on the principle. "We must put an end to the carnival of freedom of conscience," Maurras argued in a brief against secular schooling. "All power comes from God," wrote Robert Vallery-Radot, one of Maurras's most famous Catholic followers, in 1921. "The 'secularism' [*laïcité*] of a power or a doctrine is nonsense."[43]

Moenius was most impressed by two key figures in French Catholic medievalism: Maurras and Jacques Maritain (both of whom he helped introduce to a German audience).[44] The two made an unlikely but formidable pair. Maurras was not even a Catholic, although most of his supporters were. Coming more from the French sociological tradition than from scholasticism, he was personally an agnostic who had great respect for the Church as a defender of order (Auguste Comte and Émile Durkheim, the two giants of French sociology, had both emphasized the relationship between religion and social unity). Jacques Maritain was not raised Catholic, either. Born into a prominent Protestant family, he converted to Catholicism after a crisis of faith in 1906. He was less a sociologist than a scholastic, believing that the thought of St. Thomas Aquinas held the key to undoing the spiritual emptiness and chaos of modern life. Like many other Thomists, Maritain thought that Maurras's monarchism had a great deal in common with Aquinas's own veneration of order and hierarchy (Louis Billot, Réginald Garrigou-Lagrange, and Thomas Pègues, probably the three leading Thomists in France, all supported Maurras). Maritain saw the Church, as he explained in 1922, as both a "herald of supernatural order and safeguard of natural order among men."[45]

In the thought of Maritain and Maurras, French sociological and theological traditions combined into a convincing unity that was intoxicating to a generation of French Catholics. Their joint diagnosis was essentially the same as Moenius's. Like him, they believed that the problems bedeviling Europe were fundamentally political in nature and could only be solved by reversing the secular settlement that forced religion into the private sphere. Maurras's slogan, after all, was "Politics first!" (*politique, d'abord!*). "The more I think about it," Maritain wrote to a friend in 1914, "the more I am persuaded that we must have a *political doctrine,* and that this doctrine can only be anti-revolutionary, anti-republican, anti-constitutional, and therefore monarchist." The French medievalist vision had much in common with Moenius's aspirations for Central Europe. It, too, was monarchist, while being committed to a considerable weakening of central political authority in the name of more local power structures. The Action française, in Moenius's words, was a "consistently federalist" movement, committed to a "regionalist" and decentralized politics. Both Maurras and Maritain agreed with Moenius that a natural political order would be deeply federal and pluralist, respecting natural hierarchies and local power structures instead of sucking them into the maw of the centralizing state. "We suppress nothing," Maurras proclaimed, "but we order everything."[46]

As in Central Europe, Catholic medievalism provided the tools to critique capitalism as well as the secular state (Horváth's work on private property, for instance, created a firestorm of controversy in France).[47] Maurras himself pointed out similarities between his own views and those of social Catholics in Central Europe, while referring to pioneering social Catholic writer François-René de La Tour du Pin as the "direct master" of "our social politics." La Tour du Pin, also inspired by Central European social Catholics, praised Maurras in turn for championing all of the "public liberties which have disappeared since the proclamation of individual liberty."[48] Both Maritain and Maurras celebrated the work of Georges Valois, an enthusiast of Italian Fascism and the leading economic theorist of the Action française.[49] Valois tried to attract workers to the royalist movement by emphasizing that, in the "new economy" to come, neofeudalist guilds under the monarch's benevolent gaze would wrest power away from the allied forces of the state, the Protestants, and the Jews. To spread the word, Valois gave a series of lectures at Paris's prestigious Catholic Institute. He also wrote the introduction to a volume called *Political Economy and Catholic Doctrine,* which argued at length that Valois's teachings were purely in keeping with Aquinas and with the social teachings of the Vatican.[50]

In addition to the positive project of federalist anticapitalism, Maritain, Maurras, and the French medievalists blamed the same enemies as their Central European allies: Protestants, Jews, and the German nation-state. The role of Protestantism in the thought of Maritain and Maurras alike might be surprising because France had so few Protestants. Nonetheless, Protestants played an important role in the consolidation of French secularism. France had been destroyed, Maurras suggested, by a "band of Huguenot [that is, Protestant] sectarians and Bismarckean Kantians who surrounded Jules Ferry" (a prominent anticlerical politician). Maritain argued the same in his 1925 volume *Three Reformers: Luther-Descartes-Rousseau.* Maritain held that Luther was responsible for the collapse of the medieval world, and that the Protestant principles of individualism and voluntarism were at the root of the monstrous irrationality of modernity itself.[51]

In France, too, anti-Semitism was central to French Catholic political culture, and it was essentially unquestioned in the 1920s. Maurras himself was a vicious anti-Semite. La Tour du Pin, Maurras's professed master, oriented his thinking around the contrast between the "Christian city" and the "Jewish city." In his *Towards a Christian Social Order* (1905), reprinted by the Action française in 1921, he castigated usury, which he linked with the Jews, as a "parasite" on the French state. Maritain testified in court on Maurras's behalf after Maurras threatened violence against France's Jewish interior minister, Abraham Schrameck. "An essentially messianic people like the Jewish people," Maritain explained in 1921, "from the instant that it refuses the true Messiah, must play in the world a fatal role of subversion." "The Jewish spirit," he concluded, "can be found at the origin of most major revolutionary movements."[52]

Lastly, like Moenius, Maritain and Maurras were obsessed with the German state as the epitome of secular modernity (French Catholics tended to view Communism as a subsidiary of the German menace).[53] This, more than any other theme, paved the way for collaboration between French royalists and Central European medievalists, and it was also the theme of Moenius's own interventions into the French press. Maurras theorized "the *constant* historical disorder of Germany." "Disorder," he claimed, was "the intellectual and moral characteristic of Germany." Maritain agreed. During the war, he delivered a widely noted lecture series devoted to demolishing German thought. Like Maurras, he saw Germany as a metonym for everything troubling about modernity itself. "Modernism," Maritain held, "is of Germanic origin." Politically, this meant that the German project had to be abolished. "The nature of things," Maritain declared, "seems to demand that Germany be divided into multiple states."[54]

This tour through the medievalist Catholicism of the 1920s shows how adamantly medievalists rejected the modern split between private faith and public reason. Religion, they insisted, should suffuse every sphere of life, and the attempt by the secular state and the secular economy to spin free of religious oversight had led predictably to disaster. They did, from time to time, use concepts such as the "dignity of man," the "human person," or even "human rights." The Church "alone protects the dignity of man from the grasp of unspiritual power," wrote one medievalist Catholic, while another claimed that "human rights" were "a fundamental dogma" of Catholic natural law. The purpose of these invocations was not, however, to legitimate Catholic participation in secular states but rather to claim that only antimodern forms of politics could protect the dignity and rights of the person (the "human person" was a term of art in Catholic circles and was meant to distinguish the Catholic notion of the individual from the secular one). The most famous invocation of the person at this time came from Jacques Maritain, and for him, too, it first represented a form of imperial, illiberal politics.[55]

Even though the number of neomedievalist authors was rather small, their ideas circulated broadly—not only in obscure rags but also in widely circulated journals, including *More Beautiful Future* and the *Action française* newspaper. Nostalgia for the medieval trickled into the daily life of millions, many of whom were mourning lost family members and trying to understand the new Europe that had frothed into being. It found expression in novels, paintings, and plays, while medieval heroes like Joan of Arc enjoyed a renewed popularity. It circulated through educational institutions, too, as Simone de Beauvoir explained in a memoir of her childhood. She received a Catholic education in the 1920s, which meant not only instruction in Bible stories, she recalled, but also praise of the departed French monarchy and denigration of the French Revolution.[56] While Beauvoir's teachers were probably not plotting the downfall of the Republic, they were certainly not participating in the creation of a modern, democratic form of Catholicism.

Medievalist Catholicism played an outsized role in the mentality of Catholic elites, who reasonably saw in it a strategy to protect their own decaying privilege. This was true, first of all, inside the Church. Many Vatican leaders and local Church officials were convinced adherents of some version of antimodern Catholic thought. *More Beautiful Future* was, in one historian's judgment, "the most widely read weekly in Central Europe," boasting a readership of over one hundred thousand. One memoir of the period, written by a German Jesuit, recalled that it was, with its sister publications, an especially common sight in monasteries and in the hands of priests and bishops.[57] Just as it would matter, decades later, when Pope John Paul II led a crusade against Communism, it mattered in the 1920s when Pope Pius XI made common cause with Mussolini against Italy's Catholic parliamentary party, and when his encyclicals cast doubt on modern democratic states and the League of Nations (*Ubi arcano Dei* even linked political party conflict with class struggle, long rejected by the Church).[58] Medievalist Catholicism was attractive to many lay elites as well. Even if the millions of followers of France's National Catholic Federation (FNC) may have been ambivalent toward Maurras and his ideas, the FNC's leadership, both local and national, was more enthusiastic.[59] Catholic employers in France, labor leaders in Austria, and nobility in Germany were attracted to these ideas, too, which promised a restoration of the authority that seemed to be slipping through their hands.[60]

For all of that, we should be wary of overestimating the influence of Catholic medievalism. It did not dominate the 1920s Church by any means, and in some ways it was on the defensive, especially by the end of the decade. In 1926, Pope Pius XI actually condemned the Action française for attempting to link the Church too closely to a particular political project. As important as it is, the condemnation is often misunderstood. For one thing, it did not end the movement, even among Catholics. Many believers disputed the pope's authority to tell them what newspapers to read, and Moenius continued to support Maurras for years.[61] For another, the condemnation of Maurras's brand of antimodernity did not herald the victory of modernizing trends. Pope Pius XI was no celebrant of secular modernity, and outside of a scattered few intellectuals, Maurras's other opponents were not, either.[62] Maurras's condemnation was less a victory for Catholic modernizers, who remained marginal, than for a different breed of Catholic antimodernity.

Waldemar Gurian and Ultramodern Catholicism

Intellectually speaking, 1920s Catholics divided into two basic camps. Medievalism made intuitive sense to many Catholics who felt that Europe had gotten off track, and that Pope Pius IX had been right, back in 1864, to reject the idea that the Church should "come to terms with progress, liberalism and modern civilization."[63] This was not, however, the only form of Catholic antimodernism. Many argued that the Middle Ages could never come back because the process of history and the unfolding of God's plan were irreversible. The modern settlement of secular statehood and religious freedom, however, had proven disastrous. They agreed with Moenius that Catholicism could not sequester itself into the private sphere, and that society as a whole had to be suffused with Catholic values. Instead of longing for a nostalgic restoration, though, they sought to move *beyond* modernity, hurtling forward into some kind of new religious settlement that would infuse the new spirit of democracy and progress with the ancient ethos of the Church. Like contemporary Marxists, they were sometimes unclear about exactly what this new world would look like. They were clear, though, that it would involve neither a medievalist restoration nor some reformed version of secular statehood. Neither medievalist nor modern, this crop of innovative Catholic thinkers can best be described as ultramodern.

It is a mistake to confuse *pragmatic* Catholicism with *modern* Catholicism. Some Catholics, notably the French activist Marc Sangnier, did think that there was something uniquely praiseworthy in democratic, secular states, and that by organizing in Christian-inspired parties they could be properly reformed. This was a minority view, and a perilous one—especially as one of Sangnier's own political ventures had already been condemned by the Vatican.[64] The more commonplace attempt to theorize Catholic participation in modern political and economic life relied almost entirely on pragmatism. Robert Cornilleau, Marcel Prélot, Konrad Adenauer, Peter Tischleder, Josef Mausbach, and other Catholic leaders who urged participation in modern institutions argued in this way. It could take multiple forms. Some utilized the old Catholic distinction between the "thesis" (an ideal Catholic society) and the "hypothesis" (the debased modern society in which some Catholics were forced to live). Even in the latter situation, they reasoned, Catholics were duty bound to pursue Catholic values as best they could, while never losing sight of the actual goal of founding a wholly Catholic society. Others revived the Thomist tradition of accidentalism, according to which the Church is indifferent to specific questions of political arrangement.[65] Neither of these approaches required a renewed Catholic attitude toward modernity. And neither of these approaches, in the end, proved especially effective at conquering the Catholic public sphere. Pleas for moderation and pragmatism might prove inspiring in some times and places, but 1920s Europe was not one of them.[66]

Ultramodern Catholicism had, like its medievalist opponent, nineteenth-century roots. The patron saint of ultramodern Catholicism was Félicité de Lamennais (1782–1854), a pathbreaking French priest. Lamennais was no defender of secular modernity. He loathed Protestants, did not believe that the genius of Catholicism could be sequestered into a political party, and hoped for a reintegration of the faith into political and economic life alike. At the same time, he did not think that the French Revolution could or should be undone. His journal, aptly named *The Future,* envisioned a Church that would ally itself with the groundswell of revolutionary energies, inaugurating a new era on the far side of modernity. The Church should accept the spirit of liberty, he insisted, precisely because it would provide the opportunities for a new Catholic revival that would heal a decaying Europe. In *Words of a Believer* (1834), he adapted the old prophetic spirit for new times. "At present," he chanted, "the world is gloomy and cold. Our fathers have seen the sun set." And yet the dark night of the secular modern would not last forever. "Look to the east: the horizon is beginning to brighten."[67]

One of the greatest Lamennais enthusiasts of the postwar moment was named Waldemar Gurian.[68] He, too, came to believe that the time of revolutionary upheaval was far from over, and that the Church might ride the wave of liberty and democratic freedoms toward a new and ultramodern spiritual settlement. Gurian was born a few years after Moenius— not to a Catholic family in Bavaria but to a Jewish family in St. Petersburg.[69] In response to the anti-Semitic violence of late tsarist Russia, the Gurian family fled to the temporarily friendlier climes of Berlin, where they converted to Catholicism (Gurian was baptized in 1914 at the age of twelve). This did not lead to easy assimilation. Gurian was, after all, an enemy national during the war, for which he was kicked out of school. This set of experiences may have convinced him that neither the bucolic imperialism of tsarist Russia nor the modernizing German state had a place for him. In their place, like Lamennais before him, he sought something new.

Gurian eventually made his home in the Rhineland, a region in western Germany. He aligned himself with the modernizing "Cologne" orientation in German Catholicism and served as an editor at its house paper, the *Cologne People's Journal* (*Kölnische Volkszeitung*). The Rhineland, with Cologne as its chief Catholic city, played the role for Gurian that Bavaria did for Moenius. In 1945, by which point he had lived in Russia, multiple parts of Germany, France, Switzerland, and the United States, a close friend mused that if Gurian "were asked to name the piece of the earth to which he owed the most, he could only answer: the Rhineland."[70] If Bavaria allowed Moenius to glimpse Europe as it once was, the Rhineland provided Gurian a powerful vision of what it might one day become. The region, which belonged administratively to Prussia, was one of the most industrialized and confessionally mixed in Europe. Catholics in the Rhineland had spearheaded an earlier effort to bring Catholics "out of the tower," as one leader famously put it, making alliances with Protestants in the name of an interconfessional and "Christian" social project. Rhenish Catholics organized themselves to the hilt. The region was the home of the Volksverein für das katholische Deutschland (People's Union for Catholic Germany), Catholic Germany's most prominent civil society organization (Rhenish Catholics were about six times more likely to join than their Bavarian counterparts).[71] The Rhineland was also the spiritual home of the Center Party, which was central to the functioning of Weimar and shored up the republican coalition alongside social democrats and liberals.

Gurian was ensconced in a network of Catholic institutions that was trying to make pragmatic common cause with non-Catholics in the name of stability and German nationhood. They did so quite successfully, and on many fronts, notably labor politics and municipal governance, Catholics participated in the modernizing ethos of the era. They could plausibly see the Vatican as being on their side, given the Vatican's subtle maneuvering against the breakup of Germany, and the eventual signing of a concordat with Prussia.[72] Prussia loomed large in Gurian's thought, just as it did in Moenius's. As Gurian rightly saw, the Germans were not divided, as in the past, "by their interpretation of Christianity, but by their relations towards the (Prussian) German state."[73] When Moenius looked at Prussia, he saw Bismarck's anti-Church policies and the ruthless war criminals of Hindenburg's war machine. But when Gurian considered Prussia, he saw a new breed of consensus-driven, religion-friendly democracy. During the war, for instance, Gurian's editor at the Cologne newspaper published a volume of historical essays on the fruitful ties between Prussia and the Catholic Rhineland.[74] And in the 1920s, the Rhenish Center Party disavowed all forms of separatism to declare the indivisibility of the German state, while Rhenish Catholic intellectuals such as Hermann Platz and Carl Schmitt concurred that their destiny lay with Prussia.[75] Their hopes were largely met. Had medievalist Catholics been interested in Prussia as more than a symbol of secular horror, they might have seen that it actually presented quite a successful experiment. While the republic's national government staggered from crisis to crisis, Prussia itself was an oasis of stability, marked more by interconfessional governance and welfare reform than by bitter cultural conflict.[76]

All of this notwithstanding, Germany's Catholics by and large proved to be fair weather friends to the Weimar Republic—even in Prussia. The republic offered a novel political space, but Catholic institutions failed to update accordingly. Some tried to turn the Center Party into a truly interconfessional and "Christian" party, while others tried to modernize Catholic associational life along the lines of the Italian form of Catholic Action. Neither attempt worked. The Center Party did not require its members to accept republican statehood, and its leaders insisted that occasional coalitions with social democrats were entirely driven by pragmatism—not any ideological common ground. Even Adam Stegerwald, one of the few who were trying to revamp the party for a new age, insisted that it should agitate for a "Christian state," departing from the secular, centralized state birthed by the French Revolution.[77] The nonreformed institutions soon entered crises. The Volksverein entered a period of fiscal hardship and membership decline in the late 1920s. The Center Party, for its part, took a right turn in 1928 after a bitterly contested leadership dispute. It threw its support to Hitler a few years later.

The institutional stasis of German Catholicism was matched by an intellectual failure to arrive at coherent and inspiring reasons why Catholics should find a home in the republic, or why they should be willing to sequester the faith in the private sphere. If anyone was well placed to provide such a justification, it was Gurian. As a converted Jew who had already fled one dictatorship, he had a vested interest in the success of a state that protected his civil liberties. And yet he emerged as a relentless critic of the pragmatic, reformist Catholicism that had long been the hallmark of the Cologne orientation. " 'Coalitions' are necessary," he declared in 1929, "but they must not ensnare us in frivolous equation of daily necessities with eternal principles!" Like Lamennais, he believed that a defense of those principles required wholly new approaches in place of the windy moralizing that he detected in the medievalists. In a world in which "the tempo of life has become so fast, especially in industrialized and urban regions," he implored, "longwinded ethical appeals will no longer work." Instead, he thought, Catholicism "must become bound up with the times through a modernization of its most fundamental approach."[78] That modernization would not, however, lead to Weimar. Like many Catholics, Gurian saw Weimar's liberal secularism as the last gasp of an outdated secular ideology, not as the vanguard of the new.

Gurian was unimpressed with the stodginess of the traditional Catholic associations or their leaders. Like Max Kaller, whose 1927 book on the "lay apostolate" summed up this vision, he felt that Germany needed a generation of dynamic, young, and spiritually gifted elites.[79] Gurian imbibed this spirit at Quickborn, a Catholic youth group. Like many other young Germans, Catholic and non-Catholic alike, Gurian saw in the youth movement a pathway toward German regeneration. Unlike political parties or trade unions, it was aimed at transforming spirits, not winning small and pragmatic victories (Lamennais had pursued a similar strategy at La Chênais, his private home and school).

Gurian's book on the topic, written when he was just twenty-one, explained that he found in Quickborn a model of ultramodern authority that differed entirely from the clerical, authoritarian model beloved by Moenius. In the book, and throughout his life, Gurian drew on the theories of Romano Guardini, perhaps Weimar Germany's most famous theologian, and the leader of Quickborn.[80] Guardini theorized a Church that would enfold the laity into its mission and seek to turn attention away from obedience and toward embodied practice, notably through the liturgy. "The essence of order is that the individual obeys in the true sense of the word," he told an audience in 1925. This occurs only when the objective order "is made into an order of *freedom* by each individual."[81] The necessity of this free assimilation explained Guardini's obsessive focus on youth, which, he explained, is the period when we have not yet been overwhelmed by tradition and authority but still have the capacity to creatively assimilate those traditions.[82]

The Catholic youth movement was committed to a spiritual regeneration that would save the Church, and Germany, by overcoming the bankrupt secular condition. "Modernity," Guardini argued in 1923, "is over."[83] The new Germany, Guardini taught, would be born through a creative, youthful appropriation of the Catholic tradition—one that might be modeled on the medieval unity of faith and politics but would not involve a return to it. Gurian expressed this view in one of his very first publications: a fawning review for a Quickborn journal of a book by one of his friends, Paul-Ludwig Landsberg (like Gurian, Landsberg was Jewish, and while he traveled in Catholic circles, he never officially converted). The little book was entitled *The World of the Middle Ages and Us.* The book, which struck a chord in Catholic youth circles, was just as flamboyantly antimodern as anything coming out of Moenius's circles. In the Middle Ages, Landsberg dreamed, the world had been imbued with meaning and value. The Reformation, however, changed all of that, inaugurating the "heretical modernity" of the present. Landsberg, though, did not call for a return to that past. "The culture of the Middle Ages," he concluded, "was a Christian culture, but in no way was it the only one." The "culture of the future" will be Christian, too, but in an entirely new way.[84] Gurian praised Landsberg's ability to draw on history without falling into the "error" of clamoring for an "impossible restoration." In an article on historical consciousness, another youth movement intellectual concurred, drawing on Landsberg to claim both that "the imperial and chivalric Middle Ages are dead" *and* that the medieval era provides a model to follow and appropriate.[85]

Gurian and Landsberg's theory of history drew less on Guardini than on the titanic figure Gurian called "the most gifted thinker in Germany": Max Scheler. He was a Jewish convert, too—surely not a coincidence, as medievalism likely had little appeal, for obvious reasons, to Jews. And, also like Gurian, Scheler devoted himself to creating an ultramodern form of Catholic thought, in dialogue with modern philosophy and social sciences without being held hostage to them. Scheler had shot to fame during the war, urging Catholics to aid the German war effort. In its aftermath, he published voluminously on religious themes, hoping to spearhead a religious awakening that could save Europe from decadence. Scheler heavily influenced Guardini, and his archives are replete with letters from young admirers like Gurian and Landsberg. "Your ideas," Gurian gushed, "find great favor among the members of the German youth movement." "I have thought of you often these last weeks," Landsberg wrote to Scheler. "My spiritual life is very much bound up with yours."[86]

Scheler, Gurian, and Landsberg believed that modernity—understood as church-state separation, capitalism, and the rest—was out of date. "We stand," Scheler mused, "at the beginning of an age in world history that may be described as a *positive* age of *belief*." The new era, he taught, would develop organically from the spirit and dynamism of modernity, but it would also leave it behind. "The eternal," he wrote from Cologne in 1920, "is not sealed away from time in a simple juxtaposition: it timelessly embraces the content of time and its fullness, pervading each of its moments."[87] The task for the German Catholic was not, therefore, to undo the Reformation but to draw, like Lamennais, on the potentials of the modern order to vault beyond it. To quote Scheler: "It is a tragedy to be forced to expel almost the whole world from paradise, even though we [Germans] didn't want it and were only following the law and fate of its own essence. And perhaps the heart of the mythical angel sobbed behind his iron visage when he showed Adam with his sword the new path of world history. But he obeyed his Lord and God, just as we obeyed the idea and the condition of the present world, the commandments of its hour and its necessity."[88] In this extended metaphor, Scheler accepts the medievalist complaint that Germany was at fault for modernity (the expulsion from the garden). He denies, though, that this could or should be undone. Our task as Christians, and as Germans, is not to clamor back into the garden but to follow the path laid out by the mythical angel: a path that included a march through secular modernity but did not end there.

While Jewish converts were highly visible among ultramodern Catholics, they were in dialogue with broader currents in the Church, too. Gurian, for instance, was heavily impacted by both Guardini and the erstwhile Catholic jurist Carl Schmitt, an early mentor who shared his belief that liberal democracy was a relic of the past. Ideas like these were common in Weimar's Catholic circles. Ernst Michel, a Catholic socialist, was harshly critical of Moenius-style medievalists, but he, too, thought that "the modern state" was a relic of paganism and that "the future will belong to a true League of Nations" far removed from the nihilism of contemporary mass democracies. Guardini agreed that the modern state had reached its crisis. "The old world order dissolved itself," he declared, assuring readers that "a new one" is on its way. In 1926, Carl Muth published a long article in which he gave his verdict on the era. This verdict mattered a great deal, insofar as Muth and his journal (*Hochland*) were at the very center of the attempted rapprochement with German modernity. And the judgment was not a good one. "We stand," the epigraph to the essay promised, "before either a new age or a collapse."[89]

Ultramodern Catholics like Gurian were either indifferent or actively hostile to liberal democracy. Gurian personally thought that it was an unworkable system, although he did not dwell on that fact.[90] He rightly saw that the Weimar experiment was on its way out, given that its principles were outdated. He was more concerned with what would come after. His hope, like that of Scheler and Muth, was that some sort of Catholic, prophetic spirit would enliven a new generation of political and spiritual elites to lead Germany to a brighter future. His fear, which turned out to be more prescient, was that the inevitable collapse of liberal democracy would lead to "secularized religions" like Nazism and Communism (this logic led Gurian to become one of the most important founders of totalitarianism theory, which interpreted the two as twins).[91] The new age, as Scheler foretold, would be an age of belief—but perhaps not in Christ.

Not all German Catholic thinkers in the 1920s shared this skepticism of Weimar. They relied, however, on pragmatism rather than on a conceptually new defense of modernity. Note the grammar of Gurian's judgment of them: "The new democratic liberties," he explained, "in no way conflicted with Catholic political doctrine, as the theological theoreticians were able to demonstrate." The theologians Gurian had in mind provided negative defenses of the republic, arguing that political modernity was acceptable to Catholics but failing to articulate what was especially praiseworthy about it. "The Center," Carl Muth observed, "has a democratic tradition, but no affection for the republic."[92] This was the basic position of Josef Mausbach, Peter Tischleder, and Karl Neundörfer, probably the main figures Gurian had in mind (he wrote to a friend that Tischleder in particular was "extraordinarily representative of the Center's political philosophy"). They drew on accidentalism, according to which the faith can coexist with any political order, and, as one of them put it, "the democratic state form is, in certain conditions, the best." This theoretical paucity appeared in more popular venues, including future West German chancellor Konrad Adenauer's famous speeches to the 1922 Catholic Congress. In them, he called on Catholics to participate in German national life but failed to mobilize a coherent Catholic rationale for it. Banal references to strength, patriotism, and "keeping up with the times" stand in for any genuine delineation of shared values that might convince Catholic listeners to wholeheartedly work alongside socialists or Protestants (even though in his daily activities Adenauer did just that).[93]

The same dynamic was at work in German Catholic approaches to the Weimar economy and welfare state. Some Catholics were excited by Weimar's putative commitment to replacing class conflict with class collaboration through factory councils on the one hand and national economic planning on the other.[94] Some were supportive, too, of Weimar social policy. In both of these arenas, after all, Catholics played a signal role. For most of the 1920s, the minister of labor was a Catholic priest named Heinrich Brauns, who had long experience in the Volksverein and a mandate to translate Catholic social ethics into policy. Thanks largely to Brauns's initiative, the expansion of the Weimar welfare state actually ended up empowering sub-state institutions such as Catholic charities, in defiance of social democratic desires to build more centralized, statist institutions.[95]

This collaboration in Weimar's social and economic institutions, like its political counterpart, was defended in the language of pragmatism. Drawing on arguments pioneered decades before, some economic and social experts argued, as Gustav Gundlach put it, that "Catholic principles are compatible with any economic system," so long as certain principles such as private property and the common good are protected. The most influential among them was Oswald von Nell-Breuning, a Jesuit whose *Basic Principles of Stock Exchange Morality* (1928) argued for the acceptability of the stock market to the Catholic conscience, so long as it was properly regulated. Their ideas found some traction among Catholic experts connected to the Center Party, and even among some members of the hierarchy. Karl Joseph Schulte, archbishop of Cologne, sent his clergymen a document titled "Guidelines on Capital and Labor," which clarified that "capitalism" was not in itself sinful—even if it was not necessarily moral.[96]

This pragmatic version of Catholic economic doctrine, like its political counterpart, failed to gain significant traction in Catholic intellectual culture writ large. It was challenging to equate the cartel-based economy of Weimar Germany with the ethical economy of the social Catholic vision, especially once it became clear that the grand experiments in worker-employer collaboration would not amount to much. Socially and politically, Christian trade unions struggled to cohere their own teachings, aimed at class collaboration in the name of the common good, with a political and economic system that seemed to foment class conflict.[97] Even Catholics who claimed to be open to capitalism, as in the case of Nell-Breuning, found difficulties when they tried to engage with non-Catholics to solve concrete problems. This became clear when Nell-Breuning joined an inter-confessional board of experts to study the problem of unemployment. His organic economic vision, predicated on state regulation and group rights, had little in common with non-Catholic economic approaches.[98]

Catholic intellectuals like Gurian were unimpressed by this pragmatic approach to capitalism—an economic system roundly condemned by most social Catholic writers of the nineteenth century, and whose post–World War I record was not sterling enough to overcome that stigma. They continued to espouse fundamental criticisms of modern capitalism. Even those who did defend Weimar's policies often did so because they (wrongly) thought that they were designed to create a Christian economic system that would undo the capitalist excesses unleashed by the French Revolution.[99]

Gurian's view of the capitalist economy mirrored his view of democratic politics: it was a necessary but lamentable step on the way to something better. He rejected economic theorists who, like Moenius, wanted an impossible return to the days "when princes would take their questions to Thomas Aquinas." And yet at the same time he did not believe that capitalism, any more than liberal democracy, could be made acceptable to the Catholic conscience. Like Moenius, he saw "natural social groups" such as the family and the profession as the central agents of economic life. "Only a society composed of estates [Stände]," Gurian thought, "could exist without slavery." In his view, capitalism was predicated on the hegemony of the individual and his needs, constituting an entire metaphysics that was absolutely incompatible with this aspect of Catholic teaching. His critique of capitalism was not primarily ethical, as though the system was stable but legitimated certain individual moral failings. Like Rosa Luxemburg and other Marxists, Gurian linked capitalism with nationalism, imperialism, and, ultimately, war.[100]

Gurian, like many German Catholic thinkers, was committed to a form of Catholic social thought known as solidarism. Their master in this regard was Heinrich Pesch (1854–1926), a Jesuit sociologist who had studied the ravages of industrialization firsthand in Lancashire and whose textbooks were common currency in German Catholic institutions of higher learning.[101] Pesch argued that the medieval guild system was irretrievable but that modern industrial economies could potentially be reformed in kindred, and Catholic, directions. For this to happen, the state and market would have to be supplanted by the various organs that, for Pesch, made up the social body: families, trade unions, employers' associations, and so on (what Catholics called "estates"). While Pesch did accept the nation-state as a viable political form, and he called on it to engage in certain forms of welfare and regulation, he also insisted that "limited results" could be expected from state activity. Only where people have "a highly developed sense of moral responsibility" and submit to "the active dominion of the eternal and divine moral law" could the solidarist economy emerge. And when it did, capitalism would vanish, and with it the all-powerful state. "Capitalism," he declared, "is finished," and the "modern state" is not the "highest fulfillment" of political order. Like Gurian and Scheler, he rejected medievalism in the name of what he called a "*more* modern state with greater decentralization."[102]

Pesch's solidarism is often viewed as a precursor to a reformist, capitalist-friendly form of Catholic economics. It is true that Pesch believed that Catholic morality was compatible with the most advanced forms of technological progress. And yet, because he did not believe that this was possible in the particular situation of modern capitalism and secular statehood, he is better understood as ultramodern. Pesch had studied with socialists, and his writings were aimed more at thinking through a postcapitalist economic order than at blessing the one that existed. In *Ethics and the National Economy* (1918), one of his last books, he harshly criticized capitalism as an economic system that necessarily placed individual needs ahead of the common good. He even, like Gurian and Luxemburg, linked capitalism with the excesses of imperialism, which he viewed less as the beneficent spread of Christian civilization than as the lamentable result of the capitalist drive for new markets.[103]

This was not the only reading of Pesch available in the 1920s (Nell-Breuning was a disciple, too). It was, however, probably the most common. This was certainly how Max Scheler read him. Scheler built on Pesch's solidarism to call for a "prophetic socialism," which would replace the reactionary "backwards-facing utopia" of the medievalists with something new, and something beyond capitalism.[104] Many other Catholic ethicists and social scientists took it for granted that the capitalist economy was predicated on a rejection of Catholic ethics because it privileged the hedonist individual, rather than the Catholic institution, as the central agent of material reproduction. Walter Dirks, Ernst Michel, Heinrich Mertens, and others pioneered Catholic forms of socialism for just this reason.[105] Even economically trained Catholic experts such as Franz Müller and Paul Jostock, all of whom operated in Pesch's wake, agreed. In Jostock's *Way Out of Capitalism* (1928), for instance, he expressed confidence that capitalism would soon exhaust itself, and he sounded much like Gurian in his praise of the youth groups for offering an alternative mode of being.[106]

In their economics, as in their politics, Gurian's network of Weimar-accepting Catholics failed to explain how or why they would be able to collaborate with the many non-Catholics who lived in Germany. If this finding arises analytically from an exploration of those themes, it arises just as clearly from an exploration of how they thought about socialists, Jews, and Protestants (in other words, not how they *worked* with them as a matter of pragmatism but what conceptions of religious alterity were available to them). Liberals and socialists can be dispensed with easily enough: however much the Center Party may have collaborated with liberal and socialist parties, notably in Prussia, Catholic intellectuals, with few exceptions, continued to disparage both traditions as anticlerical inheritors of an Enlightenment, revolutionary legacy. Gurian himself mocked "individualist liberalism, opposed to all tradition" as a thing of the past, while even Adenauer warned his listeners that socialists sought to seize power and institute a new religion.[107]

As for the Jews, although a Jewish convert himself, Gurian did not focus on this question, likely because the Catholic faith in the 1920s did not provide the resources to critique anti-Semitism. While Adenauer and other Catholic politicians enjoyed friendly relations with Germany's Jewish community, as an intellectual matter anti-Semitism still reigned. Although Gurian did choose to write for the *Cologne People's Journal* and *Germania,* among the least anti-Semitic papers in Catholic Germany, their market shares declined during the 1920s, and regional newspapers were less temperate.[108] Even articles in forward-looking Catholic journals could offhandedly declare that the League of Nations was a creation of Jewish finance, and Max Metzger, an Austrian pacifist and priest, could declare with equal certainty that Judaism was, next to socialism and freemasonry, one of the gravest enemies facing the Church. The two most authoritative Catholic statements on race in the era—Enrico Rosa writing for *Civiltà Cattolica* and Gustav Gundlach writing for Germany's prestigious *Lexicon for Theology and Church*—concurred. In Gundlach's version, he agreed with his old teacher Werner Sombart that the Jews had too much influence on the moral and economic life of Germany and that many "assimilated Jews" had entered the service of "global plutocracy or global Bolshevism." Anti-Semitism, understood in a "social-political" sense, was therefore acceptable to the Catholic conscience so long as it did not tip into the extreme racism of those who sought an "Aryan-German religion."[109]

Gurian and other ultramodern Catholics were unable to find a common language with Protestants either. As a conceptual matter, Catholic suspicion of Protestantism remained firm in the 1920s, and even became amplified. Ecumenical movements in Weimar Germany were limited and tenuous, especially given Pope Pius XI's expressed disdain for them (one scholar has referred to the "incapacity for dialogue" among 1920s German Catholics).[110] In private discussions about the DNVP, Center Party officials admitted that while they were close on some political and economic questions, they could not move past the confessional divide. Some Catholics attempted to strike out on their own and join the party, but this effort had sputtered by the end of the decade.[111] Like most other Catholic intellectuals in his orbit, Gurian's political thought was oriented by the problem of secular individualism, which he linked above all with Protestantism.[112] In his work on the youth movements, for instance, he insisted that Protestants lacked any concept of stable, transcendent value and thus could not provide the spiritual resources for a political awakening. His last work of the Weimar era, *On the Future of the Reich* (1932), repeated the charge. While the work as a whole called for a national consensus to stave off Nazism, his critiques of Protestantism undercut any possible social basis for such a coalition.[113]

While Gurian may have been unable to build bridges to non-Catholics at home, he was fanatical about building them to Catholics abroad. Intellectually, he was especially drawn to France. As Muth noted in 1926, the French had been dealing with the secular republic for much longer than the Germans had. "Let us regard our own fortune in the mirror of France," he insisted.[114] Gurian agreed. For a period in the late 1920s, he lived in Paris as an international correspondent for *The West* (*Abendland*), an internationally minded German Catholic periodical, regularly traversing what one philosopher called the "spiritual bridge between Paris and Cologne."[115] While Gurian's time in France probably overlapped with Moenius's, it does not seem that they ever met. They looked for, and found, different versions of Catholic France, which they explained in two books on the subject that bear almost no resemblance to each other (Gurian gave Moenius's book a scathing review in *The West*).[116] Gurian celebrated the Catholic France of Lamennais, not that of Maurras—a France grappling with the revolutionary legacy of 1789 without falling prey to its secularism or anticlericalism. As a reviewer in Quickborn's journal correctly noted, Gurian meant to offer these strands of French Catholicism as a "comparison and as an example" for Germans to follow.[117] Intellectually, he was most impressed by the Semaines Sociales, or "Social Weeks," which gathered together French Catholic social scientists and clergymen who sought to infuse the faith with the most modern tools of social science. In his opening address to the first Social Week after the war, Eugène Duthoit, the meeting's organizer and presiding spirit, referred to it as "an itinerant university," charged with "observing social facts scientifically," using the tools of law, geography, statistics, and more to bring together social science and the "the moral principle" that should animate it.[118]

As in Germany, Catholics who wanted to participate in modern French political or commercial life relied on pragmatism rather than on a conceptual defense of modernity. There were some modernizing trends, to be sure, notably around the new Catholic parliamentary party (the Popular Democratic Party, or PDP). That party, however, remained vanishingly small, and even its adherents were divided about the advisability of embracing secular modernity.[119] Neither *L'Ouest-Éclair* nor *La Vie Catholique*, the premier newspapers of this tendency, developed novel approaches to modernity, either. The former continued to inveigh against Judaism, masonry, and the rights of man.[120] The latter was essentially a clearinghouse for the ideals and insights of the Social Weeks. And the Social Weeks themselves, despite their best efforts, remained either antimodern or pragmatic. Many speakers avoided ideological questions altogether, focusing instead on social-scientific investigation and piecemeal reform. Others, especially in sessions on the state and on depopulation, were flagrantly antimodern in their contention that the French Revolution had been a terrible error and that the state was bound to become tyrannical unless restrained by the specific moral influence of the Catholic Church.[121]

Most French Catholic intellectuals who rejected pragmatism opted for some kind of medievalism. Those who did not, however, theorized some kind of ultramodern Catholicism (the historian Stephen Schloesser has referred to this as "Jazz Age Catholicism").[122] This was as true for the artists and philosophers Schloesser discusses as it was for the social and economic thinkers who interested Gurian. For *The West*, for instance, Gurian interviewed Lucien Romier, editor of the *Industrial Day* and the political pages of *Figaro,* and also member of an influential group called "French Recovery" (Redressement français), made up of economic and administrative elites interested in streamlining the French economy.[123] On the one hand, and as his institutional affiliations suggest, he was allergic to nostalgic appeals to what he called "an archaic form of sovereignty." But despite all of his pretensions to technocracy, he was a critic of modernity, too. He cited Maurras positively, with the caveat that his arguments about spiritual decline and decadence should lead us forward to a new future and not backward to an outdated one. Like his German coreligionists, Romier believed that a new breed of Catholic elites would emerge to lead France into a more spiritually vital condition. He argued forcefully that "modern capitalism" had been created by the Jews, whose religious faith molded them into calculating egoists, devoid of the sentiment and tact of the native Catholic. Like Gurian and Schmitt, Romier complained that contemporary states did not understand their reason for being and were slowly transforming into mere associations of interest groups. To overcome this decadence, he suggested, some kind of ultramodern infusion of faith and politics would be required.[124]

A similar sensibility could be found in the Catholic economics textbooks published in France at the time. Pesch's solidarism found its Francophone equivalent above all in the work of another Jesuit, Albert Muller. In his *Notes on Political Economy* (1927), Muller reprised Pesch's basic themes, sketching an economic order nourished by moral regeneration and structured by Catholic institutions. Like Pesch, he stridently rejected all forms of medievalism and guild socialism as inadequate for modern industrial conditions. In place of medievalism, on the one hand, or modern capitalism, on the other, Muller imagined a pluralist economy, structured primarily by families, Catholic trade unions, and Catholic employers' associations, all of which could be trusted over the state to manage economic relations in a spirit of charity. Muller believed, for instance, that family allowances should be paid by employers voluntarily and not by a centralized welfare state. This voluntarism represented a political economy that presumed a specific moral economy in order to function, and therefore some kind of mass moral conversion away from capitalist egoism.[125]

What these analyses show is that even the apparent economic modernizers—people such as Pesch, Romier, and Muller—pursued a decentralized economic vision that was difficult to square with the realities of 1920s capitalism, marked as it was by cartelization and financial globalization. There was, in other words, no invocation of a social market economy, or anything like it, to make capitalism broadly acceptable to Catholics. This was true in Germany just as much as it was in France. And if it was true in those places, it should not be a surprise to find a similar dynamic in Austria, where Catholic intellectual culture was dominated by Moenius's brand of neomedievalism. Modern statehood was experienced in Austria as a recent trauma, and imperial nostalgia had far greater purchase there than it did elsewhere. There were exceptions, however, and Gurian gravitated to them. He was personally closest with Johannes Messner, and he chose Messner's journal, *Das neue Reich,* for the publication of a controversial essay excoriating Catholic medievalism. In response to outrage, Messner privately leaped to Gurian's defense: "A long period of education will be needed until we can overcome the social-scientific amateurism of the Catholic public sphere," he explained to one critic.[126]

Gurian's brand of prophetic ultramodernity hardly existed in Austria, where the dominant medievalism was pitted against a form of pragmatist accommodation (normally drawing on German sources, given that Austrian Catholic intellectual history offered so few resources of this sort). Messner himself was friendly with several of the Weimar pragmatists discussed earlier, and his works essentially provided an Austrian translation of its spirit. "Our task cannot be to suddenly break out of capitalism as a historically constituted form of social economy," he judged, "because we cannot simply shed historically-constituted social formations like a set of clothes. Our task, instead, is to assign to ourselves today's economy, itself, as an ethical task."[127] The German example was apparent, too, in the institutional structure of Austrian Catholic pragmatism. It found a foothold above all in the Austrian People's League (Volksbund), which was modeled directly after the German Volksverein. Heinrich Brauns himself spoke there on multiple occasions, reminding Austrian listeners that "economic and political life have their own rules"—if Catholics wished to engage in these spheres, they must study them scientifically and not resort to "dogmatics and morality."[128]

As elsewhere, this considered pragmatism never congealed into a principled form of Catholic modernity that could lend ideological coherence to the embattled First Austrian Republic. Even Messner's journal was critical of parliamentary democracy and modern individualism, while his own admission that the "Jewish spirit" was a principal cause of capitalism lent fuel to reactionary fires. He used his front-page editorials to popularize German accommodationists such as Peter Tischleder, but he was no more successful than they were at explaining why exactly Catholics should support the new states. As the First Republic descended into violence in 1927, Messner began to urge Catholics to support some kind of "true democracy," impregnated by Catholic principles instead of socialist ones.[129]

Ignaz Seipel, priest and savior of the First Austrian Republic, traveled a similar path. In the early 1920s, Chancellor Seipel guided his Catholic party toward an acceptance of the First Austrian Republic and even helped to acquire the international finance capital that kept it afloat. He did so not from any principled commitment to republicanism or capitalism but out of pragmatism. In the wake of street violence in the summer of 1927, this same pragmatic spirit brought him in a different direction. He now began to write vaguely of a "time of transition toward something new." Although he, too, called it "true democracy," in practice that "something new" involved the empowerment of the paramilitary Heimwehr and the suspension of parliamentary democracy in the name of autocratic rule that, in Seipel's eyes, could defend political justice against the machinations of socialism.[130]

Our tour of Waldemar Gurian's intellectual commitments and networks leads to the conclusion that, even among the most progressive Catholic voices, a Catholic defense of modernity, as a secular condition of religious freedom and pluralism, failed to arise in the 1920s. Gurian and the rest of the new intellectual elite hardly tried to provide one, dreaming instead of a religious renewal outside the secular modern framework. They longed for Christ to reconquer Europe, not for the Church to ally with non-Catholics in the name of human rights, religious freedom, and the social market economy.

This ideological impasse helps to explain the crises of Catholic parliamentary politics that were piling up even before the Great Depression. In the same summer that the Holy See expressed its dissatisfaction with Maurras (1926), the Center Party's relationship with its socialist partners collapsed on account of the socialist desire to expropriate Germany's former princes without compensation. The following summer, tensions between Catholics and socialists in Vienna boiled over into violence, leading Ignaz Seipel to begin questioning his commitment to parliamentary democracy. In response to *those* events, German Center Party leader Wilhelm Marx withdrew his membership from the Reichsbanner, an organization that brought together Catholics and socialists in defense of Weimar. The following year, the Center Party had a dramatic election for the party leadership. Joseph Joos, a republican and member of the Reichsbanner, lost to Ludwig Kaas, a conservative cleric more concerned with traveling to Rome and lauding Mussolini than he was in shoring up Germany's tottering democracy (in turn, and completing the cycle, Eberle and other Austrian Catholics looked on gleefully, viewing the party's authoritarian, clerical turn as a model). Meanwhile, in France, the Republican Federation was in the midst of a power struggle whose basic outlines were similar to those of the Center Party—and here, too, the new leader (Victor Perret) was a Catholic reactionary somewhere between ambivalent and hostile to the Third Republic.[131]

Scholars of the Church have lavished attention on the condemnation of Maurras, which supposedly marked the end of Catholic antimodernism. They have paid less attention to the fact that Catholic parliamentarism was entering a crisis at the same time. This fact is just as crucial, and just as telling about the state of Catholic thought in the 1920s. Since Catholic participation in secular republics was defended primarily in terms of pragmatism, Catholics mobilized little defense of those republics once circumstances began to change. Pragmatism was not enough to convince Catholics that secular modernity was worth defending. Catholics needed robust, conceptual reasons for a task like that, especially since it flew in the face of a tradition that since the French Revolution, if not before, had been calling for an end to modernist experiments. In the 1920s, those reasons were not forthcoming.

THE TRAJECTORIES OF Moenius and Gurian are radically different in almost every way, but they both ended in a strident critique of Nazism, and in the sorrows of failure and exile. Moenius spent the early 1930s fulminating against Nazism as a recrudescence of Prussian militarism. In the end, his campaign failed, as the Center Party that he had long loathed betrayed him yet again by lending its support to Hitler. He fled to Austria in disgust. Gurian, while sharing little intellectually with Moenius, was in the same predicament. By the early 1930s, he was both intellectually and personally isolated—"deeply unsettled," he wrote to a friend in 1932, by the "disorientation in German Catholicism." A few months later, after a highly successful election for the Nazis, he admitted that his attempts to become "a journalist and author in Catholic Germany had completely failed." Soon after, an important Nazi periodical singled him out in a sweeping critique of the "Jew-ization" of the German Catholic Church. Horrified, and with his opportunities rapidly shrinking, Gurian reached out to the archbishop of Freiburg for aid. The archbishop could do nothing, and his secretary suggested that Gurian try to make a life for himself in exile.[132] In the spring of 1934, Gurian accepted this limp advice. He fled Germany for good, landing eventually in Switzerland, financially broke and spiritually broken.

The failure of both projects necessitated a caesura in Catholic thinking about the problem of modernity. Each represented the continuation of a long-standing current of Catholic thought and action—two different ways to grapple with the modern, and two different ways to reject it. In the late 1920s, each was already struggling to find purchase. And when the Great Depression struck, and dangerous new political currents rushed into the mainstream, it became utterly clear that new concepts and new strategies were necessary. The postwar era had come to a close. As Nazis and Communists began to battle over the future of Weimar, a new prewar era began, and a new set of developments in the Church.

✧ 2 ✧

ANTI-COMMUNISM AND PATERNAL
CATHOLIC MODERNISM, 1929–1944

Honour your father and your mother so that you may live long in
the land that Yahweh your God is giving you.

—EXODUS 20:12

The period from 1929 to 1944 was a disastrous one for Europe, and for the
Catholic Church too. The onset of the Great Depression, quickly followed
by new threats from fascism and Communism, sent democratic polities
into crisis. Across Europe, from Spain to Hungary and most everywhere
in between, dictators came to power with the promise that they could fix
the mess that had been created by democratic failure. Generally speaking,
Catholics welcomed the new authoritarianism, even if they balked when
the regimes trampled on Church rights and liberties (as they often did).
Some Catholics did resist the new fascist movements more forcefully, and
many paid for this with their lives. They were, however, few and far between. This was certainly the case in Germany, Austria, and France. In
Germany, the Catholic Center Party gave Hitler the votes he needed to take
power in 1933. The Vatican quickly signed a treaty with Hitler, while Catholic leaders praised the new regime as an ally against Communism. The
next year, Austrian Catholics lined up behind the Catholic dictator Engelbert Dollfuss. And in France, Catholics were enthusiastic about Marshal
Pétain, another Catholic dictator who came to power after the nation fell
to Hitler's armies. In all three of these cases, there was significant church-
state conflict, but in all three cases, as elsewhere in Europe, Catholics

tended to protest individual policies without criticizing the regime as a whole. In Germany, for instance, Catholic leaders bristled at Hitler's policies toward Catholic schools, but they seldom questioned the regime's legitimacy, or its anti-Semitism. The Vatican remained silent about the Holocaust, as well, despite the fact that Pope Pius XII was privy to a great deal of information about it.

All of this is endlessly controversial, and the extent of Catholic complicity in the horrors of the period has understandably excited enormous interest. The gravitational pull of this question, however, has drawn attention away from others—less explosive, perhaps, but historically crucial. How, exactly, did Catholic *thought* about social and economic affairs evolve in the 1930s? How did Catholics themselves understand what they were doing? How did the horrific experiences of the 1930s change the shape of Catholic thinking in ways that might extend far beyond World War II? These questions have hardly been posed. So much attention has been paid to questions of complicity and guilt that historians have overlooked the conceptual transformations that took place inside the Catholic Church in the 1930s. A close attention to texts and concepts shows that those transformations were dramatic. It was during these years of chaos and bloodshed, in fact, that the Catholic Church became modern.

The word "modern" has innumerable meanings. The sense at issue here is a simple one: the Church became modern once its leaders and its intellectuals accepted that the old era of throne-and-altar fusion was never coming back, and that the Church would have to find a way to make do in a world of secular states and church-state separation. As we saw in Chapter 1, Catholics in the 1920s by and large were *not* modern in this sense. They blamed secular modernity for World War I and sought salvation in some form of Catholic antimodernity. In the 1930s, faced with the rise of fascist and Communist movements across the continent, Catholics in much of Europe gave up on that dream. While the new crop of dictators sometimes employed Christian iconography, it was obvious that they had little interest in creating the kind of antimodern social order theorized by the Catholic social tradition. As one German Catholic jurist explained in 1935, "These new states are in no way 'Christian' states in the sense of the Thomist *Communitas perfecta christiana.*"[1] That was no longer a problem. The whole panoply of prophetic or monarchist movements they had long defended seemed absurd in the wake of the Great Depression, when the molten fluidity of the 1920s gave way to a narrower and more dangerous set of political options. The goal was no longer to conquer but to retrench, forge new alliances, and survive.

Since the French Revolution, Catholics had been nostalgically pining for a return to some sort of medieval settlement, in which church and state would once again be tightly intertwined. In the 1930s, this sensibility essentially vanished. Medievalism became marginalized, the province of utopian intellectuals in non-Catholic countries or newly marginalized icons of the past such as Othmar Spann and Charles Maurras.[2] Pioneering theologians such as Marie-Dominique Chenu, Yves Congar, and Étienne Gilson were united by a desire to think more historically about the Church, dethroning the scholastic Middle Ages from their privileged status in Catholic thought. In Germany, *Hochland* published a front-page article on the "liquidation of the Middle Ages" in 1937, claiming that the "efficacy of this epoch" had reached its end. The idea that the Reformation had unleashed a temporal rupture that should be undone was no longer widely held, either. In the work of Joseph Lortz and others, even Martin Luther began to be reconsidered in Catholic circles.[3]

Once they abandoned the goal of state capture, Catholics had recourse to a new and modern language to think about political legitimacy. If the state would not itself be Catholic, and if religion would in some sense have to be restricted to the private sphere, then the task for the state was to *protect* that private sphere. Catholics, therefore, began to use a new set of concepts to rigorously delineate the private sphere into which the state could not intrude: human rights, human dignity, religious freedom, and antitotalitarianism. For the first time, therefore, they had access to a widely shared set of concepts that allowed them to be ideologically, and not just pragmatically, committed to working with non-Catholics in support of secular political projects. Even conservative Church leaders came to speak this new language fluently. In the 1930s and during World War II, Pope Pius XI and Pope Pius XII—joined by bishops such as Austria's Alois Hudal, France's Pierre-Marie Gerlier, and Germany's Clemens von Galen, alongside the collective Fulda Bishops' Conference—began to emphasize modern themes, which had been almost entirely absent from Church leadership discourse in the 1920s. In place of the rights of the Church, they spoke now of "human rights." In place of the dignity of the Church, they spoke of "human dignity," which accrued to all people, not only to Catholics. And in place of Catholicism's privileged place in the polity, they began to speak of "freedom of conscience."[4]

While the 1930s shift toward modernity and human rights discourse is sometimes recognized, it is usually presumed that the true modernizers were the minority antifascists waging battle against their reactionary opponents. This is not what happened. In most cases, in fact, Catholics turned toward modernity in an attempt to find a way to accommodate with authoritarianism. While fascists were of course not great defenders of human dignity or human rights, those concepts emerged in Catholic circles as a strategic effort to force authoritarian governments to enshrine and protect the private sphere as they understood it. Take the case of Robert Linhardt, a German Jesuit whose little book *Constitutional Reform and Catholic Conscience* (1933) did indeed herald, as one scholar has claimed, a "radical reorientation of Catholic political thought." In it, Linhardt rejected earlier forms of Catholic politics built around parliamentary pragmatism or an obsession with Catholic institutions. He suggested instead a turn toward "the inalienable human rights of the person" and "human dignity" as the cornerstone of Catholic political thinking. This was one of the first extended defenses of this turn, which would soon become commonplace, to appear anywhere in Europe. While Linhardt was certainly modern, he was not, as previous scholars have presumed, a democrat. He was a National Socialist—and precisely *because* he was modern, as he explained in a lecture entitled "On the Meaning of the New Age." Nazism, Linhardt claimed, was "powerful and historically genuine," promising a "new, modern marriage of German-ness and Christianity." The movement promised to protect an antiliberal form of "freedom," "progress," and "development of the personality."[5]

Not all Catholics in the 1930s agreed with Linhardt, to be sure. Almost all agreed that a "new age" had come, and that the new Catholic task was to shape modernity rather than to reject it. There was disagreement, however, over what that might mean. Catholic intellectuals took two basic positions, deriving from their answer to the greatest question posed to the Church in the era: given the death throes of liberal democracy, should Catholics side with the gathering forces of authoritarian nationalism or those of socialist internationalism? Or, put more boldly, should Catholics ally with fascists or Communists? The notion of alliance is crucial, because they were generally unwilling to grant unqualified support to either. Few Catholic intellectuals in the 1930s were "Catholic fascists" or "Catholic Communists," although there were far more of the former. The schools of thought in the Catholic 1930s were not therefore "fascist" and "Commu-nist" but rather *antifascist* and *anti-Communist*. Both answers were modern, both were explicable from within the resources of the Catholic tradition, and both pushed the Church toward new kinds of alliances.

For the vast majority of 1930s Catholic thinkers, Linhardt included, anti-Communism was paramount, and the task of the era was to forge a kind of modern Catholicism that could make its peace with the new authoritari-anism. The greatest Catholic innovation of the era, and the one with the most staying power, involved the creation of a new worldview in which multiple religions, along with religion-friendly secular forces, lined up against the global menace of atheistic Communism.[6] Catholics had been opposed to Communism in the 1920s, but it was a relatively marginal issue, folded into the broader critique of modernity. At the end of the 1920s, this changed as the breakdown of Vatican-USSR negotiations dovetailed with the onset of the Great Depression and the new prominence of Communist parties. For most Catholics, Bolshevism was no longer viewed as one evil among many but rather as the privileged vessel of the Antichrist. The Catholic press across Europe was filled with reports of anticlerical atroci-ties in the "triangle of suffering" that linked Spain, Mexico, and the Soviet Union. Catholics organized internationally, through an interconfessional organization called Pro Deo and elsewhere, to combat Communism, not fascism. The pope launched a "Crusade of Prayer" for victims of Soviet religious persecution in 1930, while a few years later Rome launched an unprecedented anti-Communist campaign directed by the newly created Secretariat on Atheism.[7]

There was no antifascist analogue to these efforts, an institutional reality that was reflected in dogma. While *Divini Redemptoris,* the 1937 anti-Communist encyclical, offered a sweeping denunciation of Communism in the universal language of Latin, its anti-Nazi corollary of the same year, *Mit brennender Sorge,* was written in German and was directed specifically to a German audience. It did not condemn Nazism as such, restricting itself to a criticism of Nazi excesses and violations of Church privileges. Anti-Communism became so central to 1930s Catholics that, when they wanted to critique fascism, they often did so by pointing out its similarities with Communism. German critics of Nazism referred to "brown Bolshe-vism"; Cardinals Faulhaber and Adolf Bertram, the most important Church leaders in Germany, both used this move to criticize the anti-Christian elements of Nazism. Indecent cinema was referred to as "cultural Bolshevism," another instance of a new universal signifier (Communists were never referred to as "red fascists").[8]

Crucially, Catholics did not simply accept the modern settlement from a position of weakness. Instead, they adopted modernist strategies to reform and shape it. Communism was viewed as a pathological and totalitarian form of modernity, so Catholics tasked themselves with explaining what a healthier and more acceptable form might look like. Anti-Communism was linked, therefore, with a particular form of Catholic modernism. If the basic gambit of any religious modernism is an acceptance of the split between the private sphere of religion and the public sphere of politics and economics, the best way to analyze a particular variant is to ask how that private sphere is defined. How, in other words, did religious thinkers and politicians conceptualize the space in which religion was meant to reside?

The mainstream Catholic modernism of the 1930s defined the private sphere—the space of religion—in terms of reproductive families: a unit that included a working father and a stay-at-home mother, married in the Church and bound by Catholic law to regulate sexuality and divorce, duty bound to procreate for their Church and their fatherland alike. Catholics were still interested in having their own institutions wherever possible, most notably schools and clergy-led Catholic Action organizations.[9] But in the last instance, they tended to see the nuclear family as the last redoubt of social virtue, and the institution to be protected above all else. As one German women's magazine put it in 1935, "When the whole world is in crisis" and "when all spheres of life become secularized," we Catholics have no choice but to "push for the strengthening, healing, sanctification, and consecration of family life."[10] Never before had the secularization of non-family spheres been accepted. And never before in Catholic history had so much emphasis been placed on the multigenerational family unit as the centerpiece of social order.

Of course, Catholics had long been concerned about sexuality and the family. Responding to the sexual license of the Roman empire in which Christianity had been born, titanic theologians such as St. Paul, St. John of Chrysostom, and St. Augustine forged a tight bond in Catholic thought between sex and sin. Over the centuries, however, the importance of family ethics to the Church mission had waxed and waned. In the nineteenth century, the influence of Alphonse de Liguori legitimated a somewhat lax approach to sexual issues. Dogma about divorce and infidelity was stable, but Liguori and others argued that sex had purposes other than procreation. This approach pleased many clergymen, one of whom complained that nobody would pay attention to them if they counseled the flock to "have a child every nine months." Catholic social teaching, too, was comparatively silent on family matters. While Pope Leo XIII of course criticized divorce, his great encyclicals on marriage and social welfare said nothing about contraception.[11]

Family matters became increasingly central to Catholic moralists in the 1920s, responding both to fear of depopulation and to ever-louder calls for sexual liberation. And yet, in the antimodernist years, family ethics played a limited role—not because Catholics were unconcerned with the family but because they had many concerns *besides* the family. When Catholics lambasted secular statehood and modern capitalism at every turn, family ethics remained somewhat marginal. It was between 1929 and 1934, the same years in which Catholics were convulsed by anti-Communism, that the reproductive family first emerged at the very center of social Catholic thinking. Germany's Catholic Congress focused on family issues for the first time in 1929, and the following year Pope Pius XI released the first encyclical on family issues in a half century. It became common sense to link national service, Catholic virtue, and heroic childbearing. "Our decline," one Catholic editorialist argued in 1935, "is mathematically inscribed in the annual number of births." Karl Adam, one of the most influential theologians of the era, wrote widely on marriage and the family. While recognizing that theologians had traditionally focused on sexuality and the marriage bond, he thought this was too limited: parenthood is a holy community, too, and one with a social meaning. The creation of a new Christian culture, he insisted, "stands and falls with the question of the possibility and reality of a new Christian national community, and this question is finally dependent on whether we will again have, all along the line, Christian marriages and families once again" (Adam became an enthusiastic National Socialist). Intellectually speaking, the major statement was a widely translated textbook on family affairs published in 1933 by the Belgian priest and theologian Jacques Leclercq. He, too, saw the reproductive family as the central building block of individual morality and social harmony. "Since the family is an institution extremely close to nature," he explained, "the requirements of nature are much stricter in the case of the family than they are in political matters." We are duty bound, he insisted, to procreate within the confines of Christian marriage, whether or not this gives us personal satisfaction.[12]

Only in this era did it become obvious that Catholic law should apply in questions of sexuality, marriage, and reproduction but not directly in questions of commerce or politics. Catholics called on the state to ban contraception, while presuming that Catholic doctrines of usury, private property, or trade union liberty were open to negotiation. Catholics called on the state to ban divorce, too, while abandoning the traditional insistence that the state publicly commit itself to Christ. They therefore followed a path familiar to many different religious traditions in the nineteenth and twentieth centuries. In order to make a home in a modern society, they consolidated religious law around the putatively private spaces of the body and the home, thereby permitting the economy and the state to swing free of the direct jurisdiction of religious law.[13]

The "privatization" of religion does not entail depoliticization—instead, it shapes the form that public religious action can legitimately take. This consolidation around the family generated a new form of religious engagement in the public sphere, the legitimacy of which now derived not from religious law but from its capacity to provide stability, order, and prosperity to the family unit. This took three specific forms, each of which will be considered in more detail later. In place of religious charities, Catholics came to presume that the secular welfare state would deliver aid to impoverished families. In place of Catholic professional organizations, Catholics began to trust the secular state to manage industrial relations for the common good. And in place of imperial or monarchist nostalgia, Catholics accepted the secular nation-state as a legitimate political body—so long as it respected the supposedly "European" values of the West, and so long as it properly regulated the all-important issues of marriage, divorce, homosexuality, and abortion.

The main Catholic response to the 1930s was to theorize a form of Catholic modernism in which powerful, centralized, and secular states would protect the welfare, property, and rights of religious families. I will call this strategy "paternal Catholic modernism," referring to its gendered and hierarchical account of the private sphere. For all of its affection for authority as a bulwark against the gathering threat of Communism, there was nothing intrinsically fascist or even antidemocratic about it. Versions could be found in places such as the United States and Belgium, where dictators did not come to power. It could also legitimate acts of limited protest against fascist regimes, as in the case of conservative anti-Nazi Catholics such as Bishop von Galen, Aurel Kolnai, Carl Muth, and Heinrich Rommen. Rommen's *The State in the Catholic World of Thought* (1935), for instance, made no claim that the state should explicitly recognize Church authority now that we have lived through "the great upheaval that introduced modernity." Instead, he argued that "the state is like the father," tasked with defending the people and owed authority and obedience. At the same time, the state is charged with protecting "the subjective rights" of its citizens—something that, the text strongly implied, Hitler was not doing (Rommen soon fled into exile). In Rommen's life and work, we see paternal Catholic modernism turned against Hitler—a position that was not common but that was certainly coherent.[14]

If paternal Catholic modernism was not inherently fascist, it was not inherently antifascist either. The contours of paternal modernism in fact help us to understand the basic attitude of critical acceptance that marked the 1930s Catholic response to the wave of authoritarian dictators that came to power in Catholic Europe. There was significant church-state conflict in almost all of these cases. As one recent survey of the Italian case concludes, "Historians generally agree that the vast majority of Catholics supported the regime, that fervent Catholic Fascists were a distinct minority, and that anti-Fascist Catholics were even less numerous."[15] This judgment applies equally well across Europe. Paternal Catholic modernism, as a model, cannot really help us to understand the committed fascists or ultranationalists, who were rather marginal in the Church. It helps us to understand, though, the more mainstream view that there was at least no inherent conflict between Catholicism and the new style of dictatorial rule, and that some form of fascism should be welcomed, if cautiously, as an antidote to Communism and as a spiritually healthy form of modernity. That is, it helps us to understand the many millions who accepted the basic legitimacy of the new regimes while harboring doubts about specific issues such as enforced sterilization or state regulation of marriage.

Paternal Catholic modernism was not committed to civil liberties, democracy, or, most tragically, antiracism as first-order virtues. If anything, this new set of strategies colluded in the persistence of anti-Semitism in Catholic circles. Catholics were far more willing to speak out about violations of Catholic family norms than about anti-Semitic outrages. To be fair, Catholics tended to avoid crudely biological forms of racism, which violated

the universality of the Christian message and, more proximately, threatened the rights of converts. But when they did address the Jewish question
in the 1930s, they normally gave voice to a modern form of anti-Semitism.
Catholics tended to avoid religious justifications for anti-Semitism (blaming
the Jews for the death of Christ, for instance). They justified it, instead, by
claiming that the supposed rootlessness and sexual amorality of European
Jews led them to collude with the equally rootless and amoral Bolsheviks
(indeed, the first draft of the anti-Communist encyclical *Divini Redemptoris,* the first papal encyclical in history to place human rights at its center,
included an explicitly anti-Semitic passage). This belief was codified into
the insidious notion of Judeo-Bolshevism.[16]

Paternal Catholic modernism, nonetheless, had much to offer. It appealed to Catholic elites and Church leaders struggling to imagine forms of
Catholic social action that would not directly conflict with the imperatives of states with the power to demolish the Church. It appealed, likewise, to lay Catholics and intellectuals who wanted a way to conceptualize
the new Europe and the place of the faith within it. Paternal Catholic modernism allowed them to be good citizens and good Catholics, too. This resonance in lay Catholic circles was crucial, given that the elaboration and
circulation of Catholic ideas increasingly took place in lay journals and
newspapers. The lay Catholic press survived with surprising health, too—
even during the war, and even in Nazi Germany, where Catholic journals
continued to publish longer than most, and where the Church continued to
constitute what one scholar has called an "alternate public sphere" (the
circulation of highbrow Catholic periodicals such as *Hochland* more than
doubled during the Nazi years).[17]

The emergence of paternal modernism was not a matter of high theology.
It can only be understood through a patient analysis of evolving approaches
to the three major themes of social Catholic reflection, as presented in
Marshal Pétain's famous slogan: Work, Family, Fatherland (a riposte to the
French revolutionary triptych: Liberty, Equality, Fraternity). As such, this
chapter will proceed through an investigation of three lay Catholic intellectuals, one from each of the three countries under investigation. Mina
Wolfring (Austrian) was concerned directly with the family and pioneered
the Catholic embrace of the secular welfare state. Theodor Brauer (German)
was an economist who helped Catholics make peace with modern, statist
forms of economic management. Henri Massis (French) was a political
thinker who helped Catholics to understand how and why they should embrace the secular, rights-defending nation-state. The claim is not that these

three were uniquely responsible for these shifts; although each was important, they are being used here as windows into broader transnational processes. All three were Catholic intellectuals who eventually played important political roles in secular states. All three claimed to defend human rights and family values in the name of anti-Communism, and all three ended up colluding with fascism and anti-Semitism. While each tended to stick to his or her own domain of expertise, a combined analysis of their careers, in transnational context, helps us to see how paternal Catholic modernism was forged. And while their politics were discomfiting, their joint stories help us to understand how Europe's Catholics became modern.

Family: Natalism and Welfare

The new centrality of family values to Catholic political and social thinking generated all manner of new alliances and strategies. A Catholic activist interested in returning the whole society to God acts in very different ways from one who is simply trying to ensure the safety and well-being of the Catholic family. The most obvious consequence was that Catholics celebrated secular states that imported Catholic family ideals into their legal codes. Repression of homosexuality, abortion, and contraception was a common feature of the legislative landscape, and Catholic support for it is unsurprising. The more consequential transformation of the era concerned the evolved Catholic attitude toward another interface between the law and the family: the welfare state.

Traditionally, Catholics had been wary of the centralized welfare state, which promised to bring the bureaucrats of a loathed institution into the sacred space of the home. While there were exceptions, notably in *fin de siècle* France, the social Catholic tradition, in line with the deep institutionalism that was its hallmark, had generally sought to address poverty through Catholic charities—allied with the state, perhaps, but not directed by it. As late as the 1920s, Catholics had labored to put family welfare into the hands of employers and charities. In the 1930s, though, this was clearly insufficient. The scale of suffering was too great, which was bad enough in itself but even worse when it led increasing numbers to turn to Communism. Instead of rejecting the welfare state, therefore, the new generation of Catholic family activists sought to infiltrate and reform it.

Papal encyclicals provide a rough guide to transformations in Catholic thought more broadly. In 1880, Leo XIII released an encyclical on the family called *Arcanum;* fifty years later, in 1930, Pius XI tackled the same theme in *Casti connubii,* the most extensive encyclical on family life ever released. Both encyclicals insisted that marriage was an affair for the Church to control, and not the state, and that divorce was anathema. And yet the contrasts between the two are striking. Leo XIII was primarily concerned with marriage. The only claim made about children is that they should obey their parents and receive a Catholic education. The text's claims about the state are purely negative: the state's role is merely to recognize, and not disrupt, Catholic control over marriage. When it came to social welfare, as Leo XIII explained in *Rerum novarum,* the state was only to step in "if a family finds itself in exceeding distress, utterly deprived of the counsel of friends."[18]

Pius XI, on the contrary, placed the reproductive family at the center of his theological vision and empowered the welfare state to protect that family. *Casti* considers society as a whole, arguing that the reproductive family unit—"husband, wife, and children"—is at the center of "the happiness and well being of the nation." The state, therefore, is charged with caring for the family far more than Leo ever envisioned, since "the prosperity of the State and the temporal happiness of its citizens" rest on the family. If families, "particularly those in which there are many children," could not find suitable housing, employment for the husband, or food at reasonable prices, it was up to the state to step in. Welfare policy was necessary to keep the mother from having to work outside the home, which Pius XI deemed a "great harm." It was also necessary, the text added, to keep families from turning in desperation to revolutionary doctrines. *Casti* was, notably, the first encyclical of the twentieth century to reference Communism directly, referring specifically to the "unheard of degradation of the family" in Communist nations.[19]

The great novelty of *Casti connubii* was that it legitimated Catholic collaboration with secular welfare states even if this involved the sidelining of Catholic charitable organizations. This transition can be plotted in the careers of individual social Catholic activists such as Mina Wolfring, an energetic Austrian writer and bureaucrat. Born in 1890, she began her career as an organizer in the Austrian Catholic Women's Organization (KFÖ) in the 1920s. She focused on young mothers and served as editor to numerous KFÖ publications. She was active in "Red Vienna," where socialists had control of municipal government and where socialist physician Julius Tandler, enthralled by the promise of eugenics, envisioned a state-driven reconstruction of the battle-scarred body politic. He and his allies envisioned enormous public-housing complexes, complete with child care and maternity benefits that would be delivered irrespective of marital status. These would be supplemented by marriage-counseling clinics designed to instruct working-class couples in the arts of voluntary birth control.[20]

In response to what she saw as socialist overreach, the Wolfring of the 1920s argued, as Catholics had for decades, that family welfare activities should fundamentally be handled by charitable organizations like the KFÖ, perhaps partnering with the state but not being directed by it. The KFÖ, for instance, worked with the Austrian state to administer family insurance programs. This had smaller but more concrete implications, too. In the editorial opening the first issue of a KFÖ journal under Wolfring's leadership, she explained that the social democrats were providing welcome baskets for pregnant women in the provinces. She responded viciously, complaining that the socialists were supplanting the charitable activities of Catholic women for their own nefarious, propagandizing ends. "The gifts that the Reds give to the little body of the new world citizen," she feared, "will lead to a fearful consequence for the child: the renunciation of God." As late as 1932, Catholic charitable officials were still arguing that food relief should be handled by the Church, not the state, because the Church would deliver aid in more family-friendly ways—for instance, by providing packets of food, rather than hot meals, so that the needy could spend time cooking and eating in the bosom of their family.[21]

Over the course of the 1930s, Wolfring became an apostle of the modern welfare state, whose power she believed could be used to keep women in their divinely appointed place in the home. She remained as devoutly Catholic as ever, but she and other KFÖ leaders came to believe that Austria would fall to Communists unless the state intervened to protect families from destitution.[22] She was not alone. Around 1930, many family activists followed the path laid out by *Casti connubii*, linking anti-Communism with defense of the family and finding new allies in the process. In that year, for instance, Germany's League of Catholic Women singled out Bolshevism as the major threat to the Christian family. And in that year alone, readers of *Hochland, Germania,* and *Der Volksverein* were treated to lurid accounts of marriage and family life in Soviet Russia. A Russian man who supposedly had children with twenty different women was a common fixture of the Catholic press (perhaps representing a modification of an older Catholic critique of non-Western, polygamous families).[23]

Wolfring's turn toward family-friendly welfare, like her anti-Communism, can be traced in the international spaces of the Church. The class-based internationalism of the Soviet Union, Catholics insisted, could be countered by a family-based, Catholic internationalism. A French cardinal made this explicit in an address to the International Union of Catholic Women's Organizations: "You must belong to an international," he explained, "because other international centers exist which are not Catholic."[24] A great deal of the international exchange of the 1930s focused on family matters, which provided the common ground that geopolitics sometimes could not. For instance, the first German since the war to appear at the hallowed French "Social Weeks" was a woman from Germany's Catholic Women's Union (the *Frauenbund*), while the same organization was also studied and praised in Wolfring's journal.[25]

Wolfring was personally involved with France's Women's Civic and Social Union (UFCS), the most influential Catholic women's organization in interwar Europe.[26] The organization championed stay-at-home mothers and large families, which was nothing new, but it was also committed to aggressive state policy as a necessary buttress. The primary purpose of the UFCS, in fact, was to pressure the French state for welfare policies that would allow women to stay at home. It was also a clearinghouse for Catholic family activists from across the continent who wanted to swap ideas and see what was happening elsewhere. Its journal lambasted French Catholics for their parochialism and published regular reports on family policy outside of France. The organization even published a newsletter dedicated to nothing more than a country-by-country rundown of innovations in Catholic family organization and social legislation.[27] Wolfring attended one of the UFCS's major international congresses, where she delivered a speech on Austrian welfare policy (she can be spotted in a photo in a French newspaper, listening intently in the front row of the lecture hall at the Sorbonne). The mixture of conservatism and modernism in 1930s family movements was encapsulated in the congress's title: "The Mother in the Home: A Worker for Human Progress."[28]

The UFCS was especially concerned with state-delivered family allowances, one of the central policy goals of Catholic family activists (Wolfring included). By giving cash benefits to families with multiple children, it was hoped, mothers might be able to stay out of the workplace and provide the moral instruction their children needed. In the 1920s, Catholic industrialists had pioneered family allowances that were administered without state intervention. Speakers at the 1923 Social Week on the family, including Catholic politician Jean Lerolle, celebrated this approach, presuming that a family wage would be arrived at through negotiation between Catholic workers and Catholic employers. This was all in keeping with the traditional social Catholic allergy to the welfare state. In the 1930s, however, this was clearly insufficient and Lerolle himself introduced a law that would oblige employers to pay family allowances.[29] This was one of the greatest welfare reforms of the 1930s, and social Catholics, including those at the UFCS, were largely responsible for conceiving and administering it.[30] The UFCS did not stop there. It had long pressed for an unwaged mother's allowance, another way to use state power to defend the traditional family. This, too, became French law, at least partially thanks to UFCS pressure.

While Wolfring closely followed these French developments, she was even more interested in Fascist Italy. In 1933, Catholic politician Engelbert Dollfuss sent her on an eight-day mission to Italy to explore state support of the family there. She was impressed. As she wrote to the readers of her newsletter, Mussolini, "out of concern for mother and child," had dedicated the state to their protection. "There are no more begging children on the streets," as the state was taking care of them, and she found it "exhilarating to see the honor and concern that surrounds pregnant women." She marveled at the degree of state involvement: "everything centralized, everything integrated in the simplest way." In an audience with Mussolini, he expressed to her that his "work protecting mother and child" was "the most important work of a state," as they represented "the life of the nation." Wolfring especially praised Italy's aggressive policing of abortion, reasoning that social policy ensured that it would never be economically necessary.[31]

Wolfring returned from Italy publicly calling for a similarly centralized and professionalized framework for family welfare in Austria. A few months later, by which point Dollfuss had seized power and was governing as a dictator, she got her wish. He called on Wolfring to head the new Motherhood Protection Bureau, to be based explicitly on the Italian model. That at least was the story that Wolfring fed to her followers, and it is a story that, characteristically, places her in the faithful service of the male leader. The truth was more complicated and represents the paradox that Catholic family activism, in principle dedicated to keeping women in the home, was largely the product of energetic women acting in public.[32] The idea for the bureau, and the study trip to Rome, actually came from Wolfring herself (Dollfuss privately complained that Wolfring was "a little ambitious," indicating just how steep a hill women like Wolfring had to climb even in this arena).[33]

Wolfring's bureau became a major part of the state's welfare apparatus. The regime as a whole was committed to the family, and it set up the system of family allowances that was rapidly becoming the norm. The hope was that family welfare would ensure that women would not be forced to work (in some cases they were not even allowed to work). Wolfring herself became one of the public faces of the authoritarian welfare regime. Her bureau, essentially a welfare agency, allowed her to pursue her long-standing interest in young mothers with a vastly expanded budget. By 1938, she oversaw an enormous network of charitable activities, educational facilities, and subsidized housing for young mothers.[34]

Wolfring's vision of aggressive, anti-Communist family welfare allowed her to freely combine Catholic social teaching and aggressive nationalism. This, too, was a novelty—especially in Austria, which almost entirely lacked a national consciousness of its own in the 1920s. Wolfring cited papal dogma in her speeches, appeared in public with Cardinal Theodor Innitzer, and collaborated happily with Catholic Action organizations, while the KFÖ's newsletter counseled women to laud the new regime precisely in the name of Catholic social teaching.[35] She was quick to point out the congruence between Catholic social teaching and nationalist natalism. She believed that "there must be a realization of the importance of motherhood for the future of Austria." "The protection of new life," she proclaimed elsewhere, "is not only God's command, but a problem of population politics that faces every nation that wants to secure its place in the international order." As she understood it, the bureau was designed "to further a healthy population politics" that would revalorize motherhood in the face of those who were drawing women away from their natural vocation; in her journal, she emphasized time and again that coordinated state action was necessary, as charitable activity had simply failed to solve "the catastrophic decline in births."[36] In 1937, the bureau awarded a prize to the film that best demonstrated the truth that "the healthy Christian *Volk* and healthy Christian state grows out of the healthy Christian family." Wolfring herself published a practical guidebook to child-rearing. In addition to directing women to all of the maternal services offered by the state, she admonished women for their "unwillingness to make sacrifices," drawing an explicit analogy between motherhood and military service.[37]

Wolfring interpreted the family as a site of reproduction and national service. This linkage between nationalist demography and social ethics was commonplace in Austrian Catholicism, as it was throughout Europe. In the nation's most prominent Catholic weekly, for instance, a priest argued that the old tradition of premarital counseling be reinterpreted "in the service of eugenic national education," giving the Church a role in "the hereditary makeup of the nation."[38] Wilhelm Winkler, a Catholic professor of statistics at the University of Vienna and head of the Austrian Central Statistical Office for most of the 1930s, used the language of social science to make the same point, complaining about the "useless existence" of the unmarried or childless. Church leaders agreed. In addition to a joint bishops' letter in December 1934 praising the utility of large families for national health, Cardinal Innitzer wrote a glowing foreword to Winkler's volume *The Decline of Births in Austria,* praising the "clear language of numbers and data" that demonstrated the need for a rapid regeneration to save "our Christian nation." Similarly, at the opening of an exhibit at Vienna's Natural History Museum about race and hygiene, Innitzer expressed delight that "family-biological research" was finding so much concordance with canon law.[39]

This language of race and hygiene tipped over, as it so often did in the 1930s, into anti-Semitism. The anxiety over births was racialized because foreign bodies were viewed as polluting the healthy, embattled national body.[40] While Mina Wolfring was never a Nazi, and her family organization had (illegal) competition from a Nazi counterpart, her language of organic national renewal brought her close to anti-Semitism. "Our national body," she argued in 1932, has succumbed to a "virus."[41] She spoke regularly at the Austrian Family Protection League, a state-sponsored organization with a working group on "medicine and racial hygiene." This placed her on the same stage as some of Europe's most notorious Catholic anti-Semites. The Catholic women's organization that launched Wolfring's career engaged in explicit anti-Semitism, too. An editorial in the KFÖ's journal on "Us and the Jews" worried about the overrepresentation of Jews in teaching and medicine. The author drew a connection between Vienna's high percentage of Jewish doctors and the low birthrate, which she believed resulted from the nefarious Jewish influence on the "spiritual and bodily health" of the Viennese. Our nation, the editorial concluded, "has fallen too far under the influence of the Jewish spirit."[42]

What these texts allow us to see is a flowering alliance, in the name of anti-Communism, between social Catholic ethics, nationalism, and the family-friendly welfare state. In this case, that welfare state was an authoritarian one, which was also true in Germany. Especially in the early years of his reign, many German theologians and moralists celebrated Hitler's moralizing campaigns against Communism and "smut." There were more concrete efforts, too, to find a homology between Catholic family ethics and Hitler's racialized battle for births. This sentiment reached a crescendo with a movement called "Christian People—Healthy People," under whose aegis many Catholic organizations lauded the National Socialists' campaign for, as a Catholic newspaper reported, "a healthy, plain, truly German and Christian family life." The Catholic German Women's Association was a member of that short-lived movement and of the more long-lasting Catholic Mothers' Service (Katholischer Mütterdienst), which sought to cohere Catholic family values with the Nazis' own interest in reproductive motherhood.[43] That agency in turn was propagandized in *Nature and Life of Women,* a journal of the Catholic women's movement. Editorials castigated Soviet Russia for sending mothers to the factories, while a remarkable article titled "The Woman in the New Age" praised the Nazis for their family-friendly welfare policies and their zeal for reproduction ("the purity of the race," it added, "certainly has a high value"). Another German Catholic newspaper celebrated the rise of the German birthrate and declared Catholic appreciation for "the new political will of the German nation," which has given such a "powerful stimulus" to the healthy desire to procreate (the article was also a bid for support from non-Catholics, arguing that large Catholic families were especially necessary to the national community [*Volksgemeinschaft*]).[44]

This effort largely failed. Catholics certainly appreciated the family allowances and other family-friendly welfare policies the regime put in place, but they came into regular conflict with the regime over issues such as sterilization and divorce. Nazism was still viewed as a reformable movement, though, in contrast to Bolshevism. At UFCS congresses, German representatives duly appeared to describe the family-friendly policies of the National Socialist regime, apparently without critical comment. The Bolsheviks were treated entirely differently. Their policies were discussed by anti-Communist exiles, who used their platform as an opportunity to denounce Bolshevism itself.[45] The superiority of Nazi family ethics to Communist ones was likewise taken for granted. In Austria, for instance, a 1936 editorial in the KFÖ's journal recognized that Nazism contained anti-Christian elements but still concluded that "the first and greatest danger will always be Communism."[46]

While Wolfring was not a Nazi, she was much more motivated by anti-Communism than by anti-Nazism. In some ways she even helped to lay the groundwork for the waves of support that greeted the occupying Nazis when they invaded Austria in 1938. Her insistent denigration of female economic agency, her organic language of the ailing body of the nation, and the militaristic language she used to describe motherhood paved the path for the widespread acceptance of Nazi family policy by Austrian women.[47] She was not alone, of course. Austria's bishops released a notorious declaration welcoming the Nazis. The bishops praised particularly the "social policies" of the Nazis, as well as their opposition to "Godless Bolshevism." An internal position paper clarified more fully what the bishops meant by this. The very first section praised the Nazi approach to the family, which promised to address the "crisis of declining births," a problem that had been exacerbated by the "socialist Jewish government in Vienna."[48]

Catholic familialists were in some cases collaborators with Nazis in France, too. They played a central role in the collaborationist government of Marshal Pétain, another Catholic autocrat. The pro-family legislation of the 1930s shows that the alliance of Catholic familialists and secular natalists was already bearing fruit in democratic France, but under Pétain it was able to go even further. "The rights of the family," Pétain declared, "prevail over the rights of the State and the individual."[49] Married women were essentially banned from public service, while marriage leaves and grants were promised to young women to incentivize starting a family. Divorce was rendered more difficult, while new campaigns against contraception and abortion were launched.[50] Catholics were at the heart of Pétain's considerable family welfare apparatus. The UFCS publicly praised Pétain's regime, while internal documents, too, instructed members to indulge a "prejudice in favor of authority": "better to be wrong with authority," leaders reasoned, "than against it." Its charismatic leader, Andrée Butillard, sat on Pétain's Family Council, perhaps pleased that Pétain had centralized France's panoply of family organizations into one quasi-official national federation—as the UFCS had urged. This was accomplished by the Gounot Law of 1942, known as the regime's "Family Charter" and drafted by a well-known Catholic intellectual.[51]

In the era of antitotalitarianism, Catholics now presumed that family welfare was an affair of the state, and that this was true whether or not that state had any particular alliance with the Catholic Church. Catholics no longer aimed to protect families *from* the state, or to conceptualize the body politic as one large family. Instead, they sought to influence state policy in order to protect and enshrine their own family model. This involved, especially, support for mothers with multiple children in the form of maternal education and family allowances. Fathers needed support, too, but not in the home. That kingdom belonged to women. Men needed state support in the workplace.

Work: Corporatism and the Managed Economy

From the 1890s to the 1920s, Catholic economists imagined a form of solidarism that would tame the power of the market by enmeshing the economy in a deep web of Catholic associations, nourished by the specific influence of natural law in economic institutions and in the hearts of workers and employers. This kind of moral economy and deep institutionalism was out of place in the 1930s, when Catholics tasked themselves with accepting and reforming the secular framework. This was as true of the economy as it was of the welfare state: the Vatican, after all, updated its own finances and entered global financial markets at the time.[52] Specifically, the new task was to imagine an economic structure that could provide for the needs of the reproductive Catholic family. That family did not need robust rights to free labor organizing, much less dramatic assaults on the principles of industrial society. That family needed, instead, protection of its private property and some institutional mechanism to ensure that it did not become impoverished (or "proletarianized," as Catholics meaningfully called it at the time). That basic level of social justice would require, in turn, some institutionalized way to mediate between workers and employers, given that Catholics were wary of class conflict but were also convinced that the untrammeled free market would lead to deep injustice. And if that mediation would not be carried out by organized groups of Catholic employers and workers, as Catholic intellectuals had long dreamed, perhaps the state would have to do it—using authoritarian means, if necessary. This was the essential strategy of Catholic corporatism, and under its flag Catholic economic teachings became modern.

Corporatism allowed Catholics to forge their own anti-Communist solution to the woes of the Depression. While it could plausibly be rooted in the social Catholic tradition, corporatist discourse also allowed them to forge conceptual and strategic alliances with non-Catholic thinkers—from reformed liberals to ultranationalists—who were using corporatist language for the same reason. As one Catholic industrialist put it in 1937, "Communism or corporatism: that is the question."[53] "Corporatism" is a slippery word and concept, so it is useful to pin down a bit more clearly what it meant at the time. In its 1930s Catholic guise it represented a belief that the state should be empowered to assist in the mediation of worker and employer interests, normally by creating employers' and workers' syndicates. It also signaled a belief that belonging to these syndicates should be mandatory—a position that had long precedents in social Catholic thought but had always been controversial (political scientists call this "authoritarian corporatism").[54]

While the vogue for corporatism was primarily a phenomenon of the laity, they were following a trend staked out by papal dogma (just as welfare activists such as Wolfring were). In 1891, Pope Leo XIII had released *Rerum novarum* (1891), a social encyclical that set the tone for Catholic social thought for the next four decades. Forty years later, Pope Pius XI released a new encyclical on the economy, *Quadragesimo anno* (1931). Both texts presume that the family, and not the individual worker, is the main unit of economic life, and that the index of economic justice was the delivery of a wage high enough to ensure that women would not have to work.[55] The texts differed, however, in the best means of attaining that. In *Rerum,* Leo presumed that associations of Catholic workers and employers would come together to reach agreements over wages and working conditions in the spirit of charity and the common good. For Leo, in other words, the family was only one component of a dense web of institutions, which took care of interest-group mediation without state oversight. In *Quadragesimo,* by contrast, Pius XI imagined a more central role for the state. The state, for Pius, was urged not simply to protect but to establish and create: wages were to be set, for instance, according to "the public economic good," a concept foreign to *Rerum novarum.* The "first and foremost" goal of the state, he taught, was to abolish class conflict by devoting itself to "the *re-establishment* of the Industries and Professions.*" In other words, the proper economic order had vanished, and the state was entrusted with reestablishing it. And while Leo XIII had made no reference to any particular social or economic experiment, Pius XI did. In paragraphs that he wrote himself, *Quadragesimo anno* cautiously praised the corporatist experiments of Benito Mussolini.[56]

While the corporatist turn in papal dogma is suggestive, a focus on an individual better helps us to understand when, and why, modern forms of corporatism emerged as the dominant Catholic response to the Depression.

Our focus will be on a German Catholic economist named Theodor Brauer. He had been involved in social Catholic circles for decades, editing trade union journals and serving as assistant director of the People's Union for Catholic Germany (Volksverein). In 1928, he accepted Max Scheler's old chair at the University of Cologne, becoming codirector of Mayor Konrad Adenauer's Municipal Institute for Research in the Social Sciences. As this itinerary suggests, he represented all that was most modern in Catholic economic thinking. He used the most up-to-date language of rationalization and industrial efficiency to show how Catholic politics and Christian trade unionism could yield a more moral and just economic order. But as crises in the economy and the Catholic Center Party alike rendered his vision irrelevant, he gave up on the Center Party and suffered a period of desperation.[57] Looking for new approaches, he turned abroad. In 1929, under the auspices of the International Confederation of Christian Trade Unions (CISC), he traveled to Barcelona to investigate the labor syndicates in Primo de Rivera's Catholic dictatorship. The next year, eager to learn more, he secured funds from Adenauer's institute to take a trip to Rome to study the Fascist system from within.[58]

In Spain and Rome, Brauer saw the glimmering of a new Catholic economics—one less dependent on trade unions and more in tune with the needs of the day. Soon after his trips, *Quadragesimo anno* was released. Brauer was thrilled by the encyclical, which seemed to confirm his own ideas about the economy (privately, he claimed that the encyclical so closely matched his own thoughts that it was "as though [he] had helped to write it").[59] While the encyclical, like all papal texts, could be interpreted in many ways, Brauer plausibly believed that it was meant to defend the authoritarian corporatism he was coming to cherish. Many interpreters thought this way, including Austria's chancellor Ignaz Seipel, himself an expert in social Catholic teachings.[60]

Brauer's corporatist awakening took place at a delicate time in Catholic political life. In the wake of the Depression, German politics entered a crisis period as the Nazi Party's vote skyrocketed and Chancellor Heinrich Brüning, like Brauer a devotee of the Christian labor movement, assumed emergency powers in an effort to stave off economic catastrophe. The Catholic trade unions, accepting like everyone else the need for aggressive state intervention, began to turn toward socialist ideals of nationalization and direct state planning.[61] In response, Brauer and others began to push for a more corporatist approach that could rehabilitate the Catholic ideal of interclass harmony.[62] From his leading position inside the League of Christian Unions, he argued for a National Economic Council that would represent vocational interests without recourse to class warfare. While he was not arguing (yet) for the abolition of the unions, his ideas clearly empowered the state and national planning bodies over Catholic civil society. One antagonist inside the union worried that Brauer was one of those "fanatics" who believed that "only corporatism can save us."[63]

Brauer's corporatism consisted, essentially, in a belief that interest-group mediation, in the name of anti-Communism, should be handled by the state—even if this led to the abolition of the Catholic trade unions and employers' associations that had for decades been central to Catholic economic thought. Brauer was no longer convinced of the necessity of specifically Christian institutions. With the crisis of the Center Party, the onset of the Depression, and the left turn of the Catholic unions, these institutions had proven themselves incapable, in his view, of meeting the challenges of the modern age. While Brauer did not come to these ideas as a Nazi, they did lead him to accept the Nazi takeover. Nazism never had a coherent economic platform, but in the early 1930s Nazi ideologues were certainly flirting with forms of corporatism not far removed from Brauer's. A Nazi economist named Max Frauendorfer, for instance, published a volume called *Corporatist Thought in National Socialism*—a volume that pointedly praised the Roman Catholic Church, as well as the concepts of institutional authority in the "Catholic belief community."[64] Books like these helped Brauer toward his belief that, as he wrote to a friend, "the economic-social ideas" of the Nazis "were in essence the same as those I had supported for decades," and therefore "from this perspective no intellectual sacrifice was necessary."[65]

In the end, Brauer was one of a handful of Catholic activists and thinkers to collaborate with the German Labor Front (DAF), the Nazi labor organization, accepting Robert Ley's invitation in the spring of 1933 to serve in its senate. This was not necessarily his ideal solution, but nothing in his corporatism led him to resist it either. Brauer's story is that of mainstream Catholic economic thinking in the 1930s. Many German Catholics, including industrialists such as Albert Hackelsberger and Fritz Thyssen, were convinced that Catholic social teaching endorsed Nazi-style corporatism and the abolition of trade unions. Joseph Lortz and Josef Pieper, by any measure two of the leading theologians in the country, agreed. In Pieper's pamphlet, entitled *The Labor Law of the New Reich and the Encyclical Quadragesimo anno,* he marveled at "the far-reaching, and in some points astonishing, consensus" between Nazi labor law and papal teaching. He also reminded readers that "the heart of all National Socialist social politics," as of Catholic social politics, "is the overcoming of the class struggle." A 1935 sermon, published as *Church and Economy,* instructed that "the economic life of the nation must be built from the corporatist order."[66]

An analysis of Brauer's own texts and evolution helps us to understand how this rapprochement between fascism and Catholic social teaching was possible. The first point is that, for Brauer, the natural agent of economic life was neither the individual worker, as liberals believed, nor the working class, as socialists believed. For Brauer, the "living core of human history," and the recipient of the economic justice he desired, was the family. While mainstream economists thought in terms of utility-maximizing individuals, Brauer and other Catholics peopled the economic space with single-earner families. This meant that the economy was an affair not of the individual, faced with an indifferent market, but of the father, interfacing with an economic order designed to meet his family's needs. The "wage of the breadwinner," Brauer explained, "must be sufficient for the maintenance of his family." As for married women, he insisted that they should not work outside the home—such labor, in addition to being unethical in itself, undercut the possibility that husbands would be paid a living wage.[67] This was, in his mind and in the logic of social Catholicism in general, the barometer of social justice.

The question, though, was how to *secure* the economic rights of the family. Economists of the 1920s had pursued various forms of moral regeneration, Catholic institutional consolidation, and class collaboration outside of state intervention. In the 1930s, Brauer abandoned all of this in the name of paternal Catholic modernism. In place of the chain of legitimate authorities cherished by the social Catholic tradition, Brauer now discoursed on "the two most important 'natural communities,' the family and the state." That pregnant formulation, presented as a gloss on *Rerum novarum,* was in fact a highly controversial reading of it, and one that neglected Leo XIII's own defenses of Catholic workers' right to organize. "The union," Brauer now argued, "cannot be an end in itself."[68]

Brauer's texts shied away from the *corporate* rights of the Catholic social tradition, which had proved so hard to square with modern statehood, in the name of *individual* rights. Already in 1927, he had written one of the first serious German Catholic commentaries on socialism, in which he had judged it incompatible with Catholicism because the doctrine "did violence to the rights and the freedom of the individual."[69] As Catholic institutions further declined in significance over the next six years, the rights-bearing person assumed ever-greater significance in Brauer's writings as he labored to explain the substantial differences between Catholic and Marxist social teachings. In 1933, he wrote a program for the League of Christian Unions endorsing a corporatist program that would, he promised, allow "the honor and development of the free, ethical, and professionally capable *personality*" and would ensure that the worker's "human dignity" was properly recognized. In *The Catholic in the New Reich* (1933), his most extended defense of Nazism, his turn toward the individual appeared, too: "The human individual is, from the Catholic perspective, of the highest value." In another article from this period, he reiterated his commitment to "the human personality as the bearer of responsibility."[70]

In place of the long-defended and communal right to free association, Brauer was most concerned with the individual right to private property, which had been reaffirmed in *Quadragesimo anno*. The Catholic commitment to private property was nothing new. It did, however, evolve in the 1930s, becoming more absolute and crowding out other forms of economic rights. In addition to its defense of trade unionism, *Rerum novarum*, following Aquinas, had left open the door to statist redistribution of superfluous property in the name of the common good. This had occasioned a healthy debate among Catholic economists in the 1920s, some of whom derived quite radical consequences from it. This debate was shut down with *Quadragesimo anno*, which insisted that property redistribution of this sort could only be voluntary. Its primary author, Oswald von Nell-Breuning, believed he had been chosen to put an end to that theological quarrel and its suspiciously socialist tenor. Brauer, a friend of Nell-Breuning's, celebrated the achievement. As he declared in a 1933 speech, the economy must respect "the conception of property provided by natural law." "Individual freedom," he went on, "finds its practical realization through property."[71]

The dogma of corporate rights had long urged Catholics to defend weak states, worried as they were that powerful states would dissolve, or render irrelevant, the Catholic institutions that were properly at the core of the healthy society. The new commitment to individual rights, in Brauer's case as in others, led to a new sympathy for what Brauer called the "strong state," which would be tasked with defending those rights against those who wanted to strip them away (specifically, Communists). By 1931, Brauer saw that his traditional commitment to a weak state was no longer plausible, and he began to argue for a strong state that would serve, in his words, to protect "the freedoms guaranteed by law." He learned this lesson from a man he called "one of the most important constitutional theorists of the present," Carl Schmitt. Schmitt, although no longer in his Catholic phase, still exercised considerable influence in Catholic circles. His writings of the early 1930s emphasized the need for an authoritarian leader to protect the constitution against the squabbling interest groups that were threatening the republic. Brauer's writings of the time drew heavily on this analysis. In 1931, he complained that "individual social groups consistently grab the state by the neck." Likewise, in a 1933 address to a conference of Catholic sociologists, he explained that Catholics must "repudiate" their traditional desire to "minimize the state" and instead seek a "state capable of making decisions" and devoted to "an objective social order." The strong state was not, in Brauer's view, tasked with planning the economy itself. That was socialism. It was instead tasked with overseeing and organizing the interest group mediation that he still saw as central (he hoped that non-state groups would "send distinguished personalities from their own ranks" into state service).[72]

Catholic corporatism, like Catholic family activism, was compatible with the rising tide of anti-Semitism. Both discourses relied on organic metaphors of social bodies and social health, which could easily legitimate a kindred language of contagion and impurity. Like Wolfring, Brauer showed little evidence of personal anti-Semitism—at the same time, his ideology provided no grounds to oppose anti-Semitism, and when it was politically convenient, racism began to creep into his writings. In *The Catholic in the New Reich*, he called for "the pure realization of the German nation," which required cultivation of "the natural power of blood and soil." Some races, he added, were more called to serve God than others, which required the *Volk* to remain "pure." Anti-Semitic articles appeared, too, in a regime-friendly journal that Brauer began to edit, called simply *German Nation* (*Deutsches Volk*). The journal was one of the most public efforts to find common ground between Nazism and social Catholic teaching, and articles regularly complained about the Jews as "the chief enemy of a Christian-German culture."[73]

This story extends far beyond Germany. Corporatism was a transnational response to a transnational economic crisis. Brauer himself was informed by the corporatist experiments in Italy and Spain, and by the mid-1930s, corporatism had become the common currency of Catholic economic thinking. Multiple books appeared from Catholic authors providing country-by-country rundowns of the state of corporatist politics across Europe (mirroring the UFCS publications on international welfare policy). In 1935, the Institute of Fascist Culture in Rome held a congress on corporatism, inviting French youth leaders, many of them from Catholic organizations, to parlay with Fascist luminaries (including the minister of corporations and the minister of agriculture). Austrian Church leaders punctuated the new international vogue for the corporate with an "International Conference on the Corporatist Order," held a few months after the Italian conference, which brought together Catholic social thinkers, Church officials, and political leaders from eleven nations. Brauer himself spread the gospel as widely as he could, giving lectures on the theme in France, Spain, Switzerland, the Netherlands, Austria, and eventually even the United States.[74]

Brauer was probably most excited by events in Austria, where his friend and protégé Johannes Messner was exercising decisive influence on the economic organs of Dollfuss's corporatist state. When Dollfuss seized power in 1934, he did more than attempt to empower the family. He also attempted to create a corporatist economy by fiat. He oversaw the creation of a corporatist parliament that would streamline the process of interest group bargaining by involving the state as a firm hand. The Catholic trade union was dissolved, as in Germany, and replaced by a unified workers' syndicate. The chairman of that syndicate, Friedrich Kühr, came directly from Brauer's Weimar-era circles and had been involved with the Center Party and the Volksverein (Brauer and Kühr had shared a stage at a 1932 conference on corporatism). As in Germany, corporatism was both an economic doctrine and a popular discourse. Mainstream Catholic organs such as *Reichspost* and more specialized workers' journals both praised corporatism as the proper Catholic response to economic depression. Many Catholic workers even supported the regime's dismantling of Catholic trade unions.[75]

Dollfuss was a deep student of Catholic social doctrine, especially as expressed in *Quadragesimo anno*. "We have," he exclaimed in 1933, "the ambition to be the first nation to heed the call of this powerful encyclical!"[76] Just as the encyclical was written by modernizing German economists, it was put into practice by modernizing Austrian ones. One of them was

Richard Schmitz, the mayor of Vienna, who had earlier been a minister of social welfare and an Austrian representative to the international union of Catholic parties (SIPDIC). He had close contacts with French Catholics, who wrote to him of Dollfuss's "distinguished Catholic mystique," just as Schmitz himself publicly and privately enthused that "our good old Christian workers" were coming around to his corporatist vision.[77] However Catholic Dollfuss and his experts may have been, they did not perceive themselves to be erecting a Catholic state (*Quadragesimo anno,* after all, did not call for one, and Dollfuss made no moves to declare Catholicism an official state religion). As Dollfuss's successor, Kurt von Schuschnigg, recalled in his memoirs, Austria's leaders were simply using Catholic texts to discover "the principles of a reform of society" that appealed to everyone, "irrespective of religious creed."[78]

This explains why Johannes Messner, a modernizing priest who had defended capitalism in the 1920s, emerged as the court economist of Dollfuss's regime instead of a more traditional figure such as Eugen Kogon, whose furious anticapitalism and antimodernism had been the norm in Catholic Austria. Messner's views were quite similar to those of Brauer, which is unsurprising given that the two had long known and admired one another's work. In the more Catholic-friendly Austrian state he enjoyed greater influence, and for a longer period of time (receiving a prestigious professorship, editing a journal, serving on the constitutional committee, and more). He, too, traveled to Italy to see Mussolini's corporatism in action, viewing the rights-defending corporatist state as the antidote to Communism.[79] Messner also made it clear that the right to free trade unionism was *not* one of these rights; like Brauer and a number of other Austrian corporatists, he believed that corporatism, properly understood, allowed or even mandated the suppression of the Catholic trade unions (he spoke on this issue at the 1935 international conference on corporatism, which he chaired).[80] While Messner was not a Nazi, he did believe that Catholicism and Nazism were highly compatible when it came, as he put it, to questions of "economic and social reform."[81] And while he rejected much racial science, Messner believed in a "peculiar Jewish disposition towards capitalism." "Racial hygiene" was therefore necessary to protect German racial stock and values. "Immigration," he insisted, "specifically of Eastern Jews, must be sharply policed."[82]

Dollfuss's experiments were closely watched by Catholics across Europe, including a French Catholic economist studying in Vienna with a grant from the Rockefeller Foundation. He marveled that, in the space of a few months, squads of dangerous Marxists disappeared from the streets, only to be replaced by noble parades of interclass corporations.[83] His name was François Perroux, and it was largely through his work that corporatism captured the imagination of French Catholics. As in Germany and Austria, the statist and corporatist turn only took place once the threat of Communism invalidated older Catholic strategies—in the French case, in response to the great power of the Popular Front, a socialist-Communist alliance that threatened to heal the Left's long-standing divisions and win over Catholic workers, too.

The stories were intertwined. *Quadragesimo anno* enjoyed wide circulation in Catholic France, while both Messner and Brauer gave lectures there. The 1935 Social Week featured a report on Messner's international conference on corporatism, at which a French social Catholic had given an address. In that address, J. T. Delos explained that French Catholics, in response to the crisis of liberalism and the threat of Bolshevism, were regularly calling for the state to legally organize a corporatist economy.[84] He was right. By that date, the National Catholic Federation (FNC), the Social Weeks, and the Young Christian Workers (JOC) had all begun to defend some kind of corporatism. The Church hierarchy was on board as well. An assembly of French cardinals and archbishops released a letter celebrating "the corporation, with its cadres, its hierarchy, its regulatory power, its jurisdiction, and its right of representation in government."[85]

Perroux's *Capitalism and the Community of Labor* (1937) was the capstone of the Catholic corporatist revival, offering a theoretical apparatus and a country-by-country rundown of corporatist experiments taking place across the continent. Like other corporatists, Perroux had little interest in defending the medieval guild system or a dense network of Catholic institutions. In the new age, he insisted, the secular state was absolutely required as a third partner between capital and labor, given the explosive conflicts that necessarily accompany industrial development. Perroux called for a "national revolution" that would, within the framework of the French state, create a corporatist system that would overcome the debilitating class and political divisions of the Third Republic. The revolutionary tradition of the "rights of man" would not be discarded but would be "modernized and enriched": the "rights" and "eminent dignity of the working person" would be supplemented by a concern for the legitimacy of professional groups.[86] Jean de Fabrègues, Charles Maurras's former secretary, declared both privately and publicly that Perroux was pointing the way toward a new, and more economically literate, Catholic politics.[87]

While some Catholic corporatists believed that democracy and corporatism were compatible, Perroux thought it was plain that "the parliamentary state is no longer adapted to the needs of the economy."[88] So when Pétain came to power in 1940, it is no surprise that he looked to Perroux—an educated, cosmopolitan economist hostile to liberal democracy and well versed in the continent-wide corporatist wave. Like both Messner and Brauer, Perroux began editing regime-friendly journals and abandoned his support for Catholic unions; like Messner, he served on the constitutional council. The Institute of Corporatist and Social Studies, led by one of Perroux's students, even served as a sort of official think tank for the regime.[89]

The crowning achievement of French corporatism was the Labor Charter, which promised to remake the French economy along corporatist lines through the dissolution of restive trade unions and the erection of a complex series of "Social Committees." Perroux played a role both in drafting and in publicizing the new measures (along with Lucien Romier and other technocrats, both Catholic and secular). In a propagandistic pamphlet released in 1943, he explained how the charter would play a role in "our revolutionary resurrection" by implementing the principles of corporatism and dissolving independent trade unions, which Perroux now saw as hopelessly out of touch with the realities of economic and professional life in modern economies.[90]

In France, as elsewhere in Europe, corporatism was as much a propaganda coup as a technocratic innovation. This form of modern Catholic economics, like its forebears, spread widely and found traction in the Catholic public sphere. A note prepared by Pétain's cabinet claimed that "there is currently no propaganda more urgent than that in favor of the Labor Charter and the Corporation," and, in Catholic France at least, it served its purpose. The French Confederation of Professions, a Catholic employers' body, threw its support behind the charter. The Catholic newspaper La Croix praised it not only for its "definitive break with the old system of class conflict" but also for its "spiritual element," while the secretary of the Social Union of Catholic Engineers excitedly pointed out that Pétain's economic ideas had much in common with papal teaching. The archbishop of Bordeaux declared in a pastoral letter in 1942 that Pétain's labor policies were "fundamentally in harmony with the social doctrine of the Church."[91]

The crucial commonality between Brauer, Messner, and Perroux is that all three were wary of claiming direct religious control over the economy or of relying on moral inspiration and Catholic institutionalism to reform it. All were in dialogue with secular economists: corporatism was in vogue among many in the 1930s.[92] All took a statist turn, reasoning that the secular state, by creating workers' and employers' syndicates, was acting within the bounds of economic reason and Catholic social teachings as explained in *Quadragesimo anno*. To take the French case as an example, the Labor Charter was presented not as the implementation of "Catholic social thought" but as an anti-Communist effort to protect French families and private property that was in some loose way compatible with the tradition, specifically its focus on class collaboration over class conflict. Perroux himself almost never referenced natural law theory or papal texts, even in the pamphlets that he wrote for popular consumption.[93]

Another commonality between corporatist experiments in these three countries (and others) is that they failed. This was first apparent in Germany, where as early as 1934 it was clear that Hitler and Ley had no intention of pursuing corporatist economic governance (Ley, for his part, concluded that corporatism was "an absolute chaos of ideas, a total confusion").[94] Brauer was ejected from the Labor Front just a few months after joining and spent a period in prison. Despite a letter to Ley imploring him to allow his return to the Front, Brauer remained in the wilderness, and he watched in horror as two of his supporters were murdered in the 1934 Night of the Long Knives, when Hitler ordered a number of violent assassinations to cement his hold on power. He was allowed to continue teaching at least, although his existence became increasingly precarious: students began to lodge complaints against him in 1935 for his free-flowing teaching style, in which his various criticisms of Nazi policies sometimes came to light.[95] Even in places such as France, Austria, Portugal, and Spain, where corporatist economics survived longer as a ruling ideology, the practice was a disappointment—wherever it was tried, corporatism either failed to get off the ground (France) or simply devolved into the same bureaucratic, statist economic control that it had been designed to avoid in the first place (Austria, Spain, Portugal).[96]

Authoritarian Catholic corporatism does not seem to have exercised much influence on the actual economy. It did, though, represent a major shift in the way that Catholics *thought* about the economy. The new concern for interest group mediation, organized by a secular state and between secular institutions, led Catholics to sideline much of their earlier opposition to capitalism, the market, and the very notion of state intervention. In place of the sweeping economic reorganization promised by earlier generations of Catholic thinkers, by the end of the 1930s Catholics tended to focus on the protection of individual property rights and the creation of some kind of institutional structure that could ward off Communism. In August 1943, for instance, when the war was turning against Germany and the population was reeling from bombing attacks, the German bishops released a letter expressing their support for "human rights": as in Brauer's earlier work, they focused on the right to the family and the right to property, saying nothing about the right to free association.[97]

This modernization of the Catholic view of the economy allowed for new kinds of alliances, and not only with authoritarian regimes. As recently as the 1920s, Catholic economic dogma, predicated on moral renewal and Catholic institutionalism, had helped to isolate Catholics from potential allies. In the age of corporatism it did the opposite. In the United States, many social Catholics supported Roosevelt's New Deal, which had corporatist elements. In France, both Catholic and secular technocrats looked to Hubert Lyautey, the Catholic general and poet of a revived, rationalized authority. The period's greatest hymn to the rationalizing engineer, Georges Lamirand's *Social Role of the Engineer* (1932, often reprinted), was penned by a Catholic engineer who was active in the Social Union of Catholic Engineers before entering Pétain's service in 1940. "Recent contacts," wrote Jean Coutrot, a leading technocrat, "have shown me that French Catholic thought, after two thousand years of evolution, has arrived at the exact same conclusions we engineers have arrived at, reasoning on a purely objective basis."[98]

Catholics found a new common cause with liberalism, too. Liberalism itself was evolving as its champions attempted to learn the lessons of the Great Depression (the new school sometimes called itself neoliberal, but I'll use Ordo-liberal, another contemporary term, as neoliberalism has come to mean something rather different). In place of laissez-faire attitudes and a distrust of the state, the Ordo-liberals recognized that the free market rested on an indispensable social and legal structure. They were more willing than previous liberals to defend aggressive state action to protect the market, and to champion the social utility of religion. Wilhelm Röpke, one of the founding fathers of Ordo-liberalism, began writing books aimed at Austrian Catholics in order to convince them that Catholic social teaching mandated a form of liberalism (he even wrote a praiseworthy review of

Messner's book on corporatism). In his magnum opus, *Civitas Humana* (1944), he declared that *Quadragesimo anno* was "clearly and completely" aligned with his own liberal project. "A good Christian," he instructed, "is, unbeknownst to himself, a liberal."[99]

There was not yet a genuine rapprochement between Ordo-liberalism and Catholicism, and during these years Catholics seldom even referred to the "market," much less the "social market economy." All the same, the tendrils of later cooperation were apparent in the Catholic warming toward Ordo-liberalism. Perroux had studied with prominent liberals while he was in Vienna, and in France he published the first French translations of both Ludwig von Mises and Friedrich von Hayek. Jean de Fabrègues, Charles Maurras's former secretary and an important Catholic intellectual in his own right, edited a journal called *Civilisation,* which published a number of articles on the theme. "Whereas liberalism has, for many years, been the doctrine that dare not speak its name," wrote one Catholic corporatist in 1939, "we have seen, in the last few months, the restoration of the term."[100]

The Catholic-liberal collaboration was most apparent in Central Europe. In Brauer's last article for the Christian trade union press before Hitler's seizure of power, even he praised German liberal economist Moritz Bonn in the midst of an argument that the "initiative of the entrepreneur," so long as it was tied to corporatist administration, was the path to economic recovery. Joseph Höffner, a priest and the future archbishop of Cologne, was studying with a leading Ordo-liberal named Walter Eucken and laboring to find corollaries between liberal economics and natural law theory (this would eventually become a cottage industry, but it was quite rare at the time). In Austria, too, liberal ideals looked especially appealing by the end of the 1930s, by which time the failures of statist corporatism were becoming increasingly apparent. Even an editor of the regime-friendly *Christian Corporate State* could declare that many liberal ideals were "truly a Christian inheritance."[101]

Antonio Gramsci, surveying Catholic economic thought from his prison cell in Italy, determined that the tradition was not a serious attempt to reform the economy but rather an ideological opiate designed to convince Catholics of the basic justice of modern capitalism.[102] Gramsci was wrong about the tradition in general, but he had a point about the authoritarian corporatist form traced here. For all of its revolutionary zeal, it led Catholics to abandon the more flamboyantly moralizing and anticapitalist elements of the tradition, accepting the necessity of state intervention, up to and including the dissolution of trade unions, to stave off Communism and protect private property. The homology with the Catholic approach to family welfare should be clear. In both cases, Catholics embraced anti-Communism as a bedrock political principle and in its name abandoned the dense institutionalism that had long been the hallmark of Catholic economic thinking. And in both cases, Catholics were willing to empower, like never before, the institution that had given them the greatest conceptual trouble over the years: the state.

Fatherland: The Defense of the West and of the State

In the crucial arenas of family welfare and economic management, Catholic politicians and experts were remarkably willing to grant significant power to the centralized nation-state. This was something altogether new, and it is part of what made them modern. Since the French Revolution, Catholics had normally longed for some kind of imperial restoration and some kind of weak state structure that would allow Catholic institutions to deal with economic and social questions. That antimodern political theory had been predicated on the now-abandoned notion that the entire society could be infused with Church teachings. In the 1930s, Catholics narrowed their sights to focus on the reproductive family and its needs. And in an era of exploding social tension and looming military conflict, the family could not properly be served by imperial nostalgia or by hopeless calls for the restoration of some kind of loose federal order. The 1930s was an era of secular state building, and Catholics made their peace with that fact. The new question became, what can we legitimately ask of that secular state? What, in other words, does the reproductive Catholic family *require* from the secular state?

In terms of social and economic policy, as we've seen, the answers were welfare and corporatist management. But when it came to the essence of the political itself, the family needed order, stability, and protection from Communism in order to allow those social and economic measures to do their work. This necessarily required the elaboration of an interconfessional, international kind of political community that could plausibly unite many different political groups in the anti-Communist struggle. These were the tasks that Catholic political thinkers took on for themselves in the 1930s, and by confronting them they forged a modern Catholic politics.

Viewed from the perspective of the 1920s, or even the 1820s, 1930s Catholics were remarkably willing to participate in interconfessional, broad-tent political movements, and almost unquestioningly to embrace secular statehood. There was precedent for this, of course. Throughout Europe, between the 1890s and the 1920s, many Catholics had pragmatically accepted secular nation-states. That acceptance, however, had always been tenuous and contested, as many Catholics, from the Vatican to the parish, continued to long for monarchist restoration, church-state alliance, and the return of monoconfessional civilization. The novelty of the 1930s was that this political antimodernism vanished, as Catholics stopped looking to restore ancient thrones and started thinking about which kinds of statehood would best cultivate a Catholic modernity.

In the 1930s, Catholic political thinkers finally provided a political discourse and imaginary to legitimate and encourage pragmatic cooperation with non-Catholic states. This helps to explain how freely and widely they did so. Sometimes this happened in a democratic framework. In the United States, for instance, Catholics found a welcome home in Franklin Roosevelt's Democratic Party. In Europe, however, that cooperation was more frequently in the name of authoritarianism. Catholics were doctrinally indifferent to political form, and to a surprising measure they held fast to that dogma (very few Catholics claimed that their faith was linked with any particular political form, whether it be authoritarian or democratic). In Germany, the Center Party dissolved itself, and Catholics learned to support the National Socialists. To be sure, the Nazis oppressed the Church. All the same, genuine resistance remained minimal, millions of Catholics learned to be Nazis, and the Nazi Party could be seen as the first major interconfessional party in German history. In Austria, Catholics abandoned the studiously Catholic and clerical Christian Socials in favor of the Fatherland Front, a fascist-style movement, technically interconfessional, and helmed by laymen. At the same time, they warmed to the idea of "Austria" as a nation-state of its own and not as the staging ground for Central European empire.[103] In France, in place of the National Catholic Federation and other confessional defense organizations, Catholics flocked to interconfessional national movements. The first, the French Social Party (PSF), was the largest conservative party ever founded in France—one that enjoyed tremendous Catholic support while celebrating an interconfessional national identity. The second was the National Revolution of Marshal

Pétain, which inspired the collaborationist Vichy regime in southern France during World War II.

None of these movements promised to declare Catholicism the official religion of state—long the gold standard of Catholic politics. None of the four constitutions drafted by Catholic jurists in the 1930s claimed any special relationship between the Catholic Church and the state, preferring instead to grant religious freedom (constitutions in Ireland, Portugal, Austria, and France).[104] This is remarkable because all four were majority-Catholic countries. Even in Austria and France, whose authoritarian regimes are often viewed as medievalist or clerical, the relationship between Church and state was distant and tense. These were not clerical regimes, or medieval ones, but secular states led by laymen and in conflict with the Church over fields like education and youth organizations. In Vichy France, for instance, the attempt to introduce religious education into the schools ended in failure. Pétain was a faithful Catholic, but he had no interest in upsetting the schoolteachers or presiding over a theocracy. "I do not differentiate among the French," he declared in 1940. "Catholics, Protestants and Muslims are all my children."[105]

In the 1930s, Catholics largely abandoned their dreams of church-state fusion or of legitimist imperial politics, committing themselves instead to a modern language of rights-defending secular states. As with welfare and the economy, the transformation in papal language about the state provides a rough guide to what was taking place among the laity. In 1922, Pope Pius XI released *Ubi arcano Dei consilio,* his reflection on World War I and its consequences. The encyclical was a traditional one, calling on states to publicly recognize that their power derived from God and to accept that only the Church "is able to set both public and private life on the road to righteousness."[106] The text does speak of rights, but about 80 percent of the invocations of rights granted them to institutions or to God, not to individuals. Fifteen years later, the same pope released *Divini Redemptoris,* an anti-Communist encyclical that not coincidentally represented the most up-to-date Catholic thinking on the state. This time, about 80 percent of the invocations of rights referred to the individual as their bearer. The encyclical, meanwhile, said nothing at all about the state's duty to recognize God as the source of its authority. The state's goal instead was to be "a vigilant and provident defender" of "divine and human rights"—a doctrine with great value "even in non-Christian countries."[107]

Catholic thinkers in the past had tended to draw a distinction between modern statehood, rooted in a rejection of God, and antimodern Catholic politics, often imperial in nature. In the 1930s, Catholics largely abandoned this dichotomy in place of a new one, contrasting two different *kinds* of modern states. On the one hand, "totalitarian" states were pathological and nihilistic institutions, destructive of the Church and the family alike. On the other, "Western" states belonged to the mainstream of European history, finding roots in both classical antiquity and Christendom. These states defended human rights and religious freedom, two supposed lodestars of Europe's ancient legal heritage.

This was still a conservative vision, and sometimes a fascist one, but it was certainly modern. Many Catholic political actors and theorists continued to support racist legislation and the suppression of civil liberties. They defended their politics, though, in a new way, with little recourse to natural law or the medieval model. Instead, they mobilized a vaguely articulated notion of Western culture to claim that strong leadership was necessary to protect the rights and dignities of European citizens from Bolshevik barbarians at the gates. When specifically Catholic instruction was removed from the syllabus of Vichy schools, for instance, the theme was replaced by general reflection on the virtues of Christian and Western civilization.[108]

This turn toward the West represented a sea change in how Catholics thought about themselves, the state, and the European mission. Our guide through this new political imaginary of rights-defending Westernism will be Henri Massis, who, like Wolfring and Brauer, participated in the crystallization of paternal Catholic modernism. Like them, he had been a typically Catholic critic of modernity in the 1920s, rising to prominence as a voice of Catholic monarchism and disciple of Charles Maurras. Even his early invocations of the West (*l'Occident*) were profoundly antimodern. His landmark 1927 volume, *Defense of the West*, reprised many familiar themes from Catholic medievalism, including a rejection of secularism, Protestantism, and the German national project in the name of a traditional and decentralized French monarchy. The only antidote to the unholy alliance of Jews, Protestants, and Communists, he explained, was a return to Catholicism, both because it was the true faith and because it provided resources for law, hierarchy, and order that were missing in other traditions.[109] This antimodern and antistatist understanding of the West predominated in the works of Massis and other French reactionaries until the early 1930s. After the weakening of the Action française, Massis became a mentor to a new generation of conservative thinkers known as the "Young Right" (Jeune Droite). While departing from traditionalist monarchism, their leading thinkers maintained a furious opposition to both modernity and the nation-state project as a whole.[110]

In the mid-1930s, however, Massis's understanding of the West began to evolve in more modern, interconfessional, and statist directions. The rise of the Popular Front and of a newly militarized Germany raised the stakes enormously. In the wake of the Stavisky riots of 1934, when right-wing rioters almost brought down the Third Republic, conservatives like Massis began to flock toward more practical political programs. In *Tomorrow, France,* the Young Right's main response to the riots, the quasi-anarchism of the past was replaced by a call for a "truly strong state" in place of the "totalitarian" one demanded by socialists.[111]

What "the West" allowed Catholics like Massis to do was imagine a transnational community of nation-states, including secular ones, that might stand up to the totalitarianism of Soviet Russia and Nazi Germany. Massis's imagined "Latin Alliance" could link together Austria, Italy, France, Poland, and the Iberian dictatorships against totalitarianism.[112] Massis himself traced the outlines of the new community with his own travels. He interviewed Franco, Mussolini, and Salazar in person, while he celebrated their efforts in his journal, the *Universal Review.*[113] At the time, this was a plausible exercise. Mussolini in the mid-1930s imagined himself to be heralding a Roman renaissance that would gather Latin Europe, Austria included, under his wing. Recognizing this, Engelbert Dollfuss constantly drew on the rhetoric of the West to claim that the Austrian state represented a noble Western heritage against both Nazis and Communists. The Catholic Congress of 1933, at which Dollfuss spoke, featured many paeans to "the Christian Construction of the West." After Dollfuss took power the following year, regime-supporting journals and intellectuals constantly trundled out the idea of the "West" to legitimate the Austrian nation-state. The language of the West was clearly congruent with Catholicism, and was spoken freely by Church leaders such as Cardinal Innitzer, but it was not exclusively Catholic. While most Austrian Protestants tended toward Nazism, dissident socialists like Emil Franzel could also support Dollfuss in the name of "Western Revolution."[114]

This understanding of the West became ubiquitous in French conservative circles in the 1930s. In 1935, the master-general of the Dominican order published *Latin Culture and Social Order* (1935), rehearsing many of Massis's points.[115] Three journals placed this new emphasis in their very titles: *The West, Occident,* and *S.O.S. Occident.* The masthead of the last referred directly to Massis: "Bimonthly publication consecrated to the Defense of the West." Leaders of the National Catholic Federation declared that "Christianity is the only force capable of saving Western civilization" from "the Communist revolution surging from the East." François de la Rocque, Catholic head of the quasi-fascist Croix de Feu and eventually the PSF, was prolix in defense of "Christian civilization," praising "Graeco-Roman civilization" and affirming his desire to ally France with Fascist Italy, especially given "their identical intellectual affiliations."[116]

Mussolini's 1935 invasion of Abyssinia was the high point of this form of Western consciousness. From Massis's perspective, it represented perfectly the binary between defenders and oppressors of the West. On one side, the Catholic Mussolini was attempting to revive the Roman empire in its ancestral home, bringing the faith and the fruits of civilization across the sea. On the other side, the League of Nations, the British and French parliamentary regimes, *and* Nazi Germany opposed him (Hitler was no ally of Mussolini's at the time and even helped to arm the Abyssinians). Massis reacted to the situation with gusto, penning a "Manifesto of French Intellectuals for the Defense of the West," which was eventually signed by over a thousand people, including nearly half of the Académie française and nearly all the luminaries of the French Right (including Maurras and Pétain). The manifesto expressed outrage that the French and English might place the interests of a nebulous global community above those of Rome. Unlike *Defense of the West,* however, it said nothing about the Catholic Church, which after all remained officially neutral. In Italy, a grateful parade of blackshirts marched to France's embassy in celebration of the manifesto and in protest of the actual government's continued threats of sanctions.[117]

By the mid-1930s, therefore, Massis had led French Catholics toward a more expansive and modern vision of the West, one in which Mussolini and Dollfuss had a place but Hitler certainly did not, and one in which the Catholic Church played an important but not all-important role. This understanding had for some time been shared by Germans and Austrians, too. In the 1920s, building on philosopher Oswald Spengler's famous "Decline of the West," Catholic intellectuals had latched onto the West (*Abendland*) in various ways—some in order to defend a vision of Franco-German peace inspired by the League of Nations, others to articulate a more nostalgic celebration of the Holy Roman Empire. Both of these versions had been expressed in the journal called *The West* in the late 1920s, and neither was easily assimilable into Nazism. Many writers at the journal—including Alois Dempf, Waldemar Gurian, and Hermann Platz—were firm anti-Nazis, as were the Defenders of the West at Georg Moenius's *Universal Review* (Massis specifically celebrated *The West*, while his own *Defense of the West* was translated into German by Moenius himself).[118]

The German Catholic understanding of the West, however much it might have clashed with Hitler's vision, certainly had more in common with it than it did with Communism. Beginning around 1930, when Hitler's movement gained steam and attracted many Catholics with its anti-Communist fervor, a number of theologians and writers inducted Nazism into the West. Bishop Michael von Faulhaber, although skeptical of Hitler, was pleased that he at least viewed "Christianity as the architect of the culture of the West." The German hierarchy released a pastoral letter that referred twice to the Bolshevik attack on "the Christian culture of the Western world," implying that Nazis were engaged in nothing of the sort. A Catholic jurist, to take one more example, praised the Nazis in 1936 as "pioneers of the West in the defense against culture-destroying Bolshevism."[119]

Why did German Catholics change their minds on this front? In addition to anti-Communism, Catholics noted that Hitler, like Mussolini, often described his own vision in "Western" or "Christian" terms. The Nazi Party platform promised to defend an interconfessional form of "positive Christianity." And while the regime harbored anticlerical elements, many party leaders at least claimed to defend a racially purified form of Christianity.[120] At the same time, they frequently drew on the classical legacy, viewing themselves as defenders of Europe's heritage. Even if this was not explicitly Christian, it did rhyme with the peculiarly Western tenor of Catholic appreciations of Nazism, which were more concerned with its Roman legal and cultural roots than with specifically Christian devotion.[121] Protestant supporters of Hitler published books like *Western Decision*, reviewed in the Catholic press, to explain how the Nazis were mounting an interconfessional defense of Western civilization against pagan barbarism. Joseph

Goebbels, in particular, used the concept of the West with some regularity, both in the early years of Nazi rule and during the war.[122]

The imagined community of the West allowed German Catholics to legitimate their support of Nazism by folding the movement, however implausibly, into the continent's long Christian-Roman heritage. Specifically, it helped Catholics to make common cause with Protestants. One of the crucial and often overlooked features of the Nazi era is that Catholics found themselves working alongside Protestants in support of an explicitly inter-confessional political movement and party. Anti-Communism was the impetus for this extraordinary transition, which had already begun before Hitler came to power (Heinrich Brüning, chancellor from 1930 to 1932, had already tried to gather the twin confessions into an anti-Communist and "Christian" project).[123] A German Catholic in 1933, for instance, called for an "exceptional collaboration of Christian confessions" to confront the Bolshevik menace. A theologian in 1936 enthused that "the laity from both confessions" were finding a new unity both theologically and politically, "joined in defense against common anti-Christian enemies" and seeking together "the preservation of Christianity in our *Volk*." The most pioneering Catholic ecumenical thinkers in Germany—Karl Adam, Robert Grosche, and Joseph Lortz—were all convinced National Socialists and Defenders of the West. The only Catholic journal devoted to ecumenism at the time, *Catholica,* became a centerpiece of Catholic-Nazi rapprochement. Its authors offered a newly appreciative Catholic understanding of Martin Luther, a position extended by Lortz in his pathbreaking 1939 study of the Reformation and also in a fiery wartime essay collection called *The Catholicism of the Future.* In Austria, too, furious critics of Luther such as Josef Eberle began to warm toward Protestants as allies in the anti-Communist struggle.[124]

Between 1936 and 1940, Catholics in France and Austria traveled the same path as the Germans, accepting Nazi Germany into the community of the West in the name of European heritage and anti-Communism. They did so not because they fell under Hitler's spell but because their previous forms of Westernism no longer made political sense. If the Abyssinian Crisis of 1935 fit neatly into an imagined "Latin Alliance," the Spanish Civil War of 1936–1939 did not, because Hitler and Mussolini were on the same side in defense of the devout Catholic Francisco Franco. Franco came to stand in for all of the forces of order (gender, religious, economic) that were under assault from Communists, and Hitler was supporting him. While the antifascists who flocked to fight on the Republican side are firmly embedded in historical memory of this period, it is often forgotten that many conservative Catholics from across Europe converged on Spain, too, ready to fight for the West.[125]

Massis, like many other Catholic intellectuals, was obsessed with the Spanish Civil War. He energetically cultivated Spain's image as a Western citadel against marauding hordes of Easterners, socialists, and Jews. Together with Robert Brasillach, he published a rousing volume called *Cadets of Alcazar* (1936), which treated the heroic stand of two thousand Spanish soldiers in the ancient citadel of Alcazar. Through an extraordinary historical sleight-of-hand, they folded this victory over Communism into Spain's ancient history as a defender of the West: twice before, they reminded their readers, "Spain delivered Western civilization from the Oriental peril" (against the Moors and against the Turks). Now they are doing it again, "against a subtler Orient" (Bolshevism). "The Cadets of Toledo have not fought for Spain only," Massis and Brasillach concluded. "They defended the entire Catholic Western world."[126]

Even though Hitler was supporting Franco, Catholics like Massis nonetheless remained wary of Nazism in the late 1930s (fear and loathing of Germany were embedded deeply in the DNA of the French right). During France's short war with Germany, he served as a press secretary to General Charles Huntziger, writing propaganda materials for the army about the superiority of French culture to German barbarism. This much was perfectly typical, and was not so different from French Catholic writing during World War I. But something new happened once France fell. This time, instead of reiterating his decades-old critiques of Germany, Massis urged his countrymen to collaborate with Nazi occupiers. The explanation for the shift is that, in the interim, Communism had emerged in his mind as the world-historical evil. He revealed as much in his memoirs. After the fall of France, Massis recalled, he thought back to what had happened last time France fell to Germany: the Paris Commune, in which radicalized workers had taken over the city, occasioning violence and slaughter on both sides (but primarily on the part of the anti-Communards who reclaimed it). To avoid such a terrible fate, Massis believed that a strong leader would be needed to confront the agonies of defeat. That leader, as Massis excitedly told Huntziger on a somber walk in June, could only be Marshal Pétain, ruling in unoccupied France with the support of the German victors. Huntziger agreed, and a few days later he signed the armistice himself. He became the minister of defense in the new Vichy government. Massis, too, happily embraced Pétain's rule, even writing the opening address Pétain gave to the National Council, on which he served.[127]

During World War II, especially, a Catholic understanding of the West emerged that brought together Italian, German, and French-speaking Europe, including Protestant regions, into one imagined community like never before.[128] A German Catholic soldier writing home from the front lines explained that he was fighting for "the kingdom of Christ," understood not in terms of Catholic restoration but of "occidental culture." German and Austrian newspapers employed the notion of the "West" to explain the nature of the community at stake.[129] This was most remarkable in France itself, where the whole purpose of Western rhetoric had once been to denounce Protestant-dominated Germany. Pétain placed France in "the Christian civilization of the West," while he told volunteer fighters destined for the Eastern front that they were contributing to a "crusade" against "the Bolshevik peril," "saving both your own country and the hope for a reconciled Europe." Meanwhile, articles appeared in regime-sponsored journals with titles like "Principles of a Western Order," warning darkly of massed hordes in the East before calling for a revived alliance of Catholic nations. Massis himself gave lectures in unoccupied France on the congenial theme of "Russia Against the West." His first book after the defeat rehearsed his old tropes while simply excising the anti-German animus that had animated him up until the recent past. He now blamed the French for their own decadence and linked the nefarious East with Russia and South Asia, not with Prussia. In *The Discovery of Russia* (1944), Massis reprinted passages from *The Defense of the West* alongside a familiar denunciation of Bolshevism. The book even came with a foldout map visually demonstrating his fevered Western imagination. On it, the ancient citadels of the West, which included France and Germany alike, were under siege from the barbarism of the Soviet Union and the Americans.[130]

And thus Henri Massis, paragon of the French Catholic right wing, called for an Italo-Franco-German alliance against Bolshevism under the flag of the West. This represented a fundamental shift in the Catholic understanding of European politics, and one that would survive long past the war's end. The acceptance of the Italian and, especially, the German nation-states as legitimate political bodies signaled the end of the centuries-long Catholic zeal for imperial governance. While Catholics had long championed the West, they now championed a West made up of nation-states, not feudal empires. The Roman inheritance, in turn, was now understood to mandate not the demolition of the nation-state but rather the erection of a specific form of it.

But what kind of state was acceptable to the Catholic conscience? How did Massis and others distinguish between Nazism and Communism, deeming the former potentially "Western" and the latter improperly "totalitarian"? Massis's own writings provide the answer. In his last book before World War II, he wrote hardly at all about the Church as a concrete institution, and he did not call for church-state fusion. He even praised Portugal's Catholic dictator, António de Oliveira Salazar, for keeping church and state technically separated. His language of political legitimacy, therefore, was not ecclesiastical. He praised Western states, instead, for defending the family. Like Wolfring, he was thrilled about "the primacy of the family over the state" in Mussolini's Italy. This kind of defense of the West and the family was linked in the text with a novel and modern set of keywords. Noble Western leaders such as Salazar defended, in Massis's words, "human dignity itself" and "the rights of the human person" against "totalitarianism."[131]

Western states, Massis argued, are those that protect the rights and dignity of the individual person. He meant this in a specific way, of course, and one far removed from contemporary human rights discourse. Essentially, Massis and other Defenders of the West claimed that human rights, properly understood, protected the freedom to flourish as civilized Europeans had long done. This involved amassing property, worshipping freely, and founding a family. Newfangled rights to civil liberties or sexual freedoms were not on the agenda.

This particularly conservative form of rights discourse flourished in the Catholic Church of the mid-1930s. It made sense, strategically, providing a political discourse that allowed Catholics to maintain many of their same commitments while framing them in a way that helped to build anti-Communist alliances. This is such an unfamiliar genealogy for rights discourse that it is worthwhile to give a few examples. In 1935, Raphaël Alibert, a Catholic politician and friend of Massis, wrote an "Essay on the Notion of the State," in which he condemned "totalitarian states" for their "great contempt for the rights of the person." In the West-defending *Latin Culture and Social Order* of the same year, the master of the Dominican order in France wrote admiringly of Mussolini's respect for "the enduring rights of the human person." *S.O.S. Occident* worried about "Judeo-masonry" and irreligion while heralding the West as the protector of "dignity" and the "person." The publications of the largely Catholic Young Right worried about the fate of the "human person" and his "dignity" with great regularity. The *Torch*, the mass-circulation newspaper of the quasi-fascist Croix de Feu, used this new language, too. One 1935 article proclaimed that France belonged to a "Greco-Latin" tradition, pitting "Roman law" against "barbarian force." One of the features of that tradition was the "respect and cult of the human person." "We are in the fortress of the West, of the nation of persons," another writer imagined. The manifesto of the Croix de Feu, printed in an edition of three million copies, promised to unite patriots of all faiths behind the restoration of France. As such, the text warned voters against "totalitarianism" and the global Bolshevik threat, counseling instead their own "respect for the personality." To take one final French example, and one that brings us back to Massis, the first draft of the Vichy constitution prepared in 1941 by the National Council, on which Massis sat, said nothing about the Catholic Church—but it did declare that "the state recognizes and guarantees the rights of the human person."[132]

This reframing of sovereignty around the legal person was not just a French phenomenon. It appeared, for instance, in the anti-Communist papal encyclical *Divini Redemptoris* (1937). In Austria, archconservatives like Moenius argued that the spirit of the "West" presumed respect for "the right of the individual and the personality." Defenders of Dollfuss at the regime-sponsored journal the *Christian Corporate State* celebrated the "rights of the person," distinguishing Austrian corporatism from totalitarianism. Even supporters of National Socialism such as Bishop Hudal praised ancient Rome as "the cradle of human rights and the personality."[133]

And even in Germany, Catholics in the Nazi era turned toward modern rights talk. The best example of this is Robert Linhardt, described earlier. He was one of the first Catholic thinkers anywhere in Europe to base a political theology on human rights, and he did so in the name of National Socialism. Especially after Hitler's rise to power, and the concomitant assault on Catholic institutional life, this strategy became more common. One Bavarian theologian in 1934 praised the "ineffable dignity" and "primeval rights" of the individual. Otto Schilling, a convinced Nazi and one of the leading theologians in Germany, argued along similar lines in his *Defense of Catholic Morality* (1936). "The command of the hour," he insisted in an interconfessional key, "is the integration of all Christian thinkers and friends of Christian culture in the struggle against the enemies of Christianity." Along with other Catholics across Europe, Schilling claimed that the Church respected the "dignity [and] personality of men," as mandated by natural law. "Nobody," he argued, "protects natural human rights more faithfully and loyally than the Church."[134]

Just as Catholic doctrines of rights were compatible with egregious violations of civil liberties, they helped to legitimize anti-Semitism, too.[135] The anti-Semitism of the Catholic 1930s tended to flow from Catholic modernism, rather than rehearsing the old doctrine that the Jews were eternally guilty for killing Christ, or even the more recent one that Jews were harbingers of secularism. In the 1930s, Jews were less often viewed as exemplars of secularism than as violators of it—violators, that is, of the public-private split that was now taken to be the linchpin of Western civilization. This logic was laid bare in a nasty article that Massis's *Universal Review* published on "the Jewish problem" in 1938. The problem was not that the Jews were a biological enemy of the French race or that they had conspired to murder Christ. The problem was that Jews were not properly secular, conspiring, like the Communists they served, to break down the boundary between public and private, rejecting the nation-state and its supposedly classical distinction between faith and politics. Unlike Catholics, the author argued, Jews fused religion and politics and were therefore illegitimate partners in secular polities.[136] In Germany, many rights-defending texts of the Nazi era—including the ones by Wilhelm Moock and Otto Schilling already explored—were also anti-Semitic.[137] Even in pre-1938 Austria, where the state was reasonably friendly toward the Jews, Catholics (including, in at least one case, a converted Jew) reprised this same logic: the problem for Austrian observers was that Jews refused to collaborate with modern, Western states, preferring instead to pursue anti-Western, Soviet-inspired projects.[138]

The persistence of Catholic anti-Semitism had serious consequences, helping to explain why European Catholics almost never protested racial legislation or violence. They were often trendsetters, especially in France. Although Vichy was a collaborationist regime, it began passing anti-Semitic legislation before the Germans started pressing for it. Vichy's anti-Semitism, in other words, was homegrown. Its architect was a Catholic politician named Xavier Vallat, named by Pétain as the Commissioner General for Jewish Questions. Like Massis, he linked anti-Semitism with the Defense of the West, celebrating the rise of autocratic regimes across Europe with familiar, Western language. After the election of Jewish politician Léon

Blum, for instance, he had declared on the floor of parliament that "for the first time, this old Gallo-Roman nation will be governed by a Jew." With this well-known insult, Vallat indicated a connection between an imagined Roman heritage and anti-Semitism—the same connection that Massis found, and the same one that he would mobilize to murderous ends under Vichy.[139]

Massis's strand of political thought helped to legitimate Catholic anti-Semitism and fascist collaboration. At the same time, it indicated a considerable modernization in the Catholic attitude toward the state. In the 1920s, Massis and others had defended some kind of decentralized, imperial solution that would reinstate Catholic hierarchies and institutions to their proper place. By 1944, Catholics had converged on a new account of the secular state, one that had the potential to build alliances, particularly with Protestants. For the first time, Catholics en masse imagined Europe as a community of nation-states in which Italy, France, Germany, and Austria could band together to defeat Communism. And, for the first time, Catholics understood the state to be a protector of individual rights and dignity.

PATERNAL CATHOLIC MODERNISM may have helped Europe's Catholics to understand and legitimate the new shape of Europe, but, politically speaking, it was not a great success. It did provide Catholics with a strategic way to weather the political firestorms of the era, and it is certainly true that the Church and its institutions were in general able to survive relatively well. The specific goals of paternal modernism, however, were not achieved. Catholics lent their support to regimes that were uninterested in governing in Catholic ways. Even when it came to the family, the Church clashed with authoritarian regimes across the continent, more interested in births and youth indoctrination than the niceties of Catholic doctrine. Our three protagonists suffered ironic fates. Henri Massis, poet of the West, watched American troops roll through his beloved France; Theodor Brauer, the theorist of labor, became unemployed; and Mina Wolfring, the theorist of family, was left by her husband, a Nazi sympathizer, during the war. She died in 1944, and her son, fighting at the front lines, was unable to attend her funeral.[140]

These political failures should not detract from the monumental intellectual achievement of paternal Catholic modernists (again, these three are being used as windows into an evolving Catholic world, not as world-historical figures in their own right). In a decade of horrific suffering and violence, they spearheaded a form of Catholic engagement with the modern world. They provided not just pragmatic strategies but *conceptual* reasons why Catholics should make their peace with the modern state and the secular values of religious freedom and human rights. While many paternal modernists did support some form of fascism, the ideas themselves were not intrinsically fascist or ultranationalist. They could, therefore, survive the final defeat of fascism in World War II.

The remarkable staying power of this form of Catholic modernism was signaled by the teachings of the new pope, Pius XII. From the time of *Summi Pontificatus* (1939), his first encyclical, Pius XII put rights—the rights of the family and the rights of the individual—at the center of his thinking. This invocation of rights did not lead primarily to traditional Catholic antistatism. Quite the contrary, Pius argued that the state has "wider and exceptional" capacities owing to "the exceptional conditions of the world today."[141] This understanding was pursued further in his famous Christmas messages of 1942 and 1944, which provided the clearest wartime statements of Catholic principle from the Vatican. While normally remembered for granting legitimacy to democracy, that is not their principal importance. Catholics had been participating in parliamentary governments for decades without fear of censure, and the Christmas messages simply repeated the old dictum that the Church was indifferent to questions of political form. The Christmas messages are important instead because they gave the papal imprimatur to paternal Catholic modernism, showing how it might survive beyond fascism and beyond the war. All of the central impulses of paternal Catholicism—anti-Communism, the defense of the family, the acceptance of the secular state, human rights, religious freedom—appeared in the Christmas messages.[142]

The Christmas messages reprised the remarkable feat of paternal Catholic modernism, pointing toward a Catholic acceptance of the modern world while providing a new discourse that allowed Catholics to collaborate with others in the pursuit of common goals. They reprised its limitations, too. Neither message showed any special concern with civil liberties, trade unions, or political creativity; indeed, the 1944 message was positively suspicious of the "masses" and their worrisome impact on social order. Both messages were more concerned with stabilization and the empowerment of traditional elites than they were in crafting a new Europe, and a new Church, from the ashes of the war. The messages also betrayed an unwillingness to seriously confront the depth of Catholic responsibility for the tragedies of the era. This was most apparent in one very loud silence: while "the innumerable sorrowing host of mothers" received special attention, neither message spared a word for the specific suffering of Europe's Jews. Catholics may have learned to be modern, but modernity can be cruel.

✣ 3 ✣

ANTIFASCISM AND FRATERNAL
CATHOLIC MODERNISM, 1929–1944

How good, how delightful it is to live as brothers all together!

—PSALMS 133:1

In 1933, German-Jewish philosopher Paul-Ludwig Landsberg fled from Hitler's Germany to Spain, where the Second Spanish Republic promised a more welcoming environment. Soon enough, though, a civil war broke out, and Hitler's forces appeared there, too. This time, he fled to France, where the Popular Front government of Léon Blum promised to hold the line against fascism. He was disappointed yet again: Blum chose not to aid the Spanish republicans, while inside and outside France fascism was looming. In 1940, Hitler invaded France, finding eager support from French anti-Semites. Landsberg and his wife were rounded up with other Jews in 1940, but he escaped and fled by bicycle to the unoccupied zone in the south. Rejecting friends' attempts to help him emigrate, he stayed there under a false name. A "dead lion," he had written the year before, is worth more than a "living dog." Soon enough, he was captured by the Gestapo and sent to a concentration camp, where he died of starvation and exhaustion in the spring of 1944.[1]

Landsberg had one of the border-crossing, ruinously brave, and ultimately tragic experiences shared by so many European Jews. Unlike most of them, he found spiritual and intellectual sustenance in an unlikely place: Catholicism. While he never officially converted, he moved in Catholic circles, engaged with Catholic theology, and published in Catholic journals. Why this attraction to Rome? For most of Landsberg's ill-starred life, after all, Catholics were among his persecutors. The mainstream Church was pursuing an innovative brand of Catholic modernity that I've called "paternal Catholic modernism." That strategy, which placed family ethics and anti-Communism at the center of the Catholic mission, ended up legitimating collaboration with authoritarian and anti-Semitic regimes—including those in Spain, France, and Germany. It animated Catholic politicians, some of them very powerful, and conquered the commanding heights of the Church, finding voice in bishops' letters, innumerable sermons, and lavish state-sponsored conferences and journals. But it did not conquer Landsberg, the circles he traveled in, or the comparatively grubby and low-circulation journals they wrote for. For him, the faith meant something very different.

Landsberg participated in a transnational network of Catholic antifascists. "Antifascism," he mused in 1937, "is an empty and negative concept. All the same, it acquires a concrete and positive meaning for those forced to defend their freedom and their existence."[2] It certainly did for Landsberg, just as anti-Communism did for many others. And while antifascism may have been a minority tradition within the Catholic Church, it did embed Landsberg into truly world-historical currents in the Europe of the 1930s. Landsberg's personal itinerary, spanning from Germany, to Spain, to France, to Hitler's camps, closely traces the international shape of antifascism. He joined a diverse network of Europeans, some Communist and some not, under the umbrella of the Popular Front: Josef Stalin's attempt to gather a variety of social forces together in the name of antifascist struggle. While this whole tradition has long been viewed as a Trojan horse for Stalinist influence, more recent research has shown how diverse antifascist culture truly was—and how involved Catholics were in it, in France and elsewhere.[3]

Just as Catholic anti-Communists were not generally dyed-in-the-wool fascists, Catholic antifascists were not committed Communists. There were some who believed that Catholicism and Marxism could, in some theoretical way, be combined, but this was rare. More commonly, Catholic antifascists maintained an opposition to Marxist metaphysics and Soviet politics while hoping that this would not preclude collaboration with workers' movements on worldly issues in a spirit of brotherhood. Their antifascism was not a pale reflection of a Marxist original but a unique and coherent interpretation of the Church's promise.

Sometimes, antifascist Catholics are lauded for accepting "modernity" or "human rights" against their supposedly backward antagonists. This is a misunderstanding. Catholic medievalism dwindled in the 1930s, and Catholic intellectuals who defended accommodation with fascists were just as modern as those who opposed them. The debate was not between Catholic modernism and Catholic medievalism but rather between two *forms* of Catholic modernism: two strategies, linked with two moral and political economies, to dictate how the Church should try to shape the modern condition. Landsberg aimed his pen squarely at paternal Catholic modernism. Indeed, much of his writing was concerned with uprooting the symbolic and actual authority of father figures. Every person is "irreducible," he insisted, and not a creation of their parents. He wrote sympathetically about the anarchist drive for a "fraternal humanity without a father," leading to a society organized not by paternal hierarchy but by "the equality of brothers." And in his writings on the philosophy of marriage, he criticized the mainstream Catholic writers who placed fatherhood and reproduction at the center of the family and of society. This understanding turned a community of love, sex, and spirituality into a community of law and reproduction, which in Landsberg's view "lends itself to nationalist and racist abuse."[4]

Landsberg helped to forge *fraternal* Catholic modernism, modeled less on the authoritarian role of the father than on the relationships of solidarity and cooperation found between brothers. This did not make them more modern than their foes. Ironically, fraternal Catholicism was in some ways more faithful to the antimodernism of the social Catholic tradition. It is well known that Jacques Maritain, the intellectual leader of Catholic antifascism, had been a reactionary monarchist in the 1920s before emerging as an antifascist in the 1930s. What has not been recognized is that his trajectory was a common one, representing not so much a historical irony as an evolution in the sorts of possibilities offered by the Catholic tradition. Perhaps the single defining feature of social Catholicism had long been its allergy to the centralized state and its demolition of the dense networks of Catholic institutions that, to the Catholic thinker, structured the good and meaningful life. Instead of tempering that commitment in the name of anti-Communism and a focus on the family, fraternal Catholics updated and modernized it, arriving at a pluralist account of political life that made room for, and even celebrated, religious difference.

While Catholic antifascism spread widely in many Catholic circles, it was theorized most profoundly by outsiders to the Church—by converts, especially, and often from Judaism.[5] For one thing, they were concerned with crafting a form of faith that could plausibly include them; for another, they were less committed to making compromises to protect the safety of Catholic institutions. This was certainly true for Maritain, a convert married to a Jew. He had not grown up in Catholic institutions and was more concerned with the revolutionary promise of Catholic doctrine than with the protection of a Catholic milieu supposedly under assault.

Maritain's 1936 masterpiece, *Integral Humanism,* is the clearest statement of fraternal Catholicism. Often sanitized as a paean to liberal democracy, it should instead be read as a furiously antifascist, antiracist, and anticapitalist tract. Like Landsberg's work, it is not a call for a modern Catholicism so much as a call for a specific *kind* of modern Catholicism—one modeled around fraternity rather than paternity. In the past, Maritain admitted, Catholics had viewed all power "along the lines of paternal authority": medieval forms of politics, economics, and the family itself were all derived from this fundamental model. That age, though, had passed, and he was scathing toward the mainstream approach that tried to update that paternalism instead of replacing it. This attempt, he rightly pointed out, played into the hands of fascists and legitimated what he called "totalitarian paternalism." In its place, he proposed that politics in the modern world should be based on the logic of brotherhood, replacing the paternal state with what he called "civic fraternities."[6]

Paternal Catholic modernism had three main components: an account of the enemy (Communism), an account of the private sphere (the reproductive family), and a kindred account of the public sphere (the empowerment of the secular state to defend that family). Fraternal Catholics upended each of them. As for the enemy, fraternal Catholics were willing to work with Marxists in order to found a common front against fascism, the greatest enemy of all. "A collaboration between Marxists and Christians," Landsberg concluded, "is possible" precisely because we have agreed to "a dissociation between the social and the metaphysical."[7] This did not mean abandoning Rome for Moscow, but it did mean critically engaging with Marxist organizations and theories both to focus on the fascist threat *and* to learn from their analyses of capitalism. As a German antifascist Catholic named Walter Dirks argued as early as 1931, the Catholic obsession with anti-Communism threatened to put the Church "on the wrong side of the barricades," allying with Protestants in the name of established authorities instead of with the workers in the name of social justice.[8]

Maritain, while sparing no criticism of Stalinism, was willing to dialogue with socialists and learn from Marx, presuming that a reformed socialism—not a tempered fascism—was Europe's path forward. A great deal of *Integral Humanism* is taken up with sensitive readings of Marx's texts, including his recently discovered early writings. Fascism, which in Maritain's view had "a greater historic power than the Stalinist evil," was irredeemable, while Communism, for all of its flaws, at least pointed toward a new Christendom to come (in other texts, he reaffirmed his belief that when it came to a choice between fascism, Communism, and liberalism, fascism was "certainly the worst").[9] And while he of course rejected the Marxist account of religion and metaphysics, he thought Marx had a great deal to teach Catholics nonetheless. Communism, Maritain argued, emerged from "decommissioned Christian virtues," and he urged Catholics to heed "the great lightning-flash of truth" in Marx.[10]

Antifascism was conceptually linked to a novel articulation of Catholic modernity. If Catholic modernism accepts the modern split between a private sphere of faith and a public realm of politics, it can be analyzed by exploring its particular understanding of that private sphere, which will dictate the sorts of claims that can be made in public. Paternal Catholics had envisioned the private sphere to be made up of reproductive families. They relaxed or abandoned much of the tradition's teachings on the economy and the state in order to reaffirm control over sexuality and reproduction. Fraternal Catholic modernists, in contrast, were not especially interested in the reproductive family. In its place, they focused on the marriage as a partnership of equals, structured by desire and sacrament alike. The horizontal and dialogic relationship of marriage, not the hierarchical one of the family, provided the model for a civil society made up of a teeming multiplicity of associations: Catholic, Protestant, Jewish, and secular. In short, they viewed the private sphere—the space of religion in modern polities—to be made up of civic associations, governed by solidarity.

Just as mainstream Catholic politics flowed from its elevation of the family, the minority antifascist tradition derived from this fundamental commitment to free and interfaith organizing in civil society. Regarding the economy, paternal Catholics viewed authoritarian forms of corporatism as the best way to secure family wages and stability. Fraternal Catholics, in contrast, maintained the anticapitalist elements of previous teachings and theorized an economic space made up of freely organized trade unions (interconfessional and socialist alike). And concerning the state, paternal Catholics supported a strong state that would protect families and "Defend the West" from Communism, even if this involved anti-Semitic legislation, restrictions on civil liberties, or a clampdown on civil society. Fraternal Catholics instead wanted the state to support, protect, and incorporate all of the associational activities of the private sphere, a theory that many 1930s Catholics, including Maritain, referred to as "pluralism." Pluralism can mean many things, and, like much in Maritain's work, it can be sanitized into a concern for group autonomy in a liberal society. For Maritain and other Catholic pluralists in the 1930s, though, it presumed the overturning of bourgeois civilization and its apotheosis in the state. The "pluralist city" that he sought would be a diverse and restless one. He did not seek a "minimal common doctrine" (a defense of human rights or the family, for instance) but rather sought to work with non-Catholics, including Jews and atheists, in what he called the "practical common task" of creating a humane, diverse society.[11]

It might be charged that this strategy was too utopian and dangerous for the 1930s—an era when many Catholics had legitimate fears for the survival of the Catholic institutions they dearly loved, and even for their continued ability to legally receive the sacraments. That might be, but in mobilizing otherwise neglected elements of the tradition, fraternal Catholics were able to conceptualize and protest against kinds of suffering that the mainstream tradition largely ignored. This was most apparent when it came to the Jews. Paternal Catholic modernism was both theoretically and empirically compatible with anti-Semitism. Fraternal Catholic modernism, in contrast, was fundamentally antiracist, and almost every antiracist Catholic in the 1930s traveled in Maritain's circle. For them, the linkage of "race" with governance was the greatest sin of totalitarianism. In other words, while Maritain's antitotalitarianism was shared by most Catholics, his analysis of "the racist-totalitarian conception" was the province of Catholic antifascism. Maritain worried about the growth of state power and the attempts to force a racially and religiously diverse society into an "organic unity."[12] From his pluralist perspective, interfaith collaboration was to be not only tolerated but welcomed as a beneficial component of the new Christendom. Instead of seeing Jews as wayward sons of God the Father, he and his allies viewed them as estranged brothers (this was, after all, the relationship suggested by the biblical story of Jacob and Esau).[13]

While I have used Maritain as an entry point, Catholic antifascism extended far beyond him, far beyond France, and far beyond texts. It was embedded in Catholic institutional life, most notably in some elements of Catholic trade unions and Catholic Action organizations. It certainly found a home in the place that Anson Rabinbach has called "the capital of anti-fascism": Paris. The capital cannot exist, however, without the periphery. While Maritain and his city may have been central nodes of Catholic antifascism, Central European Catholics played crucial intellectual roles, too. Maritain had been invested in German-speaking Catholic life since the mid-1920s, and some of his most important intellectual moves were pioneered there. Like antifascism more generally, Catholic antifascism was a European phenomenon.[14]

One reason that both paternal and fraternal Catholic modernism were so powerful is that they primarily emerged not from master texts or high theology but from the work of engaged intellectuals, journalists, and politicians facing concrete problems. They were less specific or complex teachings than commonplace vocabularies and strategies, circulating in political discourse and in journals that people actually read. They found purchase in dense monographs, to be sure, but also in the evolving concepts and categories that, usually without fanfare, crept into front-page editorials. Because they were concrete strategies operating in multiple countries at a complicated time, the division between paternal and fraternal Catholicism was sometimes hazy. Certain figures moved from one camp to another, or pursued idiosyncratic projects that don't seem to fit in either. Nonetheless, as a matter of conceptual history, the two forms of modernism were reasonably distinct, coherent, and cohesive—they circulated in different journals, associated with different projects, and mobilized a distinct set of keywords.

Fraternal Catholic modernism, like its antagonist, can best be explored by tracing the transnational biographies of three engaged intellectuals: one German, one Austrian, and one French, each of them grappling with one of the classic themes of social Catholic thought. All three figures stemmed from the Catholic medievalism of the 1920s and tried to update its anti-statist and anticapitalist elements in the 1930s (they all had some kind of connection to Georg Moenius, the primary medievalist traced in Chapter 1). They did so, however, in a progressive way, following the French revolutionary credo that Marshal Pétain's "Work, Family, Fatherland" was meant to supplant: "Liberty, Equality, Fraternity." The German Dietrich von Hildebrand's explosive theories of marriage and sexuality undercut the natalist, hierarchical family model of paternal Catholicism (Fraternity). By removing the reproductive family from the core of social Catholic ethics, Hildebrand's work paved the way for the more activist account of the private sphere theorized by antifascist economists and political thinkers. An

Austrian politician and intellectual named Ernst Karl Winter made the case for free trade unionism, including socialists and even Communists, as a central component of Catholic economic teaching (Equality). Jacques Maritain, for his part, gathered these threads together with a pluralist theory of politics (Liberty). Their intellectual and political dissidence brought them far from the halls of European power but close to one another. They all ended up in wartime exile in New York City, hoping against hope that the conflagration would give way to a postfascist, antiracist, and pluralist Europe.

Fraternity: Sex and the Antifascist Family

Antifascist Catholics tended not to focus a great deal on the reproductive family. "It is possible," one of them cautiously warned in 1935, "to exaggerate the meaning of the family."[15] While fraternal modernists did not question fundamental Catholic teachings on divorce, abortion, or contraception, they did focus less on them, and they did seek to dethrone reproduction from its centrality in the Catholic family imagination. As Landsberg pointed out, an obsessive focus on reproduction in practice led Catholics into alliance with fascists, concerned for their own reasons with raising the birthrate. Therefore, in place of reproduction and child-rearing, fraternal modernists focused on the *marriage* as a sacramental community of solidarity, love, and desire. By decentering the reproductive family from Catholic social thought, this account opened a space for a broader and more pluralist rendering of the private sphere.

The central figure was Dietrich von Hildebrand, in whose journal the warning against overemphasized familialism appeared. Like many other fraternal Catholics, Hildebrand was an outsider to the Church. Raised in a secular household, and with Jewish ancestry, he did not convert until 1914, when he was twenty-five years old. Like many converts, he held an exaggerated love of Catholic dogma, and an exaggerated disinterest in what more mainstream Catholics thought of him. Specifically, he was disgusted by the pride that Catholics took in cultural and political power. Like many fraternal modernists, he was fascinated by the lives of the saints, which convinced him that spiritual renewal began with the agonies of the individual soul, not with legislative triumph.[16]

Hildebrand's disdain for swaggering Catholic power made him a controversial figure in the 1920s, when many German Catholics were casting about for profoundly Catholic forms of social and cultural renewal. Like Georg Moenius, he blamed Germany for World War I—a view that made him unpopular in Nazi circles as early as 1923. Despite his respected writings and his intellectual celebrity in Munich, he was denied the prize he wanted: the chair of his venerated teacher, Max Scheler, in Cologne. Konrad Adenauer himself put an end to this dream, commenting that he had never heard of Hildebrand and he wanted a prestigious Catholic scientist to fill the slot (the future chancellor of West Germany was mayor of Cologne at the time). In the end, it went to Theodor Brauer.[17] Adenauer probably came to regret his choice. While Brauer loudly urged Catholics to support Hitler, Hildebrand emerged as one of the most prolific and insightful anti-Nazi authors in Europe.

Many fraternal Catholics experienced difficult ruptures with their mentors. In Hildebrand's case, he was forced to turn on Scheler, who had been a foundational teacher and philosophical inspiration to the young philosopher. Scheler's Catholic period was brief, however, and he began to question the Church in the years after his pathbreaking *On the Eternal in Man* (1922). Hildebrand was crushed. In the wake of Scheler's 1928 death, Hildebrand published a number of high-profile articles in which he took his former mentor to task. Scheler, he now argued, was a messy, unsystematic thinker, whose intellectual failings derived directly from his chaotic personal life. Hildebrand especially bemoaned "the profound tragedy of [Scheler's] relation to women," which "tore apart and devastated his life and which finally separated him from his knowledge of God." He was convinced that Scheler's unbridled sensuality pointed to a deeper, philosophical problem. Scheler's epistemology, in Hildebrand's telling at least, occluded the possibility of ever truly knowing another person, trapped as we are in our own fleeting impressions and drives. "Scheler," Hildebrand opined, "overlooked the possibility of an objective capturing of the uniqueness of another person in an I-Thou-Relationship."[18]

Hildebrand believed that such a relationship *was* possible, and precisely where Scheler refused to look for one: the marriage bond. Hildebrand's anguished witness of Scheler's convoluted love life, alongside his own committed and happy marriage, convinced him to turn his attention to the issues of sexuality and gender that would concern him throughout his career. His first publication on the topic, *In Praise of Purity*, appeared in 1927, while his more holistic interpretation of the marriage bond, simply called *Marriage*, came out two years later. That little book revolutionized

Catholic ethics on marriage and was the standard reference point in Catholic debates for decades.

At a time when most Catholics were beginning to theorize the reproductive family as the center of social morality, Hildebrand refused to follow suit. This forced him to disagree, at least implicitly, with papal dogma, and one striking feature of his 1930s writing is his willingness to ignore *Casti connubii*, Pope Pius XI's aggressively conservative family encyclical.[19] In both *In Praise of Purity* and *Marriage,* he argued that love and sex, quite distinct from procreation, could provide the kind of intersubjective meaning that Scheler thought impossible. In the process, he rejected out of hand the old Catholic understanding of marriage as an institution structured by canon law and oriented toward children. That model derived neatly from Thomism, which dominated Catholic intellectual production in the early decades of the twentieth century. Thomists argued that human institutions are defined by their end, or *telos*: just as the "telos" of the acorn was the oak tree, the "telos" of the marriage was procreation. Hildebrand instead urged his readers to distinguish the subjective meaning of marriage from its material or social ends. The *end* of marriage might be procreation, but from a phenomenological perspective, there was much more to the story. "Love," Hildebrand writes, "is the primary *meaning* of marriage just as the birth of new human beings is its primary *end*."[20]

Hildebrand wanted marriage to provide meaning, and not only children, to the couple. His account of marital love was only loosely related to our gauzy, everyday notion of it. For him, true love was a mystical process of communion in which husband and wife recognized the image of God, corporally and spiritually, in their partners. Intervening in legal cases that were then roiling the Catholic world, Hildebrand claimed that sex was therefore still valuable, and permissible, in cases where procreation was impossible for medical reasons. He was concerned above all with disassociating marriage, as a sacrament and love community, from any kind of biopolitical calculus. "The social function of marriage and its importance for the State," he declared, are "secondary and subordinate" to the love bond; the marriage, he emphasized, "glorifies God more" than state, nation, or even the procreative family.[21]

Hildebrand's theories struck at the very core of paternal Catholic modernism and led him to emerge as one of the most notorious anti-Nazi Catholic authors in Europe. He fled Nazi Germany to Austria, where Hitler could not reach him (even though the German ambassador to Austria complained directly to the Führer about him).[22] Together with Klaus Dohrn, another German exile and a distant relative, he began publishing an anti-Nazi journal called *The Christian Corporate State,* the premier site for fraternal Catholicism in Central Europe. It was supported by the Austrian Catholic dictator Engelbert Dollfuss, who wanted to create a rigorously anti-Nazi publishing venue to counter the influence of Joseph Eberle's more Nazi-friendly *More Beautiful Future.*[23] Especially after the murder of Dollfuss in 1934, the journal began to focus less on support for the Austrian state than on furious denunciations of Nazism, which threatened from both inside and outside Austria. Over its six-year run, the journal provided a site for hundreds of Catholic authors across the continent to express antiracist, antifascist Catholic ideas in a widely circulating German-language journal.

Hildebrand's theories of marriage were central to his antifascism. In a 1935 article called "The State and Marriage," he explained the logic. Nazis, and the Catholics who supported them, viewed everything from the standpoint of the social order as a whole. Uninterested in the marriage itself, they only cared about children—that is, they cared only for the contribution the marriage could make to social reproduction. Hildebrand, however, saw the marriage bond as a "complete, unique community" on its own, and one that was higher and more sacramental than the state or even the family. Marriage, he explained elsewhere, is in fact "the highest human community," which is why the "insulting, clueless" restrictions on marriage in the Nuremberg Laws drove Hildebrand to heights of rage: "What an egregious violation of men in their most intimate sphere of life!"[24]

Hildebrand's attack on Nuremberg shows how his theories of marriage fed his antiracism as well. The Jews, he insisted, were not disobedient sons of God but rather "beloved errant brothers."[25] That word "errant" is crucial. Like Maritain and other Catholic antiracists, Hildebrand still believed that Jews would eventually convert. He rejected, though, the political and social derivations that Catholics commonly drew from this mysterious and theological fact. Through his publishing and organizing in Central Europe, he became one of the most important of the early Catholic antiracists. When Father Georg Bichlmair, a well-known Austrian Catholic, delivered an anti-Semitic lecture on the Jewish question, Hildebrand responded in force, devoting an entire issue of his journal to the issue. His own essay savagely criticized Austrian Catholics like Bichlmair for misusing the

Catholic faith to grant a patina of piety to their mundane hatred of the Jews.[26]

Hildebrand's ideas quickly became popular, if controversial, in Central European Catholic circles. In 1930, Aurel von Kolnai, a Hungarian student of Scheler and another convert from Judaism, published a work called *Sexual Ethics* that used Hildebrand's theory. In the same year, Matthias Laros, a German priest in Scheler's circle, likewise drew on Hildebrand in his widely discussed 1930 article on marriage in *Hochland*. Herbert Doms, a Silesian priest, published *The Meaning of Marriage* in 1935, deriving inspiration from both Hildebrand and Kolnai. Even after Hitler's rise to power, these new theories of love appeared in mainstream German publications. While Karl Thieme's antifascist politics were banned from the German public sphere, he could still publish essays on the new marriage literature.[27]

Hildebrand's life and work were equally cosmopolitan. He was a polyglot who traveled throughout Europe in the 1930s, leveraging the contacts he had made as president of the foreign commission of Germany's Catholic Academic Union.[28] His texts traveled, too, especially after being translated into Italian (1931), English (1935), and French (1936). He was most interested in cultivating ties with the French. Hildebrand and Maritain first met in the late 1920s and stayed in touch for decades. Hildebrand did a great deal to publicize Maritain in German-speaking anti-Nazi circles. He personally reviewed a translation of Maritain's work, while *The Christian Corporate State* published numerous translations of his articles in two special editions devoted solely to French Catholic authors. In his own regular features, too, Hildebrand channeled Maritain in his attacks on the "politicization of religion" that had led to so many disastrous alliances.[29]

Emmanuel Mounier, one of the most influential French Catholic intellectuals of the 1930s, pursued similar ideals in his own writings and in his editorial decision-making at *Esprit,* the incendiary Catholic journal he edited. His 1936 *Manifesto in the Service of Personalism* was groundbreaking in its contention that the "family" is not necessarily good in itself, as many families "spiritually kill" the human person with their "familial inertias." "To make infants is first of all to make persons, and not primarily, or exclusively, . . . anonymous little fascists or Communists who will perpetuate the established conformism."[30] Following Mounier's lead, *Esprit* in the late 1930s focused increasingly on marriage and gender issues, publishing articles by

Paul-Ludwig Landsberg and the Catholic novelist Jacques Perret on marriage (both explained that marriage, properly understood, was an antifascist imperative).[31]

By the later 1930s, as more and more Catholics were beginning to question the aggressive natalism of authoritarian regimes, Hildebrand's ideas began to spread through a number of different venues. Marriage manuals were one of the most important. In 1936, a volume appeared in Germany called *The Secret of Marriage,* written by a Swiss bishop and aimed specifically at women. In it, he argued that conjugal love was a legitimate end of marriage and that even sterile marriages were therefore beneficial in the eyes of God and his church. Drawing clearly on Hildebrand and Doms, the text argued that marriage had both a "meaning" (love) and an "end" (children), and that it was wrong to ignore the former in the interest of the latter. A few years later, Hans Wirtz's marriage manual, *From Eros to Love* (1938), appeared in Austria with the apostolic imprimatur. In it, Wirtz counseled that "eros and sex" were "essential" to God's plan for marriage. Going further than Streng, Wirtz counseled couples to explore their sexuality, instructing the groom not to worry about overwhelming the woman with his desires, and the bride "not to deny, out of ignorance or false modesty, the thousand joys she would like to give her husband." Wirtz also recommended the rhythm method, which could bring "order and discipline" into "sexual life, which is often so chaotic." Both of these manuals were translated into multiple languages and appeared in updated editions for decades; Streng's work sold over one hundred thousand copies, and Wirtz's likely did just as well.[32]

In addition to marriage manuals, Catholic presses began to publish marriage memoirs, aimed at a wide audience. Norbert Rocholl, a German Catholic, paved the way with his *Marriage as Holy Life* (1936, translated into French in 1938): "theology for a layman, by a layman," as he put it. From Rocholl's perspective, the sociologists who focused on procreation were entirely missing the point of marriage, which was defined by "the mystery of Christian faith." Against the natalists who argued in terms of the family's social necessity, Rocholl drew heavily on Hildebrand to emphasize "conjugal love," defining the institution not by children but by "love of an entire person for another entire person." His book was soon translated into French, where it was widely reviewed by the Catholic press.[33] In 1938 alone, two Catholic marriage memoirs appeared in France. The first of them, *This Sacrament Is Great: Witness from a Christian Home,* was written by a devout

Catholic couple. While the volume did glorify procreation and was dedicated to the couple's six children, the authors nonetheless drew on Hildebrand's by now canonical work to legitimate long chapters on the phenomenology of blossoming love, both spiritual and physical. Marriage, from their perspective, was between "two persons" and required "conjugal intimacy" as "a true condition of spiritual enrichment." The other memoir, by the editor of a Catholic youth journal, was called *Eternal Companions: The Sacrament of Marriage*. Its author, too, drew explicitly on Hildebrand and focused on the psychological and physical aspects while subtly downplaying the legal, natalist elements of Catholic dogma.[34]

The new ideas about marriage coursed through lay Catholic organizations, some of which were officially affiliated with Catholic Action. In France, members of the Young Christian Workers (JOC) campaigned to reclaim marriage and the family from the natalists. Their mass-circulation journal, in its account of the "goals" of marriage, listed "the sanctification of conjugal love" first and put procreation in second place. In an article the following month, the journal complained that natalists were denying "the Christian conception of marriage. . . . The most sacred rights of the human person and of morality are sacrificed to the omnipotence of the state." The Catholic Association of French Youth (ACJF) published a special issue dedicated to the family from the same perspective. In Austria, some leaders of the Catholic Women's Organization (KFÖ) began to worry about the oppressive elements of Austrian natalism. In their journal, they questioned the notion that "a woman must be a mother," arguing that this was "in no way compatible with a Catholic outlook." They also passed a resolution opposing the notorious "Two-Income Law," which dismissed married women from government employment. In Germany, organizations such as Heliand and the Catholic German Women's League (KDF) likewise questioned the natalism of church and state, sowing doubt that Nazi calls to "return to the home" had any link with Catholic teachings.[35]

In some ways, the new Catholic approach to marriage and sexuality was beneficial for women, and it at least rhymed with the new political and economic opportunities that women were claiming.[36] It could potentially lead to the denial, as one French family expert put it, of "the idea that a free human being, generally the woman, can be obliged by moral law to suffer the movements of love without feeling the sentiment."[37] In other words, forced sex within the marriage was now theologically inadmissible. Hildebrand and his followers were not, however, feminists in the contemporary sense. Hildebrand's elevation of love and spirituality counseled a renewed, not a relaxed, hostility toward divorce, homosexuality, contraception, and abortion, all of which brought the mysteries of love and marriage into the purview of the calculating, egoist mind.[38] The conservative elements of Hildebrand's thought are important because they remind us of the very Catholic nature of Catholic antifascism. Fraternal Catholics were not socialists who happened to go to church but rather Catholics who operated within the broad but definite parameters of the Catholic tradition.

Hildebrand's ideas about marriage and sexuality, for all of their conservatism, certainly clashed with the priorities of fascism. Hildebrand had, in fact, one of the most sterling anti-Nazi records of any European intellectual, having grappled with Nazis since their origins in early 1920s Munich. When Hitler finally invaded in 1938, Austria was no longer safe for Hildebrand either. He fled to Czechoslovakia, saved only by the Swiss passport he retained from his grandfather (the Gestapo arrived at his apartment a few hours later). He made his way to southern France, where he taught in Toulouse until France, too, succumbed. Jacques Maritain secured his passage to America by ensuring that he was one of two Catholics to be included on a list of Jewish German intellectuals to be brought to America under the care of the Rockefeller Foundation.[39] Hildebrand's story might be unique in European history: attacked for his Catholicism and saved by his Jewishness.

Hildebrand showed 1930s Catholics that they could be modern *without* placing the reproductive family at the center of their social and political vision. This was a crucial lesson because paternal Catholic modernists were doing just that—a move that, while defensible from within the social Catholic tradition, was a novelty that was legitimating all manner of alliances with authoritarian states. The social ethos of the faith, Hildebrand suggested, could be found in lateral relations between consenting adults, not in vertical relations of obedience. While he left little record of his thoughts on concrete issues of social welfare, he likely balked at the Austrian regime's perpetual paeans to motherhood. After all, they legitimated a robust and interventionist welfare apparatus designed more to secure births than to cultivate spiritually sound marriages. Fraternal Catholic modernists were not opposed to the welfare state, as such, but they did not believe that it was the primary pathway to social justice because they did not believe that the child-rich family was the primary agent of social justice. They looked, instead, to another agent, one to which the childless Christ had actually belonged: the working class.

Equality: Trade Unions and the Fraternal Economy

The 1930s were a time of economic calamity, in which it was clear that the traditional Catholic zeal for paternalist employers and placid workers' clubs was out of date. There was debate, though, about how the tradition might be updated. Most Catholic economic thinkers defended some form of authoritarian corporatism, which empowered the state to create employers' and workers' syndicates that would work together to organize the economy in the interest of the common good. This solution maintained some elements of the tradition, notably, its commitment to private property, anti-Communism, and class collaboration. It had its problems, however. For one thing, it didn't work very well, leading in practice more to state meddling than to class collaboration. For another, it jettisoned what some saw as the most important elements of the Catholic tradition, namely, its antistatism and its commitment to free labor organizing. Catholic antifascists picked up and modernized those themes, arguing that Catholics should work together with Jews and socialists in the name of economic justice. The vehicle with which they would do so was the trade union.

Catholic trade unions had a long history, of course, and in Pittsburgh and Paris alike Catholic workers were organizing with enthusiasm in the 1930s (sometimes even collaborating with non-Catholics). This activism found conceptual resonance, too, as vigorous trade unionism was incorporated into the pluralism of Catholic antifascism. This innovation could be traced in many figures, but perhaps most interestingly in the life and writing of Ernst Karl Winter. Like many Austrian Catholics, he had been an uncompromising anti-Semite and antimodernist in the 1920s. As with Hildebrand and Maritain, it was precisely his intransigence and unwillingness to compromise that led him in innovative and antifascist directions in the 1930s. Over the course of that tumultuous decade, this recovering anti-Semite became an apostle for an interconfessional socialism in which Catholics, Jews, and even Communists would work together to wrest control of the economy away from capitalists and fascists alike.

Winter remained convinced that Catholicism had to offer a ruthless critique of capitalism, but he began to believe in the late 1920s that staunch conservatism, his own included, had become an apologia for that very system. We must, Winter implored, "have the courage to stand on the right and think on the left."[40] In other words, Winter sought a kind of Catholic conservatism that would intellectually appropriate the most trenchant insights of the Marxist tradition. This required an embrace of what he called "methodological dualism," distinguishing rigorously between scholasticism and sociology. Natural law could provide certain general principles about social justice and social order, but when it came to concrete issues like the gold standard or trade union policy, Catholics would have to speak the language of social science, and specifically the language of Marxism.[41]

This sensibility grew increasingly common in the Catholicism of the late 1920s, when Catholic paeans to class collaboration and charity rang hollow. Winter found a welcome intellectual home at the *Red Newsletter for Catholic Socialists,* a German publication with significant Austrian involvement (including on its editorial staff). His methodological dualism was a central element of the journal's policy. As Heinrich Mertens, a German Catholic socialist, put it, "The time is over when theologians, who concern themselves with social science for pastoral reasons, can represent Catholic social teaching." Winter's contributions focused on the economy, arguing that paternalist corporatism did no more than entrench capitalism even more deeply. Ernst Michel, a German Catholic socialist, agreed, complaining that Catholics neglected the "dynamic, historical approach" toward the economy in the name of a "static, natural law" conception. This blindness allowed social Catholicism to become a smokescreen for the interests of the ruling class instead of a ringing call for social justice. Catholics at the *Red Newsletter* were especially incensed by the authoritarian corporatism that was quickly becoming mainstream economic doctrine, and that seemed to prove Michel's point (they took special aim at Theodor Brauer, whose authoritarian leanings were evident even before he made the transition to Nazism).[42]

Catholic socialism had considerable intellectual appeal in both Germany and Austria around 1930, as the horrors of the Great Depression sent Catholics casting for novel solutions. Catholic newspapers adopted quasi-Marxist language in their attacks on private employers and coal concerns, joining their socialist brethren in calls to nationalize major sectors of the economy.[43] On the intellectual front, to take one example, Carl Muth published a blockbuster essay on "The Hour of the Middle Class" in 1930. In it, the influential editor of *Hochland* worried that the masses had diagnosed a connection between the Catholic Church, bourgeois liberalism, and the Great Depression. While he thought the masses were basically right, he also worried that the gathering counteroffensive would sweep away everything that was valuable about the Church and the middle classes alike. Only some kind of Catholic socialism, Muth mused, could reverse the tide.[44] Winter immediately wrote Muth a fawning letter expressing gratitude that Muth had turned to socialism and not toward the authoritarian corporatism that was gaining ground in many Catholic circles. He explained to Muth his notion, familiar to Marxists but still novel to Catholics, that fascism was the logical outgrowth of modern capitalism. "What could corporatist thought be," he wondered, "except fascism, which is nothing other than the contemporary adaptation of capitalism"? In the same letter, Winter explained that he had abandoned the antimodernism of his past thought. "I, who have been writing for and believing in the surviving political vocation of the nobility, realize today the absolute sterility of this class. . . . The spirit of the social aristocratic principle, embodied by [Karl von] Vogelsang, appears to finally be dead."[45]

In the early 1930s, it seemed, as Marx might have predicted, that Germany provided the best hope for a socialist renaissance. With the rise of Adolf Hitler in 1933, however, German socialism was destroyed—and its Catholic variant, too. Winter devoted himself to ensuring that the same thing would not happen in Austria. In Winter's view, the wretched relationship between Catholics and socialists would have to be healed if Austria were to put up any kind of resistance to Hitler. This was an unpopular take. For most Austrian Catholics, as for most Germans, Nazi rule was preferable to Communist dictatorship: at least Nazis claimed to support the Church. Winter chalked this up to a "lack of character amongst Catholics." He called forthrightly for a Popular Front strategy, viewing fascism as a much greater threat than Communism.[46]

When Dollfuss came to power in 1934, Winter agreed to participate in his government, serving as vice-mayor of Vienna.[47] Winter was an old war comrade of the new dictator's, but this was not primarily why he was chosen. While Dollfuss had little time for Winter's philo-Marxism, he did recognize that his friend was right about one thing: unless the new state could win the workers to its side, it would fail. Dollfuss gave Winter the nearly hopeless task of bringing the nation's disgruntled socialists into the warm embrace of the Fatherland Front. His valiant and doomed attempt to do so was known, simply enough, as the "Winter Action." The uniqueness of his project comes alive through comparison. Richard Schmitz, Winter's corporatist superior as mayor of Vienna, gave stump speeches to Austrian workers and privately was thrilled that they seemed to be excited by his authoritarian corporatist ideas. Winter's approach was different, and more democratic. He did go on lecture tours, specifically aiming at the taverns that attracted socialist workers, but he listened, too. He organized study circles with workers, both Catholic and socialist, who were encouraged to express their true opinions about the new state of affairs in Austria. His journal, called simply *Action,* published the results, even, and especially, when they were critical of the corporatists in power.

Winter's hostility to Nazism pushed him toward bold conceptual innovations, necessary if Catholic-Communist antifascism was to be defended. His writings in 1934 and 1935 represent an attempt to craft a Thomist-Marxist synthesis, and a kind of Catholic modernism that made room for a pluralist account of the private sphere. Like Aquinas, and unlike Marx, he was certain that "the state is something eternal": it is one of the divinely appointed communities that structure the natural social order. However, Winter also adopted a Marxist perspective on the state. "State constitutions," he continued, "are dependent on economic conditions." The "old democracy of the 19th century," he believed, was responsible for an epidemic of overproduction. This in turn led to a "profound economic crisis" that could only be met by an anticapitalist movement that brought Catholics and socialists together, both practically and intellectually. "It is not at all the case," he concluded, "that Christian workers are right, and socialists wrong, about all questions!" At least some socialists took the bait: one wrote in to praise Winter's organization as "the only legal path to secure workers' influence on politics."[48]

Whatever errors Communists may have made, Winter reasoned, they at least had deep roots in Austria and represented one facet of a noble European heritage (this was essentially Maritain's approach to the question, too).[49] While he believed that the economy must be investigated using modern methods and that Marxism was the best one available, he was allergic to Stalinist violence and the command economy. His version of Marx was not that of the Third International but that of the young, "humanist" Marx, whose writings Winter encountered through the pioneering edition of Siegfried Landshut and Jakob Peter Mayer.[50] This idiosyncratic Catholic Marxism yielded an unsurprisingly idiosyncratic and even utopian political program. He hoped for some kind of socialist monarchism—

essentially a constitutional monarchy—to excite patriotism and secure political legitimacy, alongside an economic order made up of freely organized trade unions and a social order enlivened by an active and organized citizenry.[51]

Winter's desire for a modern Catholic social ethics capable of staving off fascism led him to support the modern and secular nation-state: one that would enshrine "eternal human rights" and reject anti-Semitism.[52] While most Austrians thought that their national destiny lay with Germany, Winter believed that the tiny Austrian state had a mission and an identity of its own. Like Hildebrand, he thought that Austria could be a light unto the world by showing how a modern state could survive without national or racial chauvinism (there was no Austrian "nation," after all).

Winter's new conception of politics, and his new hopes for Austria, explains his antiracist turn. Anti-Semitism had been central to his writing in the 1920s, but in the 1930s, in the name of antifascism, he evolved on this front. Some of his allies did, too. "There is, properly speaking, no Jewish question in Austria," his old friend Alfred Missong argued. "There is only anti-Semitism," the dark shadow of pagan forms of nationalism.[53] Winter went even further, arguing for "a union of Christians and Jews against Nazism."[54] He became, with Hildebrand, one of the most important antiracist publicists in 1930s Europe. He founded a publishing house, Gsur Verlag, dedicated entirely to anti-Nazism. Under its imprint, he published what one historian has called "the first systematic Christian critique of racism," Walter Berger's *What Is Race?*, alongside another pioneering work of scientific antiracism, Peter Drucker's *The Jewish Question in Germany* (both Berger and Drucker were Jewish, and the former was a convert to Catholicism).[55]

However cogent Winter's theories may have been, they clashed with the priorities of a regime that never intended to allow economic power to pass into the hands of unruly trade unions. By the spring of 1935, after only about six months of feverish activity, he announced that he had "essentially changed [his] mind" about Austria's corporatist experiment: "I now believe in an expansion of parliamentary democracy through corporatist democracy, not in the replacement of the former by the latter."[56] He was not alone. Many Catholic workers, nostalgic for their union and recognizing the false promises of the system, turned on authoritarian corporatism, too.[57]

The turning point for Winter was the 1935 trial of former social democratic party leaders, condemned for inciting violence during Austria's civil war. From Winter's perspective, the trial was the perfect opportunity to win back the workers: the leaders could be set free in the name of a new understanding, and with the recognition that many conservatives had acted criminally as well (Maritain criticized their imprisonment, too). However, the trial went on and the socialists were convicted in proceedings that were roundly, and internationally, condemned as a show trial. Winter could not contain his disbelief and rage, which spilled into the columns of his newsletter. While in the past he had mainly attempted to assuage socialist doubts, he now attacked the regime head-on, advocating constitutional reform, trade union liberties, and even the return of free elections. Schuschnigg, the Austrian leader who took over after Dollfuss's assassination, wrote a blistering letter to Winter, hinting that he was an enemy of the state. His journal began to appear with significant portions censored. Increasingly hysterical counterattacks began to appear from the regime's strident right wing. "That's Enough, Mr. Winter!" exclaimed one writer in the newspaper of the Heimatschutz, the paramilitary wing of the government. Eventually, Winter was relieved of both his post and his journal.[58]

Despite his political failure, Winter showed that the Catholic tradition could generate an antifascist economic strategy, and one that wrested free of the anti-Semitism that had long dogged Catholic economic theory. He likely could not have arrived at such a position from within the conservative intellectual culture of Catholic Austria. Like Hildebrand, his trajectory was a European one. His turn against corporatism, for instance, came soon after a trip to Paris, and it is possible that his experience of the vibrant Catholic unions there impacted his hostility to state corporatism in Austria.[59]

In France, too, Catholic intellectuals moved rapidly toward a Catholic modernism that would emphasize free and interconfessional trade unionism. Auguste Cornu's pathbreaking dissertation on the young Karl Marx was discussed in a series of articles in *Esprit* in the early 1930s. These essays, in turn, were drawn on by Maritain in the lectures that eventually became *Integral Humanism*.[60] While a genuine Catholic Communism did exist, it was quite small; the union-supporting democratic socialism of Winter's imagination was more widespread. Étienne Borne's theology of labor rejected Marxist materialism, while accepting the basic socialist insight that meaningful labor was central to the good life and that dramatic social reforms would be necessary to make it possible.[61] *Esprit* published a dossier on trade unions in 1936, prefacing it all with the proud declaration that they despised corporatism and had always been "ferocious defenders of a free worker's movement." The "official" syndicates of the corporatists might adequately represent workers' concrete interests, but they could never foment the kind of working-class consciousness and organization that could transform capitalism as a whole. This sensibility was especially prevalent in Catholic Action organizations. The JOC emphasized "the right of workers to align themselves *with the syndicate of their choice*," and its older brother—the League of Christian Workers—agreed. In the *Annals of Catholic Youth*, a series of articles criticized authoritarian corporatism in the name of trade unionism. And when Marshal Pétain announced the Labor Charter, a number of Church leaders signaled their disappointment and their preference for the maintenance of syndical liberty.[62]

As in Austria, the democratic socialism of these Catholic intellectuals had a practical corollary. After the end of the Winter Action, France's CFTC (French Confederation of Christian Workers, a Catholic trade union) became the most exciting experiment in antifascist Catholic labor activity on the continent. When the Popular Front came to power in 1936 and a wave of strikes tore across France, many CFTC members collaborated with the non-Catholic unions. This was a public relations coup. Cleansed of its reputation as a white-collar, boss-coddling union, the CFTC's membership numbers skyrocketed (collaboration between the CFTC and non-Catholic unions was sporadic, to be sure, but it did exist).[63] These progressive elements came to light in the 1936 "CFTC Plan," which laid out the union's guiding philosophy. The right to freely associate, the Plan declared, was an inviolable natural right. While the Plan did envision an important role for the state, it avoided the magic word "corporatism" and focused instead on labor participation in management of the individual firm. The "organization of the profession," a valuable goal, could only be achieved through "complete liberty of constitution and recruitment" for the unions.[64]

The International Confederation of Christian Trade Unions (CISC) was stridently opposed to authoritarian corporatism, too. At its 1934 congress, Jos Serrarens, a Dutch trade unionist and secretary-general of the organization, drew explicitly on Maritain's writings in his case against corporatism, expressing outrage that a regime like Austria's could claim to act in the name of *Quadragesimo anno* (Pope Pius XI's 1931 social encyclical). Like Maritain, he was critical of Italy, Germany, and Austria for dismantling the free unions, in flat contradiction to the "theories defended over long years by Christian sociologists." While these nations wanted to construct the new economic order "one fine day, by a handful of decrees," Serrarens counseled a more bottom-up approach that would protect Catholic unions while still aiming at industry-level dialogue and regulation.[65] Serrarens spoke with some knowledge. He had recently visited Austria and reported, somewhat gloomily, that the Austrian regime was a travesty of true Catholic principles and that Catholic leaders were being dominated by more radical and "totalitarian" elements. The tension between the CISC and the Austrian experiment came up somewhat awkwardly at the 1934 meeting. Representatives from the new unified syndicate, led after all by Catholic unionists, showed up in Utrecht demanding a seat at the Congress, only to be told by the president that liberty of association was so important that this could not be allowed (the year before, the CISC had reached a similar decision about the German Labor Front [DAF], again despite the presence of Catholic unionists among its leadership).[66]

In Winter's journals, at the CISC, and in Catholic Action organizations, the vaguely worded *Quadragesimo anno* received a different interpretation from the one offered by authoritarian corporatists. This received physical form in a version of the encyclical published, in an edition of tens of thousands of copies and with copious annotations, by an association of French Catholic social scientists. The annotator glossed over the troubling passages in which Mussolini's Italy was praised, commenting only that they were "particularly delicate," thereby suggesting that Pius XI was playing a political game in those paragraphs, and one that need not interest the French. Sections that could conceivably relate to trade unions, on the other hand, were enlivened by many footnotes, reminding readers about the Church's long-standing commitment to the cause. The JOC, for its part, published a fascinating pedagogical text called *While Listening to the Pope: Interviews about Quadragesimo Anno* (1932), which broke the encyclical into chunks and tried to educate Catholic workers about its contents in colloquial terms. This interpretation, too, emphasized the pope's traditional support of trade unionism, despite the suspiciously small role of that commitment in the encyclical's text.[67]

Winter's hope that Catholic-socialist collaboration, nourished by a revived Catholic commitment to trade unionism, might hold Nazism at bay proved fruitless. By 1940, Hitler held sway over France, Germany, and Austria alike. All the same, Winter's ideas survived in various forms and venues. Many were clandestine and have left few traces. In concentration camps, for instance, Catholics and socialists found themselves in closer quarters than usual and found common cause in opposition to fascism (this became known as the "Spirit of Dachau").[68] In the German resistance, antifascist Catholic labor activists such as Jakob Kaiser and Wilhelm Elfes cultivated ties with socialists such as Wilhelm Leuschner and Carl Severing.[69]

Winter's ideas also survived in more public forums. Reprising the editorial activities of Austrian workers in the mid-1930s, Catholic workers and intellectuals in Pétain's France criticized authoritarian corporatism as a denial of CFTC and social Catholic tradition. Jeunesse de l'Eglise (Youth of the Church) was a living experiment and think tank that began publishing pamphlets on Catholic-Marxist collaboration from Lyon in 1942. The Young Christian Students (JEC) published an article by Catholic trade unionist Paul Bacon decrying the Labor Charter, Gaston Tessier attacked the charter in the name of trade unionism on the front page of *La Croix,* and the League of Christian Workers (LOC) published a series of articles in 1942 making the same points. The great text of Catholic-socialist collaboration was the "Manifesto of the Twelve," signed by Communist, socialist, and Catholic trade unionists. Unions, the joint manifesto states, must not be "absorbed by the state" but should rather follow the principle of "professional organization." The joint manifesto adopted the very slogan of the CFTC: "the free union in the organized industry."[70]

Even in Germany and Austria, while Christian trade unions had of course been destroyed, Catholics in Winter's vein continued to organize and publish. They had at least two print organs. One was the Paris-based, German-language resistance journal called *The Future,* which began publishing in 1938. While Catholics were well represented, *The Future* was not, as one Communist complained, "the organ of the conservative-Catholic emigration." Instead, it provided a space in which fraternal Catholics could appear alongside socialists such as Willi Münzenberg.[71] The other was the journal of Germany's Catholic Workers' Movement (KAB), which survived through much of the 1930s (the boundary between clandestine and public was porous: the KAB also provided a site for illicit, interconfessional discussions of Catholic social teaching).[72] The journal's implicit antifascism can be found primarily in its reporting on Catholic developments outside Germany. France's JOC was determined to be "very remarkable," a brave claim to make in a country where no such organization was possible. In 1935, a long front-page article appeared about the French Social Week on corporatism, which had been quite critical of Nazism. While those critiques were of course not reprinted, the article did report the meeting's focus on "the personality, which has duties and rights," as well as the danger of "the arbitrary power of the collective." Catholics could support "not just any corporatist order, but rather one whose spirit is that of *Rerum novarum* and *Quadragesimo anno*." The distinguishing feature of that order, the author explained, was that all members of the profession, including workers, would be consulted about questions of production and social insurance.[73] Any reader of the newspaper would have known that German workers enjoyed no such rights, and thus that the journal (eventually shut down) was using European Catholic developments to implicitly criticize Nazi policy.

While many Catholic labor leaders and economists in the 1930s opted for authoritarian corporatism in the name of anti-Communism, Ernst Karl Winter and his circles reminded Catholic workers that the social Catholic tradition had bountiful resources for free trade unionism, too. Essentially, he did little more than revive the traditional Catholic zeal for associational life, and the traditional Catholic suspicion of the overactive state. He did so, though, in a new and more modern key: less anti-Semitic, and more in dialogue with Marx. In Winter's view, freely constituted trade unions, rather than the state or the marketplace, should populate the economic sphere and bend it toward justice. His ideas, alongside Hildebrand's, help us to see the outlines of Catholic antifascism, its allergy to the state, and its commitment to a robust civil society. For a broader view of this new pluralist commonweal, we can turn to the most famous and influential Catholic intellectual of the era: Jacques Maritain.

Liberty: Pluralism and Fraternal Politics

In the 1930s, mainstream Catholic intellectuals and leaders made their peace with the secular nation-state like never before. Viewing it as the only antidote to Communism, they were willing to grant immense authoritarian power to the state apparatus, so long as the state signaled its commitment to protect religious liberty and the family while joining the cultural and legal community of "the West." To Maritain and other antifascist Catholics, this gave up too much that was distinctive about the Catholic tradition— namely, its persistent suspicion of the state, and its desire to imagine a social order defined by civil society organizations free of state domination.

Maritain's pluralist political theory of the 1930s was designed primarily to update this tradition for the modern age, salvaging and updating the most emancipatory elements of his past monarchism.

Maritain always rejected the linkage of the universal Church with the specific political and legal heritage of "the West." Unlike mainstream Catholics, in other words, he refused to salvage a Catholic politics by equating the values of the Church with those left behind by the Roman empire. In a letter to a missionary in China, he argued that "Christ's supernatural revelation puts down roots in the most native and natural way, in every nation on Earth." Therefore, he continued, "there can be no question of imposing the universal primacy of Greco-Latin culture."[74] Maritain honed his critique of the new Western consciousness on his former friend Henri Massis's bellwether volume, *Defense of the West* (1927). Even before it came out, Maritain was writing pained letters to Massis, begging him either to abandon or radically revise the project. One cannot possibly speak of "the Orient" or "German philosophy" as though they were stable entities, he wrote, adding that a book aimed at these twin targets would do more than inflame passions around the world. "Our culture is Greco-Latin," he concluded. "Our religion is not."[75]

In place of an interconfessional Defense of the West, Maritain pursued what he called a "pluralist" or "fraternal" politics—in explicit contrast to the "paternal" vision that, in his opinion, salvaged the least Catholic elements of the Middle Ages. For Maritain, the central elements to be retained were antistatism and federalism, not the zeal for authority and hierarchy. He envisioned the state giving way to an "organized political fraternity" in which "civic fraternities" enjoying their own laws and legitimacy would constitute the main institutional mediation between the citizen and the political sphere.[76] Like many contemporary thinkers, notably Georges Gurvitch and Harold Laski, Maritain rejected the sovereign state's claim to represent the political community itself. Just as he had done in his monarchist days, Maritain insisted that the sources of legitimacy and law were plural, arising from within civil society instead of being imposed from above. The novelty was that Maritain no longer believed in the necessity of installing an authoritarian or monarchist state to ratify that pluralism. The institutions of the pluralist society would arise organically, he taught, from an interfaith society of engaged laymen, working toward the common good as they understood it. As he told one authoritarian corporatist in a letter, he rejected the narrowly "technical and professional" version of corporatism offered by mainstream Catholics in favor of a "properly political" version rooted in "the political thoughts of those persons who are members of civil society."[77]

Maritain's view of civil society, however much it might have in common with secular versions, was nonetheless religious. This is most apparent in his commitment to the saints, who played a central role for him in fomenting moral transformation amongst the laity. This notion of moral elevation had always been central to social Catholic teachings but was suspiciously absent from the doctrines of paternal Catholic modernism, which was more interested in authoritarian security than in ethical cultivation of the self. "A properly Christian social renovation," he argued, "will be the work of sanctity, or it will not be." He called this "the purification of the means," a phrase that was meant as a sharp rebuke to the cynical compromises that were guiding Catholic politics at the time (Maritain wrote a great deal about Machiavelli and the baleful consequences of an instrumental notion of politics). What he meant was that Christians should concern themselves first and foremost with "thinking, living, acting politically in the Christian style" rather than attempting "to obtain from the world machinery that is only Christian in an external and illusory way." As critics pointed out, this veers close to political quietism, but Maritain didn't see it that way. He sketched out instead a political vision in which a new generation of heroic saints would conspire, through their own sacrifices and pure actions, to create a "new man" dedicated to transcendent values. He found his model with the early Christians, fleeing the authorities in the catacombs and laying the groundwork for an ethical revolution.[78]

Maritain called, in short, for a new generation of spiritual elites to lead Catholics *and others* toward a new Christendom: a pluralist commonweal structured by interfaith civil society organizations. He was not, in the 1930s, an apostle of Christian Democracy, if that refers to a kind of Catholic or interconfessional parliamentarism. This confused many readers, then and since, especially as Maritain praised "personalist democracy" in his writings. The reasoning should be clear by now, however, and Maritain spelled it out in a public letter to Paul Archambault, a Christian Democrat who tried to enlist Maritain's prestige behind his own partisan political project. Maritain had no particular affection for parliamentary democracy, which granted in his mind a patina of democratic legitimacy to a state apparatus that served primarily to suppress the civic fraternities that were the true essence of the political. The problem with Christian Democracy, from his perspective, was that it corralled the spirit of Christ, which should inflame all of society from below, into a parliamentary party aiming to conquer the sovereign power of the state.[79]

Maritain's hopes for an interfaith, pluralist renaissance militated against the prevailing culture of Catholic anti-Semitism. In a number of publications and lectures in the late 1930s, he criticized anti-Semitism as a pagan misunderstanding of the proper role of politics. The Jewish question was a matter of theology and mystery, he insisted, not one of clumsy state repression. In the here and now, the task is to work with Jews in pursuit of social justice, recognizing them as allies and brothers. As with Hildebrand and Winter, his antiracism was entwined with his anticapitalism and antifascism. Catholic anti-Semites, Maritain argued, blamed Jews for problems that were actually rooted in the logic of capitalism itself. One of those problems was the emergence of Communism. By blaming this on the Jews, Catholics were overlooking the contradictions in capitalism that Marx had diagnosed and that inevitably led to Communist insurgency unless those emancipatory energies could be harnessed by the Church. As with his account of civil society, his antiracism was profoundly Catholic. He still expected the Jews to convert, eventually, and he even argued that they were partially responsible for the waves of repression and intolerance that confronted them (they had erred, he reasoned, in accepting the bankrupt promises of bourgeois modernity instead of sticking to their authentic faith).[80]

Indifferent toward the sputtering promise of Catholic parliamentarism and the anti-Semitic celebrations of the West common in conservative circles, Maritain instead found hope in the general spirit of lay organization that traversed the 1930s global Church. While he was certainly impressed by official Catholic Action organizations, he warned that such clerical and top-down styles of activism could not replace the volcanic energy bubbling up from the laity themselves. To be sure, the organizations in practice were less clerical than they were in theory, which Maritain surely appreciated. The tables at the new organizations' meetings were often circular, eschewing the pew-and-pulpit model of the Church. "They are their own masters, aren't they?" worried one Catholic professor about the JOC.[81] He was more enchanted, though, by lay organizations that did not require direct clerical guidance, some of which he found across the ocean. Maritain began visiting the United States in the mid-1930s and was enamored, like Alexis de Tocqueville before him, with its civic life. He was most impressed, perhaps, by an organization that he frequented called the Catholic Worker. The movement was founded by Dorothy Day and a French Catholic named Peter Maurin, both of whom were devoted to bringing Catholic principles of sanctity and justice to America's cities. Like Maritain, who influenced Day and Maurin alike, they believed that Catholic principles, properly understood, mandated a robust and even revolutionary form of lay activism.

Beyond Catholic Action, Maritain found inspiration in three specific institutional settings. The first two were the same as those celebrated by Hildebrand and Winter. *Integral Humanism* celebrated the marriage as a site of moral education, intimacy, and solidarity. Maritain was conspicuously silent about the hierarchical family unit, focusing instead on the egalitarian marriage bond: "The Christian family," he insisted, is founded on "the primarily spiritual and sacramental union of two persons." He was not a feminist in the liberal sense, believing as he did that women should not have "the same economic functions as man." At the same time, he did argue for "full juridical recognition" of women, including property rights, given that housework has an economic value of its own.[82] In his own person, he enshrined similar ideals. He was inseparable from his wife, Raïssa, a considerable intellectual in her own right (whose work he cited in *Integral Humanism*). His marriage, not his family, was at the center of his family life. He and Raïssa had no children, and he never appeared at the family congresses that were such important events for more mainstream figures.

The second institution that, in Maritain's view, contained the seeds of the pluralist commonweal was the trade union. *Integral Humanism* contained quite a detailed vision of a revamped economy in which workers, organized in trade unions, would assist in managing and owning enterprises, which would in turn be administered by a national body that was "entirely different from the statist corporations of totalitarianism."[83] And while he was absent from familialist events, he was present at trade union congresses, delivering a keynote to the 1937 CISC congress mentioned earlier. In it, he declared to the assembled delegates his "sincere sympathy for the Christian union movement" and explained why neither Bolshevism nor "the anti-Communist and anti-individualistic movements of authoritarianism and dictatorship" fully protected the worker. He lambasted the authoritarian regimes for cherishing "state sovereignty" instead of "the freedom of collective men." A few years later, in the preface to a volume by a CFTC leader named Paul Vignaux, Maritain wrote that Catholic labor, unlike those who "linked [corporatism] to fascism," had devised "an entirely opposed conception, which saves what is just in the idea of the community of work and the organized profession."[84]

The third institution that fascinated Maritain was the press, an issue that he wrote about with surprising regularity. He believed in a vibrant, free press in which Catholics could afford to be independent and participate in the non-Catholic public sphere, too. Maritain himself caused enormous controversy by participating in secular or socialist publishing ventures, while his spirit inflamed the diverse and pathbreaking Catholic press environment of 1930s France. Journals such as *La vie intellectuelle* and *Sept,* often with bylines from Maritain himself, were fearlessly willing to challenge established orthodoxy, sometimes leading them to be shut down altogether (as in the case of *Sept*). In a widely cited series of articles called "Is God on the Right?," published in *La vie intellectuelle,* the anonymous author answered with a resounding "No." In place of the conservative vision offered by Massis, authors in these journals dreamed of a deep pluralism along Maritain's lines—one that would be built from the bottom up and would follow the logic of fraternal cooperation rather than patriarchal law. In Maritain's view, these journals "planted in French soil the seeds of reconciliation between two ancient opposing traditions—the France of religious faithfulness and spirituality, and the France of human emancipation."[85]

However much Maritain celebrated France's unique heritage, he was a truly European thinker, convinced that the "new Christendom," like the one before it, would be supernational. While his transatlantic connections are well known, his European itinerary was just as important. He visited Germany (multiple times), Spain, Italy, and Poland, and his works were widely translated into the languages of all of those countries. German Catholics were especially drawn to him because he provided the resources to critique the West-defending "theology of the Reich" that was legitimating so much Nazi collaboration. His most devoted German follower was Waldemar Gurian, one of the intellectual leaders of Catholic anti-Nazism. Like Maritain, Gurian was particularly scathing toward the widespread notion that Catholicism was imbricated with the West. Maritain gave Gurian the language he needed to contest the "imperial theology" that he saw as "the plague of German spiritual life." Maritain agreed, and *Integral Humanism* was scathing in its judgment of that tradition. He was perfectly aware how provocative the book would be in a German context: "If my conception of the *Reich* shocks the German public," he wrote to Gurian, "I regret it but I will change nothing."[86]

Even after Germany fell to Hitler, Maritain's star continued to rise in Central Europe. From exile in Switzerland, Gurian published an important anti-Nazi journal called *German Letters,* in which he brought Maritain's ideas to a new audience. Several of Maritain's works were translated into German, too, where they began to circulate among anti-Nazi Catholic intellectuals. Aside from Hildebrand and Gurian, Erik Peterson, Karl Thieme, and Eberhard Welty were probably the three most important anti-Nazi Catholic writers in the 1930s, and all of them were in dialogue with Maritain. Welty's *Society and the Individual Man* (1935), one of only a handful of works in the Catholic sociological tradition to appear in Germany after Hitler came to power, drew widely on both Maritain and Hildebrand (Welty soon entered the Resistance).[87] Peterson, a personal friend of Maritain's, was, like him, a convert from Protestantism (they had first met in Bonn in the late 1920s, and Maritain paid Peterson a visit in 1931, too). He described his magisterial *Monotheism as a Political Problem* (1935) to Maritain as a proof of "the impossibility of an 'imperial theology'" through "the development of theological concepts."[88] The logic of Peterson's text was of a piece with fraternal modernism. A book-length critique of Carl Schmitt, the book patiently showed how political theology could flow from monotheistic traditions, linking God the Father with the paternalist state. The Christian conception of God, however, was not monotheistic but instead pluralist—a trinity—and so the Christian state should be pluralist, too. Thieme, yet another Protestant convert, agreed with Maritain that the authority of the Church can "in no way be institutionalized, as its kingdom is not of this world." From exile in Switzerland, he closely followed Maritain's developments, writing him long letters about how transformative Maritain's work had been for him and how he, too, sought to provide "a post-totalitarian Christian political ideology on the ruins of those of the past."[89]

Even in authoritarian Austria, Maritain's thought made significant inroads in the 1930s. In Hildebrand's journal, for instance, Maritain was published and discussed regularly, and Maritain's main German translator at the time was living in Austria, too. The Austrian case shows that Catholic antifascism didn't simply flow from Paris outward. Austria was, in fact, the primary site of antiracist Catholic thinking on the continent. The leader here was a Jewish convert and follower of Maritain, Johannes Oesterreicher. Maritain and Oesterreicher met in Vienna in the mid-1930s, and they remained in close contact for decades. Oesterreicher proclaimed the German translation of *Integral Humanism* "the most valuable innovation of the year" and published an excerpt from it in his journal, *The Fulfillment* (*Die Erfüllung*).[90] That journal, which featured many Catholic antifascists from across Europe, was, next to Hildebrand's own magazine, the central site of fraternal modernism in the German language.

Oesterreicher also helped to organize the most important text in transnational Catholic antiracism in the 1930s: a manifesto called "The Church of Christ on the Jewish Question," written primarily by Maritain's acolytes Gurian and Thieme. It appeared in French, German, and English, with the signatures of Maritain, Hildebrand, and a number of other prominent German, Austrian, Belgian, Czech, Italian, French, and Polish Catholic intellectuals. The manifesto emphasized throughout that the Jewish question is a purely religious affair, and only a pagan confusion of religion and politics could lead to any other conclusion. Targeting those defenders of the West who glorified the anti-Jewish legislation of the Middle Ages, it specifically cited *Integral Humanism* to argue that "the Christian order of the Middle Ages, from which canonistic Jewish laws were derived, no longer exists."[91]

While the ideas were not all his alone, Maritain's life and work provide the clearest distillation of a transnational Catholic antifascism. In a series of indelible works, notably *Integral Humanism,* Maritain wove together ideas on the family, the economy, and race that were circulating across Catholic Europe. In response to the rise of totalitarianism and the collapse of traditional Catholic politics, he urged a form of Catholic modernism that would salvage the revolutionary, antistatist elements of the tradition for a new age, rather than its hierarchical and racist ones. This would involve, he insisted, a radical rethinking of the Church's mission in the world. "Instead of a fortified castle," Maritain urged, "we should think of an army of stars thrown across the sky."[92] He was under no illusions that this would happen quickly, or without bloodshed. An army of stars was no match for the Wehrmacht.

THE PRIMARY INSTITUTIONS of fraternal Catholic modernism—Catholic trade unions, Catholic Action organizations, freely circulating periodicals, study circles, and more—were shattered by the war. "There is nothing left but the catacombs," Maritain wrote to a friend a few days after France surrendered to Germany.[93] The foxholes of the Resistance allowed fraternal Catholicism to survive, but not flourish, on the continent. As an intellectual project, it found a happier home in exile in the United States—most notably in New York City, where Jacques Maritain, Ernst Karl Winter, and Dietrich von Hildebrand all weathered the war years.

New York was an exciting place to be an intellectual, an exile, and a Catholic during wartime. The city was home to vibrant immigrant communities of Catholic believers and to exciting, radical experiments in Catholic activism such as the Catholic Worker. It was also home to *Commonweal,* a lay Catholic journal that pursued recognizably fraternal themes (its editor, Europhile George Shuster, had warned American Catholics against Franco). New York was not the only site of the Catholic exile community, of course. Canada played host to a group of French personalists, while Waldemar Gurian found a home at Notre Dame. While he bristled at the conservative Catholic culture there, he traveled frequently to Chicago and founded the *Review of Politics,* a (still-existing) journal that put Catholic ideas into conversation with secular and socialist ones.[94]

Back in New York, Winter and Hildebrand continued to fight fascism in their own ways. Winter taught at the New School and published handwringing essays in *Social Research* about the many mistakes Austria had made in its handling of the labor question.[95] Hildebrand argued tirelessly, in lectures and radio addresses, that Nazism and fascism were antithetical to Christianity. In a country where Franco was still quite popular among Catholics, he claimed that Franco's (neutral) Spain represented "one of the forms of Fascism which we have been fighting." He published articles on "Fascism and Catholicism" in which he condemned Catholic racism in the name of democracy, personalism, human rights, and dignity. He even retained his good cheer, and a profile in the *New York Post* reported on his disastrous efforts to cook Italian food in his adopted home.[96]

Maritain threw himself into antifascist organizing with his characteristic energy. The Resistance represented to him some of the central elements of his pluralist commonweal, insofar as it brought together Communists, Catholics, and more in defiance of the common fascist enemy. Georges Bidault, one of the titanic leaders of the Resistance, was a left-leaning Catholic who had been in Maritain's orbit for years. Gaston Fessard, the intellectual leader of the Catholic resistance on the ground, was likewise a longtime friend of both Hildebrand and Maritain. Fessard had taken part in a roundtable on *Integral Humanism,* sharing with Maritain a zeal for a "new Christendom" and a rejection of the Catholic and fascist search for ersatz father figures.[97] During the war, he founded and edited *Cahiers du Témoignage chrétien* (*Notebooks of Christian Witness*), the premier Catholic publication of the Resistance—and one in which Maritain published a crusading assault on Catholic racism.[98]

Maritain wrote feverishly during the war and became something of an intellectual celebrity. Most notably, he penned a pathbreaking text called "Christianity and Democracy," in which he called for a "more human world oriented toward an historic ideal of human brotherhood."[99] The pamphlet was airdropped behind enemy lines by the American military (two American officials, in their proposal to use his writings, called him the "foremost living French philosopher").[100] He also delivered radio addresses that were beamed into occupied France, and here, too, he gave voice to fraternal Catholicism: "Christians are renouncing the old paternalist conceptions, such as the temptation of a state corporatism that turns fatally towards Fascism, in the name of a sane organization of the profession founded on syndical liberties." "Although I am not saying that Christians are becoming socialists or socialists Christians," he continued, "they are perceiving that they can work together to reconstruct the nation."[101]

Maritain and other fraternal Catholics believed that the war might clear the way for a new, more pluralist, and more federalist Europe. Maritain had been urging political federalism for years, viewing it as the geopolitical translation of his pluralism. He started to emphasize it even more during the war, writing as he was in a New York City abuzz with federalist plans for the postwar world (he was friendly with Hannah Arendt, who was imagining a federalist solution for Palestine just as Maritain was doing for Europe).[102] In lectures that were circulated throughout France as resistance tracts and reported in the *New York Herald Tribune,* he proposed a federal Germany in a federal Europe; in *Commonweal,* he even began arguing for a "federal European army or police force."[103]

For all of the energy behind Maritain's various projects, it remains the case that his positions, and fraternal Catholicism in general, remained in the minority—even among exiles and even among supporters of the American war effort. The Nazi invasion of the Soviet Union in 1941 could plausibly have led to a new hegemony for Maritain's form of antifascist Catholicism, at least among the Allies. After all, it was the Communists who were suffering and dying most atrociously. Surprisingly, it did not. "War," Maritain judged in 1943, "does not have transformative power on its own."[104] The mere fact of the war, in other words, did not necessarily alter ideas or aspirations—nor, specifically, did it necessarily privilege fraternal Catholicism over its opponent.

The continuing hegemony of paternal Catholic modernism was apparent in the pope's Christmas messages as well as in the exile community itself. The most important intellectual text of the wartime Catholic Church was probably a 1942 "Manifesto on the War," signed by about forty "European Catholics sojourning in America." Maritain eventually signed, but unhappily. The manifesto, drafted largely by exiles in Quebec, ably repeated the new lingua franca of the Catholic 1930s, making the case for religious liberty, human dignity, and human rights. This much was not surprising. The true drama concerned whether it would represent paternal or fraternal Catholic modernism. And after some behind-the-scenes wrangling, it clearly espoused the former.

Even though it urged support of an American-led war effort against fascism, which included the Soviet Union as an ally, the 1942 manifesto was more of an anti-Communist text than an antifascist one. It mentioned anti-Communism as a principle *before* anti-Nazism, and it perversely argued that the Soviet sacrifice would give the "Western world" the "freedom of action" it needed to oppose "the development within its own body of the Communist ferment by any fitting action." The manifesto presumed the survival of the nation-state in a basically unaltered form, repeating Catholic bromides about substate institutions but clearly designating them as "inferior" to the state, which was suggested as a solution to the problems of the 1930s (the text even suggested that "a particularly vigorous political authority" might be necessary). The manifesto stated explicitly, too, that capitalism was not at issue in the war.[105]

The 1942 manifesto, therefore, essentially argued that anti-Communism, corporatism, and the nation-state were solutions to wartime chaos—not, as Maritain had long believed, *causes* of it. It is surprising, then, that Maritain signed the manifesto at all, and there are indications that he was reluctant to do so. He was privately critical of it, pointing out to a friend that it was "unconsciously tending towards a corporatist state." He had, behind the scenes, forced some alterations (apparently, the first version of the text had explicitly distinguished Nazism from the "authoritarian regimes" that "Christian nations" had pursued from time to time). Nonetheless, his archives are replete with letters from antifascists complaining about the text's severe limitations. Luigi Sturzo, one of Italy's premier antifascist intellectuals, wrote to protest, reasonably enough, that the manifesto was too obviously a product of the authoritarian, antidemocratic Catholicism he had long been fighting. Yves Simon, one of Maritain's closest friends and intellectual compatriots, complained about the "idiot manifesto" that Maritain had been forced to salvage before eventually signing. Waldemar Gurian griped that the manifesto trafficked in the old "ideology of the West." "I'll give my signature out of respect for you," Gurian decided, since Maritain had "lost so much time improving the manifesto."[106]

And yet Maritain, who a few years earlier had been organizing ideologically pristine antifascist manifestos of his own, signed anyway, as did many of his comrades. During the war, and especially in the postwar era, fraternal Catholics were forced to abandon their ideological purity and make a series of compromises. The very survival of the Church was at stake, and even Maritain was not going to let his principles disrupt the formation of alliances during the greatest armed conflict the world has ever known. These compromises, which continued into the postwar era, have distracted attention from the monumental intellectual achievement of Hildebrand, Winter, Gurian, Maritain, and the other Catholic writers who forged a Catholic antifascism in the 1930s. It was not a liberalism or socialism in disguise, nor did it represent Christian Democracy *avant la lettre*. Catholic antifascism was genuinely Catholic, rooted in the antistatist and pluralist traditions of social Catholic thinking, updated in a modern and interfaith key to confront modern and interfaith problems. Then and since, some have argued that the Church's compromises with fascism and anti-Semitism reveal the secret truth of a hierarchical, obtuse, and outdated institution. Maritain and the Catholic antifascists remind us that another story is possible. They agreed with the great English Catholic writer G. K. Chesterton, who judged that "Christianity has not been tried and found wanting. It has been found difficult and left untried."[107]

4

THE BIRTH OF CHRISTIAN
DEMOCRACY, 1944–1950

If my people who bear my name humble themselves, and pray
and seek my presence and turn from their wicked ways,
then I will listen from heaven and forgive their sins and restore
their country.

—2 CHRONICLES 7:14

In the late 1940s, a Catholic politician and intellectual gave a number of speeches on "socialism, federation, and religion"—for him, the holy trinity of postwar politics. Drawing on Jacques Maritain and other antifascist Catholics from the 1930s, he imagined, as he told a constitutional assembly in 1946, a politics oriented around "human fraternity," and a faith that might inspire "brothers and sisters" to "truly live in equality."[1] This would require a continuation of the antifascist struggle, and a dramatic reordering of the political and economic status quo. Writing in *Esprit,* a left-wing Catholic periodical with mammoth circulation, he worried that the "paternalist, not to say racist, spirit" of Nazi Germany and Vichy France had survived into the postwar moment. "This war has no meaning," he declared, "if it is not anti-Nazi. Germany has been defeated, but Nazism has not."[2] The only way to eradicate the fascist spirit, he concluded, was to attack the sordid alliance of high capitalism and the sovereign nation-state.

A few years later, another Catholic politician and intellectual gave an address titled "The West under Threat" to a stadium full of sixty thousand eager Christian listeners (Catholic and Protestant alike). He had no concern with residual Nazism. He worried instead about Communism, which he folded into a long struggle between the "Christian West" and "pagan

144

Eastern hordes." This had been the great drama of European history for a thousand years—a story whose lesson was that "peaceful acts and declarations of neutrality" would not be enough to secure the "defensive front of the West." Only military power and strong states in a European alliance, he argued, could save Europe from its enemies.[3]

The first of these figures was Léopold Senghor, a Senegalese poet who emerged as a central player in post-1945 constitutional negotiations in France and went on to become the first president of independent Senegal. The second was Heinrich von Brentano, a Christian Democratic politician and foreign minister of Germany in the late 1950s. Both men hoped to pursue some form of Catholic politics. Both were "modern," in the sense that they accepted the legitimacy of interconfessional societies, church-state separation, and religious freedom. This question was essentially settled in Catholic circles, as it was in non-Catholic ones.[4] Both could plausibly enlist the faith in support of their own politics, and both had recourse to a vibrant network of Catholic activists who agreed with them. This does not mean, as it might seem, that Catholicism is endlessly protean and can be embedded in any politics whatsoever. It means instead that the twin varieties of Catholic modernism forged in the 1930s continued to exist, and continued to clash, in postwar Europe.

The Catholic transition to modernity was already well under way in the 1930s, and in the late 1940s most of the last vestiges of antimodernism in the Church were snuffed out. The venerable Belgian publication the *Christian City,* for instance, renamed itself the *New Review.* In his explanation of the shift, the editor claimed that it was because of the wartime influence of Jacques Maritain and Emmanuel Mounier, who had convinced him that "there could no longer be a Christian City, as there had never been one. The important thing is to live and act as Christians in a pluralist society."[5] In France, the medievalist vogue of the 1920s was displaced by a new fascination with the early Christians, who fought for the faith in a space of religious pluralism. The Catholic celebrities of the moment—Henri de Lubac, François Mauriac, and the rest—had none of the flamboyant atavism of their predecessors, representing instead a Church that was opening itself to the world. At the 1946 Social Week, still the central event of French Catholic intellectual life, "pluralism" was the master concept of the entire meeting. "The question is no longer about the Christian city, or the Christian social order," one intellectual declared in 1949, "but of installing a social order in which the Church can complete its mission and men can fulfill their vocation." In Germany, a book on the Middle Ages by a venerated Catholic historian appeared in the same year, reiterating that "the *Reich* and the entire Middle Ages, and all that belonged to them, are over, in every form, and are not recoverable." The new editor of *Hochland*, Catholic Germany's most prestigious journal, penned a widely noted article on "Christian politics" in a "secularized world." Catholics, he argued, had to accept the reality of modern, secular statehood.[6] Even in Austria, a hotbed of medievalism in the 1920s, the 1952 Catholic Congress released a manifesto vowing a repudiation of "the politicized Church of past centuries" in favor of a Church "with doors open to the world and outstretched arms." Johannes Messner, a priest who had supported Engelbert Dollfuss, joined the new chorus. "We live in a pluralist society," he declared. "Different groups have very different conceptions of men, even of their dignity." "The Church no longer resembles the rock of Peter, but rather the raft of Peter the fisherman, marooned in an unknown sea," rhapsodized an Austrian Catholic politician.[7]

Catholics certainly did not embrace every element of modernity: they were just as wary of provocative films and fashions as they had always been. They accepted, however, the modern *condition* of church-state separation, in which the private sphere of religion and the public sphere of politics and economics can be legitimately distinguished. As in the 1930s, a set of keywords that enshrined and defended this split were unquestioned in Catholic circles: antitotalitarianism, human rights, human dignity, and religious freedom. The last one was the most controversial. Among the laity, the issue was largely settled, and Catholics primarily talked about religious liberty to criticize Communists for denying it. Theologically, however, the doctrine found little purchase until after the war. Some Catholic thinkers, especially in Spain and Italy, continued to pursue the traditional teaching that the confessional Catholic state was the ideal, even if it was seldom attained in practice. In France, Germany, Austria, America, and elsewhere, they met stout opposition from a new generation of theologians who argued forcefully that religious liberty not only was to be pragmatically accepted but was a genuine good with deep roots in Catholic teachings.

In the 1920s, Catholics who participated in modern political life legitimated it primarily through some form of pragmatism. Some revived Thomist accidentalism, according to which the Church can participate in any political climate. Others had recourse to the old distinction between the "thesis" of a properly Catholic society, which remained the ideal, and the "hypothesis" of a non-Catholic one, in which Catholics could be-grudgingly participate. This kind of pragmatism was seldom voiced after World War II, when Catholics instead found genuine conceptual grounds to legitimate secular modernity. In France, for instance, theologian Joseph Lecler wrote widely on religious toleration, arguing that it was implicit in the Christian mission, and regretting the "dangerous confusions of the Middle Ages" on this front. The beauty of "the liberty of conscience," he concluded, was that it "could be accepted by any man of good faith"—hence its inclusion in the Declaration of Human Rights. In Germany, Albert Hartmann's *Tolerance and Christian Belief* (1955) made many of the same points.[8]

The difference between Senghor and Brentano is not, therefore, that one was modern and one was not. Like most Catholic thinkers of the era, they both were. It is not even that one was democratic and one was not. Even in the darkest years of the 1930s, Catholics had been happily democratic in Ireland, Belgium, and the United States, and Catholics rarely claimed any special resonance between their faith and a particular political form, demo-cratic or otherwise. There was, in other words, no conceptual reevaluation of "democracy" in the postwar era, because none was necessary.

The difference between them, instead, is that they disagreed profoundly over what a Catholic modernity might look like. When a religious tradi-tion "modernizes," that is not the end of the story. If modern religious fig-ures accept the seclusion of religion into the private sphere, they can still debate what precisely that means, and how that sphere might be defined. In the 1930s, Catholics had forged two forms of modernism, each a plau-sible derivation of the tradition but different in almost every other way. In the wake of World War II, both forms emerged more or less intact. World War II, like World War I, did not itself engender much intellectual cre-ativity or innovation in Catholic circles. For millions of Europeans, Cath-olics included, the late 1940s were an era of deprivation, horror, and fear—not of bold new visions and conceptual innovation.

The late 1940s restaging of this debate had exceptionally high stakes, given that Catholics emerged from the war with so much power. Not only were many drawn to religion in times of uncertainty and loss, but Catho-lics also organized with exceptional speed and took advantage of the new opportunities provided by the postwar moment.[9] In the absence of orga-nized states to provide much-needed welfare, Catholic charities rushed into the fray.[10] Pope Pius XII emerged as a moral icon, and the Catholic Action movement that he led structured the social consciousness and leisure hours of millions of Catholics across the continent. "The temporal power of Pope Pius XII," one amazed observer wrote in 1949, "is so great that it is—in a certain measure—comparable to that of Pope Innocent III."[11]

The most obvious manifestation of Catholic power was the rise of Christian Democracy. It was primarily through debating this movement that believers grappled with the meaning of postwar Catholic modernity. Catholic modernism was never confined to Christian Democracy, and it continued to gestate in all manner of venues, from trade unions to youth groups to women's organizations. While those sources will be investigated and incorporated, the analysis of Catholic modernism between 1945 and 1965 (this chapter and Chapter 5) can use Christian Democracy to organize the discussion. Catholic modernism was fundamentally a set of strategies to interface between Catholic teachings and the sociopolitical world. In these decades, those strategies almost necessarily involved the Christian Democratic parties that held enormous power, drew widely and freely on Catholic ideas, and provided avenues to power for leaders in other Catholic organizations (Christian Democratic family ministers, for instance, tended to emerge from Catholic family organizations).

While rooted in some sense in the Catholic political parties of the past, Christian Democratic parties were self-consciously new, embracing interconfessionalism and pluralism in ways that had always proven elusive to Catholic parties. While the new parties cropped up across the continent, our focus will be on three: in France, the Popular Republican Movement (MRP); in Germany, the Christian Democratic Union (CDU); and in Austria, the Austrian People's Party (ÖVP). Perhaps the biggest difference between the Christian Democratic parties and their Catholic predecessors is that they were extraordinarily successful, gathering together Catholic, Protestant, and secular voters of the center-right like no previous political movement had ever done. They were the greatest political force in the post–World War II moment, and probably the most successful political innovation in modern European history. The numbers speak for themselves. Between 1944 and 1950, the seven nations with new Christian Democratic parties held fifteen parliamentary elections. Christian Democrats won twelve of them outright. In the remaining three (France in October 1945 and November 1946, Luxembourg in 1948), they came in a close second.

The movement's successes certainly had material and geopolitical causes, notably the favor of the occupying American forces and the delegitimation of the traditional right wing.[12] And yet, as is obvious from attempts at democracy promotion elsewhere in the world, the creation of a robust parliamentary movement on either the right or the left rests on a complex, multifaceted mobilization of ideas and resources. It cannot be created from scratch by occupying powers, nor does it automatically emerge once extraparliamentary options are taken off the table. Internal traditions and institutions matter, too, and perhaps matter most. While it would be absurd to deny the role of the Americans in the creation of democratic societies in non-Communist Europe, they did not do the lion's share of the labor. Ideologically and economically, the main sources of Europe's reconstruction were native.[13]

Christian Democratic parties had multiple ideological sources, to be sure. Especially in Germany, but elsewhere too, Protestant and liberal ideas had an impact, especially on Christian Democratic economic thought. Generally speaking, however, Catholic modernism provided the single most important ideological source for Christian Democracy in the late 1940s. Christian Democratic leaders were, almost without exception, familiar faces from earlier Catholic politics. Catholic social scientists, and sometimes clergymen, played central roles behind the scenes. Only in West Germany did Protestants constitute a significant portion of the Christian Democratic electorate, and even there they complained (justly) that they were sidelined ("I am the Protestant fig-leaf of our Catholic minister," sighed one of the rare Protestant appointees to a ministerial position).[14]

The question, though, was what *kind* of Catholic modernism they would pursue: the fraternal, antifascist modernism of Senghor or the paternal, anti-Communist modernism of Brentano? Most scholars have argued that Christian Democracy emerged from the antifascist minority elements of the Church: from Senghor, that is, and not Brentano. There is good evidence for this claim. Christian Democrats, far more than earlier Catholic parties, were willing to collaborate with socialists and were staunch defenders of civil liberties. Biographically, too, many of the fraternal modernists from the 1930s could be found in key Christian Democratic positions (as politicians, but also as newspaper editors and friendly intellectuals). They included Étienne Borne, Albert Gortais, Eberhard Welty, Jakob Kaiser, and Alfred Missong, to name a few familiar names from our earlier exploration of interwar Catholic antifascism. Even when absent or in exile, their ideas sometimes became commonplace. In Austria, for instance, Ernst Karl Winter's vision of an Austrian nation-state structured by Catholic-socialist collaboration was taken for granted by the new party.[15] Jacques Maritain's ideas and insights were especially ubiquitous in the postwar moment. Italian prime minister Alcide de Gasperi and French foreign minister Robert Schuman, both Christian Democrats, were enthusiastic devotees of his thought, while his works were widely translated and discussed across the continent. This has led many historians to conclude that Maritain and his antifascist tradition represented the ideological wellspring for Christian Democracy.[16]

This antifascist, Maritain-centric genealogy of Christian Democracy is appealing because it portrays the leading party movement in postwar Europe as a direct inheritor of the heroic resistance. Moreover, it portrays a Church that learned the lessons of the war, and one that had left its sins behind. For both of these reasons, and for electoral reasons too, the parties preferred to present themselves in this way. Nonetheless, this story is implausible and misleading, resting on a misunderstanding of what had actually happened to Catholic social thought in the 1930s.

Most previous observers have presumed that mainstream Catholic social thought was antimodern in the 1930s and that only the small antifascist minority was committed to democratic politics and engagement with the modern world. Given that Christian Democrats so clearly shared those commitments, their rise must have heralded some kind of dramatic shift and an empowerment of that minority (at least ideologically). There is some truth to this narrative, especially in the Italian case, but in general this is not what happened. Mainstream Catholic social thought in the 1930s was not antimodern, nor was it especially concerned with the problem of democracy. Catholic thinkers instead were committed to a paternal form of modernism oriented around interconfessional politics, family values, anti-Communism, and a sacrosanct private sphere (denoted by human rights, human dignity, and antitotalitarianism). Likewise, antifascist Catholic thinkers had been mainly indifferent to Christian political parties, which had done so little to stave off fascism and anyhow were ancillary to their pluralist and anticapitalist commitments. Maritain had been critical of Christian political parties in 1934, and he saw little reason to change his mind after the war. He never publicly supported any of the new Christian Democratic parties, and in private he was somewhere between reticent and critical. In a 1946 letter to a friend, for instance, he disparaged the very notion of Christian Democracy: "May it be Christian in reality, without saying so!"[17]

While Christian Democratic ideology was in some ways able to co-opt the personnel and ideas of interwar antifascism, in the late 1940s the antifascist tradition was almost entirely sidelined. It was Brentano's mainstream anti-Communism, not Senghor's dissident antifascism, that came to dominate the new parties. This is not especially surprising. While Brentano's ideology had often made common cause with fascism, it was not itself fascist (it was not, that is, committed to ultranationalism, antiparliamentarism, or racism as first-order principles). Since some resisters had used it to protest certain fascist policies, there was little reason for it to lose its hegemony in the wake of the war, especially given that Pope Pius XII and his favored experts were committed to some form of it. Moreover, as a matter of electoral reality, Christian Democratic parties were not primarily driven by the largely urban, working-class, or intellectual audience for fraternal modernism. Their power rested mainly on reconstructed professional and agricultural associations, drawing more on rural voters and on white-collar workers. Christian Democrats were successful less because they forged a startling new vision than because they were able to corral religious conservatives, liberals, and secular nationalists under one center-right, constitutionalist banner. The family-friendly anti-Communism of the paternal Catholic tradition was perfectly suited to that task.[18]

The Christian Democratic parties of the 1940s, in short, essentially reiterated the mainstream Catholic ideals and strategies of the 1930s. It would be absurd to claim iron continuity. Antifascist Catholics often played important roles in the new parties, which were far more committed to trade unionism and civil liberties than the anti-Communist tradition required. That antifascist tradition, however, was a junior partner in the Christian Democratic coalition. Over the course of the late 1940s, the parties jettisoned some of the most important elements of it, while enshrining every central element of its anti-Communist antagonist.

To see how, this chapter will follow, in context, the mercurial career and the manifold disappointments of Jacques Maritain, the most intellectually sophisticated and publicly active of the Catholic antifascists. He emerged from the war with a great deal of fame, which translated into political appointments. He was courted by Charles de Gaulle, who appointed him to the highly sensitive role of France's ambassador to the Vatican, and he served as France's representative at the second UNESCO congress in Mexico City. He did not waste the opportunity, or his prestige, and he labored tirelessly to translate the central insights of 1930s antifascism into a postwar context. He had three specific projects. First, he attempted to push the Church toward a reckoning with anti-Semitism, which he saw as the greatest sin of modern Catholic history. Second, he sought to frame Catholic politics around anticapitalist solidarity rather than anti-Communist conservatism. Third, he dreamed of a form of global federalism that would abandon the conservative iconography of the West and look, instead, for novel kinds of political community that would enshrine the traditional Catholic suspicion of the nation-state. In all three cases, he failed. Christian Democrats refused to confront racism (either in the European past or in the colonial present); they revived the most exclusionary forms of anti-Communism; and they inhabited an imagined community of the "Christian West" made up of well-armed and sovereign nation-states. This does not mean that Christian Democracy was secretly fascist. It was not. It does mean, though, that Maritain and his tradition failed to break into the mainstream—and, therefore, that the ideological formation of the most successful political movement of the postwar period was not primarily rooted in the antifascist resistance.

The Eclipse of the Jewish Question

Antifascist Catholics like Maritain had long been obsessed with the issue of anti-Semitism. In addition to its violent results, they thought that it was rooted in an outdated, and even heretical, form of Catholic consciousness that sought to translate the mysteries of theology into oppressive forms of governance. Only by liberating itself from the sin of racism, Maritain believed, could the Church come into its own in the modern age, fully disentangling itself from throne-and-altar fantasies in the name of a more robust, and emancipatory, engagement with the secular world.

In the absence of a large Jewish or Muslim community in Europe, and in the years before anticolonial violence became hotly debated, the struggles over racism in the late 1940s took place largely on the perilous battlefield of memory. Maritain found himself at the center of its early skirmishes, arguing that only contrition and anguished self-examination could uproot the Church's lingering conservatism. His call was not heeded. Catholics saw little reason to confront the Church's long history of anti-Semitism, much less the myriad ways in which that history had dovetailed with and enabled the rise of fascism. The suppression of that memory, as Maritain feared, legitimated the widespread Catholic belief that the Church and its social vision had little need to evolve.

In the mid-1940s, in the midst of a continent-wide settling of scores, it briefly seemed as though the Church would not be spared and that its anti-Semitic past would be unearthed. Charles de Gaulle, chairman of the Provisional Government of France, was angry about the Church's support of Marshal Pétain, and he insisted that Valerio Valeri, the collaborationist papal nuncio, be recalled to Rome. Pope Pius XII was put off by this request, but the heady days of 1944 were no time to pick a fight with someone like de Gaulle. Pius agreed, and then some: again in response to pressure from the French government, he cleansed the French hierarchy of the most flagrant collaborationists, replacing them with icons of the Resistance. Maritain was directly involved with this effort. Working with the Secretariat of State in Rome, he passed along French demands and brought them to fruition. In the end, five of the most unpalatable French bishops tendered their resignations in November of 1945. A few weeks later, three replacements were named, all of whom had been on a list of acceptable candidates sent by the French to the Vatican (by way of Maritain).[19] As for Germany, Pius XII gave the cardinal's red hat to Clemens von Galen and Konrad von Preysing, both of whom had solid anti-Nazi credentials, at least by the standards of the German Church.

Maritain was heartened by these attempts to cleanse the Church and wanted to take them further. From his position at the heart of the Vatican, he leveraged his friendship with Giovanni Battista Montini, the Vatican's secretary of state and future Pope Paul VI, in an attempt to goad Pope Pius XII into saying something about anti-Semitism. As he wrote to Montini, the Jews were not one victim among others but a unique victim of Nazism insofar as Hitler had desired to wipe out the Jews as a people. The world needed the Vicar of Christ to "tell the truth to the world and shed light on this tragedy." Maritain's most considered statement on the question came in a 1947 text that he wrote for the Seelisberg Conference, a remarkable gathering of Jews, Protestants, and Catholics devoted to uprooting anti-Semitism. In essence, Maritain argued that the brute fact of the Holocaust did not affect the scourge of anti-Semitism. If anything, the racism gnawing away at the Catholic soul was even more deeply rooted, because the general celebration of a few heroes was unjustly obscuring the near-universal guilt of Europe's Catholics.[20]

Maritain's effort to force the Church to confront its anti-Semitic past had echoes across Europe. The occupying American forces seemed to be committed to de-Nazification. In Bavaria, Catholic politician and anti-Semite Fritz Schäffer was removed from office by Eisenhower because of his penchant for hiring and protecting former Nazis. Intellectually, too, there seemed to be a groundswell of interest in a revived Catholic antiracism. In the early months after the liberation, Europeans were discussing and reading a great deal about Hitler's crimes—a discussion that sometimes, but not always, involved special attention to the fate of the Jews.[21] Maritain himself published in the two main Catholic journals that were trying to heal relations between Catholics and Jews. In Germany, the *Freiburg Newsletter: Contributions to Christian-Jewish Understanding* began appearing in 1948. It grew from the Seelisberg Conference of the previous year, and its leading light was Maritain's longtime friend Karl Thieme. Its first issue featured a message from Maritain counseling Catholics to contemplate "the deeper meaning of anti-Semitism" and the ways it perverts the Catholic heritage, and the Catholic soul. The third issue of *The Notebooks of Zion,* a parallel French venture, featured a similar letter in the same year. "The struggle against anti-Semitism," he told his French audience, "is a fundamental obligation." "Six million Jews have been liquidated in Europe," he added. "Do Christians desire to understand? . . . How much longer will they remain asleep?"[22]

In Germany, the main site for this reconsideration was a wildly successful journal called *Frankfurter Hefte* (*The Frankfurt Notebooks*). With the enthusiastic support of the occupying Americans, who gave precious paper to the journal, it enjoyed a circulation of around seventy-five thousand copies and was perhaps the premier intellectual journal of the early postwar period. It was edited by two fraternal Catholic modernists from the interwar years: Walter Dirks, a pioneer in Catholic-Marxist dialogue, and Eugen Kogon. Kogon, one of the intransigent Catholic medievalists of the 1920s and briefly a Nazi sympathizer, had entered the resistance in the 1930s and spent much of the war in Buchenwald (his book about his experience, *Der SS-Staat,* was the first blockbuster account of Hitler's archipelago of camps—and one that, while focused more on camp functioning than on victims, did emphasize the unique suffering of the Jews). They saw Maritain as an ally, publishing translations of his works for a massive audience. "Maritain at the Vatican," Kogon exclaimed to his readers. "We can call this the right man in the right place."[23]

Kogon and Dirks, like Maritain, nourished the hope that the reconstruction would provide an opportunity to dramatically reshape the role of Catholicism in public life through an encounter with the Church's bloody history. In 1946, their journal published an incendiary article called "A Letter on the Church." Written by Ida Friederike Görres, the article was a sweeping assault on the Church and its compromises, in Germany and elsewhere. The Church, Görres despaired, had embraced the dominant ethic of martial patriotism, neglecting "the Church of Love" in the name of the "Church of Law." The Church hierarchy had subscribed to the politics of reaction, leading to "the very evil, and unfortunately not wholly unfounded, concept of clerico-fascism." In a related series of articles, Kogon himself provoked a firestorm of controversy by suggesting that Germany was failing to confront its deep complicity with National Socialism, and that the Federal Republic was repeating some of the worst sins of Nazism.[24]

And yet the Catholic Church as an institution, alongside most Catholic politicians and intellectuals on the ground, neglected to confront its past support for anti-Semitism or fascism. While the German Protestant Churches admitted their responsibility for the crimes of the Nazis in the Stuttgart Declaration of Guilt (1945), Catholics did not follow suit. In defiance of Maritain and Kogon, few Church leaders were interested in reckoning with the past, preferring to interpret Nazism as a pathology of secular materialism with no possible connection to the Church.[25] Inconvenient truthtellers like Kogon were ignored, or worse. German Catholic leaders viciously attacked him and theorized that he suffered from a "psychosis" (their implication that Kogon was suffering from his wartime experiences is all the more cruel in that he suffered more than any German bishop).[26] Also in Germany, figures such as Bishop Johannes Neuhäusler and Cardinal Josef Frings harassed the Americans with constant demands that Nazi war criminals be released. The first postwar pastoral letter of the Bavarian Bishops' Conference reassured the public that "the German people had no knowledge of the atrocities committed against innocent persons," while other statements from the bishops sought specifically to exonerate Germany's Catholics.[27] Cardinal von Galen, one of the most famous "resisters" in Germany despite his dubious record, argued that the German nation was sound and Nazism had been the result of only a few bad apples—even the minimalist Nuremberg Trials were too much for him, and he focused less on past crimes against Jews than present ones against Germans.[28]

This emerging common sense stemmed from a grassroots effort to popularize an image of the Church as one of Hitler's victims and as a shining light of the resistance. In France, books such as Jean Thosac's *Missionaries and Gestapo* (1945) and Emile Guerry's *The Church under the Occupation* (1947) defended the honor of the Church, arguing that Catholics had been targets of the Nazi regime and great friends of the Jews. In Austria, the Allies helped matters along by referring to it as "the first free country to fall to Hitler's typical aggression," rhetorically erasing the great Austrian enthusiasm for their annexation into Hitler's *Reich*. The Christian Democratic foreign minister released a volume of documents called *The Red-White-Red Book* (1946), named after the colors of the Austrian flag, which likewise sought to downplay the considerable strength of homegrown Nazis as well as burnish the record of the Church. The next year, in a volume called *National Socialism and the Catholic Church in Austria,* Jakob Fried argued that Catholics had opposed Nazism to the core of their being. "In all the years of Christian persecution," he argued, there had never been so many Christian "martyrs" as under Nazism.[29]

This narrative was hardest to sell in Germany itself, where Germans could surely remember the events and compromises of the Nazi era. Memories are fungible, however, especially when met with outright fabrication. Such was the case with the reconsideration of *Mit brennender Sorge,* Pius XI's 1937 encyclical on Nazism. The document itself had been cautious, criticizing the Nazis for specific violations of the concordat without denying the legitimacy of the movement. When the Bavarian bishops wanted to draw on it after the war to prove the Church's resistance credentials, they simply fabricated more properly antifascist quotations.[30] More often, though, Catholics turned to historical retellings that were not so much wrong as they were selective and one-sided. In Germany, there quickly appeared a series of volumes called *Christian Germany, 1933–1945,* containing every encyclical, sermon, and bishop's letter that could conceivably be read as a resistance tract. Johannes Neuhäusler's *Cross and Swastika: The Nazi Struggle against the Catholic Church and the Catholic Resistance* (1946) likewise presented a heroic and widely consumed tale of Church resistance.[31]

When it came to the specific issue of anti-Semitism, Maritain's efforts were similarly frustrated. Aside from the marginal efforts just mentioned, no reckoning was forthcoming in the postwar years. Maritain was especially exasperated by the pope's refusal to make a statement about the 1946 pogrom in Kielce, Poland, which indicated a failure to reckon with the *present* of the Church, let alone its past.[32] One of the MRP's leaders, François de Menthon, led the French prosecutorial team at Nuremberg and in his stirring opening address managed to elide Nazi crimes against the Jews, focusing instead on crimes against civilization and humanity. When Catholics did talk about the Jews, it was more often to rehash old stereotypes than it was to critically consider the Church's legacy. The most official clerical response to the Kielce pogrom was worse than silence, as Cardinal August Hlond and the Polish bishops blamed the Jews themselves for what had happened. Maritain's most powerful antagonist, within the Vatican and on the battlefield of memory alike, may have been Cardinal Aloisius Muench, an American who served as papal nuncio to Germany (Maritain met, and loathed, him in 1947). Muench's blockbuster *One World in Charity* (1946) was essentially silent about the Holocaust, focusing much more on the supposed horrors of the American occupation and the victimhood of the suffering German nation. A subtle anti-Semitism even crept into the text, as Muench contrasted Christian charity with the "Mosaic idea of an eye for an eye, and a tooth for a tooth." An analysis of Bavarian sermons in the late 1940s found almost no reference to the Jews at all, but when they did appear, they were entirely traditional. The "mistake of the Jews," one preacher in Regensburg told his flock in 1948, was "to search for heaven in material and worldly things."[33]

Catholics were under no particular pressure to confront the politically and psychologically inconvenient facts of the Church's collaboration with fascism, or its legacy of anti-Semitism. The Americans, for instance, were happy to support the myth of the resisting Church, which was both in their national interest and resonant with an American belief in the homology of Christianity and democracy (a belief especially prevalent in the early postwar years). In preparation for the Nuremberg Trials, American officials prepared a long document on "The Persecution of the Christian Churches," claiming without qualification that "National Socialism by its very nature was hostile to Christianity and the Christian churches." At the heart of America's military government in Germany (OMGUS), its Cultural and Religious Affairs Branch agitated with some success for the centrality of the churches to postwar strategy. Marshall Knappen, a political scientist from the University of Chicago and former priest, spoke for many in this division (of which he was the chief) when he declared Nazism and Christianity to be "theoretically incompatible." Their intervention ensured that the churches would not be classed as cultural organizations and would thus be spared the indignities of licensing and oversight. This was done, one of the leaders of the branch explained, so that "the churches might carry out their mission as the spiritual foundation of the new democracy." "The church emerged from the catacombs of physical ruin and spiritual disorder," reads another internal American report, as "(1) the only voice that had consistently been raised in opposition to the excesses of Nazism, (2) the strongest source of order in the early days of the occupation, and (3) almost the only remaining organization touching a majority of the people."[34]

Despite American interference, Catholic memory politics were fostered primarily by Europeans themselves. Catholics played a central role in silencing the discussion about anti-Semitism and the Holocaust that was taking place in the mid-1940s. Christian Democratic leaders had no interest in wringing their hands over sins of the past. They were, after all, simultaneously eager to claim the mantle of the resistance and to appeal to millions of voters who had, until just recently, supported authoritarian or anti-Semitic policies. In France, the MRP was notoriously committed to attracting former Vichy supporters, and its leaders colluded in the mass amnesia that descended on France about the Vichy regime's popularity. While various opinions about the amnesty laws could be found in MRP ranks, party leaders such as Georges Bidault and Menthon, alongside intellectuals such as François Mauriac, were some of their most vigorous proponents, referring both to Christian charity and to national healing. Konrad Adenauer, pioneering Christian Democrat and first chancellor of West Germany, thought that a painful trawling of past crimes would do little for his party or for his Church. "I believe that if all the bishops had together made public statements from the pulpits on a particular day, they could have prevented a great deal," he privately admitted. "But none of that happened and therefore it is best to keep quiet."[35]

The ÖVP in Austria was perhaps the worst offender in this regard. Its founders had been deeply imbued with the traditional anti-Semitism of Austrian Catholicism. Julius Raab, party founder and future chancellor, had been a member of the Heimwehr and had once inveighed against "the destructive legions of Semitic agitators" threatening Austria.[36] While he at least avoided anti-Semitic remarks after the war, not all of his colleagues did. In 1945, Leopold Kunschak, a longtime anti-Semite and another founder of the party, proudly declared that he would always remain an anti-Semite and protested the presence of Polish-Jewish refugees on Austrian soil. Kunschak's remarks caused a minor scandal, but he was far from alone: many Austrian Catholics groused about the presence of Jewish displaced persons on Austrian soil.[37] Even where explicit anti-Semitism was absent, ÖVP ideologues preferred to treat the past with a mixture of fabrication and silence. *Austrian Monthly*, the chief organ of Austria's Christian Democratic Party, published a risible series of articles on the recent past in its first two issues after the war. Six former supporters of Austria's corporatist state, most of whom also held leadership roles in the ÖVP, lauded the Dollfuss regime and crafted a narrative in which Austrian Catholics as a whole had been resisters of Nazism. Perhaps aware of the flimsiness of this narrative, future chancellor Felix Hurdes urged his readers not to dwell too much on the past, as it is "much more fruitful to turn our gaze to the future." The next year, a cringe-inducing editorial on the Jews appeared in the same journal. While "the suffering of Jewry throughout Europe has a certain amount of truth to it," the journal admitted, the Jews may not have been the "highest priority," and it was up to the Jews themselves to "prove their noble sentiments to our entire people through the temperate behavior they display to us."[38]

"The bourgeoisie," Maritain wrote to a friend in 1945, "are more sure of themselves than ever, with the competence and awful internal security that comes from refusing self-examination."[39] The next five years gave him little reason to change his mind, especially when it came to the all-important issue of anti-Semitism. Christian Democratic leaders, Catholic dignitaries, and American occupiers concurred that there was no problem with "Christian civilization"—only with those totalitarian movements, such as Nazism and Communism, that tried to overturn it. There was an opportunity, in other words, for Catholics to take part in a reimagination of Europe that would be more ethnically and culturally inclusive. This opportunity was missed. Many reasons could be adduced for this, including the psychological needs of parishioners and the political needs of Christian Democrats. But it should not be considered in isolation. After the war, as before it, the Jewish question was tied to others, which is one reason why Maritain was so convinced that it needed to be confronted. Specifically, it had long been tied to the question of Communism.

The Return of Anti-Communism

As Karl Marx pointed out long ago, the Jewish question has never been about the Jews alone but has always been entangled with broader questions of citizenship and political economy. In Catholic circles, the Jews for decades had been linked with Communism—hence the notion of "Judeo-Bolshevism" so omnipresent in interwar Catholic circles. Maritain and other fraternal modernists believed that a confrontation with the Jewish question was therefore intimately linked with a reconsideration of Marxism, which in their view had much to teach the Church. They sought not to convert the Church to Marxism but rather to extract the kernel of truth from Marxist anticapitalism—a process that was impossible if Catholics persisted in kneejerk anti-Communism. As Emmanuel Mounier put it in 1946, there was a stark divide between those "who can engage globally with Communism from a fraternal disposition, even if he disagrees" and, on the other side, "those for whom anti-Communism, whether socialist or reactionary, is the primary political reflex."[40] The former position had long been Maritain's, and after the war he urged his fellow Catholics toward fraternal engagement with Communism. In the chill of the Cold War, however, this position became untenable. By 1950, the allure of antifascism had faded and anti-Communism took its place, once again, as the "primary political reflex" of Catholic politics.

The question of Communism was far from theoretical. Catholics controlled many levers of power as Europe made its transition to Cold War division. From his position at the heart of the Vatican, Maritain allied with his close friend Montini to urge the pope to steer a neutral course in the Cold War.[41] In his writings, he pursued the explosive claim he had first broached in the 1930s: that Communists, despite their avowed atheism, were closer to God than the comfortable, anti-Communist bourgeoisie. He remained as certain as ever that Communist materialism was a self-refuting philosophical error. He despaired, though, that true saints had neglected the realm of the social, leaving it wide open for Communists, who, even though metaphysically confused, saw clearly that the deep injustice of the world called out for collective, revolutionary action. Many of today's Christians, Maritain wrote, are "practical atheists," paying lip service to God while worshiping money and power in practice. We must become truly religious, he implored, praying with our feet and in the streets, winning the workers back to the faith of the Jewish carpenter.[42]

Maritain was not necessarily urging electoral coalition with Communists—he was calling instead for broad social activism that, by avoiding dogmatic statements about Communism, could build coalitions with workers whose self-interest and passion lay in overcoming capitalism and alienation, not in empowering Soviet dictators (this was also the model pursued by Walter Dirks in Frankfurt at the same time). He certainly did not look to Christian Democracy as a model for this kind of activity. This was not so much because he opposed the parties as because their election-eering was irrelevant to his pluralist and activist social vision. He was most interested, not coincidentally, in the experiments of a Jew: a Chicago-based labor organizer named Saul Alinsky. The two met during one of Maritain's stints in the United States, and they struck up a friendship. Alinsky's brand of non-Communist, but not anti-Communist, grassroots organizing was precisely the model that Maritain had sought since the 1930s. He was espe-cially enthralled by Alinsky's *Reveille for Radicals* (1946), which quotes from his own pamphlet on democracy, and he attempted to organize French and Italian translations of it.[43]

Even more than his attempts to force a reckoning with the past, Maritain's desire to engage with Communists and socialists had transna-tional resonance. After all, the antifascist resistance had brought Catholics and Communists into close working relationships that spilled from the foxholes of Resistance, and the prison conditions of Dachau, into the postwar moment. "In the concentration camps, and in the backrooms of the inner emigration," one German Catholic wrote, "oaths were sworn."[44] In France, some Catholics participated in rallies to commemorate the Paris Commune, a heroic symbol for Communists and one loathed by conserva-tives.[45] Meanwhile, Communist and Catholic youth groups came together to form a new "Patriotic Union of Youth Organizations" (UPOJ).[46] In Aus-tria and Germany, the Christian trade unions, destroyed in the 1930s, were not revived. Instead, Catholic workers entered mighty, unified trade unions alongside their former socialist enemies—a remarkable phenomenon, sup-ported by even Pope Pius XII "as long as the extraordinary conditions of this age persist."[47] "There are only two ideas that have survived this war's hailstorm of bombs," wrote one Austrian Catholic in 1947: "the Christian idea, and the socialist. They are no longer antithetical to one another as they were before."[48]

Politically, Christian Democratic parties entered coalition governments with both socialists and Communists (Maritain welcomed this as "a new political option that would have been unthinkable ten years ago").[49] "We want a revolution," declared the first manifesto of France's MRP, signaling to voters a willingness to participate in the experimental three-party alliance in the French Parliament.[50] In Germany, too, early Christian Democrats spoke the language of socialist revolution, and throughout the late 1940s a branch of the CDU remained active in the Soviet occupied zone, where it was a member of the United Front of Antifascist Democratic Parties. The earliest public platforms of the CDU emphasized major land reform and the nationalization of coal, energy, and banking. Forthrightly critical of "the capitalist economic system," the 1947 Ahlen program called for "a socialist economic order" to ensure "economic and personal freedom." The Austrian People's Party, too, was enlivened by the "Spirit of Dachau," entering a grand coalition in 1945 with both Communists and socialists.[51]

Marxist language and tactics began to creep into Catholic writing in ways that had been uncommon even in the ranks of Catholic labor before the war. This was most apparent in the "worker-priest" phenomenon, which captured the imagination of French Catholics out of proportion to their numbers (there were only about ninety of them, but a novelization of their experiences called *The Saints Go into Hell* was a best-seller). These priests, alarmed by the secularization of the French working classes, joined the proletariat on the shop floor in an attempt to evangelize from within. This necessarily brought them into contact with Communism, leading to the spectacle of priests joining Communists on the picket lines and in some cases even joining the party. Their patron, Cardinal Emmanuel Célestin Suhard, proclaimed that the Church "denounces the proletariat as a wound . . . and as the proletariat seems to be a direct product of the liberal capitalist regime, how could the Church not desire that this regime be structurally transformed?"[52]

Fraternal modernists welcomed this kind of collaboration not out of pragmatism but rather out of a deep sense that the social Catholic tradition alone could not provide the resources to understand or manage an advanced industrial economy (and that Marxism, not liberalism, provided the most appropriate dialogue partner). "We must not allow the genesis of the Movement [MRP] to be explained solely by '50 years of Social Catholicism,'" the party's executive committee stated. Josef Dobretsberger, a Catholic economist who had supported Dollfuss in the 1930s, published a robust defense of Catholic socialism called *Catholic Social Politics at the Crossroads* (1947), in which he argued that Catholics had to overcome the musty traditions of social Catholicism, which "has for so long stood in the way of socially-progressive Catholic thought." "Catholic social teaching," he concluded, "will, in the future, have far different starting points than was common before 1939."[53]

This rethinking took place in transnational networks of left-leaning Catholic intellectuals and activists, stretching from France to Poland. Two journals were at its heart: the German *Frankfurter Hefte*, edited by Dirks and Kogon, and the French *Esprit*, edited by Mounier. Both circulated in enormous numbers and both were specifically interested in international collaboration. Jean-Marie Domenach, *Esprit*'s editor, traveled to Bavaria in 1947, asking hard questions about the Catholic Church's relation to Nazism and returning with praise for Germany's Catholic socialists, particularly the radical figures around a leftist Catholic journal called *End and Beginning*. Mounier and Dirks themselves became close collaborators. "We found ourselves in the same boat," Kogon later wrote of Mounier's visit to the *Frankfurter Hefte* headquarters in 1946, "surrounded by the same dangers and gloom, with the same beliefs and hopes in our hearts, in agreement about our positions and our goals. . . . We shook hands, as comrades." Mounier had Dirks write an essay on Catholicism and Marxism for *Esprit*, and Dirks wrote personally to his French colleague that they were united in the world-historical attempt to bring together Christ and Marx. When an author wanted to write an article for his journal critiquing *Esprit*'s philo-Communism, Dirks blocked it. "I hold this political engagement," he chided his contributor, "to be one of the most essential and important elements of the *Esprit* movement and one of our most important tasks."[54]

Both journals worked to open doors with socialists and Communists. This required a wholesale overturning of totalitarianism theory, according to which Nazis and Communists were genetically similar.[55] Jean Lacroix, another Catholic in *Esprit*'s orbit, declared that "Communism saw the problem and approached its solution." *Témoignage chrétien* (*Christian Witness*), a periodical with its origins in the Catholic resistance, had a similar position. "We observe," declared a manifesto there, "that the Communist party alone is capable of leading the struggle for the destruction of capitalism to the end." Together, all of these organs sought to forge a new Catholic avant-garde that might break, once and for all, the bonds between the Church and what Mounier called the "established disorder."[56] Dirks argued that the faith could only remain relevant if it abandoned its antiquated social ideals—what he later called "the so-called socially-harmonious social teaching, which in reality was no social-scientific theory at all, but rather an ideology." The old keywords of "solidarism" and "corporative order" had to be replaced by a new one: "socialism." "The meaning and goal of socialism," Dirks explained, "is the freedom and dignity of the person *under the conditions of an industrial economy based on the division of labor.*" This would require what Dirks openly called "the socialization of central means of production."[57]

In the mid-1940s, a space seemed to open up for anticapitalist forms of Catholic activism that would be philo-Communist without directly supporting Stalinism. By the end of the decade, that space had closed. A handful of Catholic writers opted for the pro-Soviet side in the new Cold War, penning apologetics for Stalinist show trials and seeing Hitlerian violence in the Atlantic project of European federation and capitalist consolidation. Most, though, embraced anti-Communism as the only possible option (even if they did so with sadness and unease). "The European Resistance—I repeat: as a powerful and influential political factor of determinate meaning—has become a historical memory," declared Eugen Kogon in 1949. "A mighty epic, subject-matter for poets and historians."[58]

Why did this happen? Of course, the onset of the Cold War—which likely would have happened even without Catholic anti-Communism— played a role and forced Catholics to choose sides. In non-Communist Europe, the influence of the American occupiers certainly played a part, too. Americans held a vast amount of power in postwar Europe, and Christian Democrats were well aware that Americans were not interested in pathbreaking Catholic-Communist collaboration. This was most consequential in Italy, where they used a wide variety of covert means to aid the Christian Democrats in their (victorious) 1948 electoral battle against the Communists. They were responding, perhaps, to Soviet provocation: whether true or not, internal documents indicate that American experts were under the impression that Communists were attempting "to discredit leading church personalities in the eyes of the Americans."[59]

But while American occupiers put their thumbs on the scale, European Catholics in the end made their own choices. For one thing, the Catholic Church was less a pawn of the Americans in the Cold War than is often believed. Rome and Washington clashed over the division of Germany, for instance, and the recognition of Israel.[60] More broadly, military occupation simply does not have the capability to transform ideas, especially religious ones. Pope Pius XII did not need American tutelage to pursue anti-Communism. By appointing a hard-line monarchist to a cardinal-

ship in Hungary in 1946, he signaled his rejection of the more collaborationist efforts streaming from the resistance. When this man, József Mind-
szenty, was imprisoned by the Hungarian Communists two years later, it
caused a firestorm of outrage across Catholic Europe. It was soon followed
by a Holy Office decree that forbade Catholics from joining Communist
parties. None of this required American inspiration.

Lay Catholic intellectuals and Christian Democratic leaders did not need
instruction in anti-Communism either. After all, it had been a central component of lay Catholic intellectual and political culture since around 1930,
and the new circumstances of the early Cold War were propitious for its
reactivation. As the minutes of international Christian Democratic congresses show, anti-Communism, at both the domestic and international
levels, was a central and growing concern in the late 1940s. "We are the only
ones who can give the anti-Communist struggle its true meaning," declared a leader of the MRP in a speech at an international meeting in 1950.[61]
This was clear in each domestic context, where Washington and Rome
had little direct sway. In France, *tripartisme* collapsed and, with it, the
unprecedented alliances of Communists and Catholics at the state level. In
Germany, the gambit to move the CDU leftward manifestly failed. In the
East, parliamentary politics became irrelevant, while in the West, Konrad
Adenauer and his lieutenants forged a new coalition around conservative
Catholics and bourgeois Protestants.[62] The 1949 Düsseldorf Principles announced a new dedication to private property and the "social market
economy," signaling a shift from the more radical aspirations of the Ahlen
Program just two years earlier. At the level of civil society, the happy col-
laborations of the mid-1940s quickly collapsed as the old animosities reasserted themselves, culminating in a disastrous general strike called by
Austrian Communists in 1950 and, eventually, the banning of the Communist Party in West Germany.[63]

The experiments that so engaged Maritain, Dirks, and Kogon either
faded into irrelevance or were aggressively shut down. This was most apparent in France, where Catholic-Communist collaboration had been most
exhilarating. The worker-priest experiment, for instance, was condemned
by the Vatican, while the French youth movement, which came together
into a Catholic-Communist synthesis in 1944, fractured back into its component parts. This sometimes led to bitter acrimony. Gaston Fessard and
André Mandouze had been two of the leading Catholics in the Resistance,
and yet by the end of the 1940s they were at one another's throats. Fessard,

ignoring the advice of his close friend Henri de Lubac, published a book-length anti-Communist screed as early as 1945.[64] This was not necessarily new: Fessard had published book-length denunciations of Communism before. But this time, he attempted to publish the volume under the auspices of *Témoignage chrétien,* the Resistance organ that he had helped to found and that was at the time attempting to translate the Catholic-Communist alliance of the Resistance into peacetime. André Mandouze, in his capacity as editor-in-chief, vetoed the book's publication, specifically objecting to Fessard's claim that the Soviet Union and Nazi Germany were functionally identical. The book was eventually published anyway, and it was celebrated by the most reactionary Catholics, who were thrilled that a paragon of the Resistance had turned to their side.[65] Fessard mischievously dedicated the second edition to his former Resistance comrades. This was the last straw for Mandouze, who sent Fessard a pained letter, signed by others, breaking ties for good: "We refuse to allow our Communist comrades, with whom we struggled as brothers for three years, to be insulted."[66]

The return of Catholic anti-Communism should be understood as the interaction between the long-standing commitments of the social Catholic tradition and the more contingent history of the late 1940s. Catholic modernism could certainly legitimate philo-Communism, as Mandouze demonstrated. It was not philosophical argument that turned *Témoignage chrétien* back toward anti-Communism but rather an unforeseeable event. In 1949, David Rousset, a former inmate of Buchenwald, began to draw attention to the continuing usage of concentration camps by Communists. His charges received a healthy airing in *Témoignage chrétien* and elsewhere in French Catholic circles. The Catholic concern about concentration camps, which was such a central concern of the late 1940s, transitioned from an antifascist imperative to an anti-Communist one.

The shift in discourse about the camps was especially important to the ideological evolution of Eugen Kogon, one of the most famous leftist Catholics in Europe. In the wake of World War II, he published a blockbuster book on Hitler's camps, which he had experience firsthand. The first edition, published in 1946, was a transparently antifascist text, worthy of the praise of Communist inmates (while mainly written and printed with American support, he sought to have it published in the Russian occupation zone, too). The Kogon of 1946, after all, was a Catholic socialist, hoping to overcome capitalism with the aid of Communist and Catholic forces alike. In 1948 and 1949, however, responding to various Soviet outrages but most of all to their continued usage of camps, he began to argue for the first time that Communism and Nazism were genetically identical. In his journalism, and in later editions of his book on the camps, he began to espouse totalitarianism theory, undercutting the ideological grounds of the resistance.[67]

However explicable the antitotalitarian turn may have been, it had a suffocating effect on Catholic intellectual life. Many innovations in social and economic thinking had come about through an encounter with Marxism, and after 1949 this avenue was essentially closed. Consider the trajectory of Waldemar Gurian, Maritain's greatest German-language champion in the 1930s. His story shows how the Cold War could turn mercurial intellects into ideologues. Gurian had never endorsed Communism, to be sure—he was, after all, a Russian exile himself, and his devastating 1931 volume on Bolshevism had been crucial to the development of Catholic anti-Communism. As with other Catholic antifascists, though, he had long been engaged in a broad and visionary effort to update Catholic teachings in the service of racial and economic justice. During the Cold War, however, anti-Communism became the central feature of Gurian's intellectual life, as he took full advantage of the many opportunities on offer to a polyglot intellectual willing to labor on America's behalf.[68] He played a key role in the constitution of American Sovietology, developed close ties with the Rockefeller Foundation, spoke at the University of Chicago on the virtues of the Marshall Plan, and contributed to a book called *The American Civilization,* which appeared in France and was designed to teach Europeans about the virtues of American power (Gurian discoursed on America's "mission to defend liberty" against the Soviets, which "has forced the U.S.A. to create a global politics"). He brought his new love for America back to Germany, too, speaking at the "America Houses" (*Amerika-Häuser*) set up by the occupying American forces and writing in German newspapers, both Catholic and secular, on American foreign policy. He lectured on Bolshevism in Austria and wrote in Germany for *Der Monat,* the German organ of the Congress for Cultural Freedom, an anti-Communist cultural body that was covertly funded by the CIA. By 1950, Gurian could claim in a newspaper article that the United States "is not too imperialist. On the contrary, it is not imperialist enough."[69]

Not content with his own newfound prestige and influence, Gurian also policed Catholic intellectual life to ensure there were no deviations from anti-Communist orthodoxy. When Étienne Gilson, a famous French

Catholic philosopher, visited Notre Dame, Gurian heard rumors that Gilson had privately argued for French neutrality in the Cold War and even accused Raymond Aron of being a paid American agent. Even though Gurian was not present at the dinner party, and even though there was a grain of truth to Gilson's charge against Aron, he published an open letter in the pages of *Commonweal* accusing the elderly philosopher of "spreading the sad gospel of defeatism." He used his contacts to circulate the letter throughout the Catholic intelligentsia (he even sent a copy to the editor of *Témoignage chrétien*). The affair became a scandal, almost costing Gilson his pension. He was incensed that Gurian had never bothered to confront him personally before taking a public stand—a breach of propriety that indicated how low levels of trust between former antifascist Catholics had become (both were close friends of Maritain, who could only bemoan Gurian's "unfortunate letter"). Gurian's letter, Gilson charged in his response, "forms a part of a defamation campaign undertaken in a happily restricted milieu, but virulent in the U.S.A., against every slightly well-known Catholic who does not take the war against Russia to be a sacred duty in the strictly religious sense of the term."[70] Despite Gurian's deplorable behavior, he had the winds of history at his back. Gilson was disgraced, and the whole tale revealed how impossible neutralism, let alone Communist collaboration, had become (west of the Iron Curtain, at least).

As it had been in the 1930s, the Catholic anti-Communism of the early Cold War was designed not to critique modernity but rather to enshrine a specifically Catholic form of it. This is a crucial point. Even the conservative Catholics of the Christian Democratic moment were modern, insofar as they did not call for an overturning of the French Revolution or the Reformation, nor did they call for any kind of church-state fusion. In fact, a close attention to the grammar of their arguments reveals that they critiqued Communism for being *insufficiently* modern. The problem with Communism, theoretically speaking, was that it violated the modern pact of church-state separation by setting itself up as a "political religion" and repeating the errors of the medieval Church. Gurian insisted that Communism was a "secularized politico-social religion" that denied the properly modern separation between church, society, and state. Fessard made the same claim, as did Heinrich von Brentano in the speech that opened this chapter. A Christian Democratic manifesto criticized the "secularized Messianism" of the Communists, while even a left-leaning French Jesuit could despair that Communist societies were incapable of granting true "freedom of religion" because their ideology was committed to a total victory for its own metaphysical commitments (this theory was ubiquitous in the early Cold War, being employed by non-Catholics such as Eric Voegelin and Raymond Aron, too).[71]

In the end, anti-Communism was even more hegemonic by 1950 than it had been in the 1930s. The possibilities for intellectual, social, and political collaboration between Catholics and Communists vanished, and even resistance heroes such as Maritain and Kogon joined the new anti-Communist consensus. Maritain's primary concern, though, was never with Communism itself—he had always utterly rejected Marxist metaphysics and Soviet politics. His concern was with the opening of a space for nonstatist, anticapitalist, and interfaith activism in which Catholics and workers could find common cause. The problem with anti-Communism, from his perspective, is that it shut down this space by enlisting citizens with kindred interests into geopolitical struggles that had little to do with their daily lives and concerns. For Maritain, as for Alinsky, local politics provided opportunities for charity and solidarity that national politics did not. This leads to, perhaps, the bitterest pill he had to swallow: the return, and even the apotheosis, of the nation-state on European soil.

The Return of the Nation-State

Catholics have had a long and troubled relationship with the nation-state project. Since the French Revolution, if not earlier, the Church had tried to provide an alternative political imaginary rooted in looser imperial structures that would empower local dignitaries and churches over distant parliaments. The Austro-Hungarian empire, not the French republic, represented the Catholic ideal. In the 1930s, however, only centralized nation-states provided the fiscal and military resources necessary to confront Communism and the Great Depression. In these circumstances, many Catholics made their peace with a particular vision of the state: an "antitotalitarian" institution that would protect the Church and the family while signaling an adherence to the Roman-Christian "West" as a legal and cultural community. Maritain and other Catholic antifascists were wary of this compromise, which often led to fascist collaboration. While he was aware that the imperial federalism of the Holy Roman Empire was an anachronism, he thought that some modern replacement might be found—one that would salvage the antistatism of the Catholic tradition in the service of interconfessional pluralism. In the mid-1940s, he revived his antistatism in a world that seemed poised to take the step toward global governance, leaving the nation-state behind. By 1950, however, those hopes had been dashed. If anything, the nation-state emerged from the reconstruction stronger and more unquestioned than ever.

The pluralism and federalism of antifascist Catholics found broad resonance immediately after the war. Maritain's long-standing belief that Germany should be dissolved into a number of smaller states had allies in both Germany itself and among the American occupiers (this time, Maritain meant it as an opening to a federated Europe, not as a punishment or an attempt to reinstate a medieval order). In France, many French intellectuals, including Maritain enthusiasts such as Léopold Senghor, hoped that the French empire might evolve into an innovative, "Eurafrican," and post-statist political community known as the French Union.[72]

This was the context in which Maritain became a philosopher of human rights. The Maritain of the 1930s did not focus much on rights—not because he opposed them but because the whole notion of a rights-protecting state was ancillary to his own pluralist politics. During the war, though, he turned to an expansive vision of human rights, recognizing that rights talk had the capacity to build the sorts of broad alliances he sought. His account of rights, therefore, was a capacious one, bearing as much similarity to the Soviet Constitution of 1936 as to the American Bill of Rights. As he explained in *Human Rights and Natural Law* (1942) and other texts from the period, rights represented both "political and social emancipation." He was, to be sure, concerned with civil and political rights, including the right to equality before the law, public employment without racial discrimination, freedom of expression, and freedom of association. He also defended a robust set of social rights, including the right to free trade unionism, the right to work, the right to public assistance, and the right to a just wage, defined as one that would allow the worker and his family to have a "sufficiently human standard of living." These social rights in particular, Maritain claimed, would evolve over time, given that the war was leading to enormous economic dislocations and the potential for a new and more humane reorganization of the economy.[73]

As this list might imply, Maritain saw human rights as a pathway toward collaboration with Communists and other forms of atheists. He explained this in a 1947 address delivered at the second congress of UNESCO, in Mexico City. The intellectual chaos of the postwar moment, Maritain argued, need not stand in the way of increasing political unity. Metaphysical agreement was neither possible nor necessary for global citizens to work together in the name of prosperity and justice. All that was necessary was a common practical aim—what we might now call an overlapping consensus. "I am persuaded," Maritain told his audience, "that my justification for the belief in human rights" is "the only one solidly founded in truth." However, that did not keep him from practical collaboration with those who disagreed with him about fundamental questions.[74] The Universal Declaration of Human Rights included a number of social rights, including the right to work, health care, and unemployment insurance. A well-rounded notion of rights like this one, Maritain believed, might point the way toward healthy collaboration between former ideological enemies.

While many invocations of human rights presumed the nation-state as their primary defender, Maritain's resolutely did not. His enthusiasm for human rights was coeval with a newfound enthusiasm for global government. Human rights, that is, were not vague principles to be protected by all-powerful nation-states when it suited them. They were a serious entitlement, requiring as a corollary some form of global government to enshrine and nurture them. Maritain's brief for global government received its fullest exploration in his 1949 Walgreen lectures at the University of Chicago, published as *Man and the State* in 1951. His essential point was that the rapidly accelerating economic unification of the globe had to be matched with its political unification. Otherwise, the baser instincts mobilized by economic processes could not be tamed by the nobler and more rational impulses offered by the political. The mismatch between economic globalization and political balkanization, Maritain thought, was bound to lead to disaster, and it corresponded to an unjust, irrational notion of political society. Since Jean Bodin in the sixteenth century, political theorists had made an error in their account of "sovereignty" by setting up the sovereign as an entity separate from the people. This error went so deep that the word itself would have to be excised from our common vocabulary amid a transition, however slow and painful it might be, to a global political order, one marked by a deep and fundamental pluralism of both powers and beliefs.[75]

Maritain's globalism dovetailed with a widespread notion that Europe no longer played host to a "Christian civilization" in any meaningful sense. In the 1930s, the conservative notion of the "Christian West" had led many Catholics to throw their support behind authoritarian nation-states, which they believed had the power to protect that community from its enemies. Maritain had long been critical of this idea, and after the war many agreed with him. Europe, from this perspective, was no longer viewed as a fortress of Christian truth but instead as a religiously plural continent in a religiously plural world. A blockbuster publication called *France, A Missionary Country?* (1943) claimed that France itself was in need of missionary work, no less than the overseas empire. The worker-priest experiment was designed as a sort of internal missionary movement, aimed at bringing the Christian message to non-Christian spaces at the heart of France. The same sensibility could be found in Germany. In 1947, *Frankfurter Hefte* published an essay titled "The Borders of the West," arguing forthrightly that "the West," understood as a classical, humanist, and Christian culture, "no longer exists." A new international community structured around "one world," and including Communists, must take its place. The next year, Ivo Zeiger's opening address at the first Catholic Congress after the war—a monumentally important speech—made the same point. We all live in the diaspora now, Zeiger explained, and we are all refugees from a Christian West irrevocably broken by the experience of fascism and war. "Germany," he concluded, has become a "missionary country."[76]

Maritain, like these other critics of "the West," was not seeking to abolish the state. He simply wanted to reduce the significance of the nation-state and disabuse Catholics of the notion that powerful nation-states were necessary or appropriate vehicles to defend Catholic values. As he had in the 1930s, he wanted civic fraternities and organizations, not militarized and all-powerful states, to constitute the essence of the political. While many authors in the late 1940s were pursuing similar ideals, Maritain was one of the most important. Senghor, for instance, built his crucial 1948 essay on "Marxism and Humanism" around just two authors: Maritain and Marx.[77] The fate of one text shows us the networks through which Maritain's ideas could move. In 1941, he spoke at the University of Chicago on Machiavelli and the need for a total reevaluation of modern politics, sharing the stage with Robert Hutchins, the president of the university and a famous defender of global government. Maritain's lecture appeared in the *Review of Politics*, then and now a central organ of American political thought (founded and edited by none other than Waldemar Gurian). Translated into French, it appeared both in a collection of Maritain's writings published in wartime New York and in *Nova et Vetera*, an important Swiss journal edited by his friend Charles Journet. The same essay also appeared in German translation in *Frankfurter Hefte,* where it probably received its widest readership, given that it was at the time one of the leading periodicals in the country, thanks largely to the generosity of American occupiers who provided paper.[78]

Maritain's texts traveled so freely because his ideas were so widely shared among Catholics in the mid-1940s. Many of them thought, as they had after World War I, that the war had finally demonstrated the long-standing Catholic teaching that modern statehood was the antechamber to disaster. In the opening essay of *Frankfurter Hefte,* Walter Dirks declared "the end of the sovereign national state," imagining a democratic and socialist Europe in its wake. The same issue included an editorial claiming that "human rights" and "world government" would be the logical outcomes of the Nuremberg Trials. The most influential exponent of this view, and probably the author of that editorial, was Eugen Kogon, who was more involved in the day-to-day tasks of federalist organization than Maritain was. For decades, Kogon had been inveighing against the nexus of finance capitalism and sovereign nationhood. In the 1920s, this had taken the form of anti-Semitic radicalism, but in the 1930s he had moved toward antifascist federalism. As he wrote in "Democracy and Federalism" (1946), there were two kinds of democracy: individualist democracy, which led directly to capitalism or totalitarianism, and federalist democracy, which embraced human rights and the human person by recognizing layers of authority, from the family at the bottom to the United Nations at the top.[79]

Kogon soon became one of the most famous federalists in Europe. Writing to Dirks, he referred to his activities during these years as "laying European eggs (what a dreadful image!)." Dreadful it may have been, but it captured the sense of hope that Kogon had in the project. In a 1952 letter to Konrad Adenauer, he claimed to speak for federalism "as president of the German *Europa-Union,* president of the central committee of the Union of European Federalists, and leading member of the European Movement."[80] His own activities provide a bureaucratic breakdown of the European movement as a whole. The Europa-Union was the most important federalist movement within Germany, eventually growing to twenty thousand members. It was the German branch of the international Union of European Federalists (UEF). By the late 1940s, the UEF had emerged as one of the two most important constellations of federalist activity in Europe, and it had around seventy thousand members across the continent. Kogon was elected president of the Europa-Union in 1949 and president of the UEF in

1950. The last group Kogon mentions was the European Movement, the international organization headed by Churchill and Duncan Sandys. He had been elected to head the German delegation to this movement in 1949.[81]

Kogon's institutional centrality, and the fame garnered from his writings on the camps, ensured that his evolving understanding of federalism mattered a great deal. In the mid-1940s, Kogon was, like many others, a firm believer in a "Third Force" federalism that would create a neutral Europe with a federal Germany at its heart, beholden neither to Moscow nor to Washington. In the summer of 1948, in the wake of the London 6-Power Conference about Germany's future, Kogon despaired that a remilitarized Germany would be dismembered, with two-thirds of its territory belonging to the "Atlantic–West European" powers. As he told his readers, that did not need to happen, "even if all the armor-clad 'Defenders of the West' argue the contrary."[82] In a speech delivered to an international Catholic congress the same year, Kogon declared that Europe must unify without breaking with the socialist East, finding a path toward a social democratic Europe that would dissolve national boundaries in pursuit of some sort of social democratic European Union. His hopes for a unified Europe disentangled from Moscow-Washington rivalries were common. The UEF released a position paper in 1947 in which it announced the goal of "a unified Europe in a unified world," asserting that European unity could never come about if the project was linked to one side in the Cold War. One of the UEF's early position papers sums up this stance: "Refusal of a Europe delivered to the hegemony of any power whatsoever, but also a refusal of all anti-Communist crusades, whatever the pretexts."[83]

Maritain had some reason to believe that the era of the nation-state, which, after all, was not especially old, had come to a close. Christian Democrats certainly seemed to agree with him. The MRP's Ernest Pezet, for instance, argued for turning Central Europe into a set of loose confederations, as it had been in the past. That might sound like traditional Habsburg nostalgia, but it was not—Pezet now insisted that a federated Central Europe take its place amid a European, or even global, form of federalism, in which Communists would play a role.[84] Every major Catholic newspaper frequently featured pro-federalist editorials, while every serious Catholic journal featured essay after essay on the spiritual foundations of European federalism. A full three-quarters of MRP members believed that European unity was either "indispensable" or "very useful." When Josef Müller, a Bavarian Christian Democrat, wrote in a popular magazine in

1948 to explain his party's platform, he ignored "democracy" and discoursed at length about "a federal Germany at the heart of a federal Europe." Federalist language became so common in Catholic circles that Albert Lotz, like Kogon one of the founders of the UEF, published a weary article in 1949 called "Too Much Federalism?" (referring to the discourse, not the practice, of federalism).[85]

As Maritain well knew, the question was not simply *whether* there would be federalism but *what kind*. It was not at all obvious that Europeans would federate into an anti-Communist community that served, in the last instance, to protect and stabilize the nation-state. It was not obvious, either, that the German nation-state would be divided but others would survive unscathed. Nor was it obvious that the United Nations, a grand experiment in global government, would devolve into a staging ground for renewed geopolitical struggle. That, though, is what happened, and what another crop of Catholic federalists had wanted all along. To defend it, they dusted off the hoary idea of the "Christian West," which had been so useful to legitimate anti-Communist alliances in the 1930s.

Maritain and his allies rejected the very notion of the "West," which implied that there was something uniquely Christian about Europe and its legal heritage. By 1950, however, the West had reemerged in full force.[86] The fact that it had been linked so consistently with anti-Semitism in the past was forgotten, along with Catholic anti-Semitism more broadly. While the "Defense of the West" had served to legitimate Catholic-fascist collaboration, its legacy could be recovered after the war, because it had motivated some conservative critiques of fascism, too (as in Aurel Kolnai's anti-Nazi *War against the West* [1938]). Anti-Communist Catholics regularly claimed, as the secretary-general of the ÖVP did in 1949, that they wanted to "save and renovate the cultural community of the West." Jean de Fabrègues, Charles Maurras's former secretary and a former supporter of Philippe Pétain, took over as editor of a key journal called *Catholic France,* and he used his position to reiterate the old Defense of the West in a Cold War key. Especially once the Algerian War began in 1954, the "Defense of the West" became a key concept for a revived French Catholic conservatism, and it provided cover for other recovering monarchists like Fabrègues to pursue their old concerns in the new context of the Cold War. They were not only on the Far Right, however: Robert Schuman, Georges Bidault, and other leaders of the MRP, especially when talking about imperial affairs, often had recourse to the imagery of Western Christian civilization.

In Austria, too, the ÖVP's journal regularly celebrated Austria's history as bulwark of the West against the pagan East, and one of the planks of the party platform was to secure "the sharpest emphasis on Austria's unique cultural value," defined as "Christian-Western ways of thinking."[87]

It was in West Germany that the old language of the West (*Abendland*) played the greatest role, as a divided and postfascist Germany required a new discourse of national identity and belonging.[88] Konrad Adenauer regularly spoke of the West, an imagined community that allowed him to appeal to cultural conservatives while also allying with the Americans in the name of anti-Communism. A revived Western movement was founded, too, which eventually included the Western Academy and the internationally active European Documentation and Information Center (CEDI). This allowed a number of inveterate conservatives to revive their old anti-Communism in a new key: Father Michael Schmaus, Archishop Lorenz Jaeger, and Karl Buchheim, who had all begun to "Defend the West" in the era of National Socialism, belonged to the Western Academy, as did Brentano himself.[89] The central print journal for the new Westernism was called, simply enough, the *New West* (*Neues Abendland*). With a circulation of around twenty-five thousand, it was German-speaking Catholicism's most successful new print venture, next to *Frankfurter Hefte*. It was edited by Emil Franzel, a Sudeten German convert to Catholicism who had, just a few years earlier, been an outspoken supporter of Nazism and anti-Semitism: "the Defender of the West," he wrote during the war, was embroiled in a "two-front war" against "Anglo-Saxons under Jewish-plutocratic leadership" and "Bolshevik Jews."[90]

The Defense of the West legitimated a particular form of federal organization, and a particular form of human rights, under the aegis of the nation-state.[91] West-defending federalists were concerned with salvaging the powerful nation-state in a union of Christian nations, viewing global federalism as antipatriotic and suspiciously Marxist. The first article in the first issue of *La Fédération,* one of the leading federalist journals on the continent, could have come straight from the conservative circles of the 1930s (no coincidence, as it was primarily an organ for recovering fascists and monarchists). It began with a celebration of "the rights of the individual person." While Maritain was arguing at the same time that human rights required the abolition of sovereignty, the manifesto insisted that they could be protected only in "a sovereign, but not totalitarian, state that coordinates, orients, and arbitrates between multiple private authorities (familial, professional, cultural, local)." Another essay the following year contrasted the "national state," respecting organic solidarities, and "the partisan and totalitarian state" of the Communists. At the *New West,* one author interpreted federalism as a "hierarchical system" of authorities stretching from the family to the "community of the State," rather than any global authority. Sometimes, authors in these circles were transparent about how close their ideas were to the quasi-fascist ones of the 1930s, going so far as to resurrect the language of the "corporate state" (*Ständestaat*). The "overemphasis on organic thought in the last decade," one priest wrote for the *New West,* should not lead us to "throw it overboard. Error and truth always lie near to one another."[92]

In place of Maritain's radical and global vision, Defenders of the West sought a form of human rights that, by focusing primarily on civil and political rights, would serve as an anti-Communist rhetorical and legal tool. This more conservative form of rights discourse was the one enshrined at the European Court of Human Rights. British conservatives such as Winston Churchill and David Maxwell Fyfe, convinced that European integration and human rights were the great inheritors of Europe's Christian traditions, exercised enormous sway over early federalist processes. Some of the greatest Catholic defenders of rights, in turn, came directly from monarchist or authoritarian circles. Louis Salleron, a Catholic reactionary who had helped devise Vichy's agricultural policies, emerged after the war as an ideologue for the Union of European Federalists, and as a celebrant of human rights.[93]

Christian Democrats, in turn, eventually became apologists for the nation-state. It is true that Christian Democrats were pioneering European federalists. While Jean Monnet may have been the true fount of federalist creativity, the three "fathers of Europe" who garnered public support for his proposals were all Catholics and all Christian Democrats: Robert Schuman (French foreign minister), Alcide de Gasperi (Italian prime minister), and Konrad Adenauer (West German chancellor). They mobilized long-gestating transnational ties and a shared ideology of European civilization and culture, forging the building blocks for what would eventually become the European Union. But what sort of federalism did they actually pursue? The federalism of the first postwar decade was more economic than political, and it served more to shore up tottering nation-states than to demolish the very principle of state sovereignty. Even if cynical Realpolitik is not enough to explain federalist innovation, and even if Christian

Democrats did seek limits on state power, it is clearly the case that they were uninterested in pursuing the kinds of radical federalist projects foreseen by Maritain and Kogon.[94]

If Maritain saw his pluralism as a way to diminish military tensions, the Defenders of the West saw their own form of European federalism as a way to more efficiently take arms against Communists. The resolutions of the New International Teams (NEI), the international organization of Christian Democratic parties, promised that Christian Democrats would work together against the Communist assault on "the rights of the human person" through the creation of a democratic, Christian Europe oriented toward both social justice and "the fundamental principle of private property."[95] These rights would require stout defense. "Europe," one Christian Democratic leader declared, "has become a defensive concept."[96] In the name of anti-Communism, Christian Democratic parties encouraged war in Korea and Indochina alongside a rearmament of Europe itself. This was most surprising in West Germany, where one might imagine that militarized Christianity would remain taboo. Nonetheless, in 1950, Cardinal Josef Frings urged Catholics to abandon false humanitarianism and face the reality of the Communist threat alongside the necessity of military preparedness. Jakob Kaiser and Theodor Blank, two Catholic trade unionists, emerged as prominent defenders of this line, too. Catholics hardly participated in the West German peace movement of the 1950s, tending instead toward Adenauer's zeal for a rearmed Germany. A declaration from seven prominent theologians even argued that nuclear war could be defended from the perspective of Catholic ethics. The Germans were not alone, as Adenauer's Catholic hawks were met at the negotiating table by Robert Schuman, who longed for a common army to defend the common civilization of the Christian West. Although French Catholics were more divided about rearmament than their German neighbors, the MRP leadership, especially in private, agreed in principle to the rearming of West Germany and, when that failed, the incorporation of West Germany into NATO. The entire constellation of transnational Christian Democratic parties, a recent analysis has shown, oriented itself toward European division and German rearmament.[97]

As with Catholic-Communist collaboration more generally, the notion of a "Third Force" Europe, let alone a world government, became increasingly implausible as the Cold War ramped up. Communist parties themselves began to withdraw from federalist organizing. They did so at least partially because they saw federalism as an American ploy. There was some truth to the accusation. The American Committee on a United Europe (ACUE), founded in 1948, was dedicated to European federalism precisely as a means of warding off Communism. And yet, here as elsewhere, the geopolitical answer is insufficient. Catholic attitudes were not dictated by Moscow or Washington, and European Catholics needed little instruction in adopting a militarized, anti-Communist, and "Western" political ideology that would enshrine the nation-state at its core. This had been the dominant Catholic understanding of politics since around 1930, and in the welcoming circumstances of the early Cold War it reemerged.

The Fate of Fraternal Modernism in the Early Cold War

The interesting question is not why Maritain's brand of antifascism failed to inspire Christian Democratic parties. It would have been shocking if it had, given Maritain's own disinterest in parliamentary politics, the marginality of his own tradition in the 1930s, the cautious conservatism of the Vatican, and the general collapse of the antifascist unities of the wartime resistance. The interesting question is why Maritain, or someone like him, did not emerge at the forefront of a transnational network of Catholic dissidence the way he had in the 1930s. For decades, Catholic intellectual culture had been raucous, as various camps debated fiercely over what the faith meant and how it might translate into political or social action. After World War II, these debates died down considerably. While there were still dissenters, notably in France and Poland, it is nonetheless the case that, for the first time since the French Revolution, there was widespread agreement on the basic parameters of Catholic activity in the world.

The narrowing of Catholic intellectual and political horizons had multiple causes. One was geopolitical: in the 1930s, antifascist Catholics had recourse to a plausible set of allies, arrayed against an enemy (fascism) that was worrisome to many Catholics, including Vatican leaders. This space closed in the late 1940s, as the generative "antifascist versus anti-Communist" binary gave way to the more restrictive "Communist versus anti-Communist" one. Just as importantly, however, the newly hegemonic forms of anti-Communist Catholicism were more pliable than they had been in the 1930s. Christian Democratic parties were "catch-all" movements with oppositional wings, and quite a wide range of Catholic activists were at home in them. The parties were spaces of ideological synthesis between Catholics and Protestants but also between different kinds of Catholics. Many Catholic intellectuals in the fraternal tradition found themselves on the left wing of the new parties, which provided the institutional capacity for dialogue and consensus that had been lacking in the interwar years.

Fraternal modernists, in other words, were not homeless: the intellectual and political culture of the early Cold War was remarkably capacious and inclusive, even if it did not play host to a robust anticapitalism or antistatism. Outside party politics, too, fraternal modernists like Maritain were able to find a home in a vibrant transatlantic intellectual culture. While the antifascist excitement of the 1930s did not return, there was certainly more on offer than McCarthyite paranoia. Maritain rightly saw that the intellectual landscape of the Cold War Atlantic world was more experimental and welcoming than detractors, then and since, have admitted. When fraternal Catholics like Maritain considered America and its hegemony, they did not see only imperial overreach and capitalist consolidation. Maritain was a great believer in America, but like Alexis de Tocqueville he found the America that he wanted to find. Maritain was uninterested, for instance, in the grand state building projects of the Democratic Party. He looked instead to the smaller and more grassroots projects of people such as Dorothy Day and Saul Alinsky, who showed what kinds of results the faith could have when embedded in local cultures of organizing and activism.[98]

Fraternal modernism did not vanish, nor was it summarily defeated. Christian Democratic parties made space for previously dissident insights, while intellectuals like Maritain were widely celebrated. All the same, this should not distract us from the fact that, generally speaking, Maritain's form of modernism was sidelined in the transnational spaces of the Church and in Christian Democratic parties, too (one scholar refers to this whole period in the Church as "Maritain-ism on trial").[99] The antifascist renaissance that Maritain and others hoped for did not come to pass. Some of his former enemies took the opportunity to gloat. Henri Massis, who had been crossing swords with his former friend for two decades, crowed in 1951 that the Maritain of today "is alone—not in the solitude demanded for the discovery of truth, but the solitude of a man whose pseudo-disciples have left him behind." Admirers of Maritain, such as Communist Roger Garaudy, noticed the same thing. After an interview with him near the end of his time as ambassador, Garaudy was saddened. "We leave Maritain," he sighed, "with the painful impression of having met one of those honest

Christians who sense the terrible equivocations linking their sacred beliefs to an unacceptable social regime and anti-worker struggle."[100]

As the intellectual firestorms of the mid-1940s came to a close, Catholic Europe was more intellectually and politically unified than it had been in decades. In place of the bitter disputes of the past, a settlement had been reached by 1950 that was, if not ideal, at least acceptable to most Catholic intellectuals. That outcome—in which fraternal modernism survived, albeit in a marginalized position—legitimated Christian Democracy and the postwar system in the eyes of millions of Catholics. As the austerity and crisis of the 1940s gave way to the stability and consumerism of the 1950s, however, they faced a new set of challenges. The adventure of Catholic modernism did not end with the advent of Christian Democracy. At the heart of those parties, the faithful continued to mine their tradition for new ways to be Catholic, and new ways to be modern. The solutions they found had monumental consequences for their Church and for Europe itself.

5

CHRISTIAN DEMOCRACY IN THE LONG 1950S

Work for the good of the city to which I have exiled you; pray to
Yahweh on its behalf, since on its welfare yours depends.

—JEREMIAH 29:7

The most famous electoral image from the Christian Democratic era is
beautiful in its simplicity. In it, West German chancellor Konrad Adenauer
gazes out of a white background. He does not challenge or confront the
viewer as Hitler had done in the posters that had come down just a few years
earlier. Instead, Adenauer looks at the German people from the corner of his
eye, as though he had just been working, and warmly welcomes them into
his study. He is alone, and his advanced age is emphasized by harshly outlined wrinkles. He wears a peculiar smile, enigmatic yet avuncular. The
poster bears a simple slogan: *No Experiments*. "We have lived through a
great deal, you and I," the poster seems to say. "We know that Germany
has been through enough experiments to last a lifetime, many lifetimes.
Now we need to get to work in peace. Give me your vote, and a return to
normalcy will follow." The image and accompanying campaign were
magnificently successful. In the 1957 election, for which the poster was
designed, Adenauer's Christian Democrats won a crushing victory, gar-
nering over 50 percent of the vote, and almost 20 percent more than its
closest competitor, the Social Democratic Party (SPD).

The slogan was, however, a lie. The image of the staid and conservative
1950s, which Adenauer did his part to create, has been upended by recent
scholarship. Adenauer and the other geriatric Catholics who dominated the

politics of non-Communist continental Europe oversaw a period of inter-confessional collaboration, rapid economic growth, rising consumer satisfaction, and relative social harmony. Dizzying technological progress changed the daily lives of Europeans with stunning speed: the automobile, the television, the washing machine, and the glossy tabloid heralded the advent of a new style of modernity. Politically, European states were busy acquiring nuclear weapons, gathering into an Atlantic alliance, and debating various forms of political and economic integration. All of this was novel, as was Catholic participation in it. The only reason it did not seem like an "experiment" was that it worked.

Catholics played a central role in shepherding this new Europe into being. Most prominently, they did so through the vehicle of Christian Democracy: the interconfessional but largely Catholic parties that had been founded in the late 1940s and that remained dominant throughout the long 1950s (roughly speaking, 1949–1965). How did it come to be that largely Catholic parties oversaw the creation of a fundamentally capitalist and consumerist Europe, despite the tradition's long suspicion of capitalism and consumerism alike? Did they pursue some sort of Catholic "prosperity gospel"? Was it a cynical or pragmatic attempt to gather power in an era when traditional teachings seemed unmoored? Or did it represent an abandonment of the tradition altogether? Few historians have posed these questions. Most ideological analysis of Christian Democracy has focused on the late 1940s rather than on the long 1950s.[1] The presumed narrative is that the parties began as ideologically Christian movements before slowly shedding that baggage and becoming center-right stalwarts of the status quo. While this may have happened eventually, it did not happen in the 1950s. Catholics participated in the formation of the new Europe not by abandoning their social traditions but by reforming them and creating a new style of Catholic thought and action that we can call Christian Democratic modernism.

The Christian Democratic modernism of the long 1950s represents a new chapter in the story of Catholic modernism that had begun around 1930, not a weakening or dismantling of the tradition. The usage of that moniker is not meant to imply that all Catholics were Christian Democrats or that all Christian Democrats were Catholic. It is meant, instead, to draw attention to the fact that Catholic intellectuals and social scientists crafted a new style of Catholic modernism in the long 1950s, that this vision was highly compatible with the one pursued by Christian Democratic parties, and that in practice Christian Democratic leaders tended to be direct contributors to and beneficiaries of the Catholic public sphere. This chapter will focus on Christian Democratic policymakers, but it will embed them in that public sphere by showing how their ideas emerged from broader discussions in the press, trade unions, employers' organizations, and women's movements, as well as the various social Catholic think tanks and congresses that were still central to European intellectual culture. The relations between the Catholic public sphere and Christian Democratic rule were close: this was an era in which Catholic modernism had direct and measurable impact on the governing strategies of powerful parties. Christian Democrats were not simply "conservative." They did not govern the way Dwight D. Eisenhower's Republicans did in the United States or Sir Anthony Eden's Conservative Party did in the United Kingdom. They pursued, instead, a form of moral and political economy that was directly inspired by the social teachings of the Church.[2]

Christian Democratic modernism was something new: a set of Catholic strategies that drew on the long tradition of the Church but mobilized them in new ways to respond to new challenges. Catholics in the long 1950s faced two problems in particular. First, some kind of consensus had to be reached that could bring together long-divided Catholic communities. Christian Democrats relied on the elaboration of a baseline "Christian" approach to sociopolitical affairs that could appeal to many constituencies. Historians have tended to focus on the interconfessional aspect, asking how it appealed both to Catholics and to Protestants. This is a crucial angle but not the only one (it also was not new, given that Catholics had worked freely with Protestants across Europe in the 1930s). Christian Democratic parties had to appeal as well to different kinds of Catholics, gathering together the long-warring wings of the Church into a new consensus. This was just as important, historically speaking, and was quite unprecedented. Since the French Revolution, Catholics had been firmly divided about the political and social derivations of their faith. The long 1950s was a brief interlude of consensus. Second, Catholics needed some way to understand and legitimate the most transformative element of the long 1950s: explosive economic growth and the birth of a consumer society. Catholics had long been suspicious of mass consumption and the market, a position that was no longer tenable on a continent weary of ascetic ideology and intoxicated by the new influx of consumer goods.

Christian Democrats solved both of these problems at once, and the way they did so becomes clear through a close analysis of the vast network of social Catholic thinkers, experts, journalists, and policymakers who played a role in forging a new "commonsense" form of Catholic moral and political economy. The main question to ask of any form of Catholic modernism is this one: how does it conceptualize the private sphere, in which religion supposedly lives in modern societies? Ever since making the turn to modernism in the 1930s, Catholics had been divided over the answer. In that tumultuous decade, mainstream paternal modernists had built their politics around the reproducing family, presuming that the linchpin of a healthy society was a healthy and traditional family unit: working fathers, caregiving mothers, and numerous children educated in Catholic schools. Fraternal modernists, with some justice, argued that this focus on the reproductive family was legitimating unsavory alliances. They viewed the private sphere as a space of solidarity. This began with the family itself, which they understood to be a space for love and desire rather than law and childbearing, but it did not end there. They understood the private sphere as a whole to be made up of robust civil society organizations, Catholic and interconfessional alike, which were the true building blocks of a just Catholic modernity. Neither of these competing visions survived wholesale into the Christian Democratic moment. The former was too redolent of fascist natalism, while the latter belonged to an antifascist tradition that, as we saw in Chapter 4, had been aggressively sidelined by 1950. In their place, Catholics forged something new.

Catholics in the long 1950s interpreted the private sphere as a space for *consuming* families: nuclear families, with stay-at-home mothers, tasked less with heroic childbearing than with consumption, love, and happiness. This family imaginary provides the conceptual key to Christian Democratic modernism. A Catholic modernity, it was presumed in the long 1950s, would be made up of prosperous and hygienic families following traditional gender norms and obeying Church precepts in their sexual lives. This gendered account of consumer-citizenship extended beyond the Church, to be sure, but it found tremendous traction in Catholic circles too.[3]

The genius of this understanding of the private sphere was that it solved both of the major challenges presented to Catholics at the time. It satisfied both wings of the Church, incorporating the paternal focus on family values and the fraternal emphasis on the marriage bond as a meaningful, sacramental unit that should be shielded from nationalist propaganda. It also helped Catholics to legitimate and facilitate the economic and consumer revolution that was transforming God's continent. Catholic thinkers continued to oppose a consumerist culture built around the needs of the hedonist individual. That was known as "materialism," and it remained as grave a sin as ever in Catholic circles. They could warm, though, to one that aided the traditional family in pursuit of well-ordered and morally regulated prosperity. This explains why Christian Democrats, even as they pursued all kinds of modern innovations in urban planning and consumer living, continued to defend the most traditional form of the family unit—and why they mobilized immense state resources behind the welfare of that specific family form (not with total success, it should be said, as women continued to flow into the workforce).[4]

This understanding of the private sphere, as in other forms of Catholic modernism, authorized a novel set of claims on the public sphere. The state and the economy were now tasked, above all, with enshrining the rights and needs of the consuming family. This is not to say that every Christian Democratic idea, text, or policy explicitly addressed the family, although an enormous number of them did. It is to say, instead, that at the conceptual level, the consuming family emerged as the presumed agent of social and political life. It was the entity in whose name the economy and the state should properly be organized (instead of, for instance, the individual citizen, the working class, the race, or the nation).

When Christian Democrats confronted social and economic questions, therefore, they presumed the needs of the consuming family to be paramount. And what were they? In essence, they were quite similar to the needs of the reproductive family that had structured paternal Catholic modernism in the 1930s. Media censorship and legal restrictions on divorce, abortion, and homosexuality would ensure that the state did its part to cultivate healthy family norms. In these arenas, little changed. But when it came to the crucial questions of welfare policy, economic doctrine, and political theory, Christian Democrats pursued new strategies that brought together both paternal and fraternal modernist principles. They agitated for a family-friendly welfare state that would be oriented toward consumption and housing, not simply childbearing, and would be less punitive than its predecessor. They pursued a social market economy that would champion social justice and the family wage through trade unions and workers' participation in the firm—not through aggressive state corporatism. And they no longer called for a racialized state to "Defend the West" against Bolsheviks. The Christian Democratic doctrine of the state emphasized, instead, economic growth and development.

Christian Democratic modernists, in sum, pursued robust family welfare, innovative forms of workers' participation, and a regulated form of economic development. They did so not in the name of pragmatism but in the name of a novel and coherent social Catholic vision that gathered together the more conservative and more progressive wings of the Church. While the ingenuity of Catholic thinkers should not be overlooked, the conditions in the long 1950s were uniquely well suited to such an alliance. The sexual revolution was in the future, so Catholics did not yet have to confront hard and divisive questions about women's liberation. Economic growth was stratospheric across these years—a condition that seems to generate ideological compromise. Perhaps most important of all, Christian Democrats, like other Europeans in the long 1950s, had vivid memories of the war and the destruction it had wrought. They had little appetite for deep ideological conflict, gravitating instead toward doctrines of consensus and dialogue.

To explore these themes in more detail, we can turn once again to transnationally embedded stories of significant Catholic, and Christian Democratic, intellectuals to explore the kindred themes of family welfare, economic doctrine, and political theory: a French theorist of the family who served as minister of public health, a German priest and economist who served as a key adviser to the Christian Democratic Union (CDU), and an Austrian economist and finance minister who provides access to Christian Democratic political thinking (the preponderance of economists here is indicative of the new shape of social-scientific knowledge in the postwar era). These three figures mediated between the worlds of theology, social science, and Christian Democratic governance. Their stories, in turn, will show how the long-standing cleavages in the European Church were (temporarily) papered over, with great consequences for Europe and the Church alike.

The focus of the analysis will be less on Christian Democratic policymaking as such than on the evolving sense of what a properly Catholic modernity might look like. Actual policy was hammered out in rooms filled with smoke, not incense. And while the debates about Catholic modernism largely took place around Christian Democratic parties, they were not the only site. Each section will show, too, how Christian Democratic modernism made its way into official dogma. The dogmatic apparatus of the Church changed dramatically in the 1960s, as the Second Vatican Council charted a new course for the global Church. The story of Vatican II and the story of Christian Democracy are normally understood separately, and indeed it would require a different project, paying close attention to the internal politics of the Vatican and the council, to fully understand Vatican II. At the same time, the homologies between the two are striking, and the novel analysis of Christian Democratic ideology offered here sheds light on official Church doctrine. Most of the major players at Vatican II hailed from countries with robust Christian Democratic parties. However much time the bishops spent with the *Summa Theologica,* they read newspapers and watched television, too. And, like the Christian Democrats in the media marketplace, they envisioned a modern social order based on family values and properly regulated economic development.

Christian Democratic Welfare

In the 1930s, Catholics accepted and strove to reform the centralized welfare state—an apparatus that they had long rejected. They did so by reinterpreting the welfare state as a support to Catholic families, rather than as an attempt to wrest control from Catholic charities and hand it to an anticlerical state. As such, Catholic forms of welfare were not especially concerned with measures like unemployment insurance or universal healthcare programs, which aimed to protect individuals or workers. They were interested, instead, in family allowances and other schemes designed to ease the burden of large families. At the time, they often did so in the name of authoritarian politics and reproductive motherhood, and in ways that often legitimated racist or punitive policies. These kinds of authoritarian welfare regimes were off the table in the long 1950s, so Catholics sought instead a postfascist alternative, organizing their policy around the subtly different figure of the consuming family. This allowed them to spearhead a kinder, gentler welfare state—but still one that operated according to a logic of familial citizenship.

It is perhaps not a surprise to learn that Christian Democratic welfare policy emphasized the family over other possible recipients of state support. Comparative welfare state analysts have been pointing this out for decades. What is more interesting is the pathway Catholics took to update their stodgy familialism for a new era ("family values," that is, are always evolving, even inside the Catholic Church). A speech by Helene Weber, a German Catholic politician, at Germany's first postwar Catholic congress, in 1948, shows us how. "One gigantic danger," she warned, "threatens the social order: the masses. There is one society, which the masses can never ruin, and which alone can conquer them: that is the family." The family, she argued, must be "reconstructed" through state policy in order to secure the victory of the "free market economy" over its socialist competitors. In Weber's speech, women were addressed less as mothers than as consumers, whose control of the "household economy" was central to the "national economy." By embedding themselves in Catholic women's and consumer movements, Weber concluded, they would learn to consume efficiently and morally, ensuring that "the arduous recovery would succeed without being destroyed yet again by revolutionary forces."[5]

This speech, and others like it, urged Catholics to marry their own social ethics with new cultures of consumption. Instead of reproduction as the link between the family and the national community, which had been the basis of Catholic natalism in the 1930s, Weber proposed consumption as a link between the family and the national economy. This notion of the consuming family united Catholics with secular peers, just as its natalist predecessor had done in the 1930s. Across the Cold War West, a social-scientific apparatus emerged to explain why the nuclear, consuming family was necessary to moral and economic reconstruction alike. Psychologists such as Anna Freud and Dorothy T. Burlingham were theorizing the absolute centrality of a healthy, normal home life to the development of a non-neurotic child. Secular family sociologists such as Helmut Schelsky and René König, drawing on American sociological innovations of the 1930s, likewise described the uncanny stability of the family, even amid wartime upheaval, and the necessity of a stable family life to a morally ordered society. The emerging discipline of household economics placed the consuming household, not the laboring individual, at the center of its economic theory.[6]

In this welcoming environment, the Catholic family international reactivated, as Catholics both hosted their own events and took part in congresses on family matters sponsored by institutions such as UNESCO. While the institutional environment had evolved, much was the same, too, as shown by the keynote address given at an international family congress in Vienna in 1959. In it, Catholic intellectual Hans Schmitz crowed that secular sociology and Catholic social teachings had finally arrived at "common visions of order," organized not around the class but around the family.

And while Schmitz no longer praised Italy or Portugal as he might have twenty years earlier, he focused his attention on the same site that had so enthralled Catholic family activists in the past: France.[7]

In the 1950s, as in the 1930s, France led the way in Catholic familialism. Before turning to the new consumerist ethos, it is important to stress the important continuities in Catholic family ideology across the war years. In France, where familialism was less tarred with the brush of fascism than elsewhere, this was especially notable. Charles de Gaulle and all of the major postwar parties were convinced of the importance of family stability and population growth, while familiar family activists such as Georges Pernot tried to salvage as much of the old natalism as they could.[8] Even in this crowded space, France's Christian Democratic Party, the MRP, maneuvered to present itself as the premier champion of the family. Albert Gortais, in his programmatic 1947 lecture on the MRP's platform, declared that "we recognize the *family* as the most intangible, and the most sacred" of all human groups, subtly drawing a line in the sand between the MRP and its erstwhile leftist collaborators. The MRP's newspaper regularly played up the party's dedication to the family. In the special issue devoted to the 1953 election, for instance, the recommended slate of candidates was headlined "Republican List of Familial and Social Action."[9]

Practically, much of this was familiar from the past. Maurice Schumann, in the very first article of the first issue of the party's journal, declared the MRP to be "The Great Party of the French Family." While avoiding the aggressive natalism of the recent past, Schumann pushed for many of the same policies: family allowances, affordable housing, a family wage, legislation against abortion, protection of marriage, and the family vote. The platform of the MRP's first National Council, too, declared itself in favor of a robust pro-family politics, including "the revalorization of the role of the mother in the home."[10] The MRP followed through at the policy level, working to ensure that contraception remained illegal and divorce a near impossibility. Their continued worrying about female labor outside the home took multiple forms, including a decided lack of enthusiasm for state-provided child care. They also introduced the single-wage benefit, which went only to families subsisting on a single wage, first implemented under Vichy. It thus, as the Left never tired of pointing out, discouraged women from entering the workforce and enshrined a particularly conservative model of the family: "The state knew the kind of family it wanted and adopted a coherent set of measures which favored these families and penalized others," one disappointed observer noted.[11]

This revamped Catholic familialism found its political champion in Robert Prigent, who served as minister of population for much of the late 1940s and strongly influenced the Fourth Republic's welfare state.[12] His overall political activity was deeply continuous with the tradition of French familialism as it had emerged in the Third Republic and had evolved during the Vichy years. "The family," he insisted, "is not a Vichy issue. The family is a French issue."[13] In a pamphlet on marriage loans, for instance, he displayed little desire to break with the past or even with the demographic concerns that had long undergirded French social policy. He expressed dismay at "the alarming situation of our nation from the demographic point of view" and, amazingly, discussed the Nazi system of marriage loans as a possible model for France.[14] When it came to the representation of families, Prigent recycled the Vichy-era solution to a surprising degree. Under Vichy, Catholic family associations like the Women's Civic and Social Union (UFCS) won their long-desired goal of official state recognition and representation, as the state centralized and rationalized the chaos of French family organizations. Once the Ministry of Population was in his hands, Prigent "republicanized" this system (as one French observer has termed it). The National Union of Family Associations (UNAF), founded in March 1945, restored the old pluralism of family associations while still giving them a voice in the state. While Prigent had opposed Vichy's centralized family association, he had no qualms about setting up the UNAF in the same building.[15]

Just as they had in the 1930s, Catholics like Prigent viewed family politics as an antisocialist imperative. He wanted to use social policy to protect the family, to be sure, and he oversaw enormous expansions of the French welfare state. But this was welfare of a specific sort. Prigent did not see family allowances as one component of social policy, similar in nature to unemployment assistance. They were, from Prigent's perspective, a sacrosanct state duty to the most natural and holy of social institutions. He refused, therefore, to integrate the expensive family allowance system into the more general welfare system, out of fear that family benefits would be diminished in place of other, less sacred obligations. This led to conflict with Pierre Laroque, the primary architect of the French social security system. Laroque, inspired by the British, wanted to integrate France's storied system of family allowances into a universalist, centrally administered system that would administer a wide array of social benefits. Prigent spearheaded the effort against Laroque's universalist plan, with help from the CFTC (France's Catholic trade union). Gaston Tessier, the leader of the CFTC, cast his opposition in the language of pluralism: "For us," he declared, "freedom finds its application in a form of pluralism which is rather fundamental." Prigent succeeded in securing the independence of the family benefit from the general system of social security, and his success was one of the greatest blows against Laroque's plans. As Prigent's close friend, Minister of Labor Paul Bacon, emphasized at the 1949 MRP Congress, France needed a "politics of the infant and the family," and "the autonomy of the family benefits office is the means to realize this." The MRP's commitment to independent family benefits was serious enough that a fruitful collaboration with a conservative party, led by Antoine Pinay, foundered over this very issue in 1952.[16]

A similar dynamic could be found across Europe, as Christian Democrats mobilized with great success to implement a familial form of welfare policy in place of the universalist approach of the social democrats (who often drew on the British example). In Austria, Christian Democrats agreed that "the modern state, due to economic development," must take on a great deal of responsibility for family welfare.[17] Because of this, they shepherded a system of family allowances through Parliament in 1954. Socialists and Communists, while supporting the bill, worried that it did not attack the most fundamental problems of inequality. From the perspective of the Austrian Christian Democrats (ÖVP), as they announced in Parliament, this was not the point. State policy should aim not for the chimera of social equalization but for the support of families within their own social class. As one ÖVP representative declared in Parliament, the law "is and should not be a measure for welfare." It was not even designed to raise the birthrate, a goal that reeked of Nazi population policies. Instead, it was solely concerned with "social justice": families should not be hamstrung from fulfilling their natural reproductive functions for reasons of economic need. The family, the representative insisted, is "the archetype of our entire social life," and by padding the family pocketbook the policy might help to keep women in the home.[18] "Family allowances," announced another ÖVP politician a few years later, "signify the salvation of the family as the basic cell of a society in which man can assert his value as a person." Indeed, he saw them as "without a doubt the most radical social-political renewal of the Second Republic," serving to "anchor the family in modern industrial society." Moreover, this policy represented "a decision for the free society and against the collective one, in which the unity of the family would be destroyed."[19]

In West Germany, too, Christian Democrats conspired to place the family, and not the individual or the working class, at the center of welfare policy. Franz-Josef Würmeling, West Germany's first family minister, was a devout Catholic with roots in the Center Party. He insisted, like his colleagues across Europe, that the restoration of the family was the only pathway to an antifascist future. While he spoke the language of secular social science in some settings, he was clearly most at home in Catholic circles—and, in an unpublished memoir, he later admitted that Catholic social theory was his main inspiration.[20] The stated purpose of the ministry, which Würmeling led for the first nine years of its existence, was to raise the birthrate and counter the aging of the West German population. This necessarily brought Würmeling close to fascist forms of population politics, but he steered clear, just as he had in the 1930s, when he had been unsuccessfully courted by the Nazi League of Large Families (even if he did evince bizarre praise for Vichy's family legislation in a Bundestag speech).[21] Under his guidance, and with the fearful example of East Germany present in his mind, legislative restrictions on divorce, contraception, abortion, and homosexuality remained in place. Würmeling's version of family allowances, funded primarily through income tax exemptions, was regressive, and he was proud of it. Against constant socialist attack, he explained again and again that family policy was not "welfare," nor was it aimed at income redistribution. It was simply designed to ensure that families could maintain their class standing if they had children. And despite socialist insistence that the funds be administered directly by the state, Würmeling and the CDU mobilized the ideal of subsidiarity to ensure that they were administered directly by employers. This idea entered CDU common sense through a 1948 Catholic Social Week on family issues, at which Catholic physicians and welfare experts weighed in. "We must protect ourselves from a politicization of family and youth," warned one contributor in defense of an employer-centered system.[22]

At this point, it might seem as though little had changed since the 1930s: the cautious celebrations of authoritarian family politics by Christian Democratic family ministers coincided with a continuing suspicion of working women and a basic continuity in policy goals. And yet the Catholic familialism of the Christian Democratic era was, nonetheless, organized around a novel understanding of the family unit, its purpose, and its relationship to the body politic. In the writings of Dietrich von Hildebrand and others, an antifascist conception of the family had emerged in the 1930s that refused to focus on reproduction and natalist nationalism. The marriage, a community of love and sex, was the important community from this perspective, not the reproductive family. This sensibility reemerged after the war and became more dominant than ever. Prigent himself was heir to it. In the 1930s, he had been a member of the Young Christian Workers (JOC), and as he told an interviewer years later, he had been "impregnated by its principles." Those principles were broadly antifascist: the JOC privileged gender equality and democratic norms in both theory and practice, and Hildebrand's marriage ideals were found in JOC journals. Prigent spent the war years in the resistance, owing at least partially to his rejection of Vichy's restrictive notion of the family. In 1942, he had already declared to the national council of the Popular Family Movement that women must not be confined to their reproductive role, as many in Vichy insisted, but rather that they should, with men, seize "the levers that control the world."[23]

Prigent shared the antifascist conception of the family, and after the war he enlisted it in the service of the national economy. He peddled this ideal in the premier religious and secular social-scientific venues of the era. The prestigious Social Weeks (Semaines Sociales) had long been the clearinghouse for the most advanced French Catholic social thought. And when Prigent spoke there, he celebrated the new family unit as a "unity of consumption," musing that family associations should become consumer interest groups. He explored the idea in greater depth in his contribution to a volume on family sociology that he edited for the National Institute for Demographic Studies, France's most advanced (and secular) demographic institute. Prigent's essay, significantly, was called "The Modern Notion of the Human Couple United by Marriage." Citing sociological research on modern family structures, he emphasized repeatedly that families no longer exist for society alone but should rather be understood as a site for the moral and economic fulfillment of the couple. It is therefore a totalitarian evil to pressure couples into having children—this violated the sanctity of the family unit, and it was anyhow unnecessary given that modern societies showed just how natural the urge for children is, if the proper policy environment is in place. We are experiencing, he smugly reported, "a very different evolution than the one predicted by the utopians of yesterday." While some feminists had believed that women would eventually free themselves from the home and pursue careers, the revival of the family was showing that they wanted nothing of the sort: "On the contrary, we see an important proportion of educated women . . . freely abandoning their professional activities to consecrate themselves entirely to their role as spouse and mother." This had economic benefits, in addition to the obvious moral ones. Modern women, he enthused, seek "mechanical means" to help with household labor, "giving birth to an important industry" and granting women's "daily duties the dignity of a new art."[24]

This notion of the consumer family was important because it allowed Catholics to pursue relatively traditional sorts of policies while also linking them, in ideology and in reality, to the evolving circumstances of the long 1950s. The ascetic, reproductive family of the 1930s no longer made sense for an era tired of sacrifice and nationalist ideology. The new family of intimacy, sexuality, and consumption, while fulfilling many of the same tasks from the perspective of Catholic modernists, was more compatible with the spirit of the age. And it was present well beyond Prigent, in the Catholic press and in Catholic institutional life alike. Catholic sociologists such as Jacques Leclercq began publishing books like *Changing Perspectives on Conjugal Morality* (1950) that sought to legitimate it. The JOC put out a pamphlet on marriage called, simply, *Love,* which emphasized sex, pleasure, and house hunting as the central aspects of the new couple. The organization and its rural counterpart were beginning, meanwhile, to run marriage retreats that sacralized the marriage bond without regard to children. Pius XII's acceptance of the rhythm method in a widely noted 1951 speech confirmed the notion that Catholics were full participants in the moderate sexual revolution of the postwar era, which promised to valorize conjugal sexuality within the confines of Church teachings.[25]

The Équipes Notres Dames, a Catholic society for young married couples, developed into a mass lay organization that worked to spread these new ideas among young French Catholics. Its journal, *The Ring of Gold,* had a circulation of forty thousand in the 1950s and gave the imprimatur to the new vision of the Catholic family. Its articles emphasized marriage and love at the expense of maternity. One author praised the rhythm method as a necessary form of prudence, while another assured readers that a fulfilling life was possible without any children at all. The journal's founder, Henri Caffarel, even urged married couples to "settle down" for three hours each month, *without the children*, to take stock of their love and their shared ideals. Another article dared to criticize the official French marriage liturgy for its atavistic and misogynist tone, which had no roots in "the theology that we preach."[26] Readers of *The Ring of Gold* saw advertisements for publications from the Catholic School of Family Sciences, an organization that was attempting to bring Catholic teachings and modern social science into harmony. As its secretary announced in the introduction to its magisterial *Research on the Family* (1949), the movement, while scientific in its methods, "is a tributary of the personalist movement in France, of Christian existentialism, and of the new philosophy of love."[27] Readers learned, too, about how the new family of love and intimacy was tied to consumption. One article, for instance, celebrated "the introduction of machines into the home, which increasingly reduces the burden of material necessity and housework."[28]

The image of the consuming woman was especially prevalent at the UFCS, still the most important Catholic women's organization on the continent—and one that had happily worked with Pétain just a few years earlier. It now reinvented itself as a purveyor of Christian Democratic modernism. Eight of the nine women in the MRP's first parliamentary delegation came from the organization, and its congresses now featured heroes of the resistance and victims of the camps alongside the expected parade of policy experts.[29] The 1947 international congress of the movement announced the modernizing citizen-mother as the new agent of familial reconstruction. Longtime UFCS head Andrée Butillard began the proceedings with a celebration of modern maternity. The mother of the present was meant not to labor silently beside her husband but to take an active role in social and political life, "saving her children from malnutrition just as much as from destructive ideologies." Our crisis, Butillard insisted, is both "material and moral," and by organizing the consumption and education of the household the mother becomes the true "artisan of human progress." Speakers reiterated the traditional opposition to women working outside the home, but the logic of that position now relied on the market instead of natural law. Female labor, they argued, was inefficient because it kept the household from playing its proper economic role in the life of the nation: the role of consumer and household organizer. The conference resolutions called, therefore, for "the rationalization of domestic labor," as well as "the integration of the domestic economy into the general economy," ensuring a proper relation "between the production and consumption of economic goods."[30] By the early 1950s, the UFCS was dedicating itself in innovative ways to moral forms of consumption within the family unit. By creating Buyers' Commissions and empowering housewives to monitor prices and report their findings, the UFCS dedicated itself to turning French women into "good buyers," whose wise consumption choices would benefit their families and the French nation alike.[31]

The distinguished yearly congresses of the Social Weeks celebrated the consuming family, too. In 1957, a meeting was held on "The Family of Today." The previous Social Week on family affairs had taken place in the 1920s and had been consumed by rhetoric of moral collapse and depopulation. Its successor was different, and its title alone indicated a zeal for modernity. The lectures drew freely from secular social science and demography to argue for the new relevance of the family to France's economic expansion. Alain Barrère, one of France's leading economists and a future director of the Social Weeks, gave a lecture on "The Family and Economic Evolution." He explained that, while the family of the past had been involved with both production and consumption, production had now moved outside the household. This freed the family to become a site, primarily, of consumption, leisure, and "economic decisionmaking." For this reason, Barrère concluded, the expansion of the French economy *required* healthy families. The apparent conflict between Catholic family values and the new consumer economy dissolved in the heat of the dishwasher.[32]

This evolution of the Catholic family imagination took place across Europe, albeit in different ways in different places (in France, for instance, familialists had more of a role in economic planning institutions, which were less central to the reconstruction in the economically liberal environs of Germany and Austria).[33] The transition was most remarkable in Austria, where Catholic familialists in the 1930s, led by Mina Wolfring and her Motherhood Protection Bureau, had argued for an alliance between Catholic family values and nationalist natalism. In the 1950s, this view was loudly rejected. Articles in Catholic and Christian Democratic publications emphasized the need to learn from the National Socialist experiment that the family should not be integrated into the state.[34] One Christian Democratic woman, who would eventually become minister of social affairs, argued that women are persons, deserving of their own rights, and not simply servants of the *Volk*. "We don't need the political woman of National Socialism," argued another female party member, "but rather the female personality." At a 1953 conference on pastoral care called *On the Soul of Woman,* at which Cardinal Innitzer gave the opening address, speaker after speaker addressed the need to move beyond the repressive natalism of the past. "Without a doubt," one admitted, "the emancipation of women has resulted in successes that must be welcomed." Another admonished the "men of the middle-aged and older generations" as being "too beholden to the past" on these questions. Drawing on the French Catholic literature on the family, he welcomed the new independence and freedom of women, as well as the reconceptualization of marriage as a partnership.[35]

In Germany, meanwhile, Catholic associations began to host marriage seminars, aimed at young couples, at which doctors, priests, and more experienced married couples would speak on such themes as "sex in the marriage." These were quite popular: at the first marriage seminar in Passau, the estimated crowd of 350 ballooned into a standing-only mass of 750 curious young Catholics. Meanwhile, within the Church itself, a new German marriage liturgy was approved in 1950 that allowed for far more use of the vernacular.[36] Essays with titles such as "Love as Ethical Power" appeared in major Catholic publications, bringing Hildebrand's insights into the Catholic mainstream. Intellectuals such as Josef Fuchs and Ernst Michel wrote books on marriage and sexuality, too, trying to find common ground between Catholic respect for the body and the first tendrils of the sexual liberation that would soon convulse West Germany. *Mann in der Zeit,* a Catholic men's publication with a circulation of nearly a million copies, published a number of sex-positive articles and displayed increasingly alluring photos of young Catholic couples in love (while also emphasizing that abortion and contraception were gateways to Nazism).[37]

In Central Europe, as elsewhere in Catholic Europe, the cult of young love and well-regulated sexuality was tied to glittering consumption. Even pornography, marketed as a marital aid, enjoyed a boom, and West German erotica catalogues reminded readers of the Church's support for the rhythm method.[38] The formerly staid journal of West Germany's Catholic Women's League now featured consuming housewives drinking Coca-Cola and surrounded by loving families. "The family," West Germany's Catholic family minister announced in 1961, "was once autarkic and responsible for production itself, but it has now, from an economic perspective, developed into a pure community of consumption."[39] The Catholic leader of the Austrian Women's Movement instructed in 1958 that "clever, economizing housewives build a healthy basis for all of economic life," while the journal of Austria's Catholic women's movement reminded readers that "three-quarters of the national wealth passes through the hands of the housewife."[40]

The new popular culture and social science of Catholic familialism found their way into theological reflection on the family, too. In 1960, Karol Wojtyła (the future Pope John Paul II) published *Love and Responsibility*, making many of the same points as Hildebrand had done thirty years earlier (they both applied Max Scheler's phenomenology to the marriage bond). Like Hildebrand, Wojtyła praised the sex drive as a necessary and blessed part of our being, and he even spoke warmly of "the sexual enjoyment which conjugal relations can bring." Léon Suenens, a Belgian archbishop, and an important German theologian named Josef Fuchs published kindred accounts at around the same time. This sensibility, common in Catholic family ethics by the early 1960s, was reproduced in *Humanae vitae*, Pope Paul VI's 1968 encyclical on sexuality. In some ways, it was the most sex-positive encyclical ever released by the Catholic Church. In line with the evolving Catholic image of the family, Paul VI instructed the flock that sex inside the marriage bond was a good and holy thing, even if the couple was certain, for whatever reason, that children would not result (due to, say, infertility). As such, he confirmed that Catholics could utilize the rhythm method.[41]

And yet *Humanae vitae* is most famous for outlawing artificial forms of contraception, disappointing millions of Catholics who had hoped that the pope would be flexible on this issue (the birth control pill had, after all, been partially invented by a Catholic physician who thought it might be more theologically acceptable than other contraceptive forms). Paul VI was surprised by the outrage that greeted his announcement. For one thing, even the most up-to-date Catholic family teachings, in Christian Democratic and theological circles alike, agreed that the sex drive was valuable and laudable only if it was expressed within the strict limits imposed by natural law (Wojtyła, Suenens, and Fuchs all celebrated the encyclical, as did Hildebrand himself). And for another, *Humanae* was the almost inevitable result of the family-centric strategy the Church had adopted in its transition toward modernity. From this perspective, the realms of economy and state can float free of direct theological jurisdiction so long as religious control over the private sphere of sex and family is vigorously reasserted. This conceptual history, and not any personal whim of Paul VI's, explains the drastic disjunction between *Humanae* and the other dogmatic texts of the 1960s. In general, Vatican texts of the era shied away from direct invocations of natural law. *Humanae vitae,* however, in a relatively short text, uses the phrase "natural law" more times than in all of the Vatican II documents combined. Moreover, and again departing from other texts of the 1960s, Paul VI called on "rulers of nations" to limit contraceptive use in their countries, bearing in mind that "the family is the primary unit in the state."[42]

Christian Democratic modernism enshrined the sexually satisfied and heteronormative family as the agent of welfare and ethics—a novel understanding of the private sphere that led to new forms of welfare policy, a renewed attempt to legislate family morality, and new forms of dogmatic moral teaching. This approach opened up some possibilities and foreclosed others. On the one hand, European families truly were in distress in the first postwar decades. Christian Democratic social policy delivered a great deal of resources, whether that took the form of housing assistance, housing construction, marriage loans, or child allowances. On the other hand, this model led to disinterest in other possible social agents. Most everyone, Communists included, was interested in rebuilding the family in postwar Europe. What made Christian Democrats unique was that they saw the family as the primary and even the only legitimate denizen of the social body. Christian Democrats were generally unwilling to use the powers of the welfare state to tackle inequality as such, preferring to focus instead on inequality between families (of the same class) with different numbers of children. This led to a corollary disinterest in the kinds of suffering and want that were not coded as familial or even as dangerous to the family. Christian Democrats therefore colluded in the general chill that fell on feminist and gay liberation movements in the long 1950s. They were suspicious, too, of the insistent demands coming from the working class.

The Social Market Economy

The words used to described the stratospheric economic growth of the long 1950s have a religious aura: "the miracle economy" in Germany and Austria, the "glorious" years in France. In stark contrast to the 1920s, the major institutions of Catholic social thought shared in this celebration. No major criticisms of the new economy were voiced by the Vatican, the NEI (the international Christian Democratic organization), the Social Weeks, or the Catholic Congresses of Germany or Austria.[43] Why this dramatic shift? Certainly not because of any conversion to "capitalism" in the abstract, which remained a term of opprobrium in Catholic circles (the "free market" did not fare much better). It was not because the new economic order paid any particular respect to Catholic law or institutions, either. Instead, Catholics decided that the reformed market economies of the long 1950s were valuable because they provided the resources and stability needed by the consuming family.

The new question for Christian Democrats was this one: What does the consuming family require from the economy? Above all, the consuming family needed some kind of mechanism to ensure that working fathers received a wage sufficient to maintain their wives and children at a comfortable standard of living without the mother having to work (the "family wage"). Christian Democrats knew that a free labor market would not provide this long-standing Catholic goal. "Pure capitalism," as a characteristic Christian Democratic manifesto put it in 1961, "corrupts justice, degrades liberty, and is therefore democratically intolerable."[44] Instead, they pursued what became known as the "social market economy": a reformed sort of capitalism that provided a significant safety net and balanced the rights to private property with the dignity of the worker. This term was not used everywhere in Christian Democratic Europe, but its basic outlines were nonetheless pursued quite widely by Catholic policymakers. Long pilloried by scholars as cynical representatives of bourgeois capitalism, the Christian Democratic parties of the long 1950s are now seen, more accurately, as consensus-driven parties with surprisingly robust and effective participation from trade unionists.[45] This commitment manifested in many different policy arenas, but perhaps the signal Christian Democratic commitment in the economic sphere was to codetermination: the idea that the worker, organized into free and independent trade unions, had the right to a share in either the management or the profits of his firm.

Christian Democratic economic theory drew on both the paternal and the fraternal agendas of the past. In some obvious ways, the social market economy revived the authoritarian corporatism of the mainstream paternal modernists. The political economy of postwar Europe, after all, was marked by interest-group bargaining, often mediated by the state (while the term was avoided at the time, later political scientists and historians have been happy to refer to postwar European economies as corporatist).[46] This had been the central position of 1930s corporatists, many of whom emerged after the war with reputations intact. Theodor Brauer, the Catholic corporatist who made common cause with National Socialists, was gone but not forgotten. One author for the journal of West German Christian Democratic workers wrote an article in his praise, reminding readers that "we stand on the shoulders of those who came before," adding that the interwar period was so rich in Catholic social thinking that "we practically live off of it."[47] François Perroux and Johannes Messner, two other authoritarian corporatists who had become famous in the 1930s, remained well-respected economists in the postwar era. The alliance between Catholics and the new school of liberals known as Ordo-liberals is often viewed as unique to the Christian Democratic moment. But that, too, had been pioneered in the corporatist 1930s, when each of them was looking for allies in the anti-Communist struggle. Those alliances bore fruit after the war.

However much Christian Democratic economic thought might have drawn on the mainstream corporatism of the 1930s, it was something new. Brauer, Messner, and Perroux had all argued that the state had the right and even the duty to dissolve trade unions in the name of state-sponsored syndicates. Fraternal modernists such as Ernst Karl Winter, instead, had theorized a philo-Communist form of trade unionism, hoping that robust worker organizing would unseat capitalism altogether and inaugurate a new era of social justice. This program as a whole was not on the Christian Democratic agenda, but some of its core components certainly were. Christian Democratic modernists believed that workers had the right to form their own trade unions, that employers and states should respect them, and that Catholics could and should work together with social democrats at the heart of those unions. In this way, the family wage could be secured without delivering too much power to the state.

Christian Democratic economic doctrine, like Christian Democratic family policy, should be understood as a novel alliance between formerly warring wings of the Church. The West German case provides particular insight into how this alliance emerged in practice, and how codetermination became a central component of the Christian Democratic economy. One could certainly trace a trade unionist from the unions of the 1920s, through the dissidence of the 1930s, and into the heart of Christian Democracy in the long 1950s, where many of them were committed to the social market economy and specifically to codetermination.[48] A focus on one of the more "liberal" or free market Catholics, instead, sheds a different sort of light on

Christian Democratic modernism and one that is less frequently explored. Joseph Höffner, a priest and economist, often found himself in conflict with Catholic workers. His defense of the regulated free market and regulated capitalism placed him in the conservative wing of the CDU—a wing that is sometimes viewed as the liberal and Protestant wing, in contrast to the more interventionist and Catholic one. The truth is more complicated. Höffner actually had significant policy differences with Ludwig Erhard and the largely Protestant forms of liberalism that found increasing sway inside the CDU. He was not a liberal economist in priestly garb but rather a committed social Catholic whose particular form of Catholic political economy was typical of Christian Democrats in the long 1950s.

Höffner had studied with the Ordo-liberal economist Walter Eucken in the 1930s, and he remained convinced throughout his career that some kind of regulated and reformed market was the proper pathway to social justice. His fundamental approach to postwar issues was signaled by the publication of his dissertation, "Christianity and Human Dignity" (1947), a positive account of the Spanish imperial project in the Americas and the economic consequences it had for the New World. Just as he was putting the final touches on the manuscript, his friend Oswald von Nell-Breuning wrote to him and suggested that he turn his attention toward contemporary issues. This might explain the passages in which Höffner expresses a clear hope that the American intervention in Europe would be just as beneficial. He praised the Spanish scholastics, somewhat strangely, for refusing to place "the burden of collective guilt" on the conquered Americans and for recognizing that it was their duty to avoid "plunder" by helping the conquered peoples to build up their own economies.[49]

While some German Catholics bristled at American influence, Höffner signaled his hope that the West German economy would flourish in a new-found Atlantic community. It did, and in the decades after the publication of his dissertation, his star rose precipitously. He published essays in mass-circulation newspapers on topics such as "Scholasticism and Market Economics," explaining why the Church fathers would have been convinced liberals.[50] Höffner was omnipresent in the Catholic public sphere, helping to cement the new commonsense doctrine that Catholic social thought and the social market economy were perfectly compatible. Conference after conference was held on the similarities between Catholic and liberal economic teachings, culminating perhaps in a 1963 conclave of Jesuit social theorists and secular economists in Augsburg. Although they maintained their reservations about one another, they agreed that the "social market" settlement was exemplary for both spiritual and secular reasons.[51]

Höffner's ideas mattered because CDU leaders wanted an economic theory that would build on the Catholic tradition and mobilize the Catholic electorate. This is apparent, for instance, in the internal records of the Federal Committee for Social Policy (Bundesausschuss für Sozialpolitik), the organ of the CDU tasked with social policy debates. While not officially a Catholic body, the Catholic tradition deeply inflected its meetings. Icons of Catholic labor such as Jakob Kaiser, Johannes Albers, and Anton Storch had seats on the Federal Committee, which held its first meeting in Königswinter, the symbolic home of Catholic political economy.[52] Heinrich Lünendonk, the Catholic chairman of the Federal Committee, declared at its opening meeting that the committee should avoid the twin shoals of "individualism" and "collectivism" to arrive at the healthy middle: "solidarism" (the word used by Heinrich Pesch decades earlier). He was clear, as were CDU leaders by 1950, that solidarism had little in common with socialism, either of the German or the English variety. Following a study trip to England in 1953, Lünendonk reported to the committee that the English system was too centralized and therefore "not appropriate for export" (moreover, he scoffed that it was paid for by the Americans). The next year, the committee's report on health insurance criticized England's National Health Service, and its German socialist supporters, because it "violated the principle of subsidiarity" (like solidarism, subsidiarity was a term with a long Catholic history).[53]

These meeting records show how willing the CDU was to link economic and spiritual questions. It was thus no surprise to find a priest involved with public life in all sorts of ways. Höffner was personally close with Konrad Adenauer, largely because he was serving as an academic adviser to Adenauer's son, Paul. This led him to serve on multiple government committees (work, family, and housing). He was also asked, via Paul, to gather a group of social theorists to put together a definitive statement of Christian Democratic ideology in 1954. The resulting text, authored by Höffner and three others, appeared in 1955 under the rousing title *Reform of Social Services*.[54] Höffner was renowned as an expert on social policy, and major figures such as Michael Keller, bishop of Münster, regularly wrote to him for advice.[55] Höffner founded the Institute of Christian Social Sciences, colloquially known as the "Höffner Institute," which published a journal and a series of monographs. He served as theological adviser to the *Rheinischer Merkur,* one of the largest-circulation newspapers in Germany and a staunch supporter of Christian Democracy.[56] He was also one of the founding members and directors of the Union of Catholic Employers (BKU), an employers' association that doubled as a social Catholic think tank throughout the long 1950s. Its leadership overlapped with that of *Die Waage* (*The Scales*), a massive public-relations effort designed to educate German voters about the benefits of the social market economy (its chairman, Franz Greiß, was a Catholic businessman based in Cologne and a close associate of Höffner's). Höffner's public activism coincided with recognition by the Church itself. He was eventually named archbishop of Cologne, one of the most important posts in the European Church.[57]

Höffner, therefore, was a powerful nexus between Catholic intellectuals and Christian Democratic policymakers, most of whom theorized the consuming family—not the individual worker or the working class—as the presumed agent of economic life. *Die Waage,* for instance, conducted huge advertising campaigns aimed separately at men and women: the men's advertisements emphasized wage security, while those for women celebrated consumption for the home and the children.[58] Höffner was friendly with Würmeling, the polarizing and ostentatiously Catholic family minister, and wrote privately to express support for his campaigns against "smut."[59] His *Christian Social Teachings* (1962), which became a standard text, rehearsed Prigent's views on marriage and family. His account of the marriage emphasized love and properly regulated sexuality *before* emphasizing its contractual nature. His account of the family, in turn, emphasized it as the eternal, central site of social order and moral education while also explaining how it had transitioned from a locus of production to one of consumption.[60]

Höffner further explored the importance of the consuming family in his political writings. In 1953, he published a pamphlet on family allowances for the Central Committee of German Catholics (ZdK), the nation's most important lay Catholic organization. Most modern families, he argued, have between zero and two children, and thus have extra money to chase a better life through consumption. Families with three or more children, however, are unable to do so. Families are therefore incentivized to restrict births, leading to a decline in the birthrate (a special concern of Adenauer's). Höffner was at pains to emphasize that this mattered not for nationalist reasons but rather because it hampered the expansion of the German economy as a whole. In other words, like Prigent, his notion of the family evolved from the natalist to the consumerist. As a solution, again like Prigent, he urged family allowances that would allow all families to bask in the glow of the miracle economy.[61] And in *Reform of Social Services,* he oversaw a Christian Democratic text that repeated the same theme, this time in the language of family sociology. The family, not the working class, the pamphlet emphasized, should be at the center of social politics.[62]

As with Prigent, too, Höffner's support for the family was married with a crusading anti-Communism. If in Prigent's case it manifested primarily as an opposition to universalist social insurance, for Höffner and other economists it manifested primarily as an opposition to the nationalization of industry. Many socialists and even Catholics had supported the state takeover of heavy industry and banking in the mid-1940s. Largely thanks to Christian Democratic influence, the pace of nationalizations slowed considerably in the 1950s. Catholic economists such as François Perroux and Johannes Messner traveled to England, primarily in order to report to Catholics back home how disastrous the centralizing policies of the Labour Party were. Nationalization, Höffner told an audience of Catholic employers in 1949, was the "Bolshevik solution" to economic organization. In the British occupation zone, Adenauer's CDU, with Höffner's public support, mobilized against the SPD and the British alike to ensure that coal and gas would not be nationalized.[63] Christian Democrats across Europe did the same. After a brief period of supporting the process in the mid-1940s, they tended to turn on the principle by remobilizing the old Catholic suspicion of state control of the economy. Pope Pius XII himself wrote a letter for the Social Week in 1946, declaring that "the nationalization of industry" was dangerous, tending toward "totalitarian" state control that would violate the "Christian doctrine of the person."[64] Charles Blondel, François Perroux, and Jacques Leclercq, three of the premier French-language social Catholics in the world, expressed concern at the pace of nationalizations, too. As Francisque Gay, an MRP leader, recalled in his memoirs, "The role of the MRP, faced with its Socialist and Communist associates, was often to prevent the extension of nationalizations."[65] In Austria, too, Christian Democratic politicians made a strong case against nationalizations.[66]

For Höffner and others, the social market economy, and specifically the commitment to codetermination, emerged as the Christian Democratic alternative to nationalizations. Social Catholics had long argued that worker participation in the management of the firm was an estimable way to ensure a family wage and the dignity of the worker without recourse to class conflict. The novelty of the Christian Democratic approach was that it empowered free trade unions as the proper negotiating partners—not the state-sponsored syndicates beloved by 1930s corporatists, or the Catholic workers' clubs cherished by nineteenth-century social Catholics.

This allowed Catholics to find ideological common cause with socialists. Codetermination had a long history in socialist thought, too, and it was being mobilized in the 1950s by those who were uncomfortable with the bureaucracy of the command economy and sought novel ways to empower the proletariat.[67] This newfound space for Catholic-socialist dialogue had transnational resonance. The German Trade Union Confederation (DGB) hosted a series of "European Conversations" in the early 1950s, in which the burgeoning Catholic-socialist consensus along these lines can be observed. The "conversations" were just that: lengthy, unscripted conversations between journalists and labor leaders from seven different nations who discussed codetermination as a response to the problems of managerialism, bureaucracy, and alienation (about one-quarter of the participants were Catholic).[68]

In the Christian Democratic era, this form of codetermination became central to Catholic social ethics and Christian Democratic politics alike. "The enterprise," one French priest approvingly noted, "is becoming, or becoming once again, an affair of the state with a social function." This was largely thanks to the Catholics, since the MRP controlled the Ministry of Labor for nine of the Fourth Republic's twelve years of existence. Labor Minister Paul Bacon, who had roots in the Catholic activism of the 1930s and the Resistance, helped make "workers' committees" the linchpin of the party's economic plan. A pamphlet called *The Reform of the Capitalist Enterprise* argued that the "dignity" and "personality of man" are endangered by current enterprises insofar as the worker is guaranteed no share in management or ownership. "The nationalized factory" was no better, making the worker into a slave of the state. The only solution, Bacon suggested, was to *reform* and not *abolish* the capitalist enterprise through legislation designed to create workers' committees at the heart of the workplace.[69]

The West German debates over codetermination, and Höffner's role in them, show us in granular detail how Christian Democratic economic policy emerged in a complex space of contestation and, ultimately, compromise between different wings of the Church. It was not a debate over codetermination as a general principle, which was accepted as a given even by liberal Catholics such as Höffner. "If the firm is to be a social entity," he wrote in 1949, "the worker must assume joint responsibility and codetermination."[70] The question, instead, was when codetermination was appropriate, and how far it should be extended. At the narrowest level, it could mean an unenforceable commitment by managers to consult workers about certain issues. At its broadest, it could mean that trade union representatives would have an indisputable right to a large role in decisions that affected the entire economy, and that the state would use the tools of law to ensure that workers were represented in individual firms, too.

In West Germany, the debate over codetermination was heated. The SPD, the DGB, and their Catholic allies—within the union federation itself and in the CDU—sought a far-reaching form of codetermination, arguing that workers should have the same amount of power over firm-level decisions as shareholders (parity codetermination), as well as a say in economic decisions at the industrial and national levels.[71] The gauntlet was thrown at the 1949 Catholic Congress (Katholikentag) in Bochum. The delegates passed a resolution declaring that "codetermination for all workers in social, personnel, and economic questions is a natural right in the divinely ordained social order" and therefore that "it should be anchored in law." While natural rights were being declared with abandon across the Atlantic world, this declaration was different. An august assembly of German Catholics had declared a specific, and controversial, economic policy to be a natural right on par with the divine right to property itself. Moreover, the Bochum resolution defended a particular *form* of codetermination, listing in detail the arenas in which workers' engagement was naturally mandated.[72] Catholic leaders in the Workers' Movement (KAB) and in the DGB were thrilled by Bochum, pointing as it did toward a dawning ideological consensus. At the founding congress of the DGB, a socialist dignitary proudly read the Bochum resolution alongside kindred quotations from papal social teachings.[73]

What made the Bochum resolution explosive was that it represented a reiteration of fraternal modernist principles. The resolution rejected the cardinal principle of paternal Catholic modernism: according to Bochum, the firm, like the family, was to be governed by the principles of natural law. In other words, the family was *not* the only institution about which the Church could make dogmatic claims. It should not surprise us, therefore, that Walter Dirks, perhaps Germany's most prolific fraternal modernist, emerged as a champion of codetermination. The policy, in his view, was an integral part of "the democratic movement," and he mocked anyone who thought that "democracy" was primarily about parliamentary government. Democracy, he believed, was about the increasing assertion and responsibility of the masses. While "codetermination in this or that smelting plant in the Ruhr" might seem like "a feeble thing," it was in fact an important step in reforming West German political economy in the name of Catholic ethics.[74]

The response to Bochum was ferocious despite, or because of, the fact that the declaration was firmly within the bounds of the social Catholic tradition (or at least one plausible reading of it). For another strand of German social Catholicism, the resolution was a travesty, since it seemed to leverage the tradition's commitment to class collaboration in a way that empowered trade unions beyond all reason. Internal documents from 1949–1950 show that party leaders in the CDU saw codetermination as a way to diminish the power of the trade unions, tempering their demands and keeping them at a suitable distance from the levers of power in individual firms and in the economy as a whole. Shortly before Bochum, at an international congress of Christian Democratic leaders, Adenauer himself had groused about the danger of massive trade unions, citing Britain's experience as a warning.[75]

Höffner personally led a campaign against Bochum in the Catholic public sphere and inside the Christian Democratic Party. He had actually spoken at the 1949 congress, giving an address on "Property from the Christian Perspective," and he complained that the final declaration had not taken his own address into account. Had they done so, they could not have viewed codetermination as a natural right: "Christian social teaching," he had declared in his own address, "unanimously" supports "the order of private property" against planned economies and collective property. This included the right of owners to control and dispose of that property as they saw fit.[76] And yet Höffner was ignored at Bochum, and the BKU's leadership, including the leader of *Die Waage*, feverishly corresponded about what they might do about it.[77] Höffner wrote long articles in *Rheinischer Merkur* in which he patiently quoted chapter and verse of papal dogma to explain why heavy industry should be neither nationalized nor controlled by workers, and he published a set of "theses on codetermination" that, he hoped, would quell the controversy. In them, he reiterated his belief that the long Catholic commitment to private property militated against any "natural right" to codetermination as theorized at Bochum. He also trundled out the old Catholic theory of accidentalism, according to which the Church is agnostic about the proper political form, to argue that the Church is *equally* agnostic when it comes to "the constitution of the firm."[78]

Höffner's view held sway in much of the Catholic public sphere and within the CDU. The economic committee of the party, dominated by Protestant liberals skeptical of codetermination, circulated a like-minded statement from the BKU, probably authored by Höffner. Pope Pius XII weighed in here as well, just as he had in a similar situation in France. In June 1950, he delivered a speech declaring explicitly that codetermination, unlike the right to private property, could not be grounded in natural law.[79] Gustav Gundlach, who had become Pope Pius XII's right-hand man on these issues, wrote newspaper articles explaining that the pope had indeed struck down Bochum.[80]

In the end, a number of bills were passed that struck a compromise between warring party factions, brokered against the backdrop of labor militancy, the threat of a general strike, and Adenauer's need for the SPD to support his foreign policy. The first, passed in 1951, protected parity codetermination in the iron, coal, and steel industries. The second, the Works Constitution Act of 1952, refused to extend this system to the rest of the economy, merely granting workers one-third of seats on supervisory boards of joint-stock companies with over five hundred employees. As a whole, Catholic thinkers, politicians, and institutions supported the new legislation as a compromise solution that protected the dignity of workers while respecting the sacred rights of private property. Both esteemed labor leader Jakob Kaiser and Höffner supported the compromise settlement. The KAB and many social Catholics welcomed it, too, fearing that the DGB's plan would grant too much power to unwieldy and potentially socialist labor unions.[81]

The results, however, were a mixed bag for labor, as were codetermination policies elsewhere in Christian Democratic Europe. They never went as far as socialists or progressive Catholics like Dirks wanted, and the DGB howled in protest. Taken together, the bills were a moderate concession to the labor movement and clearly indicated that the recent hopes for an anticapitalist reorganization of the economy would come to little. In Austria, Christian Democrats helped pass the work council act (Betriebsrätegesetz) into law while ensuring that the power of workers on those councils would be limited (they ensured, for instance, that it would not apply to agricultural labor and that the councils had no right to approve new hires). In France, the "workers' committees" of MRP policymaking turned out, like their Vichy predecessors, to have little impact on actual economic practice.[82]

Nonetheless, the Christian Democratic support for codetermination was genuine, and it demonstrates that the parties had not abandoned the long-standing Catholic commitment to power sharing. Höffner, that is, shored up the right wing of a Christian Democratic consensus that, as a whole, was committed to quite robust sorts of rights for workers. However "liberal" Höffner's brand of Catholic modernism might seem in comparison to the more radical voices of Bochum, the Catholicity of his vision can be seen in another venue, which has received less attention: his conflicts with Protestant Ordo-liberals such as Ludwig Erhard. Erhard was a growing force in the CDU in the long 1950s, and he had minimal interest in the niceties of the social Catholic tradition. His *Prosperity for All* (1957) was in some ways a successor to Höffner's own *Reform of Social Services* (1955). There was a key difference, however: Erhard's text only referenced the social traditions of Christianity in superficial ways.[83] And while the future of the party might have belonged with Erhard, his day had not yet come.

In the key debates of the 1950s, Höffner and other social Catholics, even the more liberal among them, clashed with Erhard. In the early 1950s, Höffner supported codetermination more than Erhard did. And in the most important debate of the later 1950s, Höffner and his allies entered into conflict with Erhard yet again—and again, Höffner's vision won. That debate concerned pension reform. For some years, the SPD had been calling for a British-style, universalist pension that would provide full income replacement and be funded from general tax revenues. Adenauer and others were worried that a pension reform along these lines would bankrupt the state, push it further down the road to serfdom, or both. The debate transformed when Adenauer's son, who was studying with Höffner at the time, alerted his father to the pension reform scheme defended by Wilfrid Schreiber, a close friend of Höffner's and a fellow leader of the BKU. A former National Socialist, Schreiber, like Höffner, had learned at the feet of an Ordo-liberal economist (Erwin von Beckerath in Schreiber's case) before beginning his climb through the institutions. In 1955, under the auspices of the BKU, he published a pamphlet called *Security of Existence in Industrial Society.* This text contained the ideas that he would present to the Ministerial Committee for Social Reform and, privately, to Adenauer himself.[84]

With some adjustments, and with the help of Höffner and the BKU, a version of Schreiber's reform was passed into law as the pension reform of 1957—against the wishes of Erhard, who thought (wrongly) that it would be a spur to inflation. Schreiber, like Höffner, spoke often about the necessary synthesis of Catholicism and liberalism. His ideas for pension reform, he believed, were "defined not only by the clear teachings of our Church, but also by our own well-understood interests." And yet that synthesis, as in the case of Höffner, left much of the social Catholic tradition intact, and the pension scheme, which emerged in a Catholic context, retained many Catholic features. Previous social insurance schemes had been based on individual compulsory savings. Workers made contracts essentially with their aged selves through the mediation of the state. There were multiple problems with this from Schreiber's perspective. For one thing, it violated the principle of subsidiarity by involving the state far too much, harming the "human dignity" and "courage to become a person" by casting the worker as a dependent on the all-providing state. For another, it violated the kindred principle of solidarity by denying the benefits of economic growth to retirees. Schreiber squared the circle by suggesting a "pay-as-you-go" system, in which the current generation of workers would fund the new generation of retirees directly, in a "contract of solidarity" between generations. Schreiber was wholly uninterested in the problems of poverty or gender equity. The current system, he insisted, was a well-oiled machine, and any residual poverty would work itself out over time. The only real issue concerned the inequality between life stages, not that between classes. Meanwhile, the system significantly disadvantaged women and served to rivet them to their husbands (who had likely been employed for longer and at higher wages, and thus earned a much greater pension).[85]

The Christian Democratic approach to the economy, like its approach to the family, found an echo in the dogmatic evolution of the Church in the 1960s. Höffner, Schreiber, and the BKU seem to have been enthused about *Mater et magistra* (1961), Pope John XXIII's social encyclical. It is not hard to see why, as the text mirrored Höffner's own views rather well. It did not criticize capitalism, holding instead that "social progress," properly regulated, would heal inequalities and raise the standard of living for all. The text was clearly anti-Communist, reprising the importance of private property in securing social health and particularly the health of the family. It celebrated personal initiative and even reminded that the worker is in the end "responsible for his own upkeep and that of his family." At the same time, *Mater* suggested that workers should have some sort of say in the management of the firm and should also have representation at the commanding heights of the economy. This much Höffner could agree to, so long as the precise nature of that collaboration was not granted the status of natural law—which it was not. In fact, in other passages *Mater* was equally supportive of the rights of employers to dispose of their firms as they saw fit, both because "unity of direction" aided economic efficiency and because their own property rights were clearly protected by natural law.[86]

In the global spaces of the Church, as in the domestic space of West Germany, codetermination was capable of narrower and broader interpretations. Höffner and *Mater et magistra* were committed to the former. A few years later, though, the Church released *Gaudium et spes* (1965), a pastoral constitution that emerged from Vatican II and dealt directly with the economy. Höffner was directly involved with the crafting of the text, but not as closely as he might have liked. The leaders of the BKU somehow got hold of a confidential draft and wrote to Höffner to express their concern. They asked him to criticize the economic portions of the text, which he did—to no avail.[87] It is easy to see why they were worried. *Gaudium et spes* did not go quite so far as Bochum, and it did not declare that codetermination was a "natural right." Such a claim was outside the bounds of Christian Democratic modernism. It did, though, go further than *Mater et magistra*. "The active sharing of all in the administration and profits" of enterprises, the text announces, "is to be promoted." While decreeing that workers should be involved at the "higher level" of the industry or the state, the text said little about the specific rights of employers. *Gaudium et spes*, therefore, gives voices to the more progressive wing of Christian Democratic modernism. It was, after all, largely written by French Jesuit Pierre Haubtmann, who was less interested in Ordo-liberalism than he was in *nouvelle théologie* (his scholarly work was largely concerned with recuperating the anarchist Pierre-Joseph Proudhon, certainly not a project that engaged Höffner).[88]

As these texts show, and as the West German debate shows, Christian Democratic modernists were not free market liberals in disguise. Catholics pursued economic reforms that were rooted in their own traditions, sometimes against the wishes of the more liberal members of the Christian Democratic coalition. And as with family welfare, Christian Democratic economic doctrine had an impact. Germany, especially, is still noted for its worker participation policies, which long remained a Christian Democratic commitment (Norbert Blüm, minister of labor from 1982 to 1998, was introduced to Christian Democracy in Höffner's era and was specifically a devotee of the person and thought of Oswald von Nell-Breuning). And yet Christian Democratic modernists tended not to question the fundamental power structure of postwar societies. When Catholics, as at Bochum, urged something more radical they were ignored, as the Christian Democratic consensus only extended so far. While aware of the remaining injustices of postwar capitalism, Christian Democrats did not believe that they required fundamental political or even economic transformations to solve them. Instead, as Schreiber's pamphlet argued, they simply needed time.

The Turn to Development

As with capitalism, Catholics had long been suspicious of the centralized, modern state (indeed, past generations of Catholic thinkers had viewed the two as twins). This impulse had largely vanished during the 1930s, as Catholics flocked to the centralizing state as the institution with the power and authority to combat Communism, and to combat the Depression. What, though, was the state meant to do? In the 1930s, mainstream Catholics had called on strong states, and often authoritarian ones, to stave off Communism and "Defend the West," by military means if necessary. In the long 1950s, this grim imaginary melted away. The consuming family did not need chest-thumping militarism in states that were reasonably stable and gathered into NATO. What the consuming family needed, above all, was income—income to purchase a home and all of the other commodities that constituted the new image of the good life. The state's new task, therefore, was economic development.

In the long 1950s, and with Christian Democrats leading the way, economic growth became a key litmus test of political legitimacy. The dogma of growth was a novelty in Catholic circles. Previous forms of Catholic political economy had been concerned to increase social justice by reshuffling power relations, not by expanding the size of the pie. It was, though, almost a necessary corollary to the evolved economic doctrine that we saw in Höffner. For if Catholics were no longer clamoring to use state power to restore departed economic hierarchies, or alternatively to empower trade unions to seize justice for themselves, what options were left to ameliorate persistent social inequalities? Properly managed growth emerged as the best solution, and one that seemed especially plausible given the fact of extraordinary economic dynamism in the long 1950s.

The turn to development required a near-truce in the long-standing battle between Catholics and socialists for control over public space (the state could not primarily focus on development if it was primarily focused on protecting the public sphere from atheist socialists). Socialist parties across Europe were abandoning their age-old anticlericalism in the name of more ecumenical and less dogmatic approaches. While this process is widely lauded or derided, depending on one's convictions, it is often forgotten that Catholics were making compromises of their own.

In two major ways, Christian Democratic modernists abandoned the more provocative elements of past Catholic politics, both of which had been central as recently as the late 1940s. In both cases, they came closer to positions long espoused by Jacques Maritain and other Catholic antifascists. First, they almost wholly abandoned the anti-Semitism that had long been central to Catholic politics. This happened quietly, and Christian Democrats were seldom apostles of antiracism. Nonetheless, the standard invective against Jews as agents of Bolshevism slipped away (even as other segments of the European right wing remained as anti-Semitic as ever).[89] Second, Christian Democratic parties increasingly abandoned the rhetoric of "the West" that had legitimated so many worrisome compromises in the 1930s and during the war. Catholic reactionaries, notably in the Bavarian Christian Social Union (CSU) or in Algeria itself, did continue to champion the West, but when they did, scandal often resulted, as when Georges Bidault gave a grandstanding address about the cross of Christianity overcoming the crescent of Islam. Even in Germany, where ideas of Western retrenchment were central around 1950, the discourse had almost entirely disappeared by 1960. The periodical called the *New West* ceased publication in 1958, and Adenauer judged that the CDU should stop talking about the West, too. It did not help that East Germans had begun to have a field day with the most reactionary Defenders of the West, publicizing their work as part of a critique of the "clerical-imperialist ideology of the West."[90]

In this newly pacified climate, even the long-standing dispute over confessional education began to subside. This happened for many reasons, but at least one of them was that Catholics were able to argue with some success that, as one French Christian Democrat put it, state control of education was the "first measure of any totalitarian regime"—and, therefore, that antifascist reconstruction required educational pluralism. In Germany, this issue was hotly debated in the late 1940s and early 1950s, as socialists sought to dismantle confessional schools and Catholics countered, with some justification, that they were reprising the anticlericalism of the Nazis (in Lower Saxony, the SPD official in charge of shuttering Catholic schools had done just the same in the Nazi era). From the mid-1950s onward, however, temperatures cooled as the Constitutional Court released an ambiguous ruling on the issue and the Vatican concluded a concordat with Lower Saxony, the heavily Protestant region that had caused the trouble in the first place. In Austria, confessional education continued despite the wishes of the Americans, who sought to export their own secular model of education, thanks largely to Felix Hurdes, the Catholic minister of education in the late 1940s. Even in France, the homeland of secularism, the Marie Law and the Barangé Law ensured state funding of confessional schools for the first time in recent history.[91]

As had happened with the antifascist account of the family, these previously dissident ideas about Catholic politics were mobilized in the name of economic growth and consumption—not of antifascist revolution. In Christian Democratic circles, this shift took place as party leadership transitioned from the sturdy, if stodgy, leaders with roots in older Catholic politics to efficient and somewhat colorless technocrats (in France, Pierre Pflimlin; in Germany, Protestant Ludwig Erhard; in Austria, Julius Raab). These leaders marked a new stage in European conservatism. Conservative leaders had traditionally come from the military, or at least had skill in populist rhetoric used to conjure a mythologized vision of the country. The conservatives of the 1950s offered nothing of the sort. Europe, they proclaimed, is open for business.

The Catholic turn to development was widespread. In postwar Europe, economic growth was not only a fact of life but one that took on a great deal of meaning. Economic growth itself was not new, but the meaning attached to it was. There was now a culture of growth, expectation of continued growth, and a linkage between growth and political legitimacy (economic historian Michael Postan suggests using "growthmanship" over "statesmanship" to discuss this period).[92] At the Organization for European Economic Cooperation (OEEC) and the Organization for Economic Cooperation and Development (OECD), economic growth came to supplant and displace questions of economic equality and justice.[93] Meanwhile, in the Third World, the familiar Western language of the "civilizing mission" gave way to a new discourse of economic and agrarian "development" as imperial hegemony came under strain. Catholics, it turns out, were central agents of this transition, and as the French imperial mission collapsed, they traveled the world, spreading the gospel of development as they understood it. François Perroux and Father Louis-Joseph Lebret, two Catholic social scientists, emerged as central figures in the new discipline of development economics.[94]

The new economic dogma appears, at first glance, like an abandonment of social Catholic teachings altogether. After all, the classic social encyclicals *Rerum novarum* and *Quadragesimo anno* only mentioned economic expansion in order to point out how dangerous it was. Catholic political and economic thinkers had traditionally been concerned with reconstructing dissolved hierarchies, not with celebrating breakneck transformation. This is too simple an explanation, however, and takes for granted the mantra that there is something apolitical or nonideological about growthmanship. While Christian Democratic parties would eventually become more secular and distance themselves from Church teachings, this was more a phenomenon of the 1960s than of the 1950s, when they first latched onto development. In that central decade, Christian Democratic parties championed a particularly Catholic form of development: an anti-Communist, and pro-family, conceptualization of economic growth.

The Austrian case is most interesting, because Austrian Catholics had long been the most furiously anticapitalist in Europe, and the most nostalgic for Catholic empire. How did it happen here that Catholic intellectuals came to accept development as the central goal of the secular state? Wolfgang Schmitz (1923–2008), who belonged to the first ranks of social Catholic royalty, was one of the loudest champions of economic development in Austria, and an exploration of his career, writings, and choices helps us to understand why.[95] His father, Hans Schmitz, had been a leader in the unified trade union under the Catholic dictator Engelbert Dollfuss in the 1930s; had shared a stage with Mina Wolfring, a Mussolini-celebrating welfare activist, at the first conference of the "Family Protection" League; and had published a pamphlet defending the authoritarian interpretation of *Quadragesimo anno*.[96] His uncle, Richard Schmitz, was a prominent social

Catholic intellectual who had served Austrian chancellor (and priest) Ignaz Seipel in the 1920s before emerging as mayor of Vienna under Dollfuss and writing books in praise of authoritarian corporatism. Johannes Messner, the priest and corporatist economist, was a family friend, and Schmitz met both Dollfuss and Schuschnigg as a young man.

Just as his uncle had visited and learned from Weimar Catholics, Wolfgang Schmitz watched and learned from the rise of the Catholic-liberal consensus in West Germany (the stories were connected: for instance, Schmitz contributed an article to a volume dedicated to Johannes Messner that was edited by Joseph Höffner). Schmitz studied with Theodor Pütz, one of the pioneering liberal thinkers in Austria. Trained in Germany, Pütz belonged to the new Ordo-liberal tradition that was so thrilling to Höffner and other Catholics on the lookout for anti-Communist allies. Pütz, like other Ordo-liberals, believed that the market mechanism was not self-sustaining and required a social commitment to ethical or religious norms that could undergird and sustain a market-based economy.[97] Schmitz also imbibed the German tradition in America. After receiving a Fulbright Scholarship to study in Washington, D.C., in 1950, he fell under the spell of Goetz Briefs, a pioneering German Catholic economist then teaching at Georgetown. Briefs had been one of the few Catholic thinkers in the 1920s to argue that increasing productivity, not the reconstruction of Catholic institutions, was the pathway to social justice. This view found increasing acceptance after the war, and Briefs labored to find common ground between Catholic social teachings and the market economy.[98]

Back in Austria, Schmitz found his first intellectual home with the Institute for Social Policy and Reform, a novel sort of Christian Democratic think tank that popularized developmentalist forms of social Catholic teachings (it was allied with the Austrian Workers and Employees Federation [ÖAAB], the workingman's wing of Austria's Christian Democratic Party, the ÖVP). Under the leadership of August Maria Knoll and Karl Kummer, the institute tried to find common ground between capitalist expansion and Catholic social teachings. Like Schmitz, both Knoll and Kummer were rooted squarely in Austria's long tradition of social Catholic thinking. Knoll had even been a member of Ernst Karl Winter's "Austrian Action" back in the 1920s. Both had been supporters of authoritarian corporatism in the 1930s before taking a liberal turn after the war. Kummer, whose dissertation was written in Nazi Germany and was surprisingly fascist in orientation, wrote the earliest and most important of the party's social programs and mentored a generation of ÖVP leaders (one of them, future minister of commerce Josef Taus, called Kummer "the one true social politician the ÖVP had").[99] Knoll, for his part, injected a new spirit into Austrian Catholic thinking with his 1953 volume *The Problem of Capitalism in Modern Sociology*, which appeared in a series that Knoll co-edited with Alfred Müller-Armack, a German Ordo-liberal. In it, Knoll turned on the Austrian social Catholic tradition, arguing that its nostalgic antimodernism had led to the failed experiment of the corporatist state. Capitalism, Knoll insisted, was acceptable to the Catholic conscience.[100]

The mantra throughout these writings was that capitalism had evolved, and specifically in ways that were supportive to the family. Schmitz focused on this in his own contribution to the institute's series, and one of his first major writings. Schmitz tackled the same topic as Höffner, and the one that most fully demonstrated the congeniality of modern economies to healthy families: family allowances. The family, he insisted, is "the most important starting point for the overcoming of the errors" of individualism and collectivism, and family allowances provided the best measures for "the strengthening of the autonomy of the family." His discussion of the measures also indicated how deeply integrated he was in transnational networks of Catholic social thinking. He drew explicitly on the family volume that Robert Prigent had recently published, while, like Höffner, he drew on non-Catholic family sociologists such as Helmut Schelsky. Like theirs, too, Schmitz's work on family allowances had an impact (one observer claimed that Schmitz's writings influenced the system that the ÖVP put into place).[101]

Schmitz's family pedigree, combined with his social-scientific expertise, made him perfectly placed to ascend the heights of power. He soon joined Austria's much-heralded Joint Committee on Wages and Prices, a corporatist institution founded in 1957 that sought to solve economic questions in an ideology-free manner. The committee was the symbol of the Austrian economic recovery, promising to move past worldview conflict and toward managed growth as a common denominator for Christian Democrats and socialists alike. This required an evolution in the ÖVP, to be sure. In the late 1940s, the party had been ostentatiously Catholic, reviving personnel from the interwar years and promising to place Catholic teachings of "solidarism" at the heart of the new Austria. In 1953, though, leadership passed from Leopold Figl, a Catholic whose progressivism had been forged in the concentration camps, to Julius Raab, a hardheaded liberal who distrusted the ÖAAB and tried to form a coalition with a neo-Nazi party. While that failed, Raab did bring in an amnestied Nazi named Reinhard Kamitz, despite ÖAAB objections, to serve as his finance minister. Together, they oversaw the "Raab-Kamitz course," which emphasized lower taxes, market-based competition, and the fight against inflation.[102] By this time, the crusading Catholic identity of the early party had melted away. "Solidarism, the slogan of 1945, has been slowly devalued," one Austrian observer noted in 1959.[103]

By the mid-1950s, the notion of the West as a Roman and Christian legal space, which had been so prominent in Catholic circles for about twenty years, faded away and was replaced by the new doctrine of development. Schmitz was no culture warrior, and he had no interest in Austria as a bastion of Western civilization against barbarian hordes. This is apparent in his writings on federalism, which were more interested in free trade and economic efficiency than cultural ramparts.[104] Meanwhile, in 1957 the Austrian bishops released a new pastoral letter on social issues. While its 1926 predecessor had inveighed against capitalism as such, the new one was careful to restrict its opprobrium to "liberal capitalism," while praising the "welfare state" and the "social partnership" model of the Christian Democrats (in the official commentary, Bishop Paulus Rusch went even further, praising the "socially tempered capitalism" of the present and emphasizing the need to "improve the productivity of the economy").[105] Internationally, too, Christian Democrats turned toward development rather than Western civilization as the benchmark of political wisdom. The NEI began orienting itself toward Africa and Latin America for the first time, choosing the rubric of "development" and committing itself to a particularly Christian Democratic version of the concept (in 1960, an international Christian Democratic conference on development took place in Germany, the first of its kind).[106]

The evolution of Catholic political thought toward a developmentalist framework can be seen especially clearly in the 1958 platform of the ÖVP, entitled simply "What We Want." The very title promised a program for an age of desire and satiation through consumption, while there was no mention of solidarism, which had been a central plank of the 1949 platform. Politics, the manifesto insisted, is concerned above all with the individual person and his or her "freedom." The first account in the platform of the *nature* of that politics is this one: "Politics, therefore, attends to the increase and proper distribution of goods." The traditional emphasis on "our

Christian-Western culture" was present but only mentioned briefly (and only one time) before a quick pivot to the more important value of "religious freedom." Moreover, the section on European integration focused above all on the economy. There was no mention of Europe as a bastion of "the West" or as a fortress of Roman virtue against American materialism. "Europe," the platform indicated, "will be our economic future" and contribute to "an increase in the standard of living."[107]

Christian Democratic parties across the continent were engaged in similar transitions. The centrality of the "miracle economy" to political legitimacy in West Germany is well known.[108] In France, too, the anticapitalist elements of the social Catholic tradition were displaced by new paeans to growth. François Perroux, in the immediate wake of the war, was arguing that capitalism could very well "turn good" and provide the path to "prosperity" and "dignity" while complaining that the French obsession with "party politics and ideological imperatives" was impeding an understanding of the autonomous laws of the economy. He found agreement from François de Menthon, a crucial MRP leader who reached the same conclusion (largely due to the influence of the Protestant liberal René Courtin). Even Gustave Thibon, a pathbreaking Catholic philosopher, was observing that "the area of maximum material prosperity and the area of maximum spiritual development coincide exactly." By 1954, Maurice Byé, the economic guru of the MRP, could give a lecture at the party congress that put "economic expansion" *before* "the liberation of the human person" as the linchpin of the party's economic policy. Party leadership soon passed from the fiery hands of Georges Bidault to those of Pierre Pflimlin, who revealed his colors in a pamphlet called "Getting Out of a Rut: For a National Politics of Productivity." The essay contained no explicit reference to Catholic social teachings at all, aligning itself instead with the new ethos of development. The same year as Pflimlin's ascendancy, Catholic growthmanship reached a pinnacle at the 1956 Social Week, entitled "The Human Requirements of Economic Expansion." Only "a politics of growth," Charles Flory declared, could respond to the needs of a growing global population.[109]

The turn to development took place in both Christian Democratic and social Catholic circles. Figures such as Schmitz, no less than Höffner and Prigent, were comfortable in both, and there were many overlaps. In clerical circles Schmitz personally found his match in Walter Riener, priest and author of a modernizing social Catholic textbook. He spearheaded Austria's

1958 Catholic Congress, entitled "The Social Responsibility of Christians in Modern Society," a congress that may have been the epitome of Schmitz's style of thought. Schmitz's father set the tone in his opening lecture, celebrating the fact that "the face of capitalism has considerably changed." Riener agreed that the renovation of capitalism and the welfare state had solved many of the burning questions of the past: "This house has been built and delivered to its inhabitants for honest use and conservation" (note the centrality of domestic spaces to this entire understanding of the economy).[110]

Schmitz's own lecture, entitled "Productivity in the Economy as an Ethical Task," was a paean to growth as the pathway to social justice. He began with a stinging critique of the tradition. The Catholic intellectual, he reported, has proven incapable of grappling with the economy, just as it has with the question of technology. He was especially scathing toward the old "social Romantics" who refused to grasp the secular processes of the economy. The Catholic task, Schmitz explained, was to administer the economy in the name of the common good, not to force it to follow anti-quated religious laws or ask it to deliver improbable levels of social equality. Since the economy was primarily to be understood in terms of increasing production, both from an ethical and a scientific point of view, the "ratio-nalization" of industrial production can be viewed as "an ethical obliga-tion," as can the market-based competition that helps to ensure it. He knew that this banal conclusion might disappoint more radical Catholic thinkers, but he was unmoved. "Anyone who expects radical or stirring slogans from Catholic social teaching," he explained, "is bound to be disappointed."[111]

Riener was significant because he oversaw the Church hierarchy's own conversion to development—in a nation whose bishops had demonized capitalism in the 1920s.[112] By now, Austrian Catholic intellectuals had largely dispensed with the old dreams in favor of a new slogan—"Christian Realism"—which was associated in the Catholic press with Riener's academy and was normally linked with relief that the socialist party had reformed into a responsible partner.[113] As was so often the case in Christian Demo-cratic circles, calls for realism and clear sight masked a rather ideological opposition to the universalist social insurance of the British and Nordic model. As Riener explained in his *Social Handbook* (1956), a "welfare state" tasked with improving living standards and providing social security was to be welcomed, but it must not become a "provider-state" that undermines the independence and autonomy of the individual.[114]

Schmitz found his new intellectual home with Riener's academy, and it was largely through Riener's help that he came to the attention of Christian Democratic powerbrokers. In 1960, Schmitz delivered a lecture on the "common good" for a Catholic Action meeting in Salzburg. Drawing on Ordo-liberal economists such as Pütz alongside social Catholic luminaries such as Gustav Gundlach and Johannes Messner, Schmitz outlined a justification for Catholics to participate in the new capitalist economy. Catholic social teaching, Schmitz instructed, has three touchstones: freedom, the common good, and subsidiarity (in that order). From that basis, the good economy can be seen to have four fundamental goals: economic growth, high levels of employment, a stable currency, and some degree of income equality. Schmitz discussed each of these in the language of postwar technocracy, which now had the aureole of Catholic teaching. Riener was thrilled about Schmitz's lecture, and he oversaw its publication as a stand-alone book, which he prefaced himself. That volume, in turn, came to the attention of Josef Klaus, then the governor of Salzburg. When Klaus ascended to the chancellorship in 1964, he remembered Schmitz, picking him to serve as his minister of finance.[115]

Wolfgang Schmitz, like his father and uncle, ascended the heights of Catholic social thinking and Catholic politics. He did it, however, in an entirely new key, in a new age. On its face, he seems to have simply abandoned Catholic social teaching entirely in the name of bland technocracy. He went on, after all, to serve as president of the Austrian National Bank and as a functionary with the IMF—neither of which were especially Catholic institutions. Closer investigation reveals, however, that he remained embedded in Catholic social doctrine, as he understood it, throughout his career: as one Christian Democrat put it in 1958, prosperity was rooted firmly in "the political and economic concepts that the ÖVP formulated on the basis of its Christian program." Schmitz, too, regularly argued, as did Pütz and his other Ordo-liberal teachers, that social politics and economic science require "a firm basis, grounded in a philosophy like that offered by Christian social teachings" and its account of "natural law." He praised Johannes Messner's textbook on natural law, which provided the kind of "meta-economic goals" he saw as necessary to economic thinkers—specifically, he pointed out Messner's depiction of the economy as rooted in the healthy family.[116]

Schmitz might not seem like a political thinker at all, and in some ways he was not. In this, though, he was entirely typical of the Christian

Democratic moment, when Catholics ceased calling on the state to Defend the West or enshrine the Church and instead began calling on it to protect religious liberty and, above all, secure the rights and prosperity of the consuming family. This political ideology, if such it was, found resonance in the evolution of official Church doctrine, too. Most obviously, the Church officially abandoned its call for a confessional state. *Dignitatis humanae* (1965) signaled the Church's final, official commitment to the principle of religious freedom, ratifying a principle taken for granted in much of Catholic Europe. *Nostra aetate* (1965) likewise signaled the end of officially sanctioned anti-Semitism by rejecting the teaching of corporate Jewish responsibility for the death of Christ. Together, these two texts placed a capstone on the Vatican's long-gestating acceptance of modern forms of statehood.

Those texts essentially ratified a consensus that had long been brewing in Catholic circles. The more remarkable novelties can be found in the implicit political theories of the two great social encyclicals of the 1960s: *Mater et magistra* (1961) and *Populorum progressio* (1967) (the texts that Schmitz celebrated as a "Copernican Revolution" in papal dogma).[117] The social encyclicals of the past had said nothing at all about economic development, which was normally viewed as a threat if it was not ignored entirely. The new encyclicals, however, held out the hope that growth, if properly managed and distributed, would heal social injustice. The moral economy, *Mater et magistra* instructed, was one in which "all classes of citizens can participate in the increased productivity" brought about by modern technology, and in which the fruits of development are shared as freely as possible.[118]

In its political dogma as in its economic doctrine, Christian Democratic modernism had room for dissent. Just as the more radical forms of codetermination were expressed in *Gaudium et spes,* the more radical forms of development found voice in *Populorum progressio* (1967). That encyclical, like *Mater et magistra,* conceptualized growth as the pathway to justice. "Development," the encyclical instructs, is "the new name for peace," so therefore "each and every nation must produce more and better goods." And yet more than *Mater* and more than most Christian Democrats, *Populorum* presented a global vision of the economy that was hard to square with organized capitalism. In place of an emphasis on individual initiative, *Populorum* explained that organized, global programs would be necessary to ensure that growth was properly regulated. Specifically, the text revived

Thomist critiques of private property—the same ones rejected by Höffner and Schmitz, as well as the German social experts who had written *Quadragesimo anno*—to claim that nations had a duty to share their own superfluous wealth with poorer nations.[119]

As Schmitz's story and the new encyclicals demonstrate, the Christian Democratic commitment to growthmanship was capable of many interpretations. And yet the apostles of development shared a presumption that the basic structure of the economy was sound—it only needed to continue expanding, and distributing the fruits of that expansion in equitable ways. This led Christian Democrats to shy away from the traditional Catholic concern for a reorientation of the power structure itself. They were loath to question the basic power differential between capital and labor, and in practice they often found themselves asking trade unions to accept smaller wage increases in order to fund investment. While these commitments helped Christian Democrats to oversee a period of stratospheric economic growth, it came at an ideological price: the abandonment of some of the more pluralist and antistatist elements of the tradition. Over the course of the long 1950s, when so many factors were urging Catholics toward compromise, this was seldom mentioned. Those conditions did not, however, hold forever.

The Limits of Christian Democratic Modernism

By crafting a synthetic "Christian" vision of political and social affairs, Christian Democratic parties played a central role in the stabilization of European democracy. If, in the 1920s, Catholics had agitated against modernity, in the 1950s they labored with great success to install their own form of it: one that would combine their version of family values with civil liberties, constitutional government, and managed economic growth. Their achievement can hardly be overstated. After decades of chaotic politics, religious and secular conservatives across Central and Western Europe banded together to create stable polities in which Christian Democrats and socialists worked together to create generous welfare regimes and manage a growing economy in ways that were at least cognizant of social inequality.

For all of its merits, Christian Democratic modernism, like any form of Catholic modernism, abandoned some elements of the tradition and therefore found itself open to legitimate critique from other social Catholics. Some Catholic critics pointed out that the very things that made Christian

Democracy successful—a commitment to stability, compromise, and the family—led to blind spots. Specifically, the commitment to party politics and state action involved a disinterest in the robust civil society organizations long central to Catholic social action. While they may have sought to smooth the rough edges of organized capitalism, Christian Democrats had little interest in fundamental transformation of the system. Economic development, they hoped, would solve problems of inequality—an ideology that occluded many forms of economic justice, a biting critique of consumerism, or a deep concern for the environment. Their focus on the nuclear, heteronormative family led to a neglect of nonnormative families, the rights of women, and kinds of suffering or social dislocation that could not be coded as familial.

In the long 1950s, these points were only made at the margins, or by figures such as Emmanuel Mounier whose intellectual celebrity was matched with increasing irrelevance. "If Christianity is going to be mistaken," he wrote, "it should err in a spirit of grandeur, bravery, defiance, adventure, and passion. What we cannot abide is that it should be confused with social timidity, the spirit of balance, and a faint fear of the people."[120] That, though, is precisely what happened, although it should be read as a creative rearticulation of the tradition and not simply as a confusion. Nonetheless, the Church is never still for long. As the war receded into the past and the global 1960s dawned, the allure of compromise began to fade.

✺ 6 ✺

THE RETURN OF HERESY IN THE
GLOBAL 1960S

Look, I am doing something new, now it emerges; can you
not see it?

—ISAIAH 43:19

The sixties began on Easter Sunday, 1950. At Notre Dame Cathedral, during Easter Mass, four young men clambered to the altar. One of them, dressed as a monk, delivered a sort of antisermon. Channeling Nietzsche, the speaker declared the death of God and implored his listeners to "till this earth anew with your bare hands, with your proud hands, with your un-praying hands." The mass was televised, and the enormous audience at home and in the pews was horrified. The officials at Notre Dame scrambled to restore order. The first blow came from the organist, who tried to drown out the offending sermon, while the next came from the cathedral's guards, who rushed at the young men with actual swords.[1] It was too late: the altar had been desecrated, the spell broken.

The stunt was an event within the history of French Catholicism, not an encounter between the Church and the secular winds of change. The ring-leader, a young man named Michel Mourré, came from a socialist family. After the war, disgusted by French decadence, he converted to Catholicism. "I recited the traditional phrases in Latin myself," he recalled, "in a voice that was choking, stammering and stuttering with emotion." He went on to read the works of Jacques Maritain and Étienne Gilson and spend time in a German monastery. And yet, he fell away. He abandoned the monastery and haunted the streets of Paris, enchanted by Heidegger, existentialism, and the "pretty little men with their powdered cheeks" in Paris's working-class bars. He decided, in the end, that the core of existentialism and Marxism retained an unavowed longing for the divine. God had not yet been truly killed, so on Easter Sunday, 1950, Mourré tried to finish the job.[2]

Mourré can best be understood as a heretic, bending the tools of the faith to new ends. While apostates reject Christ's teachings entirely, heretics accept Christ as savior but selectively adopt and manipulate Church teachings to create something new. His antisermon ended with the proclamation of "the death of the Christ-God so that finally man can live." Is this blasphemy—or is it theology? After all, this does not veer too far from the traditional dogma that the death of Christ led to redemption. Moreover, Mourré's scathing criticisms of the injustice and banality of the Church hearkened just as much to earlier saints as to atheist radicals.

Mourré's heresy pointed toward the new possibilities that would emerge for Catholic intellectuals in the global 1960s. Our image of the turbulent 1960s makes little room for the Church. We imagine free love, bearded revolutionaries, and a rock band that claimed, with some justification, to be bigger than Jesus.[3] Consider the response to Mourré's antisermon. Organs and swords were tools of the Middle Ages, and the innovative use of television did little more than add bandwidth to an institution struggling to make sense of a changing world. And yet even if the official Church and its dignitaries were sometimes caught flat-footed, Catholic students and laity were more agile. They responded creatively to the demands of a new era, forging styles of thought and activism that survive to this day.

In the long 1950s, Catholics had coalesced around a consensus form of Catholic social thought and action: the one incarnated in Christian Democratic parties and in the dogmatic evolution of the Second Vatican Council. In the later 1960s, this consensus fell apart as the material conditions that had nourished it transformed. Most notably, Christian Democratic parties ceased to play the moderating role they once had, as they either vanished or changed in character. In France, Catholics increasingly abandoned the Popular Republican Movement (MRP) in favor of Charles de Gaulle's Rally of the French People, among other parties, while the MRP itself ceased to exist in 1967. In West Germany, Chancellor Konrad Adenauer chastised some of his Catholic supporters for being "too ecclesiastical" and handed the reins of the Christian Democratic Union (CDU) to Ludwig Erhard, his Protestant economics minister, in 1963. Over the course of the 1960s, the party became increasingly less Catholic in orientation, becoming instead more of a secular conservative party (which led many committed Catholics to support the social democrats). Even though Helmut Kohl's parents had been supporters of the Center Party, he essentially abandoned any reference to Catholic social teaching once he took over the chairmanship of the CDU in 1973. By this time, the party had ceased to dominate the political system the way it once had. In Austria, the People's Party followed a similar path, as leaders such as Julius Raab and Josef Klaus, despite roots in interwar Catholicism, pursued centrist, business-friendly policies and had little time for social Catholic rhetoric. While the party held power through the 1960s, it, too, entered the political wilderness in 1970, and it would not defeat the socialists again electorally until 2002.[4]

Just as Catholic intellectuals were tied less closely to Christian Democratic parties, they were less tied to a close-knit Catholic milieu, which also began to unravel in the 1960s. This had been a long time coming, to be sure, as the dislocations and population transfers of war had already diluted the traditional power of the parish. But the dissolution of the milieu reached a new velocity in the 1960s. Church attendance in general declined, and pastoral recruitment entered a crisis. Catholic institutions such as youth groups and Catholic Action organizations tended to become smaller or fall apart altogether.[5]

This should not, though, lead to the conclusion that the Church, or its social ideals, ceased to matter. After all, Marxism did not vanish, despite the weakening of traditional socialist subcultures, whether in massive trade unions or ideologically motivated socialist parties. If anything, it experienced something of a renaissance, albeit in new, more experimental, and more global forms. Something similar happened with Catholicism, which from a different perspective was rather dynamic in the 1960s. Small groups of Catholics, led by young priests, became radicalized and embarked on the same sorts of experiments in daily life and political practice that were intoxicating their secular friends. Catholic charitable institutions remained just as important as they had ever been, and may even have grown in significance in an era of decolonization. Germany's *Caritas* continued to employ hundreds of thousands of people and aid many more, in Germany and elsewhere. In France, the Emmaus Organization, founded by the enormously popular Abbé Pierre in the wake of the war, went global (it now operates in thirty-seven countries).[6]

The weakening of the Christian Democratic consensus, dovetailing with the onset of the sexual revolution, led to a revival of the ideological turmoil of the 1930s. On the one hand, many Catholics embraced once again a confrontational politics of "family values." Like its predecessor, the new form of Catholic conservatism, which I've called paternal Catholic modernism, was resolutely modern, refusing to question human rights or religious freedom as guiding principles. Its practitioners came to believe, though, that Europe was under assault from Communists and "gender theory," and that the heteronormative family would be the first line of defense. They began to mobilize, with great success, around opposition to abortion and, eventually, opposition to gay marriage. By saving the family, they believed, a better Europe and a more Catholic form of modernity might be salvaged from the wreckage left behind by the sexual revolution.[7]

Since the new Catholic conservatism is so familiar, and it has been relatively well studied, this chapter will focus on its competitors, who may have remained more marginal but rehabilitated a different and more radical vision of Catholic modernity. The antifascist, fraternal modernism of the 1930s had never disappeared, although it had gone somewhat dormant in the long 1950s. In the late 1960s, changing conditions conspired to give it traction again. Perhaps most importantly, the centrality of anti-Communism to Catholic intellectual and political culture began to diminish, allowing Catholics to engage once again with socialist movements and thinkers (for this reason it is fair to refer to the revived fraternal modernism as the "Catholic New Left"). The twin deaths of Josef Stalin (1953) and Pope Pius XII (1958) set the stage for a wide-ranging rapprochement. Pope John XXIII had long enjoyed cordial relations with Communists, and the Second Vatican Council remained silent about Communism.[8] Meanwhile, the Church quickly made its peace with decolonization, setting up new national synods and beginning the pivot to the Third World that marks it to this day. The collapse of empire provided many opportunities to scramble accepted relationships between faith and power. In Algeria, for instance, Catholics worked together with Protestants and Muslims alike to solve concrete social problems—a relationship that led, in some cases, to widespread critiques of torture and a questioning of the imperial mission itself.[9]

Accounts of Europe's Catholic New Left often emphasize the global context, pointing out that decolonization and Latin American Liberation Theology injected new energy into the Church. While that context surely mattered, the domestic one was just as important, if not more so. The fraternal modernists of the 1930s had pioneered an antifascist form of Catholic social teaching—one that focused on civil society, rather than the family, in the private sphere, and therefore emphasized social activism, trade unionism, and pluralism in the public sphere. Each of these elements was revived and updated in the 1960s. As for the private sphere, the Catholic New Left was indelibly shaped by the sexual revolution and by the rejection, often loud and public, of *Humanae vitae*, the 1968 encyclical that reasserted the role of natural law and papal authority over conjugal sexuality. That encyclical had reasserted the central claim of paternal Catholic modernism: that the family provided the central site for social morality and Catholic ethics. The fraternal Catholics of the 1960s wholly rejected that claim, going so far as to claim that individual couples should consult their conscience, rather than natural law, when making decisions about contraception. Their rejection of *Humanae vitae*, just like their forebears' rejection of fascist natalism, freed the Catholic New Left to reimagine the private sphere as a space of solidarity and interconfessional forms of social activism (an account that rhymed, of course, with many non-Catholic social movements in the late 1960s). This account of the private sphere led to novel analyses of the public sphere, too. In the economy, the new fraternal modernists revived older traditions of Catholic anticapitalism. They engaged with non-Communist but emancipatory forms of labor politics, as they sought far more than the placid reforms on offer from Christian Democrats. And as for the state, they revived and sharpened the antiracism of the 1930s, arguing that subterranean anti-Semitism was keeping Catholics from imagining new kinds of pluralist polities in tune with a globalizing age and a revolutionary faith.

Three individual stories allow a glimpse into the inner logic of the Catholic New Left in Central and Western Europe. The focus here will be more national than transnational. The relatively coherent intellectual circuit of France, Germany, and Austria ceases to make much sense, given that Catholics everywhere were engaging with global forces. And in lieu of diffuse global stories, it is more illuminating to focus on smaller ones, uncovering global currents as they intersect in the life and writings of our three protagonists. Bernhard Häring, a German priest and the most famous moral theologian of the era, found himself swept up in the sexual revolution. Through legitimating Catholic opposition to *Humanae vitae*, he showed how a new approach to the private sphere, one in line with the spirit of the 1960s, might be articulated from within the Catholic tradition. By decentering the family, once again, from the center of Catholic ethics, Häring and others opened a space for economic and political thinkers to revive the deep pluralism that had been central to Catholic social thought from the beginning. Paul Vignaux, a French philosopher and a founder of France's largest trade union, the French Democratic Confederation of Labor (CFDT), explored the new Catholic approach to the economy. He showed how Catholic social ethics, unmoored from the tradition of corporatism, could enlist the faithful into novel forms of social democratic labor activism. Friedrich Heer, an Austrian polymath and journalist, trained his energies on the Catholic approach to racism and the state. He demonstrated that the faith could nourish a kind of politics that would move beyond the secular nation-state by totally uprooting any nostalgia for a throne-and-altar alliance (a nostalgia, he held, that continued to animate most Catholics and Christian Democrats and that could only be fully exorcised by confronting the Holocaust). Their joint stories serve as a reminder that the Lord's house has many rooms, and that there are always multiple ways to be Catholic and modern.

Sex and the Theology of Protest

The pivotal event of the Catholic 1960s was the release of *Humanae vitae,* Pope Paul VI's condemnation of artificial contraception. Catholics across the world, many of whom were already using birth control pills, reacted with rage and disbelief. Paul VI was confused by the reaction. He had done little more, after all, than reaffirm a long-standing Catholic teaching. The dogma, however, was not really at issue. Few of the Catholic opponents of *Humanae vitae* argued that contraception was moral. The issue, instead, was the nature of ecclesiastical authority. By 1968, many Catholics no longer believed that the institutional Church had the right to make legalistic pronouncements about their sexual behavior, which they saw as a matter of individual conscience. Defenders of the encyclical complained that their opponents were simply falling prey to the hyperindividualism and sexual mania of the 1960s. The truth is more complex. They were giving voice, instead, to a novel understanding of the Church, and of the very nature of Catholic modernism. The reaction to *Humanae vitae* was not sour grapes but aged wine.

The life and writings of Bernhard Häring, perhaps the most important moral theologian in post-1945 Europe, help to explain these new expectations. Born in southern Germany in 1912, he grew up in a close-knit Catholic milieu, spreading pamphlets for the local branch of the Center Party, which was chaired by his father. He decided to enter the priesthood just as Adolf Hitler was coming to power, and like many German priests he was called for war service. For a time, he was stationed in France, where he made friends with French Catholic families and priests. In 1941, he was redeployed to the far more dangerous Eastern Front, where he became a prisoner of the Russians after the German defeat at Stalingrad. Like everyone who fought in the East, he returned to Germany a changed man, and he resolved to do theology in a new way. Obedience, he came to believe, was overrated. The obedient slaughter of the innocent could not possibly mirror the proper comportment of the believer.[10]

In ways reminiscent of contemporary existentialists, Häring sought to renovate moral theology by emphasizing freedom and responsibility instead of law and obedience. This was not the only possible theological response to the horrors of Nazism: Joseph Ratzinger, Häring's contemporary and the future Pope Benedict XVI, concluded that the Church needed to reaffirm its commitment to certain bedrock principles. Häring, however, focused less on the institution than on the believer's individual conscience.[11] He did so most famously in *The Law of Christ* (1954). Quickly translated into over a dozen languages, and eventually selling over two hundred thousand copies, it became a standard textbook in Catholic circles for decades. In it, Häring pursued a situational and existential approach to Catholic ethics. Influenced by Max Scheler, the work emphasized what Häring called "the dynamic character of morality." A truly Christian morality, Häring argued, takes the form of a "dialogue" between the believer and others, with close attention to particulars and context. Despite the title of the book, "law" was not the proper grammar for Catholic morality in Häring's view, and he replaced it with "responsibility": an ethic guided by conscience that was rooted more in the imitation of Christ than in the immutable verities of natural law. He did not dispute the existence of natural law, but he did reject the notion that rational derivations from that law should guide our moral conduct. This was implicit in the architecture of the book. Häring placed his discussion of human personality, conscience, and responsibility hundreds of pages before his account of natural law.[12]

Häring derived the social and political consequences in other works. His essential point throughout was that the Church had no claim to dominate the public sphere and must embrace the fact that it represented only one voice in a cacophony.[13] This approach drew from, and helped to legitimize and explain, a crumbling of the German Catholic milieu. When Häring was born, German Catholics could live a life ensconced in the faith, reading Catholic newspapers, voting for a Catholic party, belonging to a Catholic trade union, and attending Catholic schools. By the 1960s, almost none of this was true. Catholic Action was in deep crisis, as youth groups proved unable to confront the revolutions in mass entertainment and gender relations being pioneered outside the Church. Their theological elders were helping them along: in addition to Häring, Hans Küng, Johann Baptist Metz, and Karl Rahner were giving Catholics the ammunition to accept, embrace, and even extend the secularizing trends of the 1960s. The texts of Vatican II seemed to push in the same direction, thanks largely to Häring's own work. As one of the primary editors of *Gaudium et spes* (1965), he did much to ensure that Vatican II would present an ecclesiology for a modern world, emphasizing joint action with others rather than defensive legalism (he was especially dedicated to keeping anti-Communism out of the text).[14]

When it came to sexual matters, the Häring of the 1950s and early 1960s broadly followed the consensus view of Christian Democratic modernism: acceptance of the virtues of sexuality and marital love, but only within the sharply defined limits of the Church (typically, his evolving and dialogic approach to ethics and law did not yet extend to the realm of sexuality). He certainly rejected the natalism of the past, which, like many Catholics, he had experienced firsthand. He had ten brothers and sisters, so when the Nazi official came knocking to give his mother the "Mother's Cross," she refused it. "I will not accept this honor," Häring remembered her saying, "because I have not borne and raised any of my children for National Socialism!"[15] While Häring was a priest, he encountered the evolving sexual mores of the 1950s through his pastoral work.[16] He was convinced that the sex drive was a natural, and therefore blessed, element of the human person, and he drew on Dietrich von Hildebrand (a personal friend) and others to invest sexuality and love with sacral significance. Sex, he insisted, "does not have its meaning and its total purpose in a mating and begetting" but was intrinsically valuable as part of a "personal marital fellowship." Therefore, Häring concluded that sex was lawful even when no pregnancy was possible, such as when the woman was already pregnant.[17]

As with other Christian Democratic modernists, Häring's valorization of the sex drive did not extend to a rethinking of gender roles or contraception. *The Law of Christ* argued that women, unlike men, were defined almost entirely by sex. For Häring, woman's entire being was shaped by erotic and sensual impulses on the one hand and maternal ones on the other. Consequently, women should avoid working outside the home or receiving an independent income, which together constitute a "serious hazard." Häring was also certain that public display of homosexuality "should be punished with all vigor."[18] Even though he was in general comfortable with the new positive attitude toward sexuality, he was wary of recommending the birth control pill itself and counseled his readers to wait for the pope's decision.[19]

The comfortable consensus of the long 1950s relied on the existence of a broader culture that generally supported family values and viewed sexual experimentation with suspicion. Once the sexual revolution raised new questions for Catholic moralists, the more open-minded among them began to deliver new answers. Häring first seriously dealt with these issues when he sat on the study commission on contraception that was convened by Pope John XXIII in 1963. As Häring considered the issue and talked with Catholic couples in detail about their experiences, he encountered a world in flux. His position was explained in the commission's "majority report," which was leaked to the press. It was widely misunderstood as a pro-contraception text. As Häring himself insisted, "the papal commission was not a pill-commission" and "it in no way wanted to give the Pope recommendations concerning any kind of contraceptive pills."[20] Instead, the text of the report gathered together the personalist theology of love that Häring had defended for years alongside a familiar caution against the "contraceptive mentality" that would place personal pleasure over the holy meaning of sex. It continued to claim that human sexuality is aimed primarily at procreation but that the holiness of married life does not "depend upon the direct fecundity of each and every particular act"—all positions taken up by *Humanae vitae*.[21]

The revolutionary aspect of the majority report was not its treatment of oral contraception, which it did not mention, but its treatment of authority, which seemed to follow directly from Häring's theories of responsibility in *The Law of Christ*. Decisions about responsible parenthood, the report explained, should be made by the couples themselves, in dialogue with their priest and their conscience. It would be a "grave mistake" to presume that the couple's responsibility to make crucial moral decisions constituted an "open door" to lax or egoistic morals. The commission did not seek to allow heedless use of contraceptives, and the report did argue that every use of any contraceptive device was an evil.[22] That evil, however, might have corresponding and greater benefits depending on the concrete situation of the couple—a situation that only the sacramental community of the married couple was in a position to answer.

Paul VI, of course, chose to ignore the report (or, at least, ignore the recommendation to limit his own authority). Soon after the release of *Humanae vitae,* Catholics around the world exploded in protest. The dissent focused far more on the issue of papal authority than it did on the specific theology of sexuality, which was hardly in dispute. "It could be," Marie-Dominique Chenu mused in a confidential letter to the French episcopate, "that Rome has lost, in a stroke, the authority that it took sixteen centuries to construct."[23] The response was especially heated in West Germany, where issues of sexuality and authority were entangled with the nation's wrenching encounter with its own Nazi past. While defenders of the encyclical thought that birth control was reminiscent of Hitler's biopolitics, the younger generation disagreed. For them, *Humanae vitae* represented another instance of a hierarchical, male-dominated institution seeking to control sexuality and, specifically, female sexuality. This, they believed, was the very height of fascism.[24]

A positively defiant stance toward the decision had become commonplace in Germany within about six weeks of the encyclical's release. In its first issue after the encyclical, a Catholic men's journal with an enormous circulation published an astonished front-page editorial, taking refuge in the fact that the pope had not spoken infallibly, alongside an article by a theologian called "Still Not the Last Word." Two weeks later, German bishops released the Königstein Statement, declaring that birth control should remain an affair of the individual conscience (the Austrian bishops soon followed suit). The following day, hundreds of thousands of readers of the same men's journal were treated to a compendium of lay female responses to the encyclical. The crucial fact was that the very format of the article presented the theme as a debate and not as an established moral fact. And a few days after that issue appeared, the epochal Catholic Congress of 1968 started in Essen. The congress, traditionally an opportunity for the German Church to demonstrate unity and strength, spun out of control and became a rowdy referendum on the Church's brash conservatism. While almost nobody turned out to hear Wilfrid Schreiber talk about the venerable theme of Catholic social ethics, thousands flocked to the contentious panel on sexuality. A vote was even held on the pope's new policy, translating the collegial aspect of Vatican II to the laity. About three thousand attendees voted against it, while fewer than one hundred supported it.[25]

Häring knew about the text of the encyclical before almost anyone else because it had been given to him by American journalists who had bribed their way to a copy (they wanted an interview with Häring, who had a good claim to be the most famous moral theologian in the world at the time). Therefore, when the bomb dropped, he was prepared. He immediately emerged as a dissident—and, according to one bishop at least, a "heretic."[26] His name appeared on a statement of dissent, along with those of eighty-six other theologians, that was announced in Washington, D.C., the day after *Humanae vitae* was released. (The statement was prepared by Charles Curran, a student of Häring's, and within a month, over five hundred theologians had added their names to it.) Häring began to publish an avalanche of critical commentaries, which appeared in newspapers and journals in America, Germany, and around the world. Couples, he told a willing audience, could still use contraception in good faith and need not mention it in confession. Throughout these commentaries, he focused overwhelmingly on the issue of power, arguing that the nature of the dispute was not really about Christian marriage but about the power of a small, reactionary group of curial advisers, which had used its nefarious influence over the Church to wrest authority away from the flock. In a remarkable logical somersault, Häring praised Pope Paul VI's "courage to follow his conscience," despite overwhelming opposition, and urged the faithful to learn from his example—even if it meant departing from his actual teachings.[27]

Häring's measured criticisms found a more radical echo in *Critical Catholicism*, a journal that disaffected Catholic students began circulating at the 1968 Catholic Congress and that promised to provide "a democratic alternative to the authoritarian structure of the Church." With its bright colors, intemperate tone, and zeal for uncovering the Nazi past of prominent Catholic authorities, the journal was the Catholic contribution to the freewheeling print culture of the student movement. Its authors harshly criticized the Church for its silence about the Vietnam War, and they flamboyantly published the addresses of doctors who would prescribe birth control pills. Their constant criticism of Joseph Höffner, Wilfrid Schreiber, and other Catholic luminaries was not designed to sway them to the left but rather to create a new Catholic popular culture that would deny them its support. "The Council is dead," they concluded, "because the 'laity' have not recognized their responsibility or seized the initiative." The *Critical Catholicism* team wanted to do just that, subjecting the Church to "public and independent control."[28]

The campaign against *Humanae vitae* opened a new chapter in the intellectual life of the Catholic Church, in West Germany as elsewhere. To be sure, for a number of years, the Catholic public sphere had been evolving in more critical directions. Some parishes, notably in the Netherlands, were beginning to experiment with married priests and ecumenical worship services.[29] In Germany, organized Catholic students, like their secular and Protestant colleagues, were beginning to question their elders, experiment with novel forms of socialism, and ask uncomfortable questions about Germany's past.[30] And yet it was only in the wake of 1968 that the Church became a site of genuine conflict, as a new generation of theologians, priests, laymen, and students laid claim to a Church that had, in their view, become too cozy with the establishment. The established Church attempted to harness that energy with limited success. The case of the journal *Publik* is exemplary. Founded in 1968 with support of the bishops, the journal was meant to serve as a site for critical Catholic engagement. This enterprise, however, ended up going further than bishops were comfortable with, given that members of the left-leaning Catholic intelligentsia were at the helm. The bishops accordingly withdrew their support. While decades earlier that might have been enough to scuttle the project, this was no longer the case. As with Vatican II itself, *Publik* represented an experiment in democratizing the Catholic public sphere that had uncontrollable consequences. Rebranded as *Publik-Forum,* the journal continued to appear and to represent a critical, leftist voice for German Catholics—as it does to this day.[31]

By reacting to and rejecting *Humanae vitae,* a new group of Catholics declared their unwillingness to abide by the strictures of paternal Catholic modernism and its legalist account of the private sphere. In place of the sexually regulated family, German students came to imagine, as Maritain had done decades earlier, that the private sphere was made up of a robust network of journals and civil society organizations. Häring agreed, and in his book *A Theology of Protest* (1970), he gave a theological imprimatur to the protest movements that were taking place around the world, inside and outside the Church. Christianity, he argued, was a revolutionary force, coming into its own as revolutionary nonviolence was practiced on a global scale against an antiquated, domineering paternalism.[32]

The fact that such a work could be written, and not even seem all that exceptional, signaled a dramatic transformation of the German Catholic Church, which emerged as one of the most progressive voices in global Catholicism. This happened despite the opposition of figures such as Ratzinger, who worried about Häring's influence and officially forbade his student Charles Curran from teaching moral theology. Nonetheless, Häring remained a restless, progressive voice in the Church for decades longer, making waves with his rejection of the blanket opposition to abortion that became an increasingly central part of Catholic politics. Together with German Catholics like Metz and Norbert Greinacher, he became involved with antinuclear protest, Liberation Theology, feminism, and environmentalism. Concerned with Pope John Paul II's authoritarian style and intransigence on sexual matters, he complained privately to the pope and publicly by placing his prestigious name atop a 1989 "Cologne Declaration Against Resignation and For an Open Catholicism." As his previous provocations had done, this one had a truly global reach, appearing in translation around the world and picking up tens of thousands of signatures in the process.[33] Häring's activist career shows how the issue of sex was inseparable from broader theories of the Catholic engagement with the world. For him, as for others, the new articulation of the Catholic private sphere nourished a renewed account of the public sphere, too.

The New Catholic Socialism

Häring and the other critics of *Humanae vitae* showed, once again, that it was possible to be Catholic and modern without focusing on the reproductive family and sexual ethics. This decentering of the family opened the door for a reiteration of the pluralist accounts of the private sphere that had been central to social Catholic theorizing since the late nineteenth century. Häring himself celebrated the chaotic social movement activity characteristic of the late 1960s in general, but it had more specific forms, too. When it came to the economy, a new generation of fraternal modernists revived, in a new key, one of the signal commitments of the social Catholic tradition: trade unionism. While the radical theologians in Latin America and the small group of philo-Communist Catholics in France have attracted the lion's share of historical attention, this less controversial group reminds us that this Catholic commitment, rooted in the late nineteenth century, continued to flourish even in the wake of 1968.

Many observers believed that the Catholic economic tradition essentially died over the course of the 1960s. In 1979, Marie-Dominique Chenu delivered a eulogy for social Catholicism in a short book called *The 'Social Doctrine' of the Church as Ideology*. In his view, the Church, between about 1880 and 1960, had grievously erred by linking its transcendent promise to specific social doctrine. That had been a blind alley, he suggested, leading the Church to tie itself to worldly powers and neglect its spiritual purpose. By the time his book appeared, this insight had become commonplace. "The Church's social teachings," Gustav Gundlach despaired, "stand before the ruins of their practical validity." Oswald von Nell-Breuning agreed. "Social Catholicism," he sighed, "has peacefully passed away." In France, the Social Weeks, long a premier site of Catholic political economy in Europe, began a slow decline in the mid-1960s, and their own secretary bemoaned that the long-established meetings had "lost their reason for being." Attempts to update the format, making the sessions more communal and focused on concrete issues, failed to sway the protesters who began to accumulate outside. In 1971, faced with a declining and unruly group of attendees and financial woes brought about by the poor sales of conference reports, the Social Weeks finally folded.[34]

They were right to point out that a certain form of Catholic economic dogma—one defined by corporatism or natural law—had lost its purchase. But the collapse of one form of social Catholicism should not be confused with a collapse of the tradition as a whole. For many European Catholics, faced with the slowdown of the miracle economy and the alienation of organized capitalism, the Catholic vision of trade unionism and workers' management continued to inspire. This would bear fruit most famously in Poland, where the Solidarity movement (led by Catholics and with papal support) emphasized again and again the rights to freely organize. That came later, however. In the late 1960s, the clearest example came in France.

One of the central figures was Paul Vignaux, a veteran of the fraternal Catholic modernism of the 1930s and a founder of contemporary France's largest trade union. A philosopher affiliated with the Catholic Association of French Youth (ACJF) and the Young Christian Workers (JOC), he was talking about industrial affairs at the Social Weeks as early as 1929, when he was twenty-five years old. Like his friend and interlocutor Jacques Maritain, Vignaux was inspired by the recently discovered writings of the young Marx (indeed, Maritain drew on Vignaux in his own appreciation of Marx in *Integral Humanism*).[35] Before the war, he helped to found the

General Syndicate of National Education (SGEN), a (still existing) teachers' union that was affiliated with the Catholic trade union federation (the CFTC). He spent the war years themselves in the United States, where he edited a collection of Catholic resistance essays for publication and Maritain prefaced another of his books.

Like those of Häring, Vignaux's more famous activities of the late 1960s had their intellectual roots in the superficial placidity of the long 1950s. The end of the worker-priest experiment, and the condemnation of the *nouvelle théologie,* struck Catholics like Vignaux as ill omens. Faced with the right-wing turn of Christian Democratic parties across the continent, Vignaux became acidly critical of the movement as a whole. Like Walter Dirks, he referred to the Christian Democrats as agents of "restoration." In *L'Express,* a mass-circulation magazine, he announced that he represented a minority within the CFTC that wanted to embrace decolonization and socialism, which required "a language other than Christian Democracy."[36] Vignaux's group was known as "Reconstruction," and its journal of the same name provided an important site for left Catholic reflection throughout the 1950s. Unlike the better-known *Esprit,* it was always resolutely anti-Stalinist, but it did insist that Catholics were duty bound to dialogue with revolutionary socialist partners. In 1953, for instance, an anonymous editorial in *Reconstruction,* likely written by Vignaux, complained that France's Christian Democratic Party was "chained to the representatives of the established order" and was dedicated to antiquated slogans like "Europe" and "free schooling," which bore little resemblance to the realities of the social situation. "Everyone knows that in the France of today," the editorial continued, "nobody wants to be on the right and all declare themselves 'social,' with tears in their voice." And yet by speaking the "pseudo-apostolic" language of social Catholicism, the MRP was ensuring that it could be no more than the "lackey of the traditional right wing."[37]

As a historian of theology by training, Vignaux tried to recover a form of Catholic thought that would fully and finally overcome the lingering nostalgia for natural law, which he thought led Catholics toward an acceptance of an unjust status quo. A student of Étienne Gilson's, Vignaux wrote accounts of medieval theology that bypassed Aquinas. Instead, he turned to the neglected tradition of the nominalists, most notably William of Ockham. This long-running project represented both an attempt to remind readers that the Catholic tradition had always housed immense intellectual diversity and an attempt to revive the specific theological insights of the nominalists. The nominalists, in Vignaux's telling, had granted God his proper, absolute power. In the process, they undermined the natural law tradition by distinguishing the all-powerful divine from the rhythms of the natural or social worlds. In this way, Vignaux argued, they provided an opening for humans to craft their own history, following the immanent logic of a secular sphere separated from the awesome power of God.[38]

Vignaux criticized natural law teachings not in order to adopt a purely secular view of the world but rather in order to attain more clarity about the resources that the faith could offer. When it came to social activism, he saw two in particular. The first has become known as Christian realism. Rather than specific teachings on private property, the Church in this view counseled a healthy skepticism about how much social progress or equality might be expected in a world of sin. This found its clearest expression in a 1957 essay called "Political Conscience and Religious Conscience," written in fact by Vignaux's wife, Georgette, but representing their shared approach. Her starting point was the distinction between the political and the religious conscience, which, in her view, was perpetually muddled by Christian Democratic parties. Drawing on Reinhold Niebuhr, she argued for the autonomy of the political, worldly sphere, whose perpetual clash of interests was perceptively analyzed by Marxists. The Marxists, though, did not learn their own lesson well enough. The proletariat and the bourgeoisie alike universalized their contingent interests, both sides neglecting to see how "reason is always tied to interest." The Christian conscience, while it cannot provide a coherent politics, can provide a healthy dose of Christian realism: an understanding that the world is fallen, and that no utopian kingdom is possible, alongside a faith that God has granted us the tools to improve our lot.[39]

For some, this Christian realism led to an essentially conservative and antitotalitarian form of religious politics. This was not Vignaux's view. Christian realism in his view was informed by a skepticism of the powerful, a defense of the sacred worth of the individual, and constant attention to the ways in which utopian strivings can replicate the forms of oppression they hoped to overcome. This explains his attitude toward Marxism in the 1950s. On the one hand, he was critical of those French Catholics who claimed to find no contradiction between Christ and Communism. He believed they had given up on the "realist" inheritance of the faith, refusing to see the abuses carried out by Communists once in power. On the other hand, he was *equally* critical of those French Catholics who claimed to find no contradiction between Christ and capitalism. They were not realist either, insofar as they rejected the fact that alienation and class conflict truly were central components of the capitalist order.

The second commitment that Vignaux derived from the social Catholic tradition was a staunch commitment to free trade unionism, which for him was the sure sign of a healthy civic life. His vision of dense union activity, absent any materialist metaphysics or calls for Communist insurgency, was distinctly Catholic, rooted in his own 1930s experience with Maritain and the CFTC. Like other radicals around the world, he found inspiration in the Hungarian uprising of 1956. Vignaux hoped that the restive workers would point the way toward a more humane, democratic, and reformist breed of Communism (a hope common to the New Left, Catholic and secular alike). The Hungarian workers were, in his words, engaged in a "moral struggle" for the "democratic, and even revolutionary, control of power." Support for their cause against the Soviets, Vignaux argued, required a shift away from the vanguard theories of Communism toward a more flexible theory of the proletariat: one that "defends the interests of the unqualified masses" while "rejecting racial discrimination" and supporting "the cause of 'under-developed' overseas peoples."[40]

Just as Häring had done with the fraternal vision of the family, Vignaux extended the fraternal vision of the economy for a new era. Instead of supporting CFTC collaboration with non-Catholic trade unions, as fraternal Catholics had done in the 1930s, he argued that the moment for *any* kind of Catholic trade union had passed. It had been appropriate to an earlier age, when a distinct and coherent group of Catholic workers needed representation from a union that distanced itself from socialist anticlericalism. Circumstances, however, had changed, as socialists evolved and the Catholic milieu entered its crisis.

Vignaux claimed that the CFTC had to abandon its Catholic identity if it hoped to keep pace with evolving social conditions on the ground. He hoped that a new union might gather together the many workers, Catholics included, who wanted to radically reform the economy without conforming to doctrinaire Communism as either an intellectual or a political tradition. As the head of the SGEN and a regular presence in *Reconstruction*, he was well placed to push for deconfessionalization in private and in public. In 1955, for instance, he prepared a historical overview of the CFTC after a request from an affiliated union for workers in chemical industries. Vignaux's history emphasized the collaboration of socialists and Catholics in the strike wave of 1936 and again during the war. In the process, he showed, the union had progressively distanced itself from the clergy and its laws. The completion of this process required the final jettisoning of any referent to Christian social doctrine, "if there is such a thing." A persistent attachment to it was unfaithful to the trajectory of the moment and could not possibly attract "an unbeliever or a non-practicing Catholic," whose interests qua worker were independent from his metaphysical beliefs.[41]

In the long 1950s, when the CFTC was closely allied with the Christian Democrats, Vignaux's calls for deconfessionalization went nowhere. In the 1960s, however, the collapse of the party and the new energies unleashed by the Second Vatican Council created a more propitious environment. An internal document prepared by the construction workers' union shows how far Vignaux's ideas had penetrated. The time has come, the workers declared, to deconfessionalize the union and leave behind the old references to "Christian social doctrine"—a phrase that, in the minds of most workers, committed the CFTC to apostolic action and defense of capitalism. "The Christian syndicalism of the past is out of date," the report concluded.[42] Another document prepared by Vignaux and his allies touched the third rail of Catholic social thinking by pointing out, as very few had done, that it had proven highly compatible with the authoritarianism of the 1930s. "Christian social morality," the document reminded its readers, had legitimated support for all manner of dictators in the 1930s and was therefore not a sturdy rock on which to build the democratic socialism of the future.[43] Joseph Folliet, editor of the *Social Chronicle of France* and therefore a major player in the world of social Catholicism, drew on recent papal teachings to lend his support to Vignaux and his allies in a widely quoted article on the "perhaps inevitable" deconfessionalization of the union.[44]

In 1964, Vignaux's effort to deconfessionalize the CFTC bore fruit at last, and the CFDT was born. As the story of Vignaux shows and as an interview with the CFDT's first chairman confirmed, the development of social Catholic ideals from within the Church was central to the union's transformation.[45] In its early years, CFDT activists were keen to point out the homology between their own goals and those of traditional social Catholic teaching, even while disavowing any dogmatic commitment. The newsletter of the electricity and gas union, for instance, featured a chart that showed the similarities between the union's new statutes, the UN's Declaration of Human Rights, and John XXIII's last encyclical, *Pacem in terris*. Eugène Descamps, a veteran of the JOC and new leader of the CFDT, followed suit, quoting from the pope, English socialists, and German social democrats in his report on the 1964 union congress.[46]

The CFDT's democratic spirit resonated with the events of May 1968, when millions of students and workers took to the streets and experimented with new styles of art, life, and politics. The CFDT celebrated 1968 with less anxiety than the other major trade union federations, some of which were committed to dogmatic forms of Marxism that were hard to reconcile with the student-led movement.[47] As head of the teachers' union, Vignaux in fact wrote one of the first "official" responses to the student unrest, denouncing police violence and demanding university reform. Soon afterward, once the gravity of the situation became more clear, the CFDT released a statement expressing "the entire solidarity of the workers with the students," and the union joined the General Confederation of Labor (CGT) in its call for a general strike.[48] While the CFDT was now nonconfessional, most of its leadership was still Catholic, and its pro-1968 rhetoric was matched by other Catholic workers' organizations. Workers' Catholic Action (ACO), which grew out of the JOC of the 1930s, took a similar line on the events. In the middle of May, the ACO released a statement of support for the striking workers and students. In some ways, it drew on the long legacy of Catholic social thinking, critiquing capitalism for overlooking "the value of the person" and "affirming [the ACO's] solidarity with the struggling workers."[49] Another text, written by an ACO militant in 1969, praised the French workers for seeking a non-Communist variant of democratic socialism and celebrated the Grenelle Agreements that finally ended the strikes. Like its predecessor, this internal ACO document paid little attention to traditional social teaching, seeking instead a Marxist, internationalist approach to the labor question.[50]

Vignaux was helping, that is, to craft a kind of Catholic social ethics that could find resonance with the broader worker and student movements of the late 1960s. This bore fruit above all in the characteristic commitment of the CFDT: *autogestion,* or self-management. Catholics in the orbit of Vignaux—first on the left wing of the CFTC and then in the leadership of the CFDT—were pioneers of *autogestion,* and one of the first uses of the word itself was in a speech by Eugène Descamps at the Social Week in 1960.[51] Social Catholics had long agitated for *cogestion,* or the *participation* of workers in the management of the firm. *Autogestion* merely took this a step further, and its fundamental logic of subsidiarity rhymed with longstanding Catholic concerns. The idea, which had socialist and anarchist roots too, was that workers should give up on the utopian dream of worker-management cooperation and simply run factories themselves. This reached fruition at the Lip watch factory in 1973. Upon hearing of news to shutter and restructure the factory, its workers seized control of the building and hid 65,000 watches. With support from the CFDT, they managed their own production and marketing for months until the factory was stormed by the police. The actions, which captivated French leftists reeling from the disappointments of 1968, were aided and abetted by Catholics such as Charles Piaget, a Catholic formerly affiliated with the CFTC, and Jean Raguènes, a Dominican involved with the factory workers on the ground.[52]

While Vignaux in general supported the activism and ideals of the CFDT, the new hegemony of *autogestion* made him a bit wary. For him, Christian realism counseled an experimental democratic socialism, not violence or Maoism. He feared that it was becoming another ideology, and one that violated Christian realism. His evolving views in the late 1960s can be tracked in *University Syndicalism,* the SGEN journal, in which he had a regular feature. He began the period excited about the possibility of CFDT-CGT collaboration in the name of democratic socialism. While he initially supported the students, he grew increasingly cautious and reminded his readers of the democratic, collaborationist bent of SGEN traditions. As leader of the teachers' union, he was awkwardly positioned to support student demands for control of the university, even if he had been ideologically committed to *autogestion.* In its place, he suggested *cogestion,* which had a more reliable patrimony in Catholic social teaching and would lead to power sharing between the students and the professoriate. By the end of June, he was desperately reminding his readers that power does not lay in the streets, whatever the posters might say. The essence of true syndicalism, he declared, lay in "negotiation with another power," according to "a realistic view of social facts" instead of a "mystique of 'integration' in some kind of confused community." While he continued to believe that a reform of the enterprise was central to the new economy, he did not think that a rush to *autogestion* was the answer.[53]

In other words, Vignaux tried to defend an evolved form of fraternal Catholic modernism, alive to the more radical elements of the Catholic tradition but also skeptical of Maoist direct action, which violated the spirit of Christian realism and the long-standing Catholic concern for nonviolence and social harmony. While the CFDT itself may have lost its Catholic patina in the years after 1968, many French Catholics followed Vignaux's lead and began to vote for the socialist party (in 1976, almost one-third of practicing Catholics voted for leftist parties).[54] Vignaux personally inspired a broad range of Catholic thinkers who did not wear their faith on their sleeve but were nonetheless impressed by the antiutopianism of the tradition and its focus on civil society activism. Jacques Julliard, for decades one of the most influential political editorialists in France, was introduced to syndicalism through Vignaux's SGEN, and he remained touched by his old mentor's example throughout his life.[55] Vignaux was also a major infleunce on Pierre Rosanvallon, one of the most influential thinkers of the Fifth Republic (in Rosanvallon's inaugural lecture at the Collège de France, he especially thanked Vignaux for showing that there need be no distinction between the contemplative and the active life). Rosanvallon got his start in the JOC and the CFDT, and his calls to revive the social democratic tradition through the remaking of civil society embody the economic tradition of fraternal Catholic modernism. In *The Demands of Liberty*, for instance, Rosanvallon sounded much like Vignaux in his celebration of trade unions and civil society on the one hand and his warning against utopianism and statism on the other.[56]

Vignaux's complex itinerary and influence reveal an important, and often overlooked, truth about the fate of Catholic social ethics in the 1960s. Much attention has been focused, and rightly so, on the adventures and trials of Liberation Theology, a novel and controversial form of social Catholic thinking birthed in Latin America but influential across the Catholic world. More quietly, Catholics such as Vignaux updated the social Catholic tradition in ways that were continuous with the fraternal modernism of the 1930s (in which he had been personally involved). He caused less controversy than the theologians of liberation because he was not a priest and had little interest in conquering the institutional Church. For him, as for many other European Catholics, the era in which explicitly Catholic organizations would play a major social role had come to a close. The spirit of the Church would, instead, encourage the faithful toward various forms of experimental, collaborative, and democratic socialism. As he explained in 1972, Catholicism did not provide a dogmatic social theory, but it did provide a space of possibilities and aspirations, alongside a realist sense of limitations.[57] In this sense, diffuse but real, the tradition of social Catholicism survived the collapse of the postwar social compact.

Political Theology, Race, and the Critique of the State

In 1965, with *Dignitatis humanae,* the Second Vatican Council declared that the Church was firmly and officially in favor of religious freedom. This seemed to put an end to the long-standing belief that some form of "Catholic state" was the ideal form of political organization. Catholics now called on the state to protect religious liberty and human rights, thereby protecting a stable social order in which the Church could flourish without clamoring for political power. Meanwhile, Christian Democratic modernists called on the state to pursue socially just forms of economic development, which would address social inequality without the need for dangerous or socialist forms of political action. This ideal of political community, which promised to protect the family without indulging in dangerous political experiments, helped to underwrite the extraordinary Catholic participation in the creation of a new Europe of democratic nation-states (west of the Iron Curtain, at least).

For many, however, this political vision was insufficient for the needs of the time. In the global South, especially, the dogma of development reached a crisis in Catholic and non-Catholic circles alike. Gustavo Gutiérrez's *Theology of Liberation* (1973), for instance, patiently demolished the myth of development, arguing that the project did little more than empower global elites. He suggested "liberation" over "development" as the new keyword of Catholic politics.[58] This sensibility found a foothold in Europe, too, as a new generation of fraternal modernists began to reframe the Church's mission from the perspective of the downtrodden.

One of the central figures, theologically speaking, was Johann Baptist Metz, a pioneering German Catholic who was an inspiration to European and Latin American theologians alike. Metz sought to recover the tradition of political theology in a modern and antifascist key. In his 1968 book *Theology of the World,* he argued that the faith, by restricting itself to a narrow private sphere, had abandoned the revolutionary spirit of Christ. Metz hoped that, by recovering the spirit of the early Christians, Catholics might finally shed the many compromises that had marked Church history over the centuries. He did not seek a medieval style of church-state fusion, to be sure: he insisted that Christ had called on us to legitimate and sanctify the fallen and secular world. He did, though, seek a new style of witness and action that would follow Christ's model and infuse political action with the spirit of eternal justice and equality. As he explained in later works, this recovery would happen primarily by harnessing the power of memory: memory of Christ's sympathy with the poor but also and especially the memory of Christianity's Jewish roots, the Church's turn toward anti-Semitism, and the great horror of Auschwitz. Through confrontation with the Holocaust, Metz suggested, the Church could overcome its long and disastrous experiment with political power and become once again a force for revolutionary disruption.[59]

A surprising number of Metz's insights were prefigured, if in less polished form, by an Austrian layman named Friedrich Heer (1916–1983) (the two crossed paths at an Austrian journal named *Neues Forum*). Although little known in the United States, Heer was, in the words of one historian, "the central figure in the intellectual life of Austria's Second Republic."[60] An art critic, historian, and journalist of indefatigable energy, he was a constant presence in the Austrian conversation, regularly pushing the boundaries of what it could mean to be a Catholic: an important task in a heavily Catholic nation. Through encounters with Karl Marx, Sigmund Freud, and the "Jewish question" more generally, Heer crafted a restless, global, and experimental Catholic faith that drew on the Catholic past while speaking to the new world of the 1960s. If Pope John XXIII wanted to "throw open the windows of the Church," Heer wanted to tear down the walls.

The first element of Heer's project was simply to declare that the present articulation of modernity, crowned by the secular state and family-defending Catholics, was inadequate and would be overwhelmed by its contradictions. Like other thinkers of the New Left, he was unimpressed by Cold War ideology, arguing that both the Soviet Union and the United States were overseeing the installation of a global managerial elite that was bringing the world under unprecedented forms of domination.[61] To imagine an alternative to the creeping domination of capitalist modernity, Heer looked to Teilhard de Chardin, a mercurial French thinker who was enjoying a global vogue in the 1960s. Chardin, Heer announced in a 1962 radio address, is "*the* pioneering thinker of Christendom." What Chardin offered Heer was a vision of the future: "legitimate hope," along the utopian lines of Ernst Bloch.[62] "We live in an axial age," Heer declared. This concept, popularized by Karl Jaspers, referred to the ancient period in which the major religious traditions were forged and the intellectual apparatus of man's prehistory seemed to vanish. It was Heer's firm contention that the late twentieth century was another one of these global turning points, and one whose precise shape was still unknown and unknowable.

"The era which has just begun," he insisted, "is a time of new struggles, of new experiences, of new sufferings."[63]

Heer believed that Europe had something to offer at this new historical conjuncture. But the message of Europe had nothing to do with the noble legacy of antiquity, the tangled web of treaties, or even "the Europe of sermons, of the numerous and well-meaning tracts on the Christian West." Like Maritain a few decades earlier, Heer thought this form of European consciousness, far from representing an overcoming of nationalism, was "one of its spoiled fruits, the old nationalism in new clothes." He enthused instead about what might now be called global Europe: the Europe of border-crossing migrants and cultural exchange in what he called "a new age of encounter." For Heer, Europe's true beauty comes in its plurality, and in the hope that its "wounds, sensitivity, and great weakness" might push its inhabitants to a new moral awakening. The European consciousness of the past, pious as it might have been, was not up to the task. "The bankruptcy of this Europeanism," Heer concluded, "is a necessary act of clarification."[64] Pius XII, Adolf Hitler, and Benito Mussolini all "conceived a typically continental, European, and isolated entity," Heer mused. "A historical epoch has, with these three men, come to a close."[65]

If the first element of Heer's project was a sort of messianic expectation in the axial age of the late twentieth century, the second was a prescription for how the Church should respond: through dialogue. Heer thought that the Church could continue to lead this new world if it could break free of its Eurocentric pretensions and conservative impulses. To stay relevant, and to redeem the time, the Church would have to engage in deep and profound dialogue with the "atheist" currents in contemporary thought and culture. In *The Hour of Christians* (1947) and *Conversation between Enemies* (1949), Heer called for a new Christianity that might, through collaboration with socialism, point the way toward a sort of permanent revolution in our hearts and our social structures alike. And in *The Europe Experiment: One Thousand Years of Christendom* (1952), he retold the history of the Church as one of constant evolution and encounter, in which the Church incorporated insights from all of its so-called opponents.

But as the molten 1940s gave way to the long 1950s, Heer became pessimistic about the Church. He was especially bothered that, with all of the suffering in the world, Catholics continued to place so much emphasis on sex. "The modern clergy," he acidly judged, "has developed an obsession with the crudely sexual"—an obsession that in Heer's view had legitimated the "unholy alliance between the German bishops and Hitler."[66] This sexual obsession was busying Catholics with self-laceration and dogmatic proclamation in place of encounter and dialogue with existentialism, psychoanalysis, and Marxism. Like Maritain before him, Heer thought that these intellectual trends had a kernel of Christian truth at their core— otherwise, how could they exist, and to what element of the soul would they speak? By turning its back on them, the Church was abandoning its heritage. "European Christianity," Heer wrote in a Nietzschean mood, "does not smell good."[67]

The reason that the Church was being left behind, Heer argued, was that the Church had yet to confront its own past, and specifically the legacy of anti-Semitism. If most Catholics had quietly abandoned public anti-Semitism in the long 1950s, this was not the result of agonized reckoning or reflection. Through his constant writing and his editorship of *The Furrow* (*Die Furche*), one of the most important publications in Catholic Austria, Heer sought to remind his coreligionists of the Church's bloody hands. Adolf Hitler, he wrote in a front-page 1958 article for *The Furrow,* presents "a social and world-political problem that concerns us all and has not been solved after a quarter century," while in 1962 he claimed that "Nazism corresponds both internally and externally to collective European history, especially since the sixteenth century." In a front-page editorial called "Algeria and Us," he expressed great sorrow at the revival of imperial, racist Catholicism among settler Catholics in Algeria. While admitting that the Algerian struggle was a French affair, the editorial drew a comparison with Austria, where "thirty years ago, young men and good Catholics prepared themselves to build a 'new order.' They failed."[68]

Heer was part of a sea change of Catholic culture in the early 1960s, as a new generation of Europeans, Catholics included, began to ask challenging questions about their parents' generation. In Austria, two of Heer's Catholic friends—Günther Nenning and Wilfried Daim—were drawing attention to the Church's anti-Semitic history.[69] In France, Pierre Duquesne's *French Catholics under the Occupation* (1966) cast doubt on the myth of Catholic resistance. In Germany itself, Ernst-Wolfgang Böckenförde, a jurist and a student of Carl Schmitt's, wrote an explosive essay in *Hochland* in 1961, reminding readers that many Catholics had welcomed Hitler and that the Church's natural law theory and furious anti-Communism had paved the way. Two years later, Rolf Hochhuth's widely translated 1963 play, *The Deputy*, condemned Pius XII for his silence about the Holocaust, casting a pall on his reputation from which neither he nor his Church have ever quite recovered.[70]

In some ways the Church of the 1960s did address the Jewish question. Thanks to the long and subterranean influence of a group of Catholic converts, Maritain included, the Second Vatican Council released a document called *Nostra aetate*.[71] For many Catholics, the grappling with these issues at the Second Vatican Council was sufficient. *Nostra aetate*, after all, signaled the Church's total opposition to any form of racial anti-Semitism. In Heer's eyes, however, even that declaration did not go far enough. The text is ambiguous, for instance, about whether the Church still seeks to convert Jews. Moreover, the text was still compatible with a new culture war that would pit religious communities, now united, against secular or atheist opponents. That possibility is implicit in the text, and Heer could also see evidence of it in the Church leadership of his own country. When Austria's Cardinal Franz König went on a lecture tour of Egypt and India in 1964–1965, he showed unprecedented respect for non-Christian religions while also calling on a joint effort against the common enemy of atheism.[72]

The third plank of Heer's intellectual project concerned the nature and purpose of the memory politics and Christian-Jewish dialogue that he saw as the key components of Catholic renewal. Like Metz, Heer believed that a more agonized and transformative encounter with the fascist past, and especially with the legacy of Catholic anti-Semitism, was necessary. He was convinced that only a recovery of that memory, and in more painful ways than *Nostra aetate* authorized, would cleanse the Church of its fortress mentality and recover the true Church of fraternal solidarity. "Catholicism," he wrote, "will become believable again only when it takes its place squarely in the world's solidarity in guilt."[73]

Heer was fascinated by the moral significance of the 1961 trial of Adolf Eichmann, a key architect of the Holocaust who was brought to justice in Israel. Many observers viewed the trial as an exhibition of the unique evil of Nazism. Like Hannah Arendt, though, Heer saw something different—and more troubling. "Today it is our duty to ask if there is a bit of Eichmann in each of us," Heer thought. Disgusted by the many Austrians who believed they had nothing to do with the Holocaust, Heer reminded readers that anti-Semitism had been ubiquitous in Austria and in fact remained that way. Austrians had yet to confront their residual hatreds—their "anti-

Semitism without Jews" that manifested in all sorts of antagonisms and kept Austria from participating in "the dawning global culture." The kind of pluralism Heer recommended went far beyond toleration, and Heer ended by suggesting that the Star of David was a symbol of redemption—even for Catholics.[74]

Heer's grappling with Eichmann shows that he saw the Holocaust less as a specific wartime event than as the horrific crystallization of genocidal impulses that long predated and postdated it. He expended a great deal of time and energy making this case. Heer did not simply argue that the Church could have done more or that Pius XII had been too cautious—he argued for the direct and massive culpability of the Church, during the war but especially in the preceding centuries when the Church had done so much to legitimate anti-Semitism. He defended this claim in two audacious, encyclopedic works of history. The first, *God's First Love* (1967), was the most scathing and well-sourced indictment of Catholic anti-Semitism that had ever been written. "The prime responsibility" for the Final Solution, Heer thundered, "lay with ten centuries of Christian tradition." "World history," he went on, "has smashed the illustrious thousand-year-old tradition of Christianity."[75] *The Belief of Adolf Hitler: Anatomy of a Political Religiosity* (1968) made much the same argument, showing that "the Austrian Catholic Adolf Hitler" should be viewed as the very epitome of the Christian West—not as its antagonist. In it, Heer reviewed the Church's wretched legacy of anti-Semitic and authoritarian politics, especially in Austria, with a sweep and intensity that has not been matched since. Everything that Catholics preferred to forget about—the Catholic anti-Semitism of Hitler's Vienna, the philo-Nazism that swept Bavarian Catholics in the 1920s and Austrian Catholics in the 1930s, the silence of European Catholics, most notably the Vatican, in the face of the Holocaust—was ruthlessly exposed. In Heer's view, this sad tale pointed to the utter bankruptcy, both theological and moral, of the "theological traditionalism" based around eternal Rome and any notion of "Christ the king and judge of the world."[76]

The confrontation with the history of Catholic anti-Semitism, Heer hoped, would open the pathway to Catholic-Jewish dialogue and, specifically, a transformation of the Church, through the insights of two secular Jews: Karl Marx and Sigmund Freud. Heer's interest in Marx was commonplace among the Catholic New Left, and like Vignaux he sought an encounter with Marxism that would salvage elements of the Catholic tradition, too.

His usage of Freud was more original. Heer believed that Freud inherited his fearless plumbing of the depths, including his own, from the Jewish tradition, and that Catholics had to follow suit. This would not be easy. "Self-analysis," Heer reminded his readers, "is a journey through hell, the hell of one's own subconscious depths."[77]

Heer used Freud to mount an unprecedented frontal assault on the shibboleths of paternal Catholic modernism. When he psychoanalyzed the Catholic believer, he discovered a neurosis occasioned by an unresolved relationship with God the Father. The cult of obedience at all costs was a scourge of modern bureaucratic culture, and one that Catholics were unfortunately facilitating by erecting and worshiping a vast bureaucratic apparatus stocked with father figures calling for unqualified deference. In place of a clear-eyed confrontation with a changing world, believers embraced a "neurotic" and "psychopathic" form of "obedience-Christianity."[78] Heer argued that, for the true Catholic, the greatest sin was complicity in a world of violence, fear, and unfilled potential. And yet, "in the confessional," only the "petty sins," "sexual anxieties," and "sins of 'the flesh,'" were broached, thus keeping the believer from understanding his proper relationship to an evolving world.[79]

The failure of Catholics was not the fault of God the Father, who was after all a God of love and acceptance rather than law and punishment. It was instead the fault of the believer, and his neurotic relationship to him. This indifference to the "real" was not truly a love of God—the Catholic God had been made flesh—but was instead a symptom of an inability to psychologically cope with the fallenness and otherness of creation. "The word 'God,'" Heer explained, "is a cipher for the imaginings and fears and dreams of the Ego confronted with a confusingly different world." Likewise, the willingness of Catholics to imagine a third world war against Communism was chalked up to the "death wish" and a "collective neurosis (the devilish and subversive Jews have now been replaced by Socialists and Communists)." Anti-Communism, for decades the core of Catholic political economy, was in Heer's view a childish fantasy, part and parcel of the anti-Semitic outrages of the Catholic past.[80]

Heer hoped that a confrontation with Catholic anti-Semitism would cleanse the Catholic conscience of its nostalgia for authoritarian father figures in the Church and in the state alike. This would, he hoped, pave the path toward a more restless and robust Church, and one more alive to the realities of suffering and inequality. Heer's reckoning with Freud gathers together the fraternal modernism of the Catholic New Left: its opposition to authoritarian father figures, its rejection of sexual prurience, its desire to transform the Catholic soul through encounters with Jewish and secular trends, and its hope that this might lead to a less bureaucratic Church more in keeping with Christ's original message. Heer's project can be summed up as the exorcism of Catholic paternalism in the name of "true Christian brotherhood," as he put it in 1960, or a "new fraternalism," as he called for in 1962.[81]

Even as Austria remained home to a relatively traditional Catholic culture, Heer opened the door for a new generation of progressive Catholic intellectuals. Historians such as Anton Pelinka and Erika Weinzierl, as well as activists and politicians such as Norbert Leser and Günther Nenning, viewed Heer as a guiding light. This group of Catholic activists helped to found Austria's Green Party and wrote pioneering critical histories of the Catholic Church. Beyond his avowed Austrian followers, Heer pointed the way toward an important component of today's European Church: those Catholics who abandon the Church's fortress mentality, and especially those who are on the front lines of caring for refugees, providing asylum and refuge, and washing the feet of those discarded by the nation-state. Heer would have appreciated their effort and contrasted it with the general Catholic indifference toward the suffering of the Jews, both before and immediately after the Holocaust. Heer wanted a Church oriented toward "global responsibility, love, sex, fraternity, political partnership, national and international responsibility, humanity, [and] universal mankind."[82] This would require the final dissolution of any alliance between Catholicism and any political commitment—be it to the West or to international development—that placed the Church on the side of the powerful. By breaking the centuries-old alliance between the Church and worldly power, Heer hoped, a new institution might be born that would take its rightful place with the wretched of the earth.

Catholic Modernism and Its Legacies

Since the 1930s, Catholics have debated, sometimes viciously, the proper form of Catholic modernity. Those debates extended well beyond that disastrous decade, and even well beyond the 1960s. Fraternal modernism, of the sort explored in this chapter, has found expression in all manner of lay movements since Vatican II, and in the papacy of Pope Francis, which began in 2013, it is finding a foothold at the Vatican, too.[83] While Pope

Francis emerges from a distinctly Latin American tradition, he does embody some of the principal positions of fraternal modernism. In a 2013 interview, for instance, he explained that while he accepted Catholic teachings on sexuality and the family, "it is not necessary to talk about these issues all the time." His pathbreaking encyclical on environmental stewardship, *Laudato si'* (2015), says nothing at all about sexual decadence, worrying instead that the modern family inducts children into habits of "wasteful consumption" (he thus criticized the notion of the "consuming family" so central to Christian Democracy). The path toward a more just future, the encyclical instructs, requires a rekindling of civic activism. Through the defense of natural sites or public places, Francis argues, communities "can break out of the indifference induced by consumerism." This activism will in turn create a new shared identity, a new set of narratives to be passed on, and will provide "intense spiritual experiences" for its participants.[84]

This is not, however, the only way to be Catholic and modern. Many Catholics have been drawn, instead, to a set of strategies that I've called paternal Catholic modernism. From this perspective, the central site of social virtue is the reproductive family, and the threats to that family from divorce, abortion, and homosexuality accordingly assume great significance. Paternal Catholic modernism might seem like an imposition of the Church elite against the wishes of a more progressive laity. It certainly does enjoy the support of many in the hierarchy. Pope Francis's two predecessors—John Paul II and Benedict XVI—were both European thinkers clearly embedded in the paternal modernist tradition (in fact, we have already met them both in their pre-papacy guise: Karol Wojtyła as an expert in family ethics and defender of *Humanae vitae*, Josef Ratzinger as a leading theologian in conflict with Bernhard Häring and his students).

And yet one of the central findings of this book is that paternal modernism of this sort is not an imposition from the hierarchy. A focus on "family values" has been inspiring to many in the laity, women included, and through the elaboration of welfare programs it has been a path to social justice, too. It has served Catholics well over the years and provides many with a compelling and plausible interpretation of their political and social environment. Since the 1970s, as Christian Democratic parties have either collapsed or become less Catholic, sexual politics has galvanized Catholics around the world—and with great success. Even in relatively secular and Protestant-dominated countries such as Germany, Catholics have exercised decisive influence on abortion legislation. In France, opposition to gay marriage in 2013 led to one of the broadest mobilizations of the Catholic community in memory (the Manif pour Tous).

Much of this book has been consumed with telling the story of these two strategies—how they were birthed, how they fused in the anomalous era of the Christian Democratic 1950s, and how they were torn apart again in the shadow of the sexual revolution. This should not distract us from what is, in some sense, the largest and most surprising finding. It was not a given that the Catholic Church would be able to make the transition to modernity with success. Indeed, from the vantage point of 1900, it seemed to many that it would not, which is one reason why Catholic leaders were reluctant to do so for so long. It is certainly possible to imagine a world in which the Church slowly dwindled in significance, unable or unwilling to grapple with the new problems posed by the twentieth century. That is not, however, the world that we live in.

In the decades and countries covered in this book, the Catholic Church confronted huge and apparently insurmountable challenges. It proved astonishingly resilient, rising from the ashes when so many other political and even religious projects could not. There were many reasons for this, but the intellectual history recounted in this book provides a major one. Human beings require moral and social stories to make sense of their world and their activities within it. For millions of Europeans living through desperate times, the Catholic Church provided those stories. It offered grand and plausible theories to explain the violence and trauma of the century, and it offered strategies to heal and to progress. It offered a theory of human flourishing, and it offered a way to link the most intimate sexual and domestic affairs to the most public questions of justice and civil society. It was able to offer these things because so many intellectuals and writers, primarily among the laity, were able to use the varied resources of a long tradition to create them.

By engaging fully with the political and social transformations of twentieth-century Europe, Catholics were able to show that there is no necessary contradiction between Catholicism and modernity. Like European modernity itself, the Catholic participation in it took many forms. Some modern Catholics enlisted their faith in the name of racial violence, discrimination against homosexuals, or repressive dictatorships. Others played a signal role in the democratic reconstruction of postwar Europe, and in the creation of family-friendly welfare states. Yet others dedicated their lives to brave acts of resistance, or to creative forms of social activism. Catholic modernism has been a force for good, and a force for evil, but above all it has been a force that mattered.

It will be a force that matters in the future, too. There are over one billion Catholics, and the Church is still one of the most effective purveyors of ideas and concepts the world has ever known. The Church of the twenty-first century, of course, is not the same as the one charted in this book. The demographic and even intellectual center of gravity of the Church has swung toward the global South. The Church is confronting a phalanx of issues—including climate change and mass refugee flow—that were hardly on the agenda for the modern Catholic pioneers of the twentieth century. As this book has shown, though, Catholic ideas can have tremendous power. And as this book has shown, the shape of Catholic engagement is not set in stone. The Church, despite its reputation as a site of quiet obedience, is a space of contestation and argument, especially among the laity. This was true in the early Church, and it is true today. The shape of the debate has changed, however. Catholics no longer struggle over the proper alternative to modernity, nor do they even struggle over the legitimacy of modernity. The twentieth-century experience put an end to that. The important question now is not *whether* but *how* the Church will be modern. The answer to that question will have an immense impact—not only on the Church but also on our common world.

Abbreviations

Notes

Acknowledgments

Index

Abbreviations

ACJF   Catholic Association of French Youth

ACO   Workers' Catholic Action

ACUE   American Committee on a United Europe

BKU   Union of Catholic Employers (German)

BVP   Bavarian People's Party (Bavarian equivalent to the Center Party)

CDU   Christian Democratic Union (German Christian Democratic Party)

CEDI   European Documentation and Information Center

CFDT   French Democratic Confederation of Labor
        (deconfessionalized CFTC)

CFTC   French Confederation of Christian Workers (Catholic trade union)

CGT   General Confederation of Labor (French trade union)

CIA   Central Intelligence Agency (U.S.)

CISC   International Confederation of Christian Trade Unions

CSU   Christian Social Union (Bavarian partner to the CDU)

DAF   German Labor Front (Nazi labor organization)

DGB   German Trade Union Confederation

DNVP   German National People's Party

FNC   National Catholic Federation (mass French Catholic organization)

JEC   Young Christian Students

JOC   Young Christian Workers

KAB   Catholic Workers' Movement (German)

KDF   Catholic German Women's League

KFÖ   Austrian Catholic Women's Organization

LOC   League of Christian Workers

MRP   Popular Republican Movement (French Christian Democratic Party)

NEI   New International Teams (Christian Democratic international
          organization)

ÖAAB   Austrian Workers and Employees Federation (affiliated with ÖVP)

OECD   Organization for Economic Cooperation and Development

OEEC   Organization for European Economic Cooperation

OMGUS   Office of Military Government, United States

ÖVP   Austrian People's Party (Austrian Christian Democratic Party)

PDP   Popular Democratic Party (French Catholic party)

PSF   French Social Party (mass conservative party)

SGEN   General Syndicate of National Education (French national
          teachers' union)

SIPDIC   International Secretariat of Christian-inspired Democratic Parties

SPD   Social Democratic Party of Germany

UEF   Union of European Federalists

UFCS   Women's Civic and Social Union (French Catholic
          women's organization)

UNESCO   United Nations Educational, Scientific, and Cultural Organization

USSR   Union of Soviet Socialist Republics

Notes

Introduction

1. The literature I'm referring to here is far too voluminous to cite in any detail, but for examples see Urs Altermatt, *Katholizismus und Moderne. Zur Sozial- und Mentalitätsgeschichte der Schweizer Katholiken im 19. Und 20. Jahrhundert* (Zurich: Benziger, 1989); David Blackbourn, *Marpingen: Apparitions of the Virgin Mary in a Nineteenth-Century German Village* (New York: Random House, 1995); Ruth Harris, *Lourdes: Body and Spirit in the Secular Age* (New York: Viking, 1999); Pamela Voekel, *Alone before God: The Religious Origins of Modernity in Mexico* (Durham, NC: Duke University Press, 2002).

2. There were certainly exceptions, notably in the eighteenth century, but in the wake of the French Revolution antimodernism took hold once again. Ulrich L. Lehner, *The Catholic Enlightenment: The Forgotten History of a Global Movement* (New York: Oxford University Press, 2016), esp. chap. 2.

3. For an influential statement of this view, see Mark Lilla, *The Stillborn God: Religion, Politics, and the Modern West* (New York: Vintage, 2007).

4. Charles Taylor, *A Secular Age* (Cambridge, MA: Harvard University Press, 2007).

5. For one example of a massive literature, see Joan Scott, *The Politics of the Veil* (Princeton, NJ: Princeton University Press, 2007).

6. For two distinguished examples of this approach, see Jean L. Cohen and Cécile Laborde, eds., *Religion, Secularism, and Constitutional Democracy* (New York: Columbia University Press, 2015); Elizabeth Shakman Hurd, *Beyond Religious Freedom: The New Global Politics of Religion* (Princeton, NJ: Princeton University Press, 2015). On varieties of secularism, see Michael Warner, Jonathan VanAntwerpen, and Craig Calhoun, eds., *Varieties of Secularism in a Secular Age* (Cambridge, MA: Harvard University Press, 2010).

7. Ari Joskowicz and Ethan Katz, eds., *Secularism in Question: Jews and Judaism in Modern Times* (Philadelphia: University of Pennsylvania Press, 2016); Mayathi Fernando, *The Republic Unsettled: Muslim French and the Contradictions of Secularism* (Durham, NC: Duke University Press, 2016); Jeanette S. Jouili, *Pious Practice and Secular Constraints: Women in the Islamic Revival in Europe* (Palo Alto, CA: Stanford University Press, 2015); John Lardas Modern, *Secularism in Antebellum America* (Chicago: University of Chicago Press, 2011); Elizabeth Pritchard, *Religion in Public: Locke's Political Theology* (Palo Alto, CA: Stanford University Press, 2013); Voekel, *Alone before God.*

8. Peter Fritzsche, "Nazi Modern," *Modernism / Modernity* 3 (1996): 1–22 at 2.

9. David Kertzer, *The Pope and Mussolini: The Secret History of Pius XI and the Rise of Fascism in Europe* (New York: Random House, 2014); Hubert Wolf, *Pope and Devil: The Vatican's Archives and the Third Reich,* trans. Kenneth Kronenberg (Cambridge, MA: Harvard University Press, 2010).

10. For versions of this argument in various national contexts, see Christian Baechler, *Clergé catholique et politique en Alsace, 1871–1940* (Strasbourg: Presses universitaires de Strasbourg, 2013); Kristian Buchna, *Ein klerikales Jahrzent? Kirche, Konfession und Politik in der Bundesrepublik während der 1950er Jahre* (Baden-Baden: Nomos, 2014); Thomas Forstner, *Priester in Zeiten des Umbruchs. Identität und Lebenswelt des katholischen Pfarrklerus in Oberbayern 1918 bis 1945* (Göttingen: Vandenhoeck & Ruprecht, 2014); Maximilian Liebmann, *'Heil Hitler'—Pastoral bedingt. Vom politischen Katholizismus zum Pastoralkatholizismus* (Vienna: Böhlau, 2009).

11. For excellent and important studies of those texts, though, see Etienne Fouilloux, *Une église en quête de liberté. La pensée catholique française entre modernism et Vatican II, 1914–1962* (Paris: Desclée de Brouwer, 1998); Fergus Kerr, *Twentieth-Century Catholic Theologians* (Malden, MA: Blackwell, 2016). For an account that marries theological and political thought, see Sarah Shortall, *Soldiers of God in a Secular World: The Politics of Catholic Theology in Twentieth-Century France* (Cambridge, MA: Harvard University Press, forthcoming).

12. For precedents, see John Connelly, *From Enemy to Brother: The Revolution in Catholic Teaching on the Jews* (Cambridge, MA: Harvard University Press, 2012); Brenna Moore, *Sacred Dread: Raïssa Maritain, the Allure of Suffering, and the French Catholic Revival (1905–1944)* (South Bend, IN: Notre Dame University Press, 2012).

13. There are exceptions, notably Lukas Rölli-Alkemper, *Familie im Wiederaufbau. Katholizismus und bürgerliches Familienideal in der Bundesrepublik Deutschland, 1945–1965* (Paderborn: Schöningh, 2000); Mark Ruff, *The Wayward Flock: Catholic Youth in Postwar West Germany, 1945–1965* (Chapel Hill: University of North Carolina Press, 2004).

14. For recent examples of the former, see Véronique Auzépy-Chavagnac, *Jean de Fabrègues et la jeune droite catholique. Aux sources de la révolution nationale* (Pas-de-Calais: Presses universitaires de Septentrion, 2002); Moore, *Sacred Dread*. For the latter, see John T. McGreevy, *American Jesuits and the World: How an Embattled Religious Order Made Modern Catholicism Global* (Princeton, NJ: Princeton University Press, 2016); Albert M. Wu, *From Christ to Confucius: German Missionaries, Chinese Christians, and the Globalization of Christianity, 1860–1950* (New Haven, CT: Yale University Press, 2016).

15. Edward Baring, "Ideas on the Move: Context in Transnational Intellectual History," *Journal of the History of Ideas* 77 (2016): 567–587; Wolfram Kaiser, *Christian Democracy and the Origins of European Union* (New York: Cambridge University Press, 2007); Piotr H. Kosicki, *Catholics on the Barricades: Poland, France, and 'Revolution,' 1891–1956* (New Haven, CT: Yale University Press, 2018); Paul Misner, *Catholic Labor Movements in Europe: Social Thought and Action, 1914–1965* (Washington, DC: Catholic University of America Press, 2015).

16. On the role of European Catholic exiles in the United States, see John T. McGreevy, *Catholicism and American Freedom: A History* (New York: Norton, 2003), chap. 7.

17. Some version of this story has been pursued by Urs Altermatt, Noel Cary, Michael P. Fogarty, R. E. M. Irving, Wolfram Kaiser, Maria Mitchell, Mario Einaudi and François Goguel, Jean-Marie Mayeur, Thomas Nipperdey, Franz-Josef Stegmann, Rudolf Uertz, Maurice Vaussard, and in a number of edited collections.

18. Emma Fattorini, *Hitler, Mussolini, and the Vatican: Pope Pius XI and the Speech That Was Never Made*, trans. Carl Ipsen (Malden, MA: Polity, 2011), xiii.

19. Michael Geyer and Sheila Fitzpatrick, eds., *Beyond Totalitarianism: Stalinism and Nazism Compared* (New York: Cambridge University Press, 2009); James Chappel, "The Catholic Origins of Totalitarianism Theory in Interwar Europe," *Modern Intellectual History* 9 (2011): 261–290.

20. For an introduction to these debates, see Michael Warner, *Publics and Counterpublics* (Brooklyn: Zone Books, 2002), chap. 1. My argument is indebted to, but departs from, the approach laid out in José Casanova, *Public Religions in the Modern World* (Chicago: University of Chicago Press, 1994).

21. The gendered nature of secularism has attracted a great deal of attention in recent years. See, for instance, Linell E. Cady and Tracy Fessenden, eds., *Religion, the Secular, and the Politics of Sexual Difference* (New York: Columbia University Press, 2013).

22. See, for instance, Anna Grzymała-Busse, *Nations under God: How Churches Use Moral Authority to Influence Policy* (Princeton, NJ: Princeton University Press, 2015).

1. Catholic Antimodern, 1920–1929

1. Anson Rabinbach, *In the Shadow of Catastrophe: German Intellectuals between Apocalypse and Enlightenment* (Berkeley: University of California Press, 1997), 2.

2. Jacques Maritain, *Oeuvres complètes*, ed. Cercle d'études Jacques et Raïssa Maritain (Paris: Éditions Saint-Paul, 1982–2007), 1:928; Joseph Eberle, "Die neue Wochenschrift *Schönere Zukunft*," *Schönere Zukunft* 1, no. 1 (1 October 1925): 1–3 at 1; Max Scheler, "Prophetischer oder marxistischer Sozialismus," *Hochland* 17, no. 1 (1919): 71–84.

3. The culture wars of the late nineteenth century, it now appears, were as much about mutual learning and exchange as they were about contestation. See, for instance, Oliver Zimmer, "Beneath the 'Culture War': Corpus Christi Processions and Mutual Accommodation in the Second German Empire," *Journal of Modern History* 82 (June 2010): 288–334. My point is that this accommodation had little intellectual or even rhetorical rationale beyond the occasional references to a shared "Christian" heritage. Ulrich Lehner has shown how it did have one in the "Catholic Enlightenment" of the eighteenth century. Religious freedom under the umbrella of the Austro-Hungarian empire was quite a different thing, however, from religious freedom in a secular republic. Ulrich L. Lehner, *The Catholic Enlightenment: The Forgotten History of a Global Movement* (New York: Oxford University Press, 2016).

4. On economic thinking, see Paul Misner, *Social Catholicism in Europe: From the Onset of Industrialization to the First World War* (New York: Crossroad, 1991), esp. chaps. 12–13 on early Christian Democrats; on political thinking, see Borja Villalonga, "The Theoretical Origins of Catholic Nationalism in Nineteenth-Century Europe," *Modern Intellectual History* 11 (2014): 307–331.

5. *Pascendi domenici gregis*, esp. secs. 24–25, available at http://w2.vatican.va /content/pius-x/en/encyclicals/documents/hf_p-x_enc_19070908_pascendi -dominici-gregis.html.

6. On the resurgence of antimodernism in the 1920s, see, for instance, Klaus Große Kracht, "Von der 'geistigen Offensive' zur neuen Unauffälligkeit. Katholische Intellektuelle in Deutschland und Frankreich (1910–1960)," in *Religion und Gesellschaft. Europa im 20. Jahrhundert*, ed. Friedrich Wilhelm Graf and Klaus Große Kracht (Cologne: Böhlau, 2007), 223–246, esp. 226–234; Thomas Ruster, *Die verlorene Nützlichkeit der Religion. Katholizismus und Moderne in der Weimarer Republik* (Paderborn: Schöningh, 1994), summarized on 391–392. For three studies that find a broad continuity in Catholic cultural and intellectual life across the war years, see Margaret Stieg Dalton, *Catholicism, Popular Culture, and the Arts in Germany, 1890–1930* (South

Bend, IN: Notre Dame University Press, 2005); Patrick Houlihan, *Catholicism and the Great War: Religion and Everyday Life in Germany and Austria-Hungary, 1914–1922* (New York: Cambridge University Press, 2015); Otto Weiß, *Kulturkatholizismus. Katholiken auf dem Weg in die deutsche Kultur, 1900–1933* (Regensburg: Pustet, 2014).

7. Victor Bucaille, "L'inquiétude présente," *La Vie Catholique* 1 (20 September 1924): 3. For another example, see A. Felden, "Der Beginn des neuen Kulturkampfes in Deutschland," *Die Monarchie* 1, no. 16 (16 January 1919): 274–276.

8. "Das Linzer Programm," available at http://www.marxists.org/deutsch /geschichte/oesterreich/spoe/1926/linzerprog.htm; Ch. Seignbobos, "Histoire du parti républicain," in *La politique républicaine,* ed. Michael Augé-Laribé et al. (Paris: Felix Alcan, 1924), 11–60 at 56–59.

9. See, for instance, Joseph Eberle, "Meinungsverschiedenheiten katholischer Sozialwissenschaftleer," *Schönere Zukunft* 4, no. 9 (25 November 1928): 184–187; Arthur Vermeersch, S.J., "Soziale Krise und Reformtheorien," *Theologisch-praktische Quartalschrift* 82 (1928): 687–724.

10. Joseph Eberle, "Wenn Christus König des öffentlichen Lebens ware," *Schönere Zukunft* 3, no. 5 (30 October 1927): 93–95 at 93.

11. Stefan Goebel, *The Great War and Medieval Memory: War, Remembrance and Medievalism in Britain and Germany, 1914–1940* (New York: Cambridge University Press, 2007); Jay Winter, *Sites of Memory, Sites of Mourning: The Great War in European Cultural History* (New York: Cambridge University Press, 1995).

12. Accounts of Austria, in particular, urge a continuity between the 1920s and 1930s in this regard. See Julie Thorpe, "Austrofascism: Revisiting the 'Authoritarian State' 40 Years On," *Journal of Contemporary History* 45 (2010): 315–343; Janek Wassermann, *Black Vienna: The Radical Right in the Red City, 1918–1938* (Ithaca, NY: Cornell University Press, 2014).

13. Joseph Eberle, "Die neuen Staatsregierungen Mitteleuropas und ihr Rechtscharakter (Zur Kontroverse Domdekan Dr. Kiefl und Dr. Tischleder)," *Schönere Zukunft* 3, no. 35 (27 May 1928): 752–755.

14. Wassermann, *Black Vienna,* 194.

15. Mona Hassan, *Longing for the Lost Caliphate: A Transregional History* (Princeton, NJ: Princeton University Press, 2017), chaps. 5–6.

16. For an unparalleled examination of the Church's aggressive role in the formation of a Bavarian identity, see Werner K. Blessing, *Staat und Kirche in der Gesellschaft. Institutionelle Autorität und mentaler Wandel in Bayern während des 19. Jahrhunderts* (Göttingen: Vandenhoek & Ruprecht, 1982).

17. For the controversy over Hildebrand's remarks in Paris, see the documents in Nachlaß Franz Xaver Münch, Historisches Archiv des Erzbistum Köln, Box

126; Benjamin Ziemann, *War Experiences in Rural Germany: 1914–1923*, trans. Alex Skinner (Oxford: Berg, 2007), chap. 4 on this theme, esp. 142–144 (this quotation is at 142). For Catholic memory of the war, see Houlihan, *Catholicism and the Great War*, chap. 7.

18. Gregory Munro, *Hitler's Bavarian Antagonist: Georg Moenius and the Allgemeine Rundschau of Munich, 1929–1933* (Lewiston, NY: Edwin Mellen, 2006), 21.

19. Jacques Bainville, *Les conséquences politiques de la paix* (Paris: Nouvelle Librairie Nationale, 1920).

20. Otto Kunze, "Großdeutsch und kleindeutsch," *Allgemeine Rundschau* 20, no. 39 (27 September 1923): 462–463 at 462.

21. This is explored in Gregory Munro, "The Holy Roman Empire in German Roman Catholic Thought, 1929–33: Georg Moenius' Revival of Reichsideologie," *Journal of Religious History* 17 (1993): 439–464. For an overview of specifically Bavarian conservative thought, and one that places Moenius and the *Allgemeine Rundschau* into context, see Friedhelm Mennekes, *Die Republik als Herausforderung. Konservatives Denken in Bayern zwischen Weimarer Republik und antidemokratischer Reaktion (1918–1925)* (Berlin: Duncker & Humblot, 1972).

22. Förster quoted in Munro, *Hitler's Bavarian Antagonist*, 97; Georg Moenius, "Frankreichs Jugend zwischen Scylla und Charybdis," *Schönere Zukunft* 2, no. 17 (23 January 1927): 329–330 at 330.

23. Otto Sachse, "Katholizismus und Faschismus," *Allgemeine Rundschau* 20, no. 2 (13 January 1923): 13–14; Georg Moenius, "Nationalsozialismus, Action française und Faschismus," *Allgemeine Rundschau* 28, no. 10 (7 March 1931): 145–150 at 145. On Catholic support for early National Socialism, see Derek Hastings, "How 'Catholic' Was the Early Nazi Movement? Religion, Race and Culture in Munich, 1919–24," *Central European History* 36 (2003): 383–433. On the *Universal Review*'s anti-Nazi polemics, see Munro, *Hitler's Bavarian Antagonist*, chap. 4.

24. Robert Moeller, *German Peasants and Agrarian Politics, 1914–1924: The Rhineland and Westphalia* (Chapel Hill: University of North Carolina Press, 1986), esp. chap. 6.

25. Georg Moenius, "Zentralismus in Deutschland—zugunsten der Trusts?," *Schönere Zukunft* 2, no. 3 (17 October 1926): 45.

26. For two treatments of anti-Semitism's centrality to earlier Catholic thought and action, both of which trouble the apologist distinction between modern "anti-Semitism" and traditional "anti-Judaism," see Olaf Blaschke, *Katholizismus und Antisemitismus um Deutschen Kaiserreich* (Göttingen: Vandenhoeck & Ruprecht, 1997); Vicki Caron, "Catholic Political Mobilization and Antisemitic Violence in Fin de Siècle France: The Case of the Union Nationale," *Journal of Modern History* 81 (2009): 294–346.

27. Georg Moenius, *Italienische Reise* (Freiburg im Breisgau: Herder, 1925), 317; Heinrich Wartberg, "Nationalsozialismus, Marxismus und moderne Judentum," *Allgemeine Rundschau* 20, no. 51/52 (22 December 1923): 608–609. On the *Rundschau* circle more broadly, see Munro, *Hitler's Bavarian Antagonist*, 221. On the Weimar Catholic press, see Ulrike Ehret, *Church, Nation and Race: Catholics and Antisemitism in Germany and England, 1918–45* (New York: Manchester University Press, 2011), 58–72.

28. *Die Reden. 62. General-Versammlung der Katholiken Deutschlands* (Würzburg: Fränkische Gesellschafts-Druckerei, 1923), 3–4. For Moenius on Faulhaber, see Georg Moenius, *Kardinal Faulhaber* (Vienna: Reinhold, 1933).

29. D. R. Dorondo, *Bavaria and German Federalism: Reich to Republic, 1918–33, 1945–49* (New York: St. Martin's, 1992), chap. 1.

30. Benedikt Schmittmann, *Wirtschafts- und Sozialordnung als Aufgabe*, 2nd ed. (Freiburg: Karl Alber, 1948), 44–46; Anonymous [presumably Schmittmann], "Was wir erstreben," *Reich- und Heimatblätter* 1, nos. 5–6 (1925): 35.

31. On the political history of right-wing Catholics like Spahn, see above all Christoph Hübner, *Die Rechstkatholiken, die Zentrumspartei und die katholische Kirche in Deutschland bis zum Reichskonkordat von 1933* (Berlin: Lit, 2014). On their ideas, see Gabriele Clemens, *Martin Spahn und der Rechts-Katholizismus in der Weimarer Republik* (Mainz: Mattthias-Grünewald, 1983), 98–144.

32. Moenius, "Zentralismus in Deutschland—zugunsten der Trusts?"

33. Tait Keller, "Eternal Mountains—Eternal Germany: The Alpine Association and the Ideology of Alpinism, 1909–39" (PhD diss., Georgetown University, 2006), chap. 4. On Salzburg, see Michael Steinberg, *Austria as Theater and Ideology: The Meaning of the Salzburg Festival* (Ithaca, NY: Cornell University Press, 1990), esp. 70–72. The archbishop quoted in Heinrich Lutz, *Demokratie im Zwielicht. Der Weg der deutschen Katholiken aus dem Kaiserreich in die Republik 1914–1925* (Munich: Kösel, 1963), 95.

34. Eberle, "Die neue Wochenschrift *Schönere Zukunft*," 2; Karl Debus, "Neues zur deutschen Geschichts- und Kulturauffassung," *Schönere Zukunft* 1, no. 11 (13 December 1925): 274–278 at 276; Hans Pfeiffer, "Politische Fragen der reichsdeutschen Katholiken," *Schönere Zukunft* 3, no. 18 (29 January 1928): 373–374. For circulation, see Wassermann, *Black Vienna*, 197.

35. Anton Orel, *Oeconomia perennis. Die wirtschaftslehre der menschheitsüberlieferung im Wandel der Zeiten und in ihrer unwandelbaren Bedeutung*, Bd. 1 (Mainz: Mathias-Grünewald, 1930); Sándor Horváth, *Eigentumsrecht nach dem h. Thomas von Aquin* (Graz: Ulrich Moser, 1929); Friedrich Gustav Piffl et al., *Lehren und Weisungen der österreichische Bischöfe über soziale Fragen der Gegenwart* (Vienna: Typographische Anstalt, 1926), 5.

36. Karl Lugmayer, *Das Linzer Programm der christlichen Arbeiter Österreichs* (Vienna: Typographische Anstalt, 1924), 11, 15; Ernst Karl Winter, "Die österreichische Aktion," *Allgemeine Rundschau* 26, no. 36 (7 September 1929): 685–690; Eugen Kogon, *Die Idee des christlichen Ständestaats. Frühe Schriften,* ed. Gottfried Erb and Michael Kogon (Berlin: Ullstein, 1999), 232; E. K. Winter, "Die Juden und das letzte Jahrhundert Weltgeschichte," *Das Neue Reich* 1 (1918–1919): 270–273 at 273; E. K. Winter, *Nibelungentreue—Nibelungenehre: Ein katholisches, österreichisches, deutsches Kulturprogramm* (Vienna: Vogelsang, 1921), 11.

37. Moenius, foreword to Henri Massis, *Verteidigung des Abendlandes, Mit einer Einführung von Georg Moenius,* trans. Georg Moenius (Hellerau: Jakob Gegner, 1930), 17; Moenius, *Italienische Reise,* 312–318. "Looks to" is quoted from Munro, *Hitler's Bavarian Antagonist,* 226; Otto Kunze, "Am Meilenstein 1923," *Allgemeine Rundschau* 20, no. 1 (6 January 1923): 1–2.

38. For an account, see Hubert Wolf, *Pope and Devil: The Vatican's Archives and the Third Reich,* trans. Kenneth Kronenberg (Cambridge, MA: Harvard University Press, 2010), chap. 2.

39. David Kertzer, *The Pope and Mussolini: The Secret History of Pius XI and the Rise of Fascism in Europe* (New York: Random House, 2014), chap. 14.

40. Georg Moenius, *Paris, Frankreichs Herz* (Munich: Limes, 1928), 26.

41. On Moenius and the French context more generally, see Joris Lehnert, "Rome ou la solution à tous les problèmes européens: Georg Moenius et le concept de romanité durant l'entre-deux-guerres," *Amnis* 11 (2012), available at http://amnis.revues.org/1844. For Moenius's French writing, see Georg Moenius, "Slaves, Germans, Latins," *Cahiers* 2, no. 2 (1929): 116–132; Georges Moenius, "Le germanisme contre la romanité (Témoignage d'un catholique allemand)," *La Revue Universelle* 37 (1929): 641–658 (and for Jean-Pierre Maxence's praise of Moenius's journal, the editorial preface to the former).

42. Heinrich Staab, "Der Großdeutsche Gedanke," *Allgemeine Rundschau* 9, no. 3 (21 January 1922): 26–27 at 26; E. K. Winter, foreword to *Die Österreichische Aktion. Programmatische Studien* (Vienna: Selbstverlag, 1927), 5–10 at 8. For more on the movement, see Janek Wassermann, "Österreichische Aktion: Monarchism, Authoritarianism, and the Unity of the Austrian Conservative Ideological Field during the First Republic," *Central European History* 47 (2014): 76–104.

43. Charles Maurras, "L'école laïque contre la France," *Almanach de l'Action française* 20 (1928): 69–79 at 69; Robert Vallery-Radot, *Devant les idoles* (Paris: Perrin, 1921), 6.

44. Moenius, "Nationalsozialismus, Action française und Faschismus"; Georg Moenius, "Jacques Maritain über Thomas von Aquin als 'Apostel unserer Zeit,'" *Schönere Zukunft* 3, no. 39 (24 June 1928): 837–838.

45. Maritain, *Oeuvres complètes,* 3:1280.

46. Jacques Maritain to Henri Massis, 3 April 1914, Archives of the Centre d'études Jacques et Raïssa Maritain, Kolbsheim (emphasis in original); Moenius, "Nationalsozialismus, Action française und Fascismus," 146; Joseph Paul-Boncour and Charles Maurras, *La République et la Décentralisation: Un Débat de 1903* (Paris: Nouvelle Librairie Nationale, 1923), 78.

47. A. M., "Droit de propriété," *Bulletin Thomiste* 9 (1932): 602–606; J. Tonneau, review of Horváth, *Eigentumsrecht, Bulletin Thomiste* 8 (1931): 373–376.

48. For Maurras and Vogelsang, see Michael Sutton, *Nationalism, Positivism and Catholicism: The Politics of Charles Maurras and French Catholics, 1890–1914* (Cambridge: Cambridge University Press, 1982), 78–79. For Maurras and La Tour du Pin, see Matthew Elbow, *French Corporative Theory, 1789–1848* (New York: Columbia University Press, 1953), 79, 119.

49. Jacques Maritain, "En lisant Georges Valois," in *Oeuvres complètes,* 16:320–323. Originally from *La Gazette Française,* 28 May 1925.

50. Nel Ariès, *L'économie politique et la doctrine catholique* (Paris: Nouvelle Librairie Nationale, 1923), preface by Georges Valois.

51. Maurras, "L'école laïque contre la France," 70; Maritain, *Oeuvres complètes,* 3:435–658. For the reality, see Dale K. Van Kley, *The Religious Origins of the French Revolution: From Calvin to the Civil Constitution, 1560–1791* (New Haven, CT: Yale University Press, 1996); Philip Nord, *The Republican Moment: Struggles for Democracy in Nineteenth Century France* (Cambridge, MA: Harvard University Press, 1995), chap. 5.

52. Marquis de La-Tour-du-Pin, *Vers un ordre social chrétien* (Paris: Nouvelle Librairie Nationale, 1921), 71–104; Maritain quoted in Bernard Doering, "The Origin and Development of Maritain's Idea of the Chosen People," in *Jacques Maritain and the Jews,* ed. Robert Royal (Milwaukee: American Maritain Association, 1994), 17–35 at 27.

53. Henri Massis and Léon Daudet both interpreted Communism through the lens of the German peril. See Henri Massis, *Défence de l'Occident* (Paris: Plon, 1927), chaps. 2–3; Olivier Dard, *Charles Maurras. Le maître et l'action* (Paris: Armand Colin, 2013), 140. For the centrality of Germany to Maurras's worldview, see Michel Grunewald, "De Luther à Hitler. Maurras et l'Allemagne éternelle," in *Charles Maurras et l'étranger, l'étranger et Charles Maurras,* ed. Olivier Dard and Michel Grunewald (New York: Peter Lang, 2009), 339–358.

54. Charles Maurras, "Gaulois, Germains, Latins," *La Revue Universelle* 27 (October–December 1926): 385–419, esp. 407 (emphasis in original); Maritain, *Oeuvres complètes,* 1:906, 1082.

55. Otto Kunze, "Katholikentag—Weltrundschau," *Allgemeine Rundschau* 19, no. 34 (26 August 1922): 399–400 at 400; Kogon, *Die Idee des christlichen Ständestaats,* 147; Sachse, "Katholizismus und Faschismus," 13; Oscar von Soden, "Der

abstrakte Staat," *Allgemeine Rundschau* 26, no. 38 (21 September 1929): 742–745 at 742; Maritain, *Oeuvres complètes,* 1:964 (for one striking and early example of Maritain's antimodern discourse of rights).

56. Simone de Beauvoir, *Memoirs of a Dutiful Daughter* (New York: Harper-Collins, 1959), 127.

57. Wasserman, *Black Vienna,* 197; Friedrich Muckermann, *Im Kampf Zwischen zwei Epochen. Lebenserinnerungen* (Mainz: Matthias-Grünewald, 1973), 476.

58. *Ubi arcano dei consilio,* sec. 12, available at http://w2.vatican.va/content/pius-xi /en/encyclicals/documents/hf_p-xi_enc_23121922_ubi-arcano-dei-consilio .html.

59. Eugen Weber, *Action Française: Royalism and Reaction in Twentieth-Century France* (Stanford, CA: Stanford University Press, 1962), 244.

60. On aristocracy, see Larry Eugene Jones, "Catholic Conservatives in the Weimar Republic: The Politics of the Rhenish-Westphalian Aristocracy, 1919–1933," *German History* 18 (2000): 61–85. They were joined by some titans of industry such as Eugène Mathon who saw in social Catholicism a means to halt the spread of socialism.

61. Weber, *Action Française,* chap. 13.

62. For an account that gives significantly more explanatory power to this condemnation, see Philippe Chenaux, *Entre Maurras et Maritain: une generation intellectuelle catholique (1920–1930)* (Paris: Éditions du Cerf, 1999).

63. "Syllabus of Errors" (1864), sec. 80, available at http://www.papalencyclicals .net/Pius09/p9syll.htm.

64. Yves Palau, "Approches du catholicisme républicain dans la France de l'entre-deux-guerres," *Mil neuf cent* 13 (1995): 46–66.

65. On the role of pragmatism, and its contestation, in Weimar Catholicism, see Stefan Gerber, *Pragmatismus und Kulturkritik. Politikbegründung und politische Kommunikation im Katholizismus der Weimarer Republic (1918–1925)* (Paderborn: Schöningh, 2016).

66. For one example of when pragmatism can inspire, see Aurelian Craiutu, *A Virtue for Courageous Minds: Moderation in French Political Thought, 1748–1830* (Princeton, NJ: Princeton University Press, 2012).

67. Félicité de Lamennais, *Paroles d'un croyant* (Paris: Eugène Renduel, 1834), 2.

68. Gurian planned an entire book on Lamennais, but it never came to fruition. He did write about him at length, however. See, for instance, Waldemar Gurian, *Die politischen und sozialen Ideen des französischen Katholizismus, 1789–1914* (Mönchengladbach: Volksverein-Verlag, 1929), chaps. 5–6; Waldemar Gurian, "Lamennais," *Heilige Feuer* 7, no. 6 (November 1927): 499–517.

69. The best biographical source for Gurian's life is Heinz Hürten, *Waldmar Gurian. Ein Zeuge der Krise unserer Welt in der ersten Hälfte des 20. Jahrhunderts* (Mainz: Matthias-Grünewald, 1972).

70. Part of a biographical sketch that Karl Thieme sent to Gurian, apparently destined for *Kölnische Rundschau*. Karl Thieme to Waldemar Gurian, January 1947, Folder 163/28, Nachlaß Thieme, Institut für Zeitgeschichte, Munich.

71. A great deal of work has been done on Catholic culture in the Rhineland before World War I. Especially relevant is Claudia Hiepel, *Arbeiterkatholizismus an der Ruhr. August Brust und der Gewerkverein christlicher Bergarbeiter* (Stuttgart: Kohlhammer, 1999). For membership figures in the Volksverein by *Land*, see Helmut Walser Smith, *German Nationalism and Religious Conflict: Culture, Ideology, Politics, 1870–1914* (Princeton, NJ: Princeton University Press, 1995), 110.

72. For an exploration of the Vatican's engagement in the Ruhr Crisis, and its subtle aid to the Germans, see Stewart A. Stehlin, *Weimar and the Vatican, 1919–1933: German-Vatican Diplomatic Relations in the Interwar Years* (Princeton, NJ: Princeton University Press, 1983), chap. 5.

73. Waldemar Gurian, *Hitler and the Christians*, trans. E. F. Peeler (New York: Sheed & Ward, 1935), 25.

74. Julius Bachem, ed., *Zur Jahrhundertfeier der Vereinigung der Rheinlande mit Preußen* (Cologne: Bachem, 1915).

75. Ellen Lovell Evans, *The German Center Party, 1870–1933: A Study in Political Catholicism* (Carbondale: Southern Illinois University Press, 1981), 226; Hermann Platz, "Um die preußische Frage," *Abendland* 2, no. 4 (January 1927): 103–105; Carl Schmitt, *Die Rheinlande als Objekt internationaler Politik* (Cologne: Verlag der Rheinischen Zentrumspartei, 1925).

76. Dietrich Orlow, *Weimar Prussia, 1918–1925: The Unlikely Rock of Democracy* (Pittsburgh: University of Pittsburgh Press, 1986); Eric Kohler, "The Successful German Center-Left: Joseph Hess and the Prussian Center Party, 1908–32," *Central European History* 23 (1990): 313–349.

77. Margaret Lavinia Anderson, "Interdenominationalism, Clericalism, Pluralism: The Zentrumsstreit and the Dilemma of Catholicism in Wilhelmine Germany," *Central European History* 21 (1988): 350–378; Noel Cary, *The Path to Christian Democracy: German Catholics and the Party System from Windthorst to Adenauer* (Cambridge, MA: Harvard University Press, 1996), 66, 85; Klaus Große Kracht, *Die Stunde der Laien? Katholische Aktion in Deutschland im europäischen Kontext, 1920–1960* (Paderborn: Schöningh, 2016), chap. 4.

78. Waldemar Gurian, "Der Katholizismus im Urteil der Zeit," *Das Neue Reich* 11 (1929): 693–695 at 695; Waldemar Gurian, "Lebensaufgabe der katholischen Presse," *Das Neue Reich* 12 (1930): 445–446 at 445.

79. Max Kaller, *Unser Laienapostolat* (Leutesdorf: Verlag des Johannesbundes, 1927), 18–21.

80. "Writings Keep Dr. Gurian Busy." *Tribune.* Undated. Waldemar Gurian Papers, Library of Congress, Box 18, Folder 1. For a particularly clear evocation of Guardini, see Waldemar Gurian, *Die deutsche Jugendbewegung,* 3rd ed. (Habelschwerdt: Frankes Buchhandlung, 1924), 26.

81. Romano Guardini, "Über Sozialwissenschaft und Ordnung unter Personen," *Die Schildgenossen* 6, no. 2 (March 1926): 125–150 at 148. He explored this tension further in Romano Guardini, *Der Gegensatz. Versuche zu einer Philosophie des Lebendig-Konkreten* (Mainz: Matthias-Grünewald, 1925).

82. Romano Guardini, *Neue Jugend und katholischer Geist* (Mainz: Matthias-Grünewald, 1920), 12.

83. Quoted in Weiß, *Kulturkatholizismus,* 151.

84. Paul-Ludwig Landsberg, *Die Welt des Mittelalter und Wir* (Bonn: F. Cohen, 1922), 105, 103.

85. W. G. [almost certainly Gurian], review of Landsberg, *Die Welt des Mittelalter und Wir, Die Schildgenossen* 3 (1922): 44–45 at 44; Anton L. Mayer-Pfannholz, "Paul Ludwig Landsberg und das Mittelalter," *Hochland* 20 (1923): 319–322; Heinrich Getzeny, "Was ist uns Geschichte?," *Die Schildgenossen* 4 (1924): 430–435 at 435.

86. Waldemar Gurian to Jacques Maritain, 25 May 1928, Maritain Archives, Kolbsheim; Waldemar Gurian to Max Scheler, 5 September 1921, and Paul-Ludwig Landsberg to Max Scheler, n.d. [early 1920s], both in Nachlaß Scheler, Bayerische Staatsbibliothek München, Ana315.E.II. Per his matriculation records at Universität Köln, Gurian took courses on Kant, metaphysics, and epistemology with Scheler, and another from his disciple Dietrich von Hildebrand (on the foundations of sociology, which we know from his other writings of the time were strongly rooted in Scheler's theory of value). See Gurian Papers, Box 18, Folder 4.

87. Max Scheler, *On the Eternal in Man,* trans. Bernard Noble (Hamden, CT: Archon, 1972), 379 (emphasis in original), 12 (from preface to first German edition).

88. Max Scheler, *Politisch-Pädagogische Schriften,* ed. Manfred Frings (Munich: Francke, 1982), 322.

89. Waldemar Gurian, "Das geistige Gesicht unserer Zeit," *Abendland* 5, 2 (November 1929): 53–56; Ernst Michel, *Politik aus dem Glauben* (Jena: E. Diederichs, 1926), 12, 144; Romano Guardini, "Die Gefährdung der lebendigen Persönlichkeit," *Die Schildgenossen* 6 (1926): 33–51 at 46–47; Carl Muth, "Res Publica," *Hochland* 24 (1926–1927): 1–14 at 1.

90. For Gurian's Schmittean critique of parliamentarism, see Waldemar Gurian, "Zur Soziologie der Wahlpropaganda," *Archiv für Politik und Geschichte* 3, no. 8 (June 1925): 585–589.

91. On Gurian, secular regions, and conservative nihilism, see James Chappel, "Nihilism and the Cold War: The Catholic Reception of Nihilism between Nietzsche and Adenauer," *Rethinking History* 17 (2014): 95–110. On Gurian and totalitarianism theory, see James Chappel, "The Catholic Origins of Totalitarianism Theory in Interwar Europe," *Modern Intellectual History* 9 (2011): 261–290.

92. Muth, "Res Publica," 12.

93. Gurian, *Hitler and the Christians*, 29; Waldemar Gurian to Jacques Maritain, 24 September 1927, Maritain Archives, Kolbsheim; Karl Neundörfer, "Politische Form und religiöser Glaube: Eine Bücherbesprechung," *Die Schildgenossen* 5, no. 4 (July 1925): 323–331 at 327. See also Karl Neundörfer, "Die politisch-religiöse Basis der Zentrumspartei," *Die Schildgenossen* 4 (1924): 135–138. On Mausbach and Tischleder, see Rudolf Uertz, *Vom Gottesrecht zum Menschenrecht. Das katholische Staatsdenken im Deutschland von der französischen Revolution bis zum II. Vatikanische Konzil* (Paderborn: Schöningh, 2004), 312–323. Adenauer's speeches are available in *Die Reden* 62.

94. Franz-Josef Stegmann, *Der soziale Katholizismus und die Mitbestimmung in Deutschland* (Paderborn: Schöningh, 1974), 141–157.

95. Young-Sun Hong, *Welfare, Modernity, and the Weimar State, 1919–1933* (Princeton, NJ: Princeton University Press, 1998), chap. 2; Hubert Mockenhaupt, *Weg und Wirken des geistlichen Sozialpolitikers Heinrich Brauns* (Munich: Schöningh, 1977), esp. 205–207.

96. Gustav Gundlach, "Zur Christianisierung unseres Wirtschaftslebens," *Stimmen der Zeit* 109 (1925): 268–280 at 271; Oswald von Nell-Breuning, *Grundzüge der Börsenmoral* (Freiburg: Herder, 1928); Otto Schilling, *Christliche Gesellschaftslehre* (Freiburg: Herder, 1926), 91; Karl Joseph Schulte, "Richtlinien über Kapital und Arbeit," *Soziale Kultur* 47 (1927): 81–83.

97. William Patch, *Christian Trade Unions in the Weimar Republic: The Failure of Corporate Pluralism* (New Haven, CT: Yale University Press, 1985).

98. Noah Strote, *Lions and Lambs: Conflict in Weimar and the Creation of Post-Nazi Germany* (New Haven, CT: Yale University Press, 2017), chap. 2.

99. For an example of this antimodern defense of Weimar, a position that quickly became untenable, see Robert Grosche, "Die neue Demokratie," *Hochland* 17, 1 (1919): 1–8.

100. Waldemar Gurian, "Die Gestaltungskraft sozialer Theorie der Katholiken," *Soziale Revue* 30 (1930): 241–249 at 243; Waldemar Gurian, "Faschismus und Bolschewismus," *Heilige Feuer* 15 (1928): 197–203 at 200; Hürten, *Waldemar Gurian*, 24n for "slavery" quotation; Waldemar Gurian, "Der kapitalistische Unternehmer (Aus Anlaß der Schrift von Franz Müller)," *Heilige Feuer* 14, no. 6 (March 1927): 218–226.

101. Ralph Bowen, *German Theories of the Corporative State* (New York: Whittlesey House, 1947), 118.

102. Heinrich Pesch, *Teaching Guide to Economics,* trans. Rupert J. Ederer (Lewiston, NY: Edwin Mellen, 2003), 1:331, 2:257, 1:212 (emphasis added).

103. Heinrich Pesch, *Ethik und Volkswirtschaft* (Freiburg: Herder, 1918), chap. 5 on capitalism, 146–147 on empire.

104. Scheler, "Prophetischer oder marxistischer Sozialismus," 78.

105. Ulrich Bröckling, *Katholische Intellektuelle in der Weimarer Republik* (Munich: Fink, 1993), chap. 5.

106. Paul Jostock, *Der Ausgang des Kapitalismus* (Munich: Duncker & Humblot, 1928), 288.

107. Gurian, "Das geistige Gesicht unserer Zeit," 56; Adenauer, *Die Reden 62,* 48. See also, for another example, Karl Neundörfer, "Die Kirche als gesellschaftliche Notwendigkeit," *Hochland* 20, no. 1 (1922–1923): 225–237.

108. Ehret, *Church, Nation and Race,* 61.

109. R. Kuenzer, "Deutschland und der Völkerbund," *Abendland* 2, no. 1 (1926): 7–8; Gustav Gundlach, "Antisemitismus," *Lexikon für Theologie und Kirche* (Freiburg im Breisgau: Herder, 1930), 1:504–505. The best analysis of this phenomenon remains Hermann Greive, *Theologie und Ideologie. Katholizismus und Judentum in Deutschland und Österreich, 1918–1935* (Heidelberg: Lambert Schneider, 1969) (Metzger quoted at 3). For an analysis of Rosa's article, see Wolf, *Pope and Devil,* 116–117.

110. Ruster, *Die verlorene Nützlichkeit der Religion,* 173–179.

111. Moeller, *German Peasants and Agrarian Politics,* 125; Larry Eugene Jones, "Catholics on the Right: The Reich Catholic Committee of the German National People's Party, 1920–33," *Historisches Jahrbuch* 126 (2006): 221–267.

112. Walter Dirks, "Primat der Politik: Zur politischen Aufgabe der Zentrumspartei," *Heilige Feuer* 13, no. 4 (January 1925): 129–140, esp. 131; Hermann Platz, "Die Zerspaltung des Abendlands," *Heilige Feuer* 14, no. 7 (April 1927): 262–264; Scheler, *Politisch-pädagogische Schriften,* 434–435, 465–467; Scheler, *On the Eternal in Man,* 292; Carl Schmitt, *Roman Catholicism and Political Form,* trans. G. L. Ulmen (Westport, CT: Greenwood, 1996), 8–10.

113. Gurian, *Die deutsche Jugendbewegung,* 33n, 61–71; Walter Gerhart [i.e., Gurian], *Um des Reiches Zukunft. Nationale Wiedergeburt oder politische Reaktion* (Freiburg: Herder, 1932), chaps. 9–10.

114. Muth, "Res publica," 3.

115. Peter Wust, *Ein Deutsch-Französisches Gespräch. Peter Wusts Briefwechsel mit Frankreich,* ed. Johannes Bendiek und Hildebert Huning (Münster: Regensburg, 1968), 309.

116. Waldemar Gurian, "Das Frankreichbuch von Georg Moenius," *Abendland* 4 (1929): 220–221.

117. Bernhard Braubach, "Der französische Katholizismus zwischen Staat und Gesellschaft," *Die Schildgenossen* 9, 5 (September 1929): 393–406 at 393.

118. Eugène Duthoit, "Déclaration d'ouverture," in *Semaine sociale de France, Metz 1919* (Lyon: Chronique sociale de France, 1919), 13–37, at 18, 21.

119. R. William Rauch Jr., "From the Sillon to the Mouvement Républicain Populaire," *Catholic Historical Review* 58 (1972): 25–66 at 49–50.

120. Oscar L. Arnal, "The Nature and Success of Breton Christian Democracy: The Example of *L'Ouest-Éclair*," *Catholic Historical Review* 68 (1982): 226–248.

121. See, for instance, Eugène Duthoit, "Comment adapter l'Etat à ses fonctions economiques," in *Le role économique de l'état* (Semaines Sociales de France) (Lyon: Chronique sociale de France, 1922), 33–60 at 58–60; R. P. Gillet, "Les doctrines individualistes et leur influence néfaste sur l'état," in ibid., 201–218.

122. Stephen Schloesser, *Jazz Age Catholicism: Mystic Modernism in Postwar Paris, 1919–1933* (Buffalo: University of Toronto Press, 2005).

123. Waldemar Gurian and Werner Becker, "Deutschland und Frankreich im neuen Europa: Ein Gespräch mit Lucien Romier," *Abendland* 2, no. 6 (March 1927): 169–172.

124. Lucien Romier, *Explication de notre temps* (Paris: Grasset, 1925), 245, 242, 95–98, 244.

125. Albert Muller, *Notes d'économie politique* (Paris: Spes, 1927), 397, 211, 255–257, 6–7, 25.

126. Johannes Messner to Pius Fink, 8 February 1930, Historisches Archiv des Erzbistums Köln, Archiv der Görres-Gesellschaft, Nr. 216, 1.

127. Johannes Messner, *Sozialökonomik und Sozialethik. Studie zur Grundlegung einer systematischen Wirtschaftsethik* (Paderborn: Schöningh, 1927), 54.

128. Heinrich Brauns, "Ziele und Methoden der sozialen Reformarbeit," in *Die soziale Woche,* ed. Zentralstelle des katholisches Volksbundes (Vienna: Volksbund-Verlag, 1911), 21–27 at 23.

129. On *Neue Reich* in general, see Wassermann, *Black Vienna,* 193. For the Jewish spirit, see Johannes Messner, "Das Werden des Kapitalismus," *Das Neue Reich* 8 (1926): 646–650 at 648. For Tischleder and true democracy, see Johannes Messner, "Unsere Aufgaben im heutigen Staate," *Das Neue Reich* 9 (1927): 45–46; Johannes Messner, "Das erste and letzte Gesetz im Staate," *Das Neue Reich* 9 (1927): 149–151 at 151.

130. Klemens von Klemperer, *Ignaz Seipel: Christian Statesman in a Time of Crisis* (Princeton, NJ: Princeton University Press, 1972), 181, 273–290.

131. On the relations between the Reichsbanner and the *Schutzbund* in Austria, see Karsten Ruppert, *Im Dienst am Staat von Weimar. Das Zentrum als regierende Partei in der Weimarer Demokratie 1923–1930* (Düsseldorf: Droste, 1992), 268–270. On the mutual learning process between the Center Party and the Christian Socials, see Barbara Haider, "'Die Diktatur der Vernunft.' Die

Präsidialkabinette Brüning und das christlichsoziale Lager in Österreich," *De-mokratie und Geschichte* 2 (1998): 194–227. On Perret and the Federation, see Kevin Passmore, *From Liberalism to Fascism: The Right in a French Province, 1928–1939* (Cambridge: Cambridge University Press, 1997), chap. 5.

132. Waldemar Gurian to Karl Thieme, 23 May 1932 and 15 August 1932, Nachlaß Thieme, Folder 163 / 2; Albert Wiedemann, "Stimme aus der katholischen Jugend," *Deutsches Volkstum* 15 (1933): 567–568 at 568; Hürten, *Waldemar Gurian*, 90.

2. Anti-Communism and Paternal Catholic Modernism, 1929–1944

1. Heinrich Rommen, *Der Staat in der katholischen Gedankenwelt* (Paderborn: Bonifacius-Druckerei, 1935), 304.

2. It became convenient after the war to link Maurras with Vichy, but this myth has been unraveled. See Jean-Louis Clement, "The Birth of a Myth: Maurras and the Vichy Regime," *French History* 17 (2003): 440–454.

3. Wilhelm Hoffmann, "Liquidation des Mittelalters? These," *Hochland* 35, no. 1 (1937–1938): 1–11 at 1. Lortz and other interconfessional pioneers are considered later.

4. *Divini redemptoris*, sec. 14, available at https://w2.vatican.va/content/pius-xi /en/encyclicals/documents/hf_p-xi_enc_19370319_divini-redemptoris.html; Alois Hudal, *Deutsches Volk und Christliches Abendland* (Vienna: Tyrolia, 1935), 28; Pierre-Marie Gerlier, "L'action du chrétien au service de la Patrie souffrante," *La Croix*, no. 17837 (20 March 1941): 3; Bischof Clemens August Graf von Galen, *Akten, Briefe und Predigten 1933–1946*, ed. Peter Löffler (Paderborn: Schöningh, 1996), 1:444–445; Ludwig Volk, ed., *Akten deutscher bischöfe über die Lage der Kirche, 1933–1945* (Mainz: Matthias-Grünewald, 1985), 6:199. See also "Gemeinsame Hirtenbriefe der am Grabe des hl. Bonifatius versammelten Oberhirten der Diözesen Deutschlands 1942" and "Mitteilungen des österreichischen Episkopates zur Frage: Kirche und Bolschewismus," 1 December 1941, both available in Diözesanarchiv Graz, 45-e-10 / 2.

5. On Linhardt, see Rudolf Uertz, *Vom Gottesrecht zum Menschenrecht: Das katholische Staatsdenken im Deutschland von der französischen Revolution bis zum II. Vatikanische Konzil* (Paderborn: Schöningh, 2004), 347–359; on his Nazism, see Thomas Forstner, *Priester in Zeiten des Umbruchs: Identität und Lebenswelt des katholischen Pfarrklerus in Oberbayern 1918 bis 1945* (Göttingen: Vandenhoeck & Ruprecht, 2014), 214–216. For the quotes here, see Robert Linhardt, *Verfassungsreform und katholisches Gewissen* (Munich: J. Pfeiffer, 1933), 4–7, 14, 24–28, 35–36; Robert Linhardt, "Von dem Sinn der neuen Zeit," *Bayerischer Kurier* 77, nos. 364–365 (31 December 1933): 1–2. The

turn to rights is equally apparent in Linhardt's previous volume, *Die Sozial-prinzipien des heiligen Thomas von Aquin* (Freiburg im Breisgau: Herder, 1932). For another account of Catholic rights talk that focuses on minority currents in the 1930s, see Samuel Moyn, *Christian Human Rights* (Philadelphia: University of Pennsylvania Press, 2015).

6. Communism was not a central concern for most Catholic thinkers in the 1920s: while they opposed it, it was not yet the universal signifier of evil. For a Catholic take on Bolshevism in the 1920s, arguing that it was not currently attempting to export revolution, see Waldemar Gurian, "Politische Bilanz des Bolschewismus," *Abendland* 3 (1927): 82–84. One interesting source comes from the Austrian bishops, who in 1941 tried to explain how long the Church had been against Bolshevism. The text subverts itself, though, because almost all of the examples from the first thirteen years of the USSR's existence concerned famine relief. See "Mitteilungen des österreichischen Episkopates zur Frage: Kirche und Bolschewismus," 1 December 1941, available in Diözesenarchiv Graz, 45-e-10 / 2. The centrality of the 1930s to the making of anti-Communism has been widely recognized by other scholars. For a sample, see Giuliana Chamedes, "The Vatican, Nazi-Fascism, and the Making of Transnational Anti-Communism in the 1930s," *Journal of Contemporary History* 51 (2016): 261–290; Philippe Chenaux, *L'église catholique et le communisme en Europe (1917–89). De Lénine à Jean-Paul II* (Paris: Cerf, 2009), 86; Lauren Faulkner Rossi, *Wehrmacht Priests: Catholicism and the Nazi War of Annihilation* (Cambridge, MA: Harvard University Press, 2015), 23–24; Peter Kent, *The Lonely Cold War of Pope Pius XII: The Roman Catholic Church and the Division of Europe, 1943–1950* (Montreal: McGill–Queen's University Press, 2002), 12; Herbert Smolinsky, "Das katholische Rußlandbild in Deutschland nach dem Ersten Weltkrieg und im 'Dritten Reich,'" in *Das Rußlandbild im Dritten Reich* (Cologne: Böhlau, 1994), 323–355; Todd Weir, "A European Culture War in the Twentieth Century? Anti-Catholicism and Anti-Bolshevism between Moscow, Berlin, and the Vatican 1922 to 1933," *Journal of Religious History* 39 (2015): 280–306; Antoine Wenger, *Rome et Moscou (1900–1950)* (Paris: Desclée de Brouwer, 1987), 385–386. It is worth noting, too, that Communism was not mentioned in any encyclicals of the 1920s, but it appeared multiple times in the 1930s (and was even the subject of its own encyclical in 1937).

7. Stéphanie Roulin, *Un credo anticommuniste: La commission Pro Deo de l'Entente internationale anticommuniste, 1924–1945* (Lausanne: Antipodes, 2010); Giuliana Chamedes, "Reinventing Christian Europe: Vatican Diplomacy, Transnational Anticommunism, and the Erosion of the Church-State Divide (1917–1958)" (PhD diss., Columbia University, 2012), 189. See also Klaus

Große Kracht, *Die Stunde der Laien? Katholische Aktion in Deutschland im europäischen Kontext, 1920–1960* (Paderborn: Schöningh, 2016), 247–248.

8. For Bertram and Faulhaber, see Peter Godman, *Hitler and the Vatican* (New York: Free Press, 2004), 110, 134, respectively. For a broader version of this claim, see Waldemar Gurian, *Bolschewismus als Weltgefahr* (Luzern: Vita Nova, 1935). For a secondary source, see Björn Laser, *Kulturbolschewismus! Zur Diskurssemantik der 'totalen Krise' 1929–1933* (Frankfurt am Main: Peter Lang, 2010).

9. On Catholic Action, see above all Kracht, *Die Stunde der Laien?*

10. "Klarheit und Kraft," *Frauenart und Frauenleben* 25 (1935): 111–114 at 112.

11. On Liguori and the nineteenth-century approach, see John T. Noonan, *Contraception: A History of Its Treatment by the Catholic Theologians and Canonists* (Cambridge, MA: Belknap Press of Harvard University Press, 1986), chap. 13. On the diversity of approaches in France before 1920, see Martine Sevegrand, *Les enfants de bon dieu: Les catholiques français et la procreation au XXème siècle* (Paris: Albin Michel, 1996), 23, for the clergyman referenced here. As for the papal tradition, Leo XIII's encyclical *Arcanum* on marriage, released in 1880 when contraception and onanism were already widely discussed, is silent on the issue.

12. *Casti connubii,* available at https://w2.vatican.va/content/pius-xi/en/encyclicals /documents/hf_p-xi_enc_19301231_casti-connubii.html; *Die 68. Generalversammlung der Deutschen Katholiken zu Freiburg im Breeisgau* (Freiburg im Breisgau: Herder, 1929); Civis, "Natalité," *La Vie Intellectuelle* 30 (1934): 586–588 at 586; Karl Adam, *Die sakramentale weihe der Ehe* (Freiburg im Breisgau: Herder, 1930), 29; Jacques Leclercq, *Marriage and the Family: A Study in Social Philosophy,* 2nd ed., trans. Thomas Hanley (New York: Frederick Pustet, 1942), 2, 207. For the American version of this story, likewise emphasizing 1930 as a turning point, see Leslie Woodcock Tentler, *Catholics and Contraception* (Ithaca, NY: Cornell University Press, 2004), chaps. 2–3. For a revisionist account of Weimar Germany that emphasizes how much Catholics were willing to compromise on family affairs, see Laurie Marhoefer, *Sex and the Weimar Republic: German Homosexual Emancipation and the Rise of the Nazis* (Toronto: University of Toronto Press, 2015), chap. 6.

13. Among other sources, see Linell E. Cady and Tracy Fessenden, eds., *Religion, the Secular, and the Politics of Sexual Difference* (New York: Columbia University Press, 2013).

14. Rommen, *Der Staat in der katholischen Gedankenwelt,* 266, 354, 162.

15. Walter L. Adamson, "Fascism and Political Religion in Italy: A Reassessment," *Contemporary European History* 23 (2014): 43–73 at 63. For a similar assessment of the German case, see Olaf Blaschke, *Die Kirchen und der Nationalsozialismus* (Stuttgart: Reclam, 2014), 86–90.

16. Étienne Fouilloux, *Les chrétiens français entre crise et libération, 1937–47* (Paris: Seuil, 1997), 97. On the Polish version of this story, see Piotr H. Kosicki, "Masters in Their Own Home or Defenders of the Human Person? Wojciech Korfanty, Anti-Semitism, and Polish Christian Democracy's Illiberal Rights-Talk," *Modern Intellectual History* 14 (2017): 99–130. On Judeo-Bolshevism, see Paul Hanebrink, "Transnational Culture War: Christianity, Nation and the Judeo-Bolshevik Myth in Hungary, 1890–1920," *Journal of Modern History* 80 (2008): 55–80.

17. Winfried Süß, "The Catholic Church, Bishop von Galen, and 'Euthanasia,'" in *Protest in Hitler's National Community: Popular Unrest and the Nazi Response,* ed. Birgit Maier-Katkin and Nathan Stoltzfus (New York: Berghahn, 2016), 55–75 at 64; Gilbert Merlio, "Carl Muth et la revue *Hochland:* Entre catholicisme culturel et catholicisme politique," in *Le milieu intellectuel catholique en Allemagne, sa presse et ses réseaux (1871–1963),* ed. Michel Grunewald and Uwe Puscher (Bern: Peter Lang, 2006), 191–210 at 203.

18. *Arcanum,* sec. 13, available at http://w2.vatican.va/content/leo-xiii/en/encyclicals /documents/hf_l-xiii_enc_10021880_arcanum.html; *Rerum novarum,* sec. 14, available at http://w2.vatican.va/content/leo-xiii/en/encyclicals/documents/hf _l-xiii_enc_15051891_rerum-novarum.html.

19. *Casti connubii,* secs. 37, 123, 120, 92.

20. Britta McEwen, *Sexual Knowledge: Feeling, Fact and Social Reform in Vienna, 1900–1934* (New York: Berghahn, 2012).

21. Anonymous [presumably Wolfring], "Wenn zwei dasselbe tun," *Frauen-Briefe* 34 (October 1928): 2. While Wolfring may not have written these editorials, which appeared on the front page, she at least subscribed to them: the back page says that Wolfring was "responsible" for the contents. The insurance program is discussed in *Frauen-Briefe* 39 (March 1929): 5; for the charitable recommendations, see Herr Propst (Caritas official) to unnamed "friend," 24 December 1932, available in Diözesenarchiv Graz, 44-d-2 / 2. See also "Denkschrift über Armenpflege" in the same folder.

22. Anonymous [presumably Wolfring], "Was wir wollen!," *Frauen-Briefe* 59 (November 1930): 1–2; Alma Motzko, "25 Jahre Frauenorganisation," *Frauen-Briefe* 73 (January 1932): 1–2; anonymous [presumably Wolfring], "Politisch oder unpolitisch?," *Frauen-Briefe* 78 (June 1932): 1–2.

23. Alexander Maklezow, "Ehe und Familie in Sowjetrußland," *Hochland* 28, no. 1 (1930–1931): 506–524; "Sowjet-Russland, ein Menschheitsproblem," *Der Volksverein* 40, no. 1 (1930): 10–16. On the League of Catholic Women rally and *Germania,* see Marhoefer, *Sex and the Weimar Republic,* 192. For the earlier critique, also in its way a critique of supposed socialist family mores, see Agostino Gemelli, *Origine de la famille,* trans. R. Jolivet (Paris: M. Rivière, 1923).

24. "Discours du cardinal Dolci," *La bonne parole* 38, no. 5 (May 1939): 6–8 at 7.

25. Thérèse Doneaud and Christian Guérin, *Les femmes agissent, le monde change. Histoire inédite de l'Union féminine civique et sociale* (Paris: Cerf, 2005), 68; "Die Errichtung katholischer Eheberatungsstellen," *Frauen-Briefe* 81 (September 1932): 5.

26. Susan Pedersen, "Catholicism, Feminism, and the Politics of the Family during the Late Third Republic," in *Mothers of a New World: Maternalist Politics and the Origins of Welfare States,* ed. Seth Koven and Sonya Michel (New York: Routledge, 1993), 246–276.

27. Mairie de Tailhandier, "Le Corporatisme dans les États modernes," *La Femme dans la Vie Sociale* 8, no. 76 (January 1935): 2–3 (the first in a series of articles); *Documentary Notes* can be viewed in 16AF356, UFCS Archives, Centres des Archives du Féminisme, Angers.

28. For the photograph, see "Le Congrès de la Mère au Foyer, ouvrière de progrès humain," *La Mère au Foyer* 3, no. 20 (July–August 1937), 1. For Wolfring's address, see Mina Wolfring, "Mesures légales prises en Autriche pour la famille et la mère," in *La Mère au Foyer, Ouvrière de Progrès Humain* (Paris: Union Féminine Civique et sociale, 1937), 176–177.

29. Jean Lerolle, "Les réformes politiques qu'exige la restauration de la famille," in *Le Problème de Population* (Semaines Sociales de France) (Lyon: Chronique sociale France, 1923), 369–384. He did not dwell on the theme himself, but he did refer readers to other essays that took this approach. For more on the specific context, see Paul V. Dutton, *Origins of the French Welfare State: The Struggle for Social Reform in France, 1914–1947* (New York: Cambridge University Press, 2004), 118–122.

30. See the correspondence in "Relations entretenues avec le ministre du travail," 16AF355, UFCS Archives. For the story of these allowances, which built on a longer history of Catholic industrial experimentation, see Susan Pedersen, *Family, Dependence, and the Origins of the Welfare State: Britain and France, 1914–1945* (New York: Cambridge University Press, 1993).

31. Mina Wolfring, "Besuch des Mutterschaftsinstitutes in Rom," *Das Blatt der Mutter* 5, no. 12 (February 1934): 1–2.

32. This was neither new nor explicitly Catholic, although it did have special resonance in the 1930s as Catholic women struggled to find a place in conservative political movements. See Seth Koven and Sonya Michel, "Womanly Duties: Maternalist Politics and the Origins of Welfare States in France, Germany, Great Britain, and the United States, 1880–1920," *American Historical Review* 95 (1990): 1076–1108; Laura Lee Downs, "'Each and Every One of You Must Become a *Chef*': Toward a Social Politics of Working-Class Childhood on the Extreme Right in 1930s France," *Journal of Modern History* 81 (2009): 1–44; Kevin Passmore, "'Planting the Tricolor in the Citadels of Communism':

Women's Social Action in the Croix de feu and Parti social français," *Journal of Modern History* 71 (1999): 814–851.

33. The revised story comes from her traveling companion, interviewed decades later. See Irene Schöffmann, "Organisation und Politik katholischer Frauen im 'Ständestaat,'" *Zeitgeschichte* 11 (1984): 349–375 at 362–363. For this period more broadly, see above all Irene Bandhauer-Schöffmann, "Der 'Christliche Ständestaat' als Männerstaat? Frauen- und Geschlechterpolitik im Austrofaschismus," in *Austrofaschismus. Politik-Ökonomie-Kultur, 1933–1938,* ed. Emmerich Tálos and Wolfgang Neugebauer (Vienna: Lit, 2005), 254–281.

34. For the legislation, see Laura S. Gellott, *The Catholic Church and the Authoritarian Regime in Austria, 1933–1938* (New York: Garland, 1987), 308.

35. For Wolfring on the encyclicals, see Mina Wolfring, *Erziehung zur Elternschaft* (Vienna: Vaterländische Front, 1935), 10; for Innitzer and Wolfring together, see the cover of *Das Blatt der Mutter* 6, no. 9 (November 1934); for collaboration with Catholic Action, see Mina Wolfring, *Das Mutterschutzwerk der Vaterländischen Front. Seine Entstehung, sein Zweck, sein Ziel* (Vienna: Selbstverlag des Mutterschutzwerkes der Vaterländischen Front, 1938), 38; for a general elaboration of the homology between Austrian policy and Catholic social teaching, see "Die Frau im neuen Ständestaat," *Frauen-Briefe* 102 (June 1934): 2.

36. Gellott, *Catholic Church and the Authoritarian Regime in Austria,* 311; Mina Wolfring, "Zum neuen Jahr," *Das Blatt der Mutter* 6, no. 11 (January 1935): 1–3 at 3; Mina Wolfring, "Der Sinn des österreichischen Mutterschaftswerkes," *Das Blatt der Mutter* 6, no. 7 (September 1934): 1–2 at 1.

37. Wolfring, *Das Mutterschutzwerk der Vaterländischen Front,* 10–11, 39; Mina Wolfring, *Sorgenbirkels erste Lebenszeit. Einfache Anleitungen zur richtigen Säuglings- und Kinderpflege,* 3rd ed. (Vienna: Das kleine Volksblatt, 1936), 5, 8.

38. Monika Löscher, '*. . . der gesunden Vernunft nicht zuwider . . . ?' Katholische Eugenik in Österreich vor 1938* (Vienna: Studienverlag, 2009), 123.

39. Wilhelm Winkler, *Geburtenrückgang in Österreich* (Vienna: Österreichischer Bundesverlag, 1935), 38 (Innitzer's foreword not paginated); "Mendel-Gedächtnisausstellung im Dienste der Familie," *Reichspost* 41, no. 200 (22 July 1934): 13.

40. See, for instance, Elisa Camiscioli, *Reproducing the French Race: Immigration, Intimacy, and Embodiment in the Early Twentieth Century* (Durham, NC: Duke University Press, 2009); Sandrine Sanos, *The Aesthetics of Hate: Far-Right Intellectuals, Antisemitism, and Gender in 1930s France* (Stanford, CA: Stanford University Press, 2012).

41. "So kann es nicht weitergehen," *Frauen-Briefe* 83 (November 1932): 1–2. On Nazi women's organizations in Austria, see Johanna Gehmacher, '*Völkische*

Frauenbewegung.' Deutschnationale und nationalsozialistische Geschlecht-spolitik in Österreich (Vienna: Döcker, 1998).

42. Löscher, '. . . *der gesunden Vernunft nicht zuwider . . . ?,'* 136–142; "Wir und die Juden," *Österreichische Frauen-Zeitung* 124 (April 1936): 2.

43. Dagmar Herzog, *Sex after Fascism: Memory and Morality in Twentieth-Century Germany* (Princeton, NJ: Princeton University Press, 2005), 42–44; Ingrid Richter, *Katholizismus und Eugenik in der Weimarer Republik und im Dritten Reich. Zwischen Sittlichkeitsreform und Rassenhygiene* (Paderborn: Schöningh, 2001), 337–349.

44. "Die Frau in Sowjetrußland," *Frauenart und Frauenleben* 11 (1933): 27; "Die Frau in der neuen Zeit," *Frauenart und Frauenleben* 11 (1933): 129–134 at 133; "Wer schenkt uns das dritte und vierte Kind?," *Katholische Kirchenzeitung* 24, no. 22 (31 May 1936): 408.

45. Mlle. Fink, "Mesures prises en Allemagne pour développer le rôle de la mère au foyer," in *La Mère au Foyer*, 178–182; Helen Iswolski, "La femme et la mère en Russie," in ibid., 77–81.

46. Anonymous, "Die erste und größte Gefahr ist noch immer der Kommunismus," *Österreichische Frauenzeitung* 126 (June 1936): 1.

47. Karin Berger, "'Hut ab vor Frau Sedlmayer.' Zur Militarisierung und Ausbeutung der Arbeit von Frauen im nationalsozialstsichen Österreich," in *NS-Herrschaft in Österreich*, ed. Ernst Hanisch, Wolfgang Neugebauer, and Emmerich Tálos (Vienna: Verlag für Gesellschaftskritik, 1988), 141–161 at 142.

48. Stefan Moritz, *Grüß Gott und Heil Hitler. Katholische Kirche und Nationalsozialismus* (Vienna: Picus, 2002), 63–64.

49. Pétain quoted in Rémi Lenoir, "Family Policy in France since 1938," in *The French Welfare State: Surviving Social and Ideological Change*, ed. John S. Ambler (New York: New York University Press, 1991), 144–186 at 151.

50. On the 1940 law, see Miranda Pollard, *Reign of Virtue: Mobilizing Gender in Vichy France* (Chicago: University of Chicago Press, 1998), chap. 6.

51. On UFCS pressure to centralize and politicize family organizations, see the proposition to Pétain 16AF87, Propositions de l'UFCS et de sa Commission familiale (1932–43), UFCS Archives. For their appreciation and participation in the new order, see "Note sur la représentation de Mères dans les divers Organismes," June 1941, 16AF87, UFCS Archives; A. Butillard, "Comité Consultatif de la Famille," *La mère au foyer* 60 (September–October 1941): 5. For these quotations, see "La France au service de la Société Chrétienne, du Monde, 1941–1942," 16AF1, 5, UFCS Archives.

52. John F. Pollard, *Money and the Rise of the Modern Papacy: Financing the Vatican, 1850–1950* (New York: Cambridge University Press, 2005), chaps. 6–7.

53. Paul Chanson, *Communisme ou corporatisme?* (Paris: Cerf, 1937), 1.

54. On the varieties of corporatism, and for a fuller definition of its authoritarian variant, see Philippe C. Schmitter, "Still the Century of Corporatism?," *Review of Politics* 36 (1974): 85–131. On earlier debates, see Paul Misner, *Social Catholicism in Europe: From the Onset of Industrialization to the First World War* (New York: Crossroad, 1991), 177.

55. *Rerum novarum*, sec. 13; *Quadragesimo anno*, sec. 71, available at http://w2.vatican.va/content/pius-xi/en/encyclicals/documents/hf_p-xi_enc_19310515_quadragesimo-anno.html.

56. *Quadragesimo anno*, secs. 74, 81–82 (emphasis added), 91–95.

57. For Brauer's negative judgment of the Center Party, see Theodor Brauer, "The Present Condition of the Centrum," *World* 152 (1928): 309–314. For his depression, see Ludwig Heyde, "Theodor Brauer. Leben und Werken eines christlichen Sozialreformers," in *Theodor Brauer. Soziale Kämpfer*, ed. Bernard Ridder and Ludwig Geck (Cologne: Kolping, 1952), 5–15 at 11.

58. For his trip to Barcelona, see Patrick Pasture, *Histoire du syndicalisme chrétien international. La difficile recherche d'une troisième voie* (Paris: L'Harmattan, 1999), 136. For his trip to Rome and its funding, see Theodor Brauer to Christian Eckert, 30 January 1930, Forschungs-Instutut für Sozialwissenschaft, University Archives, Cologne, Zugang 9 / 339.

59. Theodor Brauer to "Direktor [?]," 8 October 1934, Nachlaß Theodor Brauer, University Archives, Cologne, Zugang 54 / 6.

60. Ignaz Seipel, "Die neue Gesellschaftsordnung nach der Enzylika *Quadragesimo Anno*," in *Die soziale Botschaft des Papstes. Vorträge über Quadragesimo Anno* (Vienna: Volksbundverlag, 1931), 81–90.

61. William Patch, *Christian Trade Unions in the Weimar Republic: The Failure of Corporate Pluralism* (New Haven, CT: Yale University Press, 1985), 178–181.

62. Josef van der Velden, ed., *Die berufsständische Ordnung* (Cologne: Bachem, 1932).

63. Theodor Brauer, *Sozialpolitik und Sozialreform* (Jena: Gustav Fischer, 1931), for his general views at this time; Röhr quoted in William Patch, *Christian Democratic Workers and the Forging of German Democracy, 1920–1980* (New York: Cambridge University Press, 2018), 30.

64. Max Frauendorfer, *Der ständische Gedanke im Nationalsozialismus* (Munich: Franz Eher Nachf, 1932), 28–29, 6.

65. Theodor Brauer to Pius Fink, 21 September 1933, Nachlaß Brauer, Zugang 54 / 5.

66. Albert Hackelsberger, *Die Enzyklika Quadragesimo Anno und die neue Wirtschaftsordnung* (Essen: Fredebeul & Koenen, 1933); Franz Andreas Huber and Ferdinand Kudjelka, *Grundriss einer christlich-ständischen Wirtschaftsordnung auf der Grundlage der katholischen Sozialidee und der*

Arbeitswährung Berthold Ottos (Graz: Ulrich Moser, 1934), 4; Joseph Lortz, *Katholischer Zugang zum Nationalsozialismus* (Münster: Aschendorffschen Verlag, 1934), 23; Josef Pieper, *Das Arbeitsrecht des Neuen Reiches und die Enzyklika Quadragesimo Anno* (Münster: Aschendorffschen Verlagsbuchhandlung, 1934), 1, 5; P. Frist Vorspel, S.J., *Kirche und Wirtschaft* (Cologne: Bachem, 1935), 7.

67. Theodor Brauer, *Der moderne deutsche Sozialismus* (Freiburg im Breisgau: Herder, 1929), 128, 368–374; Theodor Brauer, *Der soziale Katholizismus in Deutschland im Lichte von Quadragesimo Anno* (Düsseldorf: Religious Quellenschrifte, 1935), 59; Theodor Brauer, *Christentum und öffentliches Leben* (Mönchengladbach: Volksverein-Verlag, 1927), 195–200.

68. Brauer, *Der soziale Katholizismus,* 8; Theodor Brauer, "Das Schicksal der Gewerkschaften," *Deutsches Volk* 1 (1933): 99–105 at 105.

69. Brauer, *Der moderne deutsche Sozialismus,* 306.

70. On Brauer and Essen, see Patch, *Christian Democratic Workers,* 40. For these quotations, see *Die Essener Richtlinien 1933 der christlichnationalen Gewerkschaften* (Berlin: Christliche Gewerkschaftsverlag, 1933), 10–11, 13 (emphasis in original; the text references dignity and personality again on 18–19); Theodor Brauer, *Der Katholik im neuen Reich. Seine Aufgabe und sein Anteil* (Munich: Kösel, 1933), 41; Theodor Brauer, "Leistungsgemeinschaft—der Kern der berufsständischen Wirtschaftsordnung," *Deutsches Volk* 1 (1933): 20–28 at 26.

71. *Quadragesimo anno,* sec. 47; *Die Essener Richtlinien,* 49. On all of this, see James Chappel, "The Thomist Debate over Inequality and Property Rights in Depression-Era Europe," in *What's So New about Scholasticism? How Neo-Thomism Helped Shape the Twentieth Century,* ed. Rajesh Heynickx and Stéphane Symons (Berlin: Walter de Gruyter, forthcoming).

72. The "freedoms guaranteed" quotation can be found in Patch, *Christian Democratic Workers,* 40. For the others, see Brauer, *Sozialpolitik und Sozialreform,* 55; Theodor Brauer, "Der Staat," in *Der katholische Gedanke und die Neuordnung von Wirtschaft und Gesellschaft* (Augsburg: Verlag Haas & Grabherr, 1933), 11–15 at 13, 14.

73. Brauer, *Der Katholik im neuen Reich,* 27–28; Wilhelm Reinermann, "Judentum und christliche Kultur," *Deutsches Volk* 1 (1933): 209–217 at 213.

74. For one example of the continental approach, see Albert Muller, S.J., *La politique corporative* (Brussels: Rex, 1935). On the Franco-Italian conference, see the account in "*Esprit* au congrès franco-italien sur la corporation," *Esprit* 3 (1935): 474–480. For a list of foreign attendees at the Viennese conference, see *Volkswohl* 26, nos. 11–12 (1934–1935): 5–6. On Brauer's international activities, see Brauer to "Direktor [?]," 8 October 1934, Nachlaß Brauer, Zugang 54 / 6.

75. "Der christliche Gewerkschaften und die neue Verfassung," *Reichspost* 41, no. 150 (3 June 1934): 2–3; "2 März 1934!," *Christlichsoziale Arbeiter-Zeitung* 39, no. 10 (10 March 1934): 1. On Catholic labor in Austria, see above all Anton Pelinka, *Stand oder Klasse. Die christliche Arbeiterbewegung Österreich 1933–1938* (Vienna: Europaverlag, 1972). On Kühr, see Elke Seefried, *Reich und Stände. Ideen und Wirken des deutschen politischen Exils in Österreich, 1933–1938* (Düsseldorf: Droste, 2006), 304–317.

76. *Allgemeiner deutscher Katholikentag, Wien 1933* (Vienna: Verlag des Katholikentagkomitees Wien, 1934), 55.

77. Lothar Höbelt, "Richard Schmitz als Protagonist der internationalen Kontakte der Christlichsozialen in der Zwischenkriegszeit (1931–1934)," *Demokratie und Geschichte* 13–14 (2009–2010): 159–171. For Pezet's praise of Dollfuss, see Ernest Pezet to Richard Schmitz, 24 October 1933, in Nachlaß Richard Schmitz, Österreichische Staatsarchiv, E/1786:78. On his private ideas, see Richard Schmitz to Sebastian Rieger, 3 February 1934, Nachlaß Schmitz, E/1786:79; for his public ones, see Richard Schmitz, *Der Weg zur berufsständische Ordnung in Österreich* (Vienna: Manzsche, 1934). For his influence, see Helmut Wohnout, *Regierungs-Diktatur oder Ständeparlament. Gesetzgebung im autoritären Österreich* (Vienna: Böhlau, 1993), 82.

78. Kurt von Schuschnigg, *My Austria* (New York: Knopf, 1938), 213.

79. Johannes Messner, *Dollfuss: An Austrian Patriot* (Norfolk, VA: IHS Press, 2004), 128. On the trip to Italy, see Jakob Strieder to Pius Fink, 13 April 1931, Archiv der Görres-Gesellschaft, Historisches Archiv des Erzbistum Köln, Nr. 143. For Messner's influence, and that of papal teaching more broadly, see Alexander Novotny, "Der berufsständische Gedanke in der Bundesverfassung des Jahres 1934," *Österreich in Geschichte und Literatur* 5 (1961): 209–220. On Brauer's esteem for Messner, see "Rücksprache des Vizepräsidenten der Görreselsschaft mit Professor Dr. Theodor Brauer," April 1930, Archiv der Görres Gesellschaft, Historisches Archiv des Erzbistum Köln, Nr. 143. On Messner's esteem for Brauer, see the references peppered throughout Johannes Messner, *Sozialökonomik und Sozialethik: Studie zur Grundlegung einer systematischen Wirtschaftsethik* (Paderborn: Schöningh, 1927).

80. Johannes Messner, "Das Sozialproblem im berufsständischen Aufbau des neuen Oesterreich," *Volkswohl* 26, nos. 11–12 (1934–1935): 23–27 at 25–26. This was extremely controversial and required a full-court press from Catholic luminaries. See Leopold Kunschak, "Die Klärung schreitet weiter," *Österreichische Arbeiter-Zeitung* 40, no. 5 (2 February 1935): 1; E. K. Winter, *Arbeiterschaft und Staat* (Vienna: Reichhold, 1934), 51, 55. For Johannes Staud, erstwhile Catholic labor leader, see Pelinka, *Stand oder Klasse*, 89.

81. Quoted in Helmut Rumpler, "Der Ständestaat ohne Stände. Johannes Messner als 'Programmatik' der Berufsständischen Idee in der Verfassung des Jähes

1934," in *Der Forschende Blick. Beiträge zur Geschichte Österreichs im 20. Jahrhundert,* ed. Reinhard Krammer et al. (Vienna: Böhlau, 2010), 229–246 at 234.

82. Johannes Messner, *Die Soziale Frage der Gegenwart* (Vienna: Tyrolia, 1934), 28, 559.

83. François Perroux, *Capitalisme et communauté de travail* (Paris: Recueil Sirey, 1937), 123.

84. Charles Poisson, "Les réalisations étrangères des régimes dénommés 'corporatifs,'" in *L'organisation corporative* (Semaines Sociales de France) (Lyon: Chronique sociale de France, 1935), 151–186 at 171; J. T. Delos, "Frankreich," *Volkswohl* 11–12 (1935): 9–10.

85. For the FNC, see "La lutte contre le communisme, la rénovation corporative," *Credo* 128 (November 1936): 9–29; Jean Le Cour Grandmaison, *Comment envisager un programme de restauration sociale par les corporations* (Paris: Fédération Nationale Catholique, 1934); Corinne Bonafoux, "Les corporatistes catholiques de l'entre-deux-guerres et La Tour du Pin," in *Le corporatisme dans l'aire francophone au XXème siècle,* ed. Olivier Dard (New York: Peter Lang, 2011), 11–28. For the Social Weeks, see *L'organisation corporative.* For the JOC, see "Des arguments pour les militants! Pourquoi nous allons à Rome!," *L'équipe ouvrière* 5, no. 12 (November 1930): 90–91; "Pour un ordre social chrétien," *L'équipe ouvriere* 8, no. 99 (July 1934): 115. The ecclesiastical assembly is quoted in Maurice Eblé, "Les Catholiques sociaux et le corporatisme," *Politique* 8, no. 5 (May 1934): 396–402 at 402 (this entire issue, featuring a representative from Salazar's Portugal, was dedicated to an exploration of corporatism).

86. Perroux, *Capitalisme et communauté de travail,* 18–20, 286, 267; François Perroux, "La personne et le droit du travail," *Esprit* 42 (1936): 866–898 at 879, 881.

87. Jean de Fabrègues to Alexandre Marc, undated [July 1938], AM-123 (1938–1939), Fonds Alexandre Marc, EUI Florence.

88. Perroux, *Capitalisme et communauté de travail,* 172–173.

89. Steven Kaplan, "Un laboratoire de la doctrine corporatiste sous le régime de Vichy: l'Institut d'études corporatives et sociales," *Le Mouvement Social* 195 (2001): 35–77. See also Jean-Pierre Le Crom, *Syndicats, nous voilà! Vichy et le corporatisme* (Paris: Editions Ouvrières, 1995). For specifics of his role on the constitutional council, see Michèle Cointet, *Le Conseil national de Vichy: Vie politique et réforme de l'Etat en régime autoritaire, 1940–1944* (Paris: Aux amateurs de livres, 1989), 152–156.

90. François Perroux and Yves Urvoy, *Le Charte du travail. Son contenu et son esprit* (Lyon: Impr. nouvelle lyonnaise, 1943), 12–14.

91. Kaplan, "Un laboratoire de la doctrine corporatiste sous le régime de Vichy," 42–43; M. J. Garnier [USIC secretary], as quoted in "L'organisation sociale

dans la France nouvelle," *La Croix*, no. 17956 (7 August 1941): 3; Marcel Gabilly, "L'esprit de la charte du travail," *La Croix*, no. 18025 (28 October 1941): 1. For more, including this quotation from Maurice Feltin, see Jacques Julliard, "Charte du Travail," in *Le gouvernement de Vichy, 1940–1942: Institutions et politiques,* ed. Janine Bourdin and René Rémond (Paris: Presses de la Fondation nationale des sciences politiques, 1972), 157–211, esp. 173–175.

92. Le Crom, *Syndicats, nous voilà!,* is the leading study of French corporatism. Catholicism is present but is not a major theme.

93. Perroux and Urvoy, *La Charte du travail.*

94. Timothy Mason, *Social Policy in the Third Reich: The Working Class and the 'National Community,'* trans. John Broadwin (Providence, RI: Berg, 1993), 90.

95. Brauer mentions the letter to Ley in his letter to Pius Fink, 21 September 1933, Nachlaß Brauer, Zug. 54, 5. For the murders of Jung and von Bose, see Patch, *Christian Democratic Workers.* For Brauer's troublesome student, see Wener Doyé, "Beschrift über das sozial-politische Seminar am Donnerstag, den 24.1.35," in Nachlaß Brauer, Zug. 54.

96. On France, see Richard F. Kuisel, *Capitalism and the State in Modern France: Renovation and Economic Management in the Twentieth Century* (Cambridge: Cambridge University Press, 1981), chap. 5. On Austria, see Wohnout, *Regierungsdiktatur oder Ständeparlament?,* 429; Helmut Rumpler, "Der Ständestaat ohne Stände." On Portugal, see Nuno Luís Madureira, "Cartelization and Corporatism: Bureaucratic Rule in Authoritarian Portugal, 1926–45," *Journal of Contemporary History* 42 (2007): 79–96. On Spain, see J. Martinez-Alier and Jordi Roca, "Spain after Franco: From Corporatist Ideology to Corporatist Reality," *International Journal of Political Economy* 17 (1987–1988): 56–87, esp. 64–65.

97. Volk, *Akten deutscher bischöfe über die Lage der Kirche,* 6:199–205.

98. Philip Nord, *France's New Deal: From the Thirties to the Postwar Era* (Princeton, NJ: Princeton University Press, 2010), 263–264 for Lamirand, 57 for Coutrot.

99. Wilhelm Röpke, "Die Neuordnung von Gesellschaft und Wirtschaft," *Monatsschrift für Kultur und Politik* 2 (1937): 325–332; Wilhelm Röpke, *Civitas Humana. Grundfragen der Gesellschafts- und Wirtschaftsreform* (Erlenbach-Zürich: Rentsch, 1944), 96, 18. On Röpke in the 1930s more generally, see Noah Strote, *Lions and Lambs: Chaos in Weimar and the Creation of Post-Nazi Germany* (New Haven, CT: Yale University Press, 2017), chap. 7.

100. Louis Salleron, "Faut-il encore parler du libéralisme?," *Civilisation* 2, nos. 10–11 (April–May 1939): 26–30. He was referring especially to the Colloque Walter Lippmann, which played such a crucial role in renovating the tradition.

101. Theodor Brauer, "Ende des Kapitalismus?," *Zentralblatt der christlichen Gewerkschaften Deutschlands* 33, no. 2 (15 January 1933): 13–15 at 15; Klaus

Dohrn, review of R. N. Coudenhove Kalergi, *Totaler Staat—Totaler Mensch, Christliche Ständestaat* 4, no. 5 (26 December 1937): 1221–1223 at 1221.

102. Antonio Gramsci, *Prison Notebooks: Volume 2*, ed. and trans. Joseph Buttigieg (New York: Columbia University Press, 1996), 273–275.

103. On the unsteady formation of a "national consciousness" in 1930s Austria, see Ernst Bruckmüller, "Österreich—eine 'katholische' Nation?," in *Religion und Nation. Katholizsmen im Europa des 19. und 20. Jahrhunderts,* ed. Urs Altermatt and Franziska Metzger (Stuttgart: Kohlhammer, 2007), 69–93; Albert Reiterer, "Vom Scheitern eines politisches Entwurfes. 'Der österreichische Mensch'—ein konservatives Nationalprojekt der Zwischenkriegszeit," *Österreich in Geschichte und Literatur* 30 (1986): 19–36.

104. This paragraph draws on Articles 27 and 29 of the Austrian constitution (available at http://www.verfassungen.de/at/at34-38/oesterreich34.htm); Article 8 of the Portuguese constitution (http://www.cphrc.org/index.php/documents /docnesta/167-1933-02-22-political-constitution-of-the-portuguese-republic -part-1); Article 44 of the Irish constitution (https://www.constituteproject .org/constitution/Ireland_2012.pdf); Article 35 of the never-enacted Vichy constitution (Cointet, *Le Conseil national de Vichy,* 416).

105. Quoted in Ethan Katz, *Burdens of Brotherhood: Jews and Muslims from North Africa to France* (Cambridge, MA: Harvard University Press, 2015), 116. On Austria and the insufficiency of "clerical fascism," see Julie Thorpe, "Austrofascism: Revisiting the 'Authoritarian State' 40 Years On," *Journal of Contemporary History* 45 (2010): 315–343. On Vichy schools, see Nicholas Atkin, "Church and Teachers in Vichy France, 1940–1944," *French History* 4 (1990): 1–22.

106. *Ubi arcano Dei consilio,* secs. 28, 43, available at http://w2.vatican.va/content /pius-xi/en/encyclicals/documents/hf_p-xi_enc_23121922_ubi-arcano-dei -consilio.html.

107. *Divini redemptoris,* secs. 33, 35.

108. Atkin, "Church and Teachers in Vichy France, 1940–1944," 13.

109. Henri Massis, *Défense de l'Occident* (Paris: Plon, 1927).

110. The paradigmatic text of the early Jeune Droite was almost anarchist. Robert Aron and Arnaud Dandieu, *La révolution nécessaire* (Paris: Grasset, 1933).

111. Robert Francis, Thierry Maulnier, and Jean-Pierre Maxence, *Demain la France* (Paris: Grasset, 1934), 175.

112. For one example, see Gregorio Marnon, "Front Latin," *Occident* 1, no. 5 (December 1937): 3. On Massis's continuing hatred of the German national project, see Massis, *Défense de l'Occident,* 19–59, and on the German-USSR comparison, 113.

113. Christine Foureau, "La revue universelle (1920–1940): aux origines intellectuelles du pétainisme" (PhD diss., Princeton University, 1999), 197–221.

114. *Allgemeiner deutscher Katholikentag*, 22; Emil Franzel, *Abendländische Revolution* (Bratislava: Prager, 1936). For a classic Catholic example, see Otto Marie Fidelis [i.e., Otto Maria Karpfen], *Österreichs europäische Sendung. Ein außenpolitischer Überblick* (Vienna: Reinhold, 1935).

115. Martin-Stanislaus Gillet, *Culture latine et ordre social* (Paris: Flammarion, 1935).

116. On the FNC, see Bruno de Solages, "L'Eglise et l'Occident," *Irénikon* 4, no. 9 (1928): 3; François de la Rocque, *The Fiery Cross: The Call to Public Service in France* (London: Lovat Dickson, 1936), 132, 144. On the PSF and "Christian civilization," see Sean Kennedy, "Defending Christian Civilization: The Evolving Message of the Parti social français, 1936–1939," in *The French Right between the Wars*, ed. Samuel Kalman and Sean Kennedy (New York: Berghahn, 2014), 180–194.

117. Manifesto reproduced in Yves Simon, *The Ethiopian Campaign and French Political Thought*, trans. Robert Royal, ed. Anthony O. Simon (Notre Dame, IN: University of Notre Dame Press, 2009), 94–97; "Coupures de presse sur la défense de l'Occident," press clipping in Fonds Mounier, IMEC, MNR2.D4–03.03.

118. Henri Massis, *Verteidigung des Abendlandes, Mit einer Einführung von Georg Moenius*, trans. Georg Moenius (Hellerau: Jakob Gegner, 1930). On the fate of *Abendland* in these years, see Vanessa Conze, *Das Europa der Deutschen. Ideen von Europa in Deutschland zwischen Reichstradition und Westorientierung (1920–1970)* (Munich: Oldenbourg, 2005), 57–63; Dagmar Pöpping, *Abendland. Christliche Akademiker und die Utopie der Antimoderne 1900–1945* (Berlin: Metropol, 2002), chap. 4. On the diversity of opinions in the Weimar-era *Abendland*-Kreis, see the very different stances taken by its two lead editors: Hermann Platz, "Bierville," *Abendland* 2 (1926): 10–12; Friedrich Schreyvogl, "Genf und der abendländische Gedanke," *Abendland* 1 (1926): 210–211.

119. Faulhaber quoted in Gerhard Besier, *Die Kirchen und das Dritte Reich. Spaltungen und Abwehrkämpfe, 1934–1937* (Berlin: Econ Ullstein List, 2001), 763; pastoral letter quoted in Gerhard Besier, "Bolshevism and Antisemitism: The Catholic Church in Germany and National Socialist Ideology, 1936–37," *Ecclesiastical History* 43 (1992): 447–456 at 454–455; Karl Gottfried Hugelmann, "Die Gestalt des Reiches in Idee und Wirklichkeit im Wandel der deutschen Geschichte," *Zeitschrift für öffentliches Recht* 16 (1936): 433–447 at 445.

120. For two sides to this debate, see Richard Steigmann-Gall, *The Holy Reich: Nazi Conceptions of Christianity, 1919–1945* (New York: Cambridge University Press, 2003); Wolfgang Dierker, *Himmlers Glaubenskrieger. Der Sicherheitsdienst der SS und seine Religionspolitik, 1933–1941*, 2nd ed. (Paderborn: Schoningh, 2002).

121. Johann Chapoutot, *Greeks, Romans, Germans: How the Nazis Usurped Europe's Classical Past*, trans. Richard R. Nybakken (Oakland: University of California

Press, 2016); Philipp Gassert, "No Place for 'The West': National Socialism and the 'Defence of Europe,'" in *Germany and 'The West': The History of a Modern Concept,* ed. Riccardo Bavaj and Martina Steber (New York: Berghahn, 2016), 216–229.

122. Hermann Sauer, *Abendländische Entscheidung. Arischer Mythus und christliche Wirklichkeit* (Leipzig: J. C. Hinrichs, 1938); Joseph Goebbels, *Communism with the Mask Off* (Berlin: M. Müller & Sohn, 1935), 9.

123. Strote, *Lions and Lambs,* 47–50.

124. Konrad Algermissen, *Die gottlosenbewegung der Gegenwart und ihre Überwindung* (Hannover: Joseph Giesel, 1933), 305; Alois Dempf, "Begegnung der Konfessionen?," *Hochland* 33, no. 1 (1935–1936): 481–490 at 490; Damasus Winzen, "Gedanken zu einer 'Theologie des Reiches,'" *Catholica* 2 (1933): 97–116; Joseph Lortz, *Die Reformation in Deutschland* (Freiburg: Herder, 1939); Hermann Mulert, ed., *Der Katholizismus der Zukunft. Aufbau und kritische Abwehr* (Leipzig: Klotz, 1940); Peter Eppel, *Zwischen Kreuz und Hakenkreuz. Die Haltung der Zeitschrift 'Schönere Zukunft' zum Nationalsozialismus in Deutchland 1934–1938* (Vienna: Böhlau, 1980), 193–196. The clear political-national implications of Lortz's work were drawn out, among other places, in Hans Eibl, "Reformationsgeschichte und Wiedervereinigungsfrage," *Schönere Zukunft* 15, nos. 39–40 (23 June 1940): 462–463.

125. Judith Keene, *Fighting for Franco: International Volunteers in Nationalist Spain during the Spanish Civil War, 1936–39* (New York: Leicester University Press, 2001).

126. Henri Massis and Robert Brasillach, *The Cadets of the Alcazar* (New York: Paulist, 1937), 61.

127. Henri Massis, "Huntziger, Weygand, de Gaulle," *Hommes et Mondes* 101 (December 1954): 1–12 at 4, 9; Cointet, *Le Conseil national de Vichy,* 91, 283.

128. Some Defenders of the West refused to take the bait. See, for instance, Aurel Kolnai, *War against the West* (New York: Viking, 1938).

129. For Austria, see, for instance, "Europa—eine volkische und kulturelle Einheit," *Neues Wiener Tagblatt* 344 (12 December 1941): 3. For Germany, see Pilgrim, "Zum Gespräch zwischen den Konfessionen," *Hochland* 38, no. 4 (January 1941): 176–178. This soldier is quoted in Rossi, *Wehrmacht Priests,* 187–188.

130. Pétain on front page of *La Croix,* no. 17772 (3 January 1941), and in "Deux messages du maréchal Pétain," *Figaro* 116, no. 304 (7 November 1941); Armand Petitjean, "Principes d'un ordre occidental," *Idées* 3, no. 22 (August 1943): 1–14; "Une conférence de M. Henri Massis," *Le Journal,* no. 18344 (16 April 1943): 2; Henri Massis, *Les idees restent* (Lyon: H. Lardanchet, 1941), 74, 135, 237; Henri Massis, *Découverte de la Russie* (Lyon: H. Lardanchet, 1944), 24.

131. Henri Massis, *Chefs. Les dictatures et nous* (Paris: Plon, 1939), 66, 92, 17, 121. For Massis on the individual / person distinction, see Foureau, "La revue universelle," 119.

132. Jacques de [i.e., Raphaël] Alibert, "Essai sur la notion d'Etat," *Revue du XXème Siècle* 3 (January 1935): 15–23 at 19; Gillet, *Culture latine et ordre social*, 234; "Le Pays des 'personnes,'" *S.O.S. Occident* 4, no. 86 (1 November 1935): 4. For the Young Right, see "Manifeste," *Réaction pour l'ordre* 1, no. 1 (April 1930): 1–3; Louis Salleron, "Réflexions sur le régime à naître," *Combat* 3, no. 30 (December 1938): n.p. For the Croix de feu, see Gaston Rageot, "Regroupement," *Le Flambeau* 7, no. 2 (9 March 1935): 1; Gabriel Boissy, "Latinité," *Le Flambeau* 7, no. 10 (4 May 1935): 1; "Manifeste Croix de Feu," supplement to *Le Flambeau* 8, no. 53 (11 April 1936): 8, 6. For the constitution, see Cointet, *Le Conseil national de Vichy*, 413.

133. Moenius cited in Seefried, *Reich und Stände*, 190; Walter Münster, "Das Wesen des Föderalismus," *Christliche Ständestaat* 4, no. 33 (22 August 1937): 784–786 at 784; Hudal, *Deutsches Volk und Christliches Abendland*, 28.

134. Wilhelm Moock, "Der Einzelne und die Gemeinschaft," *Hochland* 32, no. 1 (1934–1935): 193–203 at 194, 198; Otto Schilling, *Apologie der katholischen Moral* (Paderborn: Schöningh, 1936), 5, 240, 238.

135. See also Kosicki, "Masters in Their Own Home or Defenders of the Human Person?"

136. "Le problème juif," *Revue Universelle* 77 (1939): 418–433.

137. Schilling, *Apologie der katholischen Moral*, 110; Moock, "Der Einzelne und die Gemeinschaft," 196, 203.

138. Otto Maria Karpfen, "Die Juden und der Sozialismus," *Die Erfüllung* 2 (1935): 23–29; Emmerich Czermak, "Verständigung mit dem Judentum," in *Ordnung in der Judenfrage* (Vienna: Reinhold, 1933), 1–72 at 9. The same logic can be traced in H. de Vries de Heekelingen, *Israël. Son Passé. Son Avenir* (Paris: Perrin, 1937).

139. On Vallat, see Laurent Joly, *Xavier Vallat. Du nationalisme chrétien à l'antisémitisme d'État, 1891–1972* (Paris: Grasset, 2001). Paeans to the West can still be found in his work after the war. See Xavier Vallat, *Le Nez de cleopatre. Souvenirs d'un Homme de droite (1919–1944)* (Paris: Editions Les Quatre Fils Aymon, 1957), 163–179, 229, passim.

140. I am grateful to Irene Bandhauer-Schöffmann for the information about her divorce. For her funeral notice, including her son's whereabouts, see *Neues Wiener Tagblatt* 232 (23 August 1944): 5.

141. *Summi Pontificatus*, secs. 35 and 65, available at http://w2.vatican.va/content/pius-xii/en/encyclicals/documents/hf_p-xii_enc_20101939_summi-pontificatus.html.

142. The Christmas messages are available at https://www.ewtn.com/library /PAPALDOC/P12CH42.HTM; https://www.ewtn.com/library/PAPALDOC /P12XMAS.HTM.

3. Antifascism and Fraternal Catholic Modernism, 1929–1944

1. Paul-Ludwig Landsberg and Jean Lacroix, *Problèmes du personnalisme* (Paris: Seuil, 1952), 168; Emmanuel Mounier, "Paul-Louis Landsberg," *Esprit* 118 (January 1946): 155–156.

2. Paul-Ludwig Landsberg et al., "D'un nouvel humanisme ou d'un humanisme intégral," *Union pour la vérité* 44, nos. 9–10 (June–July 1937): 351–418 at 401.

3. For a general consideration of antifascism, see Anson Rabinbach, "Paris, Capital of Anti-Fascism," in *The Modernist Imagination: Intellectual History and Critical Theory*, ed. Warren Breckman et al. (New York: Berghahn, 2009), 183–209. On Catholic participation in the Popular Front, see Paul Christophe, *1936: Les catholiques et le front populaire* (Paris: Desclée de Brouwer, 1979); for their role in the Resistance, see, among other sources, Robert Gildea, *Fighters in the Shadows: A New History of the French Resistance* (Cambridge, MA: Belknap, 2015), chap. 7.

4. Paul-Ludwig Landsberg, "Quelques réflexions sur l'idée chrétienne de la personne," *Esprit* 27 (December 1934): 386–399 at 391; Paul-Ludwig Landsberg, "L'anarchiste contre dieu," *Esprit* 55 (April 1937): 75–91 at 85–86, 91; Paul-Ludwig Landsberg, "Notes pour une philosophie du mariage," *Esprit* 79 (April 1939): 48–57 at 51.

5. For another monograph on this period emphasizing the doctrinal centrality of converts, see John Connelly, *From Enemy to Brother: The Revolution in Catholic Teaching on the Jews* (Cambridge, MA: Harvard University Press, 2012).

6. Jacques Maritain, *Oeuvres complètes,* ed. Cercle d'études Jacques et Raïssa Maritain (Paris: Éditions Saint-Paul, 1982–2007), 6:462; Maritain's preface to Paul Vignaux, *Traditionalisme et syndicalism: Essai d'histoire social (1884–1941)* (New York: Éditions de la maison française, 1943), 7–16 at 14; Maritain, *Oeuvres complètes,* 6:485.

7. Landsberg, "D'un nouvel humanisme ou d'un humanisme intégral," 401.

8. Walter Dirks, "Was ist 'Kulturbolschewismus'?," *Zeitschrift für Religion und Sozialismus* 3 (1931): 220–225 at 221.

9. Maritain, "Europe and the Federal Idea," *Commonweal* 31 (1940): 544–547 at 545; Maritain, *Oeuvres complètes,* 7:646.

10. Maritain, *Oeuvres complètes,* 6:341, 347–348.

11. Ibid., 485, 522.

12. Maritain, *Oeuvres complètes,* 7:645–646, 6:457.

13. Malachi Hacohen, *Jacob and Esau between Nation and Empire* (New York: Cambridge University Press, forthcoming).

14. Hugo García et al., eds., *Rethinking Antifascism: History, Memory and Politics, 1922 to the Present* (New York: Berghahn, 2016); special issue on transnational antifascism, *Contemporary European History* 25, no. 4 (November 2016); papers presented at "Trajectories of Antifascism," Rutgers University, March 2017.

15. Karl Gustav Bittner, "Katholizismus gegen Kapitalismus," *Christliche Ständestaat* 2, no. 23 (9 June 1935): 541–544 at 544.

16. Denis Kitzinger, "Dietrich von Hildebrand: A Catholic Intellectual in the Weimar Republic" (PhD diss., University of St. Andrews, 2017), chap. 2.

17. For his agitation in Cologne, see Franz Xaver Münch to Dietrich von Hildebrand, 15 February 1928, Historisches Archiv des Erzbistum Köln, Nachlaß Franz Xaver Münch, Box 140.

18. Dietrich von Hildebrand, "Max Scheler als Persönlichkeit," *Hochland* 26 (1928–1929): 70–80 at 78, 77.

19. Kitzinger, "Dietrich von Hildebrand," chap. 3.

20. Dietrich von Hildebrand, *Marriage* (New York: Longmans, Green, 1942), 4 (emphasis in original).

21. Ibid., 23, 55. On the legal and theological issues at play, see Norbert Lüdecke, *Eheschließung als Bund. Genese und Exegese der Ehelehre der Konzilkonstitution 'Gaudim et spes' in kanonistischer Auswertung* (Würzburg: Echter, 1989), 118–209.

22. Franz von Papen to Adolf Hitler, 30 April 1937. I am grateful to John Henry Crosby for sending me this remarkable document.

23. Rudolf Ebneth, *Die österreichische Wochenschrift Der Christliche Ständestaat. Deutsche Emigration in Österreich 1933–1938* (Mainz: Matthias-Grünewald, 1976), 22.

24. Dietrich von Hildebrand, "Staat und Ehe," *Christliche Ständestaat* 2, no. 42 (20 October 1935): 1002–1004 at 1002; Dietrich von Hildebrand, *Memoiren und Aufsätze gegen den Nationalsozialismus, 1933–1938,* ed. Ernst Wenisch (Paderborn: Schöningh, 1994), 353.

25. Dietrich von Hildebrand, *My Battle against Hitler: Faith, Truth, and Defiance in the Shadow of the Third Reich,* trans. John Henry Crosby (New York: Image, 2014), 268.

26. Dietrich von Hildebrand, "Falsche Antithesen," *Christliche Ständestaat* 3, no. 17 (26 April 1936): 391–394 at 394.

27. Aurel Kolnai, *Sexual Ethics: The Meaning and Foundations of Sexual Morality,* trans. Francis Dunlop (Aldershot: Ashgate, 2005); Matthias Laros, "Revolutionierung der Ehe," *Hochland* 27 (1930): 193–207 at 198–200; Herbert Doms, *The Meaning of Marriage,* trans. George Sayer (New York: Sheed &

Ward, 1939), 25–26; Karl Thieme, "Neubegründung der Ehe aus Natur und Übernatur," *Hochland* 34, no. 1 (1936–1937): 459–466.

28. On his travels, see Alice von Hildebrand, *Soul of a Lion* (San Francisco: Ignatius, 2000), 206–207; Hildebrand, *My Battle against Hitler*, 168–169; Johannes Oesterreicher to Waldemar Gurian, 29 July 1937, Waldemar Gurian Papers, Library of Congress, Box 6, Folder 10.

29. Dietrich von Hildebrand, review of Maritain, *Von der Christlichen Philosophie, Christliche Ständestaat* 2, no. 51 (22 December 1935): 1234–1235; Dietrich von Hildebrand, "Quietistische Gefahr," *Christliche Ständestaat* 2, no. 10 (10 March 1935): 227–228 at 227.

30. Emmanuel Mounier, *Oeuvres* (Paris: Seuil, 1961), 1:565.

31. Paul Landsberg, "Notes pour une philosophie du mariage," 51; Jacques Perret, "La femme mariée personne humaine," *Esprit* 45 (June 1936): 311–329.

32. Franz von Streng, *Das Geheimnis der Ehe. Eine Braut- und Ehebelehrung* (Cologne: Benziger, 1936), 13–18; Hans Wirtz, *Vom Eros zur Ehe. Die naturgetreue Lebensgemeinschaft* (Innsbruck: Tyrolia, 1938), 225, 229–230, 253. For the circulation of Streng, see Martin Tschirren, *Ehe- und Sexualmoral im Schweizer Katholizismus 1950–1975* (Freiburg, Switzerland: Paulusdruckerei, 1998), 52n.

33. Norbert Rocholl, *Le mariage, vie consacrée* (Ramgal: Thuilles, 1938), 12, 29, 86–87; for a review, see Benoit Lavaud, "Recension de Norbert Rocholl *Die Ehe als geweihtes Leben*," *Revue Thomiste* 43 (1937): 303–316.

34. A. Christian [Georges Gallichet], *Ce sacrement est grand. Temoignage d'un foyer chretien* (Montreal: Editions Familiales, 1938), 244, 47. For Hildebrand, see A.-M. Carré, *Compagnons d'eternite. Le sacrement de mariage* (Paris: Cerf, 1938), 45. Carré, incidentally, had an office right next to Father Marie-Vincent Bernadot, editor of *La Vie intellectuelle*, as reported in Helen Iswolsky, *Light before Dusk: A Russian Catholic in France, 1923–1941* (New York: Longmans, Green, 1942), 120.

35. On France, see "Les sacrements pour la conquête," *L'équipe ouvrière* 11, no. 123 (September 1936): 3; "Le mariage: Sacrement de la famille et de l'amour," *L'équipe ouvrière* 11, no. 124 (October 1936): 15; P. Rousset, "Le mariage, mystère de la vie (Introduction à l'étude du mariage, mystère de la vie, union de deux personnes)," *Les Annales de la jeunesse catholique* 66 (May–June 1938): 147–152. On Austria, see Laura Gellott, "Defending Catholic Interests in the Christian State: The Role of Catholic Action in Austria, 1933–1938," *Catholic Historical Review* 74 (1988): 571–589; Laura Gellott and Michael Phayer, "Dissenting Voices: Catholic Women in Opposition to Fascism," *Journal of Contemporary History* 22 (1987): 91–114 at 108. On Germany and Heliand, see Michael E. O'Sullivan, "A Feminized Church?," in *Beyond the Feminization Thesis: Gender and Christianity in Modern Europe*, ed. Patrick Pasture et al. (Leuven: Leuven University Press, 2012), 191–211 at 206–209.

36. Susan B. Whitney, *Mobilizing Youth: Communists and Catholics in Interwar France* (Durham, NC: Duke University Press, 2009), chap. 4; Kevin Passmore, " 'Planting the Tricolour in the Citadels of Communism': Women's Social Action in the Croix de feu and Parti Social Français," *Journal of Modern History* 71 (1999): 814–851.

37. E. Jordan, "Le monde moderne et le mariage chrétien," *La Vie intellectuelle* 38, no. 2 (25 October 1935): 211–218 at 214.

38. Hildebrand, *Marriage*, 21.

39. Hildebrand, *My Battle against Hitler*, 243.

40. E. K. Winter, foreword to *Die Österreichische Aktion: Programmatische Studien* (Vienna: Selbstverlag, 1927), 5–10 at 9.

41. E. K. Winter, *Die Sozialmetpahysik der Scholastik* (Vienna: Franz Deuticke, 1929), 164–176.

42. Heinrich Mertens, "Katholizismus, Klasse, Klassenkampf," *Das rote Blatt* 1 (1929): 66; Ernst Karl Winter, "Was ist Kapitalismus?," *Das rote Blatt* 1 (1929): 7; Ernst Michel, "Das Eigentumsrecht in der Reichsverfassung," *Das rote Blatt* 2 (1930): 80–86 at 81. For two critical perspectives on Brauer, see Franz Müller, "Karl Marx. Wie Katholiken heute urteilen," *Das rote Blatt* 1 (1929): 7; Hendrik de Man, "Professor Brauer und der Sozialismus," *Das rote Blatt* 1 (1929): 29–31.

43. William Patch, *Christian Trade Unions in the Weimar Republic: The Failure of Corporate Pluralism* (New Haven, CT: Yale University Press, 1985), 176–187.

44. Carl Muth, "Die Stunde des Bürgertums," *Hochland* 28, no. 1 (1930): 1–14.

45. Ernst Karl Winter to Carl Muth, 16 October 1930, Nachlaß Muth, II.A., Bayerische Staatsbibliothek München.

46. E. K. Winter, *Monarchie und Arbeiterschaft* (Vienna: Gsur, 1936), 51, 65; Ernst Karl Winter, "Monarchie, 'Faschismus' und 'Bolschewismus,' " *Christliche Ständestaat* 3, no. 34 (23 August 1936): 799–801.

47. For one account, see Anton Pelinka, *Stand oder Klasse? Die christliche Arbeiterbewegung Österreich 1933–1938* (Vienna: Europaverlag, 1972), 129–141.

48. Anonymous [presumably Winter], "Für ein freies, unabhängiges Österreich," *Die Aktion* 1, no. 1 (14 September 1934): 1–3 at 2; Anonymous [presumably Winter], "Wir und die christliche Arbeiterschaft," *Die Aktion* 1, no. 1 (14 September 1934): 2–3; Fritz-Piccardi, "Warum wir mittun?," *Die Aktion* 1, no. 4 (6 October 1934): 2–3.

49. Winter, "Monarchie, 'Faschismus' und 'Bolschewismus.' "

50. Ernst Karl Winter, *Rudolf IV. von Österreich* (Vienna: Reinhold, 1936), 2:467–468.

51. Winter, *Monarchie und Arbeiterschaft*, 77, 52.

52. E. K. Winter, "Christentum oder Sozialismus?," *Wiener Politische Blätter* 4 (1936): 1–11 at 6.

53. Otto Brunner [i.e., Missong], "Antisemitismus in Österreich," *Christliche Ständestaat* 3, no. 17 (26 April 1936): 396–398.

54. Anonymous [almost certainly Winter], "Die Judenfrage," *Wiener Politische Blätter* 4 (1936): 183–195 at 191.

55. Walter Berger, *Was ist Rasse? Versuch einer Abgrenzung ihrer Wirksamkeit im seelischen Bereich mit berucksichtigung des jüdischen Rassenproblems* (Vienna: Gsur, 1936); Peter Drucker, *Die Judenfrage in Deutschland* (Vienna: Gsur, 1936).

56. E. K. Winter, "Wahlrecht und Wehrpflicht," *Die Aktion* 2, no. 19 (11 May 1935): 1–2.

57. See the voices collected in Ludwig Reichhold, *Opposition gegen den autoritären Staat. Christlicher Antifaschismus, 1934–1938* (Vienna: Europa-Verlag, 1964); Pelinka, *Stand oder Klasse?*, 85–88. For a primary source, see "Die berufständische Ordnung," *Österreichische Arbeiter-Zeitung* 42, no. 6 (6 February 1937): 3–4.

58. Ernst Karl Winter, "Nach den Schutzbundprozeß," *Die Aktion* 2, no. 18 (4 May 1935): 1–4; Winter, "Wahlrecht und Wehrpflicht"; R. Poukar, "Nun aber Schluß, Herr Winter!," *Der Heimatschützer* 4, no. 11 (14 March 1936): 2. For internal records, including Schuschnigg's 5 March 1935 letter to Winter, see Nachlaß Richard Schmitz, Österreichische Staatsarchiv, E / 1786:314.

59. The trip is reported in Winter, "Nach den Schutzbundprozeß."

60. On the intellectual relationship between Catholicism and Marxism at the time, see David Curtis, "True and False Modernity: Catholicism and Communist Marxism in 1930s France," in *Catholicism, Politics and Society in Twentieth-Century France*, ed. Kay Chadwick (Liverpool: Liverpool University Press, 2000), 73–96.

61. Etienne Borne, "Les catholiques, le communisme et les crises du moment présent," *La Vie intellectuelle* 48, no. 1 (25 February 1937): 9–31.

62. Anonymous [presumably Mounier], "Préface a quelques témoignages," *Esprit* 46 (1936): 486–488 at 487; "À propos des grèves, faison le point," *L'équipe ouvrière* 10, no. 53 (July 1936); Jules Zirnheld, "Pour nous documenter: Quelques principes essentiels pour reconstruire l'Économie," *Meneurs* 8 (September 1935): 33–34; Albert Gortais, "Efforts pour la Paix sociale," *Annales de la Jeunesse Catholique* 64 (March 1938): 83–90; Albert Gortais, "Corporatisme?," *Les Annales de la Jeunesse Catholique* 68 (September–October 1938): 238–245, 300–312; Jean-Louis Clément, *Les évêques au temps de Vichy. Loyalisme sans inféodation* (Paris: Beauchesne, 1999), 121–127. On Maritain's influence in the ACJF and throughout Catholic Action, see Arthur Plaza, "From Christian Social Order to Humane Democracy: Three Itineraries Leading to the MRP 1936–1948," *Chrétiens et Sociétés* 12 (2005), paras. 11–12, available at http://chretienssocietes.revues.org/2214?lang=en.

63. Kevin Passmore, *From Liberalism to Fascism: The Right in a French Province, 1928–1939* (Cambridge: Cambridge University Press, 1997), 257.

64. Jules Zirnheld, *Cinquante années de syndicalisme chrétien* (Paris: Spes, 1937), 265.

65. Quoted in Patrick Pasture, *Histoire du syndicalisme chrétien internationale. La difficile recherche d'une troisième voie* (Paris: L'Harmattan, 1999), 177.

66. On the CISC and the Austrians, see *L'Oeuvre de l'internationale syndicale chrétienne, 1932–1934* (Utrecht: Confédération internationale des syndicats chrétiens, 1934), 7–8, 47, 188; on the CISC and the DAF, see William Patch, *Christian Democratic Workers and the Forging of German Democracy, 1920–1980* (New York: Cambridge University Press, 2018), 46–47.

67. *L'encyclique Quadragesimo Anno sur la restauration de l'ordre social (15 Mai 1931)* (Paris: Spes, 1936), 80, 25n; *En écoutant le pape. Entretiens sur l'encyclique Quadragesimo Anno* (Paris: Editions Jocistes, 1932), 49.

68. Ludwig Reinhold, *Geschichte der ÖVP* (Vienna: Verlag Styria, 1975), 44.

69. Wolfgang Schroeder, *Katholizismus und Einheitsgewerkschaft. Der Streit um den DGB und der Niedergang des Sozialkatholizismus in der Bundespreublik bis 1960* (Bonn: Dietz, 1992), 61; Albert Eßer, *Wilhelm Elfes, 1884–1969. Arbeiterführer und Politiker* (Mainz: Matthias-Grünewald, 1990), 115–123.

70. For Bacon, see Arthur Plaza, "From Christian Militants to Republican Renovators" (PhD diss., New York University, 2008), 53; Gaston Tessier, "Les Syndicats et la Charte du Travail," *La Croix,* no. 18072 (23 December 1941): 1. For an example from the LOC, see "Formation et information: Notre attitude vis-à-vis de la Charte du travail," *Meneurs* 78 (January 1942): 14–15. Manifesto reproduced in Val Lorwin, *The French Labor Movement* (Cambridge, MA: Harvard University Press, 1954), 315–320. See further Jacques Julliard, "Charte du Travail," in *Le gouvernement de Vichy, 1940–1942: Institutions et politiques,* ed. Janine Bourdin and René Rémond (Paris: Presses de la Fondation nationale des sciences politiques, 1972), 157–211, esp. 163–165.

71. "Das Echo bei den Diktaturen," *Die Zukunft* 2, no. 8 (24 February 1939): 6 (citing a Communist judgment of the journal). For Catholic participation, see, among others, "Der Weg zu einer neuen Demokratie: Von einem rheinischen Katholiken," *Die Zukunft* 1, no. 4 (4 November 1938): 7; Otto Maria Fidelis, "Verfolgte Katholiken," *Die Zukunft* 2, no. 4 (27 January 1939): 5; Landsberg's contribution to "Ein Jahr 'Zukunft,'" *Die Zukunft* 2, no. 41 (13 October 1939): 4.

72. Vera Bücker, *Nikolaus Gross. Politischer Journalist und Katholik im Widerstand des Kölner Kreises* (Münster: Lit, 2003), 142, 184–188.

73. On the JOC, see "Die Welt im sozialen Blickfeld," *Ketteler Wacht* 37, no. 9 (2 March 1935): 63. On the Social Week, see "Neue Form, neuer Geist," *Ketteler Wacht* 37, no. 35 (31 August 1935): 241.

74. Jacques Maritain, *Oeuvres complètes,* 16:411–414 at 411.

75. Jacques Maritain to Henri Massis, undated [1927], Archives of the Centre d'études Jacques et Raïssa Maritain, Kolbsheim; Jacques Maritain to Henri Massis, 4 March 1927, Maritain Archives, Kolbsheim.

76. Maritain, *Oeuvres complètes,* 6:484–485.

77. Jacques Maritain to Alexandre Marc, 19 March 1935, Historical Archives of the European Union, Fonds Alexandre Marc, HAEU AM-118.

78. Maritain, *Oeuvres complètes,* 6:430, 564, 572, 399.

79. "Au Sujet de 'La Démocratie et la Révolution': Une Lettre de M. Jacques Maritain," *L'Aube,* 25 January 1934, 2.

80. Jacques Maritain, *A Christian Looks at the Jewish Question* (New York: Longman's, 1939), 10–16.

81. Gerd-Rainer Horn, *Western European Liberation Theology: The First Wave (1924–1959)* (New York: Oxford University Press, 2008), 16, 29. See Maritain, *Oeuvres complètes,* 6:590–592, for his view of Catholic Action.

82. Maritain, *Oeuvres complètes,* 6:511–513.

83. Ibid., 505.

84. Jacques Maritain, "Der Vorrang der menschlichen Persönlichkeit," in *Von Montreux bis Paris. Die Arbeit der christlichen Gewerkschafts-Internationale, 1934–1937* (Utrecht: Internationaler Bund der Christlichen Gewerkschaften, 1937), 107–123 at 107, 118, 119; Maritain's preface to Vignaux, *Traditionalisme et syndicalisme,* 10.

85. Anonymous, "Dieu est-il à droite?," *La Vie intellectuelle* 41, no. 1 (25 February 1936): 49–72; Aline Coutrot, *Sept, un journal, un combat (mars 1934–août 1937)* (Paris: Editions Cana, 1982), 77–92; Jacques Maritain, "Religion and Politics in France," *Foreign Affairs* 20 (1942): 266–281 at 273.

86. Waldemar Gurian, "Die Abendlandideologie als Maske des französischen Nationalismus," *Abendland* 2, no. 9 (June 1927): 277–279; Waldemar Gurian to Karl Thieme, 9 July 1932, Nachlaß Thieme, Folder 163 / 28, Institut für Zeitgeschichte, Munich. For Maritain's willingness to shock the Germans, see Jacques Maritain to Waldemar Gurian, 19 July 1935, Gurian Papers, Library of Congress, Box 5, Folder 18.

87. Eberhard Welty, O.P., *Gemeinschaft und Einzelmensch. Eine Sozialmetaphysische Untersuchung* (Salzburg: Pustet, 1935). The subtlety of the text is remarkable: in a footnote (435n21), Welty actually cites *Mein Kampf* to make an argument *against* collectivism.

88. The first meeting is mentioned in Erik Peterson to Jacques Maritain, 17 August 1935, Maritain Archives, Kolbsheim, while Peterson described his project

in Erik Peterson to Jacques Maritain, 3 September 1935, Maritain Archives, Kolbsheim. The book is Erik Peterson, *Der Monotheismus als politisches Problem* (Leipzig: Hegner, 1935).

89. Karl Thieme, *Deutsche evangelische Christen auf dem Wege zur katholischen Kirche. Akten und Abhandlungen* (Schlieren-Zürich: Verlagsanstalt Neue Brücke A.G., 1934), 50; Karl Thieme to Jacques Maritain, 24 April 1939, Nachlaß Thieme, Folder 163/51.

90. Johannes Oesterreicher to Jacques Maritain, 22 December 1937, Maritain Archives, Kolbsheim. On their meeting, see "Jacques Maritain," Radio WSOU (1992), an interview transcript in Oesterreicher Archives, Seton Hall, Box 2. On all of this, see Connelly, *From Enemy to Brother*.

91. "Die Kirche Christi und die Judenfrage," *Die Erfüllung* 2, nos. 5–6 (February 1937): 3–32 at 16.

92. Jacques Maritain, *Oeuvres complètes*, 4:94.

93. Jacques Maritain to Mortimer Adler, 26 June 1940, Mortimer J. Adler Papers, Box 29, Special Collections Research Center, University of Chicago Library.

94. On Gurian's perpetual clashes with Notre Dame's Catholic culture, see, for instance, Arnold Lunn to Waldemar Gurian, 7 November 1938, Gurian Papers, Library of Congress.

95. Ernst Karl Winter, "The Rise and Fall of Austrian Labor," *Social Research* 6 (1939): 316–340 at 337.

96. Dietrich von Hildebrand, "Fascism and Catholicism," *Free World* 1 (1941): 197–199; Dexter Teed, "A Price on His Head," *New York Post*, 3 December 1943.

97. "D'un nouvel humanisme ou d'un humanisme intégral," *Union pour la vérité* 44, nos. 9–10 (June–July 1937): 351–418; Gaston Fessard, "Pour une chrétienté nouvelle," *Temps Présent* 3, 66 (17 February 1939): 4, 8; Danilo Scholz, "Alexandre Kojève et Gaston Fessard sur l'autorité et la politique," *Revue philosophique de la France et de l'étranger* 141 (2016): 343–362.

98. "Un message de Jacques Maritain," *Cahiers du Témoignage chrétien* 6–7 (April–May 1942): 3.

99. Maritain, *Oeuvres complètes*, 7:762.

100. M. Rapaport and J. L. Brown, Foreign Language Section, U.S. Government Coordinator of Information, to Dr. Fry and Mr. Stanley, 7 May 1942, Jacques Maritain Papers, Jacques Maritain Center, University of Notre Dame, Box 18, Folder 3.

101. Maritain, broadcast delivered 30 September 1943, transcript in Maritain Papers, Notre Dame, Box 16, Folder 2.

102. Gil Rubin, "From Federalism to Binationalism: Hannah Arendt's Shifting Zionism," *Contemporary European History* 24 (2015): 393–414. On Maritain's earlier calls for federalism, see Maritain, *Oeuvres complètes*, 4:1144.

103. Jacques Maritain, *L'Europe et l'idée fédérale* (Paris: Mame, 1993), 31; "Maritain Sees Europe United by Religious Tie," *New York Herald Tribune,* 24 March 1940; Jacques Maritain, "Europe and the Federal Idea," *Commonweal* 31 (1940): 544–547 at 547.

104. Maritain, *Oeuvres complètes,* 7:702.

105. "Manifesto on the War," *Commonweal* 26, no. 18 (21 August 1942): 415–420 at 415, 417, 418.

106. Jacques Maritain to Yves Simon, n.d. [November 1941], in *Jacques Maritain-Yves Simon Correspondance. Les années americaines,* ed. Florian Michel (Tours: CLD, 2012), 80. On the alterations, see Manuel M. de Ynchausti to C. G. Paulding, 31 January 1942, in Maritain Papers, Notre Dame, Box 18, Folder 3; and in the same collection, Luigi Sturzo to Jacques Maritain, 8 March 1942 (Box 18, Folder 5); Yves Simon to Jacques Maritain, 6 November 1941 (Box 18, Folder 4); Waldemar Gurian to Jacques Maritain, 8 February 1942 (Box 18, Folder 3).

107. G. K. Chesterton, *What's Wrong with the World* (New York: Dodd, Mead, 1912), 48.

4. The Birth of Christian Democracy, 1944–1950

1. Léopold Senghor, *Liberté II. Nation et voie africaine du socialisme* (Paris: Seuil, 1971), 101–109, 28.

2. Léopold Sédar-Senghor, "Défense de l'Afrique noire," *Esprit* 13, no. 112 (July 1945): 237–248 at 238, 248.

3. Heinrich von Brentano, "Innere und äußere Einheit Europas bringt Frieden," *Bulletin des Presse- und Informationsamtes der Bundesregierung,* no. 128 (14 July 1955): 1069–1070. For the context and fallout, see "Die missionäre Monarchie," *Der Spiegel,* 10 August 1955, 12–14.

4. Anson Rabinbach, *In the Shadow of Catastrophe: German Intellectuals between Apocalypse and Enlightenment* (Berkeley: University of California Press, 1997), 8–9.

5. Jean-Louis Jadoulle, *Chrétiens modernes. Les engagements des intellectuels catholiques "progressistes" en Belgique francophone (1945–1958)* (Louvain-la-Neuve: Academia-Bruylant, 2003), 55.

6. Pierre-Henri Simon, "La Semaine Sociale de Strasbourg," *La Vie intellectuelle* 14, no. 10 (October 1946): 74–78 at 75; René Rémond, "Les surprises d'une méthode: L'Action Catholique," *La Vie intellectuelle* 17, no. 1 (January 1949): 17–25 at 24–25; Michael Seidlmayer, *Das Mittelalter. Umrisse und Ergebnisse des Zeitalters unser Erbe,* 2nd ed. (Göttingen: Vandenhoeck & Ruprecht, 1967; originally published 1949), 31; Franz Josef Schöningh, "Christliche politik?," *Hochland* 41 (1948–1949): 305–320 at 308.

7. "Eine freie Kirche in einer freien Gesellschaft," in *Österreichischer Katholikentag* (Vienna: Generalsekretariat d. Österr. Katholikentages, 1952), 29–32; Messner quoted in Robert Kriechbaumer, *Von der Illegalität zur Legalität. Die ÖVP im Jahr 1945* (Vienna: Multiplex, 1985), 218; Alfred Maleta quoted in David Neuhold, *Franz Kardinal König—Religion und Freiheit* (Fribourg: Kohlhammer, 2008), 218. On the retreat of the clergy from politics, even in West Germany, see Kristian Buchna, *Ein klerikales Jahrzent? Kirche, Konfession und Politik in der Bundesrepublik während der 1950er Jahre* (Baden-Baden: Nomos, 2014).

8. Joseph Lecler, S.J., "La papauté moderne et la liberté de conscience," *Etudes* 249 (1946): 289–309 at 306, 308; Albert Hartmann, S.J., *Toleranz und christlicher Glaube* (Frankfurt: Josef Knecht, 1955). For an overview, see Joseph A. Komonchak, "Religious Freedom and the Confessional State: The Twentieth-Century Discussion," *Revue d'Histoire Ecclésiastique* 95 (2000): 634–650.

9. Thomas Brodie, "The German Catholic Diaspora in the Second World War," *German History* 33 (2015): 80–99, makes this case for West Germany.

10. Ewald Frie, "Zwischen Amtskirche und Verbandswesen: Der deutsche Caritasverband, 1945–1949," in *Siegerin in Trümmern. Die Rolle der katholischen Kirche in der deutschen Nachkriegsgesellschaft*, ed. Joachim Köhler and Damian van Melis (Stuttgart: Kohlhammer, 1998), 161–174.

11. Roger Garaudy, *L'Eglise, le Communisme et les Chrétiens* (Paris: Éditions Sociales, 1949), 9. See also Wilhelm Damberg, "'Radikal katholische Laien an die Front!' Beobachtung zur Idee und Wirkungsgeschichte der katholischen Aktion," in Köhler and Melis, *Siegerin in Trümmern*, 142–160.

12. Martin Conway, "The Rise and Fall of Western Europe's Democratic Age, 1945–73," *Contemporary European History* 13 (2004): 67–88 at 81.

13. See, for instance, Noah Strote, *Lions and Lambs: Conflict in Weimar and the Creation of Post-Nazi Germany* (New Haven, CT: Yale University Press, 2017).

14. Frank Bösch, *Die Adenauer-CDU. Gründung, Aufstieg und Krise einer Erfolgspartei, 1945–1969* (Munich: Deutsche Verlags-Anstalt, 2001), chap. 3; Protestant minister quoted in "Des Papstes Garde," *Der Spiegel*, 15 September 1954, 8–15 at 12.

15. Fritz Fellner, "The Problem of the Austrian Nation after 1945," *Journal of Modern History* 60 (1988): 264–289.

16. For the general consensus view of the significance of the 1930s minority currents, see Wolfram Kaiser, *Christian Democracy and the Origins of European Union* (New York: Cambridge University Press, 2007). On Maritain in particular, see Mario Caciagli, "Christian Democracy," in *The Cambridge History of Twentieth-Century Political Thought*, ed. Terence Ball and Richard Bellamy (New York: Cambridge University Press, 2003), 165–181 at 174; Jan-Werner

Müller, *Contesting Democracy: Political Ideas in Twentieth-Century Europe* (New Haven: Yale University Press, 2011), 135–138.

17. Jacques Maritain to Charles Journet, 2 June 1946, in *Journet-Maritain Correspondance,* ed. Mgr. Pierre Mamie and George Cottier, O.P. (Fribourg: Editions Universitaires, 1998), 3:409.

18. For one interpretation along these lines, see Emiel Lamberts, "La démocratie chrétienne en Europe comme expression politique des religions chrétiennes: Essor et déclin (1945–2000)," *Social Compass* 47 (2000): 113–125.

19. Peter Kent, *The Lonely Cold War of Pope Pius XII: The Roman Catholic Church and the Division of Europe, 1943–1950* (Montreal: McGill–Queen's University Press, 2002), 132–133.

20. Michael Marrus, "A Plea Unanswered: Jacques Maritain, Pope Pius XII, and the Holocaust," in *Jews, Catholics, and the Burden of History,* ed. Eli Lederhendler (New York: Oxford University Press, 2006), 3–11 at 6; Jacques Maritain, *Mystère d'Israel* (Paris: Desclée de Brouwer, 1990), 223–231.

21. David Cesarani and Eric J. Sundqist, eds., *After the Holocaust: Challenging the Myth of Silence* (New York: Routledge, 2012).

22. Jacques Maritain, "Eine Botschaft Jacques Maritain," *Freiburger Rundbrief* 1 (1948), available at http://www.freiburger-rundbrief.de/de/?item=941; Jacques Maritain, "Lettre de son exc. Jacques Maritain," *Cahiers Sioniens* 2 (1948): 186–193 at 187, 189.

23. Eugen Kogon, *Der SS-Staat* (Stockholm: Bermann-Fischer, 1947), 37, 214, passim; Eugen Kogon, "Jacques Maritain—Frankreichs Botschafter beim Vatikan," *Frankfurter Hefte* 1, no. 3 (June 1946): 77–79 at 77. In its internal memoranda regarding paper supplies, OMGUS designated *Frankfurter Hefte* as a "priority German magazine." See "List of Priority German Magazines," National Archives, OMGUS, Publications Control Branch, 6 February 1948, Information Control Division, Records of the Press Branch, 260/390/42/19/4, Box 238, Folder 48.

24. Ida Friederike Görres, "Brief über die Kirche," *Frankfurter Hefte* 1, no. 8 (November 1946): 715–734 at 726, 730; Eugen Kogon, "Das Recht auf den politischen Irrtum," *Frankfuter Hefte* 2, no. 7 (July 1947): 645–649.

25. Maria Mitchell, "Materialism and Secularism: CDU Politicians and National Socialism, 1945–1949," *Journal of Modern History* 67 (1995): 278–308.

26. "The Catholic Bishops and Dr. Kogon," 3, report prepared by OMGUS on this matter, dated 23 August 1947 and available in John Riedl Papers, Marquette University, Box 3 of Series 2.5, Folder 11.

27. Suzanne Brown-Fleming, *The Holocaust and Catholic Conscience: Cardinal Aloisius Muench and the Guilt Question in Germany* (Notre Dame, IN: University of Notre Dame Press, 2006), 17.

28. This account is based on Beth A. Griech-Polelle, *Bishop von Galen: German Catholicism and National Socialism* (New Haven, CT: Yale University Press, 2002).

29. Fried quoted in Robert Kriechbaumer, *Von der Lagerstraße zum Ballhausplatz. Quellen zur Gründungs- und Frühgeschichte der ÖVP, 1938–1949* (Salzburg: IT-Verlag, 1995), 33. For more, see Pfarrer Leopold Arthofer, *Als Priester im Konzentrationslager. Meine Erlebnisse in Dachau* (Graz: Ulrich Moser, 1947); Leonhard Steinwender, *Christus im Konzentrationslager. Wege der Gnade und des Opfers* (Salzburg: Otto Muller, 1946). For an overview of Austrian memory in the early years of the Second Republic, see the essays collected in *Austrian Historical Memory and National Identity*, ed. Gunter Bischof and Anton Pelinka (New Brunswick, NJ: Transaction, 1997).

30. Joel Davis, "Rebuilding the Soul: Churches and Religion in Bavaria, 1945–1960" (PhD diss., University of Missouri-Columbia, 2007), 54–55.

31. This series appeared under the title *Christliche Deutschland 1933 bis 1945. Katholische Reihe* in multiple issues, with multiple editors, between 1945 and 1947 (published by Herder). For more on this, see Mark Ruff, *The Battle for the Catholic Past in Germany* (New York: Cambridge University Press, 2017), chap. 1.

32. Marrus, "A Plea Unanswered," 9.

33. Menthon's speech in Nuremberg Trial Proceedings, Volume 5, Transcript of thirty-sixth day (17 January 1946), available at http://avalon.law.yale.edu/imt /01-17-46.asp. On Hlond, see Kent, *The Lonely Cold War of Pope Pius XII*, 128, and on Muench and Maritain, see ibid., 145; Muench quoted in Brown-Fleming, *The Holocaust and Catholic Conscience*, 143; sermon analysis in Davis, "Rebuilding the Soul," 45.

34. "The Nazi Master Plan, Annex 4: The Persecution of the Christian Churches," 6 July 1946, available at http://library2.lawschool.cornell.edu/donovan/pdf /Nuremberg_3/Vol_X_18_03_02.pdf, p. 3; Marshall Knappen, "The Christian Churches in Germany," February 1946, National Archives, Religious Affairs Branch, 615 (A1), General Records, 1946–9, 390 / 46 / 15–16 / 5–4, Box 158, Folder 7, p. 3; incomplete essay by C. Eagan, June 1947, National Archives, Religious Affairs Branch, 615 (A1), General Records, 1946–9, 390 / 46 / 15–16 / 5–4, Box 158, Folder 6, p. 8; Report on the U.S. Occupation of Germany, Religious Affairs Program, 23 September 1947, National Archives, Religious Affairs Branch, 615 (A1), General Records, 1946–9, 390 / 46 / 15–16 / 5–4, Box 165, Folder 3, pp. 1–2.

35. Quoted in Griech-Polelle, *Bishop von Galen*, 148.

36. Oliver Rathkolb, *The Paradoxical Republic: Austria 1945–2005* (New York: Berghahn, 2010), 101.

37. Thomas Albrich, "Fremd und jüdisch. Die osteuropäischen Überlebenden des Holocaust—erste Projektionsziele des Nachkriegsantisemitismus," in *Antisemitismus in Österreich nach 1945,* ed. Heinz Wasserman (Innsbruck: Studien Verlag, 2002), 66–95.

38. Walter Manoschek, "How the Austrian People's Party Dealt with the Holocaust, Anti-Semitism and National Socialism after 1945," in *Austro-Corporatism: Past, Present, Future,* ed. Günter Bischof and Anton Pelinka (New Brunswick, NJ: Transaction, 1996), 317–335 at 322–323. For the Hurdes quotation given here, see "Wie kam es 1934/38 zur Krise der österr. Demokratie?," *Österreichische Monatshefte* 1, no. 1 (1945): 26–34 at 28. The series is finished up in *Österreichische Monatshefte* 1, no. 2 (1945): 15–20.

39. Jacques Maritain to Yves Simon, 8 January 1945, *Cahiers Jacques Maritain* 4 (1982): 11–14 at 12.

40. Emmanuel Mounier, "Débat à haute voix," *Esprit* 119 (February 1946): 164–190 at 165.

41. Kent, *The Lonely Cold War of Pope Pius XII,* 180–183.

42. Jacques Maritain, *Oeuvre complètes,* ed. Cercle d'études Jacques et Raïssa Maritain (Paris: Éditions Saint-Paul, 1982–2007), 9:232, 464, 445.

43. Bernard Doering, ed., *The Philosopher and the Provocateur: The Correspondence of Jacques Maritain and Saul Alinsky* (Notre Dame, IN: University of Notre Dame Press, 1994), 11. On Dirks and the Frankfurt activists, see Klaus Große Kracht, *Die Stunde der Laien? Katholische Aktion in Deutschland im europäischen Kontext, 1920–1960* (Paderborn: Schöningh, 2016), chap. 9.

44. Walter Dirks, "Der restaurative Charakter der Epoche," *Frankfurter Hefte* 5, no. 9 (September 1950): 942–954 at 947.

45. Discussed in Gaston Tessier to Robert Lecourt, 10 June 1947, Fonds Gaston Tessier, CFDT Archives, 1P2. Tessier was furious and threatened to organize a counterdemonstration to the tomb of Archbishop Georges Darboy, massacred by the Communards.

46. Alain-René Michel, *Catholiques en démocratie* (Paris: Cerf, 2006), 427–428.

47. See the essays collected in *Between Cross and Class: Comparative Histories of Christian Labour in Europe 1840–2000,* ed. Jan de Maeyer, Patrick Pasture, and Lex Heerma van Voss (Bern: Peter Lang, 2005), and William Patch, "The Legend of Compulsory Unification: The Catholic Clergy and the Revival of Trade Unionism in West Germany after the Second World War," *Journal of Modern History* 79, no. 4 (December 2007): 848–880, Pius XII quoted at 849.

48. Joseph Dobretsberger, *Katholische Sozialpolitik am Scheideweg* (Vienna: Ulrich Moser, 1947), 8.

49. Jacques Maritain, "Réconciliation pour la liberté," *Cahiers Jacques Maritain* 4 (1982): 62–66 at 63.

50. Manifesto quoted in Gerd-Rainer Horn, "Left Catholicism in Western Europe in the 1940s," in *Left Catholicism, 1943–1955: Catholics and Society in Western Europe at the Point of Liberation,* ed. Gerd-Rainer Horn and Emmanuel Gerard (Leuven: Leuven University Press, 2001), 45–63 at 55.

51. Andreas Lienkamp, "Socialism out of Christian Responsibility: The German Experiment of Left Catholicism (1945–1949)," in ibid., 196–227 at 203–206. The Ahlen Program is available at http://www.kas.de/upload/themen /programmatik_der_cdu/programme/1947_Ahlener-Programm.pdf.

52. Quoted in André Deroo, *L'épiscopat français dans la mêlée de son temps* (Paris: Bonne Presse, 1955), 115. See also Thierry Keck, *Jeunesse de l'Église (1936–55), aux sources de la crise progressiste en France* (Paris: Karthala, 2004), pt. 2.

53. MRP Executive Committee quoted in Isser Woloch, "Left, Right and Centre: The MRP and the Post-War Moment," *French History* 21 (2007): 85–106 at 89; Dobretsberger, *Katholische Sozialpolitik am Scheideweg,* 99–100.

54. Jean-Marie Domenach, "Rencontre avec la jeunesse allemande," *Travaux de l'Action Populaire* 13 (November 1947): 813–818; Eugen Kogon, *Dieses merk-würdige, wichtige Leben,* ed. Michael Kogon (Berlin: Weinheim, 1997), 128–129; Emmanuel Mounier to Walter Dirks, undated [1947] and Walter Dirks to Emmanuel Mounier, 20 November 1947, both in Archiv der sozialen Demokratie der Friedrich-Ebert-Stiftung, Personenbestand Walter Dirks, Signatur 1 / WDAC000018 (for the finished version, see Walter Dircks [*sic*], "Le marxisme dans une vision chrétienne," trans. Paul Thisse, *Esprit* 145 [May–June 1948]: 783–798); Walter Dirks to Aloys Leber, 2 June 1950, Personenbestand Walter Dirks, Signatur 1 / WDAC000018.

55. For some examples, see Walter Dirks, "Das Wort Sozialismus," *Frankfurter Hefte* 1, no. 7 (October 1946): 628–642 at 641; Eugen Kogon, "Über die Situation," *Frankfurter Hefte* 2, no. 1 (January 1947): 17–37 at 26; Pierre Emmanuel, "Le dialogue interrompu," *Temps Présent* 10, no. 120 (6 December 1946): 1–5 at 5; "Antinomies soviétiques et conscience chrétienne," *La Vie intellectuelle* 14, no. 4 (April 1946): 54–62 at 59.

56. Jean Lacroix, "Dépassement du Communisme," *Esprit* 105 (December 1944): 56–64 at 59; Jean Baboulène, "La main tendue," *Témoignage chrétien* 4, no. 154 (18 June 1947): 3.

57. Walter Dirks, *Für eine andere Republik* (Zurich; Ammann, 1991), 251; Dirks, "Das Wort Sozialismus," 631 (emphasis in original), 642.

58. Eugen Kogon, "Der Politische Untergang des Europäischen Widerstandes," *Frankfurter Hefte* 4, no. 5 (May 1949): 405–412 at 407. On the fate of Buchenwald and antifascism, see *Der 'gesäuberte' Antifaschismus. Die SED und die roten Kapos von Buchenwald. Dokumente,* ed. Lutz Niethammer (Berlin: Akademie Verlag, 1994).

59. MG Weekly Intelligence Report for Württemberg-Baden, n.d. [between 1945 and 1948], National Archives, Records Relating to the Cultural Exchange Programs of the Catholic Affairs Section, 1946–1950. 260/390/46/16-/4-, Box 202, Folder 23.

60. This is the fundamental argument in Kent, *The Lonely Cold War of Pope Pius XII.*

61. Paolo Acanfora, "Christian Democratic Internationalist: The Nouvelles Equipes Internationales and the Geneva Circles between European Unification and Religious Identity, 1947–1954," *Contemporary European History* 24 (2015): 375–391 at 382. For another example of anti-Communism in the NEI, see "Niederschrift über die Sitzung vom 8.März 1949 in Genf," Institut für Zeitgeschichte Wien, Nachlaß Felix Hurdes, NL48, Carton 356, Mappe Coordinationkomittee, p. 3.

62. For a masterful account, see Bösch, *Die Adenauer-CDU,* chap. 2.

63. On the French youth groups, to take one example, see Michel, *Catholiques en démocratie,* 441–445. For the Italian version of this story, see Rosario Forlenza, "The Enemy Within: Catholic Anti-Communism in Cold War Italy," *Past and Present* 235 (2017): 207–242.

64. Fessard to the *Témoignage chrétien* editorial staff, 22 October 1945, Archives Jésuites (Vanves), Fonds Fessard, Box 3, Folder 24.

65. All of the reviews—including raves from reactionaries in *La France catholique* and *Paroles françaises*—are collected in Fonds Fessard, Box 3, Folder 24. See also Louis Salleron to Fessard, 19 February 1949, and Henri Rambaud to Fessard, 15 February 1949, both in Fonds Fessard, Box 5, Folder 28.

66. For the veto, see André Mandouze, "Note à l'usage de quelques pères sur la question Communiste," n.d. [but probably October 1945]. For Mandouze's rejection of Fessard's totalitarian theory, see Gaston Fessard to André Mandouze, 29 November 1945. For the rejection of Fessard, see joint letter (Mandouze et al.) to Gaston Fessard, n.d. [but presumably 1946, when the second edition of Fessard's book appeared]. All are in Fonds Fessard, Box 3, Folder 24.

67. David Rousset, "David Rousset propose une enquête sur les 'Camps de travail correctif' en U.R.S.S.," *Témoignage chrétien* 5, no. 280 (18 November 1949): 4. On Kogon's ambitions for the Russian zone, see Walter Dirks to Eugen Kogon, 8 March 1946, Personenbestand Walter Dirks, Signatur 1/WDAC000010. For the antifascism of the early texts, see Kogon, *Der SS-Staat,* 16–18, 322–326; Eugen Kogon, "Der Weg zu einem Sozialismus der Freiheit in Deutschland," *Frankfurter Hefte* 2, no. 9 (September 1947): 877–896. For the antitotalitarian turn, see Eugen Kogon, "Der Terror als Herrschaftssystem," *Frankfurter Hefte* 3, no. 11 (November 1948): 985–1000 (this was appended to later editions of *Der SS-Staat*). On the effects of camp knowledge in

political thought, see Emma Kuby, "In the Shadow of the Concentration Camp: David Rousset and the Limits of Apoliticism in Postwar French Thought," *Modern Intellectual History* 11 (2014): 147–173.

68. Udi Greenberg, *The Weimar Century: German Émigrés and the Ideological Foundations of the Cold War* (Princeton, NJ: Princeton University Press, 2014), esp. chap. 3.

69. Waldemar Gurian, "La politique étrangère," in *La civilisation américaine*, ed. Yves Simon (Paris: Desclée de Brouwer, 1950), 169–190 at 184, 189. His talk at Chicago is described in Notre Dame's press release PNDP PR 47–206 (17 July 1947). These are available in the reading room of the Notre Dame Archives. See also Waldemar Gurian, "Drei Korrespondenten über Deutschland," *Der Monat* 2 (1950): 546–548. The program for the Salzburg lectures is contained in an 18 March 1949 letter from W. Reinermann to Waldemar Gurian, Library of Congress, Waldemar Gurian Papers, Box 17, Folder 11. For the imperialism quotation, see Waldemar Gurian, "Die Weltpolitik der USA," *Rheinischer Merkur* 5, no. 37 (9 September 1950): 5.

70. Waldemar Gurian, "Europe and the United States: An Open Letter to Etienne Gilson," *Commonweal* 53 (1950): 250–251 at 250; Gurian to Robert Barrat, 16 January 1950, Gurian Papers, Box 2, Folder 6; Jacques Maritain to Gurian, 9 November 1951, Gurian Papers, Box 5, Folder 18; Gilson's response collected in "Le Cas Gilson," dossier available in Gurian Papers, Box 16, Folder 10, pp. 8–10.

71. Waldemar Gurian, "Totalitarianism as Political Religion," in *Totalitarianism*, ed. Carl J. Friedrich (Cambridge, MA: Harvard University Press, 1952), 119–129 at 123; Gaston Fessard, *Le Communisme va-t-il dans le Sens de l'Histoire?* (Paris: Études, 1948), esp. 4 and 17 for these arguments; Brentano, "Innere und äußere Einheit Europas bringt Frieden," 1069; Hans Achinger et al., *Neuordnung der sozialen Leistungen. Denkschrift auf Anregung des Bundeskanzlers* (Cologne: Greven, 1955), 28; Jean Boulier, "Rome et Moscou," preface to Pierre Debray, *Un catholique retour de l'U.R.S.S.* (Paris: Pavilion, 1950), 7–32.

72. Gary Wilder, *Freedom Time: Negritude, Decolonization, and the Future of the World* (Durham, NC: Duke University Press, 2015).

73. Jacques Maritain, *Oeuvres complètes* 7:643, 675–676, 678–679, 691, 682–685.

74. Ibid., 9:159.

75. Jacques Maritain, *Man and the State* (Chicago: University of Chicago Press, 1951), chap. 2.

76. Clemens Müster, "Grenzen des Abendlandes," *Frankfurter Hefte* 2, no. 7 (July 1947): 776–787 at 785; Ivo Zeiger, S.J., "Die religiös-sittliche Lage und die Aufgabe der deutschen Katholiken," in *Der Christ in der Not der Zeit. Der 72. deutsche Katholikentag* (Paderborn: Bonifacius-Druckerei, 1949), 24–39 at 26–27, 35. On the German reception of the more famously French notion of

Europe as a space of missionary encounter, see Benjamin Ziemann, *Encounters with Modernity: The Catholic Church in West Germany, 1945–1975* (New York: Berghahn, 2014), 73–80.

77. Léopold Senghor, "Marxisme et humanisme," *La revue socialiste* 19 (1948): 201–216.

78. Jacques Maritain, "The End of Machiavellianism," *Review of Politics* 4 (1942): 1–32; Jacques Maritain, "La fin du Machiavélisme," *Nova et Vetera* 17 (1942): 113–145; Jacques Maritain, *Principes d'une politique humaniste* (New York: Editions de la Maison Française, 1944), chap. 5; Jacques Maritain, "Das Ende des Machiavellismus," *Frankfurter Hefte* 1, no. 5 (August 1946): 15–21.

79. Walter Dirks, "Die zweite Republik," *Frankfurter Hefte* 1, no. 1 (April 1946): 12–24 at 16; Anonymous [probably Kogon], "Nürnberg und die Geschichte," *Frankfurter Hefte* 1, no. 1 (April 1946): 3–5 at 3, 4; Eugen Kogon, "Demokratie und Föderalismus," *Frankfurter Hefte* 1, no. 6 (September 1946): 66–78.

80. Eugen Kogon to Walter Dirks, 23 August 1949, Personenbestand Walter Dirks, Signatur 1/WDAC000040; Eugen Kogon to Konrad Adenauer, 8 July 1952, enclosed in letter from Kogon to Staatssekretär Otto Lenz, 8 July 1952, Archiv der sozialen Demokratie der Friedrich-Ebert-Stiftung, Sammlung Personalia, Signatur 6/SAMP005391.

81. For a guide to all of this, see Bertrand Vayssière, *Vers une Europe fédérale?* (Brussels: Peter Lang, 2006).

82. Eugen Kogon, "Der entscheidende Schritt," *Frankfurter Hefte* 3, no. 7 (July 1948): 586–591 at 586.

83. Eugen Kogon, "Les perspectives de paix en Europe," *Documents* 5 (1949): 56–72; "Positions de l'Union Européene des federalists [1947]," in Historical Archives of the European Union, EUI Florence, Box UEF-91.

84. Walter Lipgens and Wilfried Loth, eds., *Documents on the History of European Integration,* trans. Paul Falla (New York: de Gruyter, 1988), 2:39–41.

85. For the newspapers, see, for instance, F. A. Kramer, "Gegenwart oder Vergangenheit?," *Rheinischer Merkur* 2, no. 12 (12 April 1947): 1; "Neugliederung des Reiches: Vereinigte Staaten von Deutschland?," *Süddeutsche Zeitung* 1, no. 2 (9 October 1945), 1; polling data from Pierre Letamendia, *Le Mouvement Républicain Populaire: Histoire d'un grand parti français* (Paris: Beauchesne, 1995), 114; Josef Müller, "Bayerische Temperament," *Der Spiegel,* 10 April 1948: 20; Albert Lotz, "Zuviel Föderalismus?," *Föderalistische Hefte* 2 (1949): 316–317.

86. On the clash between different concepts of "the West," and the temporary victory of a particularly conservative, anti-Communist form, see Vanessa Conze, *Das Europa der Deutschen. Ideen von Europa in Deutschland zwischen Reichstradition und Westorientierung (1920–1970)* (Oldenbourg: de Gruyter, 2005).

87. ÖVP leader quoted in Kurt Skalnik, "La démocratie chrétienne," *Etudes* 320, no. 6 (1964): 792–807 at 799; Jean de Fabrègues, "Le christianisme n'est pas

l'occident, mais l'Occident est la clé de la Maison chrétienne," *La France Catholique* 23, no. 77 (7 May 1948): 1, 3; Étienne Fouilloux, "Ordre social chrétien et Algérie française," in *La Guerre d'Algerie et les Chrétiens, Cahiers de l'institut d'histoire du temps present* 9 (1988): 63–88; ÖVP platform quoted in Werner Suppanz, *Österreichische Geschichtsbilder. Historische Legitimationen in Ständestaat und Zweiter Republik* (Vienna: Böhlau, 1998), 87.

88. Axel Schildt, *Zwischen Abendland und Amerika. Studien zur westdetuschen Ideen-landschaft der 50er Jahre* (Munich: Oldenbourg, 1999), 24–38.

89. Johannes Großmann, *Die Internationale der Konservativen. Transnationale Elitenzirkel und private Außenpolitik in Westeuropa seit 1945* (Munich: de Gruyter, 2014).

90. Quoted in Trautl Brandstaller, *Die zugepflügte Furche. Geschichte und Schicksal eines katholischen Blattes* (Vienna: Europa, 1969), 97.

91. Marco Duranti, *The Conservative Human Rights Revolution: European Identity, Transnational Politics, and the Origins of the European Convention* (New York: Oxford University Press, 2016).

92. Anonymous, "L'Homme et la Société," *Circulaire intérieure de La Fédération,* March–April 1945, 1–3; A. Gautier-Walter, "Contre l'Etat partisan et totalitaire. Pour l'Etat national et fédéral," *Circulaire intérieure de La Fédération,* April 1946, 9–10; Walter Ferber, "Paul Jostock," *Neues Abendland* 1, no. 7 (September 1946): 23–26 at 24; F. [probably Franzel], "Der 'Ständestaat,'" *Neues Abendland* 1, no. 12 (February 1947): 22–24; Pater Heinrich Hansen, S.V.D., "Res publica sub Deo," *Neues Abendland* 1, no. 9 (November 1946): 14–21 at 15.

93. Duranti, *The Conservative Human Rights Revolution,* 261–266 on Salleron, chap. 6 on this phenomenon more broadly.

94. Compare Kaiser, *Christian Democracy and the Origins of European Union;* Alan Milward, *The European Rescue of the Nation State,* 2nd ed. (New York: Routledge, 2000).

95. "Objectifs de la Démocratie Chrétienne dans l'Europe actuelle. Les résolutions du congrès de Sorrento, 12–14 Avril 1950," Nachlaß Felix Hurdes, NL48, Carton 366, pp. 1, 3.

96. Bavarian minister-president Hans Ehard, in Lipgens and Loth, *Documents on the History of European Integration,* 2:509.

97. Alice Holmes Cooper, *Paradoxes of Peace: German Peace Movements since 1945* (Ann Arbor: University of Michigan Press, 1996), 64 (on Catholics and peace movement), 67 (on Frings). For this revisionist account of French policy, see Michael Creswell and Marc Trachtenberg, "France and the German Question, 1945–1955," *Journal of Cold War Studies* 5 (2003): 5–28. On transnational Christian Democracy and its support for German rearmament, see Kaiser, *Christian Democracy and the Origins of European Union,* 273–281.

98. For an account that stresses the intellectual creativity of this supposedly "post-ideological" moment, see Howard Brick, *Transcending Capitalism: Visions of a New Society in Modern American Thought* (Ithaca, NY: Cornell University Press, 2006), chap. 5. For Maritain on America, see above all Jacques Maritain, *Reflections on America* (New York: Scribner's, 1958).

99. Philippe Chenaux, *L'église catholique et le communisme en Europe (1917–89). De Lénine à Jean-Paul II* (Paris: Cerf, 2009), 196.

100. Henri Massis, *Maurras et notre temps* (Paris: La Palatine, 1951), 175; Garaudy, *L'Eglise, le communisme et les chrétiens*, 331–332.

5. Christian Democracy in the Long 1950s

1. There are exceptions, notably Emiel Lamberts, ed., *Christian Democracy in the European Union* (Leuven: KADOC, 1997), chap. 5; Albrecht Langner, ed., *Katholizismus, Wirtschaftsordnung und Sozialpolitik, 1945–1963* (Paderborn: Schöningh, 1980). For a claim that Christian Democracy did not have an ideology to speak of, see Harold L. Wilensky, "Leftism, Catholicism, and Democratic Corporatism," in *The Development of Welfare States in Europe and America,* ed. Peter Flora and Arnold J. Heidenheimer (New Brunswick, NJ: Transaction, 1981), 345–382 at 351–353.

2. The literature on welfare state typology is vast and heavily contested, but see above all Gøsta Esping-Andersen, *The Three Worlds of Welfare Capitalism* (Princeton, NJ: Princeton University Press, 1990). That text emphasizes the uniqueness of Christian Democratic welfare policy. For a more detailed version of that claim, see Kees van Kersbergen, *Social Capitalism: A Study of Christian Democracy and the Welfare State* (London: Routledge, 1995).

3. This literature is large and growing. For samples, see Erica Carter, *How German Is She? Postwar West German Reconstruction and the Consuming Woman* (Ann Arbor: University of Michigan Press, 1997); Steven Zdatny, "The French Hygiene Offensive of the 1950s: A Critical Moment in the History of Manners," *Journal of Modern History* 84 (2012): 897–932. On the Catholic story, see, for instance, Lukas Rölli-Alkemper, *Familie im Wiederaufbau. Katholizismus und bürgerliches Familienideal in der Bundesrepublik Deutschland, 1945–1965* (Paderborn: Schöningh, 2000). The old idea of the family as a model for an authoritarian society as a whole was extremely rare in the postwar era, and especially in the 1950s. For one late example, though, see Gustav Ermecke, *Der Familiarismus als Ordnungsidee und Ordnungsideal des sozialen Lebens* (Paderborn: Schöningh, 1947).

4. Klaus-Jörg Ruhl, *Verordnete Unterordnung. Berufstätige Frauen zwischen Wirtschaftswachstum und konservativer Ideologie in der Nachkriegszeit (1945–1963)* (Munich: R. Oldenbourg, 1994).

5. Helene Weber, "Die katholische Frau im wiederaufbau Deutschlands," in *Der Christ in der Not der Zeit. Der 72. deutsche Katholikentag* (Paderborn: Bonifacius-Druckerei, 1949), 150–153 at 152. For evolving family norms in Catholic Germany, see above all Till van Rahden, "Fatherhood, Rechristianization, and the Quest for Democracy in Postwar West Germany," *Raising Citizens in the "Century of the Child": Child-Rearing in the United States and German Central Europe in the Twentieth Century,* ed. Dirk Schumann (New York: Berghahn Books, 2010), 141–164.

6. James Chappel, "Nuclear Families in a Nuclear Age: Theorising the Family in the Federal Republic of Germany," *Contemporary European History* 26 (2017): 85–109; "Domestic Dreamworlds: Notions of Home in Post-1945 Europe," special issue of *Contemporary European History* 40, no. 2 (2005); Tara Zahra, " 'The Psychological Marshall Plan': Displacement, Gender, and Human Rights after World War II," *Central European History* 44 (2011): 37–62.

7. Hans Schmitz, "Ziel und Weg des Familienlastenausgleichs," speech given at XI. Internationalen Familientagung in Vienna, 7 September 1959, copy in Konrad Adenauer Stiftung, Bonn, Nachlaß Franz-Josef Würmeling, 01-221-020, 7, 1.

8. Paul V. Dutton, *Origins of the French Welfare State: The Struggle for Social Reform in France, 1914–1947* (New York: Cambridge University Press, 2004), 212.

9. *Forces Nouvelles* numéro special (April 1953): 1.

10. Maurice Schumann, "Le grand parti de la famille française," *Forces Nouvelles* 1 (10 February 1945): 1; "La motion générale du 1er Conseil National du Mouvement," *Forces Nouvelles* 10 (14 April 1945): 4–5.

11. Pierre Laroque quoted in Claire Duchen, *Women's Rights and Women's Lives in France, 1944–68* (New York: Routledge, 1994), 3 (103–106 provide a more thorough overview of the legislative interventions).

12. Rémi Lenoir, "Family Policy in France since 1938," in *The French Welfare State: Surviving Social and Ideological Change,* ed. John S. Ambler (New York: New York University Press, 1991), 144–186, esp. 159.

13. Quoted in Camille Robcis, *The Law of Kinship: Anthropology, Psychoanalysis, and the Family in France* (Ithaca, NY: Cornell University Press, 2013), 59.

14. Robert Prigent, *Le Prêt au marriage?* (Paris: Éditions familles de France, 1946), 7, 17–20.

15. Robcis, *The Law of Kinship,* 56–60. The term "republicanize" comes from Michel Chauvière.

16. Tessier quoted in Eric Jabbari, *Pierre Laroque and the Welfare State in Postwar France* (New York: Oxford University Press, 2012), 134; Paul Bacon, "La politique économique et sociale," in *En marche vers l'Avenir,* MRP Congress, 1949 (Strasbourg: MRP, 1949), 39–57 at 54. The party's commitment to the indepen-

dence of the *caisses* was so staunch that some viewed Pinay's decision to raid them to cover a shortfall in the social security system as, in essence, a trap. J. Fontanet, "M. Pinay a-t-il voulu partir?," *Forces Nouvelles* 28 (January 1953): 6–7.

17. Franz Ritschl, "Familienförderung im neuen Oesterreich," *Österreichische Monatshefte* 2 (1946–7): 159–161 at 160.

18. Stenographisches Protokoll, *VII. Gesetzgebungsperiode des Nationalrates (1953–1956)* (Vienna: Österreichische Staatsdruckerei, 1956), 2764–2766. The speaker here is Representative Reich of the ÖVP.

19. Erwin Altenburger, "Von der Sozialpolitik zur Gesellschaftspolitik," *20 Jahre Österreichische Volkspartei,* ed. Ludwig Reichhold (Vienna: Herder, 1965), 55–57 at 57.

20. Franz-Josef Würmeling, "Nach dem Zusammenbruch von 1945," Nachlaß Würmeling, 01–221–002 / 5, p. 1.

21. [Illegible] to Franz-Josef Würmeling, 10 January 1938; SS-Sturmbannführer [illegible] to Franz-Josef Würmeling, 17 February 1938, Nachlaß Würmeling, 01–221–002 / 1; Franz-Josef Würmeling, "Zur inneren Ordnung der Familie," in *Familie Gabe und Aufgabe* (Cologne: Luthe, 1963), 15–23 at 17.

22. This quotation in Karlheinz Groebmair, "Familienzulagen durch Familien-ausgleichskassen," in *Die Familie, ihre Krise und deren Überwindung,* ed. Arbeitsgemeinschaft der Katholischen Sozialen Woche (Augsburg: Winfried-Werk, 1951), 102–113 at 108. On Würmeling's ideology, see Chappel, "Nuclear Families in a Nuclear Age," 88–95. On the influence of the 1948 conference, see Christiane Kuller, *Familienpolitik im föderativen Sozialstaat. Die Formierung eines Politikfeldes in der Bundesrepublik 1949–1975* (Munich: Oldenbourg, 2004), 125.

23. Michel Chauvière, "Entretien avec Paul Bacon, Charles Bonnet et Robert Prigent," *Cahiers du G.R.M.F.* 3 (1984): 177–89 at 178. The 1942 quotation is from Arthur Plaza, "From Christian Militants to Republican Renovators: The Third Ralliement of Catholics in Postwar France, 1944–1965" (PhD diss., New York University, 2008), 381.

24. Robert Prigent, "Perspectives et méthodes de l'action familiale," in *Famille d'aujourd'hui, situation et avenir* (Semaines Sociales de France) (Lyon: Chronique sociale de France, 1958), 399–417 at 410; Robert Prigent, "Notion moderne du couple humain uni par le mariage," in *Renouveau des idées sur la famille,* ed. Robert Prigent, cahier 18 of the Institut national d'études démographiques (Paris: Presses universitaires de France, 1954), 304–318 at 315.

25. Jacques Leclercq, *Changements de perspectives en morale conjugale* (Paris: Association du mariage chrétien, 1950), 12; *Amour,* supplement to *L'Équipe ouvrière* 35, no. 138 (January 1964); Rebecca J. Pulju, *Women and Mass Consumer Society in Postwar France* (New York: Cambridge University Press, 2011), 109.

26. Roger Pons, "Fécondité," *L'Anneau d'or* 2–4 (1945): 114–120; "Foyers sans enfants," *L'Anneau d'or* 2–4 (1945): 121–122; Caffarel quoted in Agnès Walch, *La spiritualite conjugale dans le catholicisme francais* (Paris: Éditions du Cerf, 2002), 433–434.

27. Henry Duméry, "De la Méthode dans les Sciences Familiales," in *Recherche de la famille*, ed. Gabriel Marcel et al. (Paris: Éditions Familiales de France, 1949), 13–26 at 16.

28. Paul Archambault, "Destin de la famille," *L'Anneau d'or* 33 (May–August 1950): 177–182 at 178.

29. Naomi Black, *Social Feminism* (Ithaca, NY: Cornell University Press, 1989), 196.

30. *La Mère, ouvrière de progrès humain* (1947), 1–2, 9, available in Centres des Archives du Féminisme, UFCS Archives, Angers 16AF400.

31. Pulju, *Women and Mass Consumer Society in Postwar France*, 47–48.

32. Alain Barrère, "La famille et l'écolution économique," in *Famille d'aujourd'hui*, 55–73 at 56–57, 72.

33. Pulju, *Women and Mass Consumer Society in Postwar France*, 33.

34. Helmut Schelsky, "'Unsere Kinder sollen es besser haben.' Eine Bestandsaufnahme der Familie in Westdeutschland," *Wort und Wahrheit* 3 (1953): 201–209; Wolfgang Schmitz, *Der Ausgleich der Familienlasten. Allgemeine Theorie und Praktische Vorschläge in Österreich*, Schriftenriehe des Institus für Sozialpolitik und Sozialreform 2 (Vienna: Carl Ueberretuer, 1954), 46; Franz Ritschl, "Familienförderung im neuen Oesterreich," *Österreichische Monatshefte* 2 (1946–1947): 159–161.

35. Grete Rehor, "Die Frau in Gesellschaft und Staat," in *Um die Seele der Frau. Die Frau von heute in pastoraler Schau*, ed. Karl Rudolf (Vienna: Herder, 1954), 68–77 at 68; Nadir Paunovic, "Was erwartet die Frau vom neuen Österreich?," *Österreichische Monatshefte* 1, no. 2 (October 1945): 21–22 at 21; Albert Mitterer, "Was ist die Frau?," in Rudolf, *Um die Seele der Frau,* 19–33 at 32; Franz M. Kapfhammer, "Die Frau als Gattin. Psychologie und Ethik des Man-Frau-Verhältnisses," in ibid., 34–43 at 34, 37.

36. Joel Davis, "Rebuilding the Soul: Churches and Religion in Bavaria, 1945–1960" (PhD diss., University of Missouri-Columbia, 2007), 385–386, on the marriage seminars; A.-M. Roguet, "Le nouveau rituel allemand du mariage," *L'Anneau d'or* 36 (1950): 397–401.

37. Josef Endres, "Die Liebe als sittliche Grundmacht," *Neue Ordnung* 1 (1946–1947): 242–262; Josef Fuchs, *Die Sexualethik des Heiligen Thomas von Aquin* (Cologne: Bachem, 1949); Ernst Michel, *Ehe. Eine Anthropologie der Geschlechtsgemeinschaft* (Stuttgart: Klett, 1948); Jakob David, S.J., "Die Kirche ist für Ehenot nicht blind," *Mann in der Zeit* 15, no. 8 (August 1964): 3. For an

especially pro-sex article, see Ingrid Bergmann, "Eheliche Pflicht oder Liebe?," *Mann in der Zeit* 10 (May 1968): 38–39.

38. Elizabeth Heineman, "The Economic Miracle in the Bedroom: Big Business and Sexual Consumption in Reconstruction West Germany," *Journal of Modern History* (2006): 846–877 at 872.

39. Coca-Cola ad in *Frau und Mutter,* April 1956, 14; Franz-Josef Würmeling, "Die Familie von heute und ihre Erziehungskraft," *Bulletin* 238 (21 December 1961): 2241–2243 at 2241.

40. Hertz Baczynski, "Konsumentenberatung und Lebenshaltung," *Österreichische Monatshefte* 13, no. 2 (February 1957): 17–19 at 17 (preface by Lola Solar); Helga Lechner, "Hauswirtschaftliche Fragen," *KFÖ Führungsblatt* 5, no. 2 (Spring 1957): 23–25 at 24.

41. Karol Wojtyła, *Love and Responsibility,* trans. H. T. Willetts (New York: Farrar, Straus and Giroux, 1981), 61; *Humanae vitae,* secs. 11, 16, available at http://w2.vatican.va/content/paul-vi/en/encyclicals/documents/hf_p-vi_enc _25071968_humanae-vitae.html. See also Fuchs, *Die Sexualethik des heiligen Thomas von Aquin*; Josef Fuchs, "Moraltheologisches zur Geburtenregelung," *Stimmen der Zeit* 170 (1961–1962): 354–371; Léon Suenens, *Love and Control: The Contemporary Problem,* 2nd ed. (Westminster, MD: Newman, 1962).

42. *Humanae vitae,* sec. 23.

43. Examples from domestic contexts will be given later, but for the Vatican and the NEI, see Pius XII quoted in Monseigneur Guerry, *La doctrine sociale de l'église. Son actualité, ses dimensions, son rayonnement* (Paris: Bonne Presse, 1957), 127; "Ein NEI-Treffen in Paris," *Union in Deutschland* 5, no. 41 (9 June 1951): 5; "Projet de Rapport de synthèse des Travaux de la Session Extraordinaire des NEI pour la Conference Economique du Mouvement Européen" (1949), in Institut für Zeitgeschichte Wien, Nachlaß Felix Hurdes, Box 366, 1.

44. *Le MRP, cet inconnu,* supplement to *MRP vous parle* 159 (April 1961): 37.

45. William Patch, *Christian Democratic Workers and the Forging of German Democracy, 1920–1980* (New York: Cambridge University Press, 2018); Isser Woloch, "Left, Right and Centre: The MRP and the Post-war Moment," *French History* 21 (2007): 85–106.

46. For France, see Philip Nord, *France's New Deal: From the Thirties to the Postwar Era* (Princeton, NJ: Princeton University Press, 2010). For Germany, see Werner Abelshauser, "The First Post-liberal Nation: Stages in the Development of Modern Corporatism in Germany," *European History Quarterly* 14 (1984): 285–318. For Austria, see Emmerich Tálos and Bernhard Kittel, "Roots of Austro-corporatism: Institutional Preconditions and Cooperation before and after 1945," in *Austro-corporatism: Past, Present, Future,* ed. Günter Bischof and Anton Pelinka (New Brunswick, NJ: Transaction, 1996), 21–52.

47. Wilhelm Reinermann, "Theodor Brauer zum Gedenken," *Soziale Ordnung* 6, no. 4 (April 1952): 2.

48. This has been done to great effect in Patch, *Christian Democratic Workers*.

49. Joseph Höffner, *Christentum und Menschenwürde* (Trier: Paulinus, 1947), 302, 283–289. For Nell-Breuning's intervention, see Oswald von Nell-Breuning to Joseph Höffner, 7 July 1946, Historisches Archiv des Erzbistum Köln, Nachlaß Joseph Höffner, NH1402.

50. Joseph Höffner, "Marktwirtschaft und Scholastik," *Rheinischer Merkur* 4, no. 18 (30 April 1949): 9.

51. On this meeting, see Erik von Kuehnelt-Leddihn, "Die Augsburger Begegnung zwischen Ordo-Liberalen und katholischen Sozialethikern," in *Perspektive 2000. Der ökonomische Humanismus im Geiste Alexander Rüstows*, ed. Lothar Bossle (Würzburg: Creator, 1987), 91–99. For another example, see *Ökonomischer Humanismus. Neoliberale Theorie, Soziale Marktwirtschaft und christliche Soziallehre* (Cologne: J. P. Bachem, 1960).

52. "Besprechung: Bundesausschuß für Sozialpolitik und Sozialausschuusse am 11.10.1952 in Königswinter," Konrad Adenauer Stiftung, 007-001-8702.

53. "Niederschrift über die konstituierende Sitzung des Bundesauschusses für Sozialpolitik der CDU in Bonn am 3.10.1951," Konrad Adenauer Stiftung, 007-001-8702, p. 2; Lünendonk, "Kurzbericht über die soziale Sicherung in England," p. 1; "Niederschrift über die Sitzung der Kommission 'Krankenversicherung' am 30.6.1954," p. 2, both in Konrad Adenauer Stiftung, 007-001-8704.

54. Norbert Trippen, *Joseph Kardinal Höffner, 1906–1987* (Paderborn: Schöningh, 2009), 1:257–270.

55. For one example, see Michael Keller to Joseph Höffner, 17 June 1949, Nachlaß Höffner, NH1401.

56. Trippen, *Joseph Kardinal Höffner*, 1:97.

57. Mark E. Spicka, *Selling the Economic Miracle: Economic Reconstruction and Politics in West Germany, 1949–1957* (New York: Berghahn, 2007), chap. 4.

58. Ibid., 185–186.

59. Trippen, *Joseph Kardinal Höffner*, 1:282.

60. Joseph Höffner, *Christliche Gesellschaftslehre* (Kevelaer: Butzon & Bercker, 1963), 78–79, 103–107.

61. Joseph Höffner, *Ausgleich der Familienlasten* (Paderborn: Bonifacius-Druckerei, 1953), 8–11.

62. Hans Achinger et al., *Neuordnung der sozialen Leistungen. Denkschrift auf Anregung des Bundeskanzlers* (Cologne: Greven, 1955), esp. 24–25.

63. Johannes Messner, *Das englische Experiment des Sozialismus* (Vienna: Tyrolia, 1954); François Perroux, "Sur la politique du plein emploi," *Economie appliquee. Archives de l'ISEA* 8 (1955): 285–306; Joseph Höffner, "Der christliche

Unternehmer in der kommenden Wirtschaftsordnung," in *Joseph Höffner (1906–1987). Soziallehre und Sozialpolitik,* ed. Karl Gabriel and Herman-Josef Große Kracht (Paderborn: Schöningh, 2006), 107–116 at 109–110; Joseph Höffner, "Die Sozialisierung der Grundstoffindustrien in der Bundesrepublik Deutschland, beurteilt nach den Grundsätzen der katholischen Soziallehre (1951)," in Gabriel and Kracht, *Joseph Höffner,* 117–127.

64. "Lettre de S.S. Pie XII à M. Charles Flory," in *La communauté nationale* (Semaines Sociales de France) (Lyon: Chronique sociale de France, 1947), 5–8 at 6–7. For an example of the MRP's early enthusiasm for nationalizations, see "Nationalisations," *Forces Nouvelles* 5 (10 March 1946): 1.

65. François Perroux, *Les comptes de la nation. Apparences et réalités dans notre comptabilité nationale* (Paris: Presses universitaires de France, 1949), 193; Charles Blondel, "Structure democratique de l'état," *Communauté Nationale et jeunesse: semaine sociale de France de Strasbourg* (Lyon: Chronique Sociale de France, 1947), 170–188; Jacques Leclercq, *Propriété et nationalisation* (Antwerp: Lux, 1946); Gay quoted in Richard Vinen, *Bourgeois Politics in France, 1945–1951* (New York: Cambridge University Press, 1995), 144.

66. Eugen Margarétha, "Die Verstaatlichung und Sozialisierung in Oesterreich," *Österreichische Monatshefte* 1 (1946): 464–470 at 470. For further statements on this issue from Austrian Christian Democrats, see the compendium in Ludwig Reichhold, *Geschichte der ÖVP* (Graz: Styria, 1975), 454–457.

67. I am grateful to Sean Forner for guidance on this theme, which will be explored in his forthcoming work.

68. For an example of Kogon's antitotalitarianism in this context, see Ernst von Schenk, ed., *Arbeiter, Manager, Kultur. Zweites Europäisches Gespräch* (Cologne: Bund, 1952), 4.

69. R. P. Tonneau quoted in Francois Villey, *Le complement familial du salaire. Étude des allocations familiales dans leurs rapports avec le salaire* (Paris: Les éditions sociales francaises, 1946), 163; Paul Bacon, *La Réforme de l'entreprise capitaliste* (Paris: Société d'éditions républicaines populaires, 1947), 3–4, 41.

70. Höffner, "Der christliche Unternehmer in der kommenden Wirtschaftsordnung," 114.

71. An excellent guide to all of this can be found in James C. Van Hook, "From Socialization to Co-determination: The US, Britain, Germany, and Public Ownership in the Ruhr, 1945–1951," *Historical Journal* 45 (2002): 153–178. On codetermination's ability to provide a common language for German workers, see William Patch, "The Legend of Compulsory Unification: The Catholic Clergy and the Revival of Trade Unionism in West Germany after the Second World War," *Journal of Modern History* 79, no. 4 (December 2007): 848–880.

72. "Die Entschliessung des 73. Deutschen Katholikentag," in *Gerechtigkeit schafft Frieden. Der 73. Deutsche Katholikentag* (Paderborn: Bonifacius, 1950), 110–18 at 114.

73. Patch, "The Legend of Compulsory Unification," 856–859.

74. Walter Dirks, "Mitbestimmung—Aktuell und mehr," *Frankfurter Hefte* 10 (1955): 346–354 at 347.

75. "Besprechung: Bundesausschuß für Sozialpolitik und Sozialausschuusse am 11.10.1952 in Königswinter"; "Niederschrift über die 2. Sitzung des Bundesausschuss für Sozialpolitik der CDU, 18.10.1951," both in Konrad Adenauer Stiftung, 007–001–8702; "Mitbestimmungsrecht—Gewerkschaften—Betriebsräte," Konrad Adenauer Stiftung, 007–001–3410; "Protokoll der Zusammenkunft vom 22. Dezember 1948 in Genf," Nachlaß Hurdes, Carton 356, Mappe Coordinationkcomitee, p. 3.

76. Joseph Höffner, "Eigentum in christlicher Sicht," in *Gerechtigkeit schafft Frieden,* 215–218 at 216.

77. For one example, see Franz Greiss to Joseph Höffner, 29 September 1949, Nachlaß Höffner, NH-1400.

78. Joseph Höffner, "Soziale Gerechtigkeit statt Sozialisierung," *Rheinischer Merkur* 6, no. 42 (12 October 1951): 4; Joseph Höffner, "Zehn Thesen zur Mitbestimmung," orig. 1949, rpt. in *Gesellschaftspolitik aus christlicher Weltverantwortung* (Münster: Regensburg, 1966), 440–442.

79. "Wirtschaftsausschuß der CDU, Rundschreiben Nr. 19 / 49, 17 November 1949," Konrad Adenauer Stiftung, 007–001–3410. For the pope's response, see Andreas Lienkamp, "Socialism out of Christian Responsibility: The German Experiment of Left Catholicism (1945–1949)," in *Left Catholicism, 1943–1955: Catholics and Society in Western Europe at the Point of Liberation,* ed. Gerd-Rainer Horn and Emmanuel Gerard (Leuven: Leuven University Press, 2001), 196–227 at 224.

80. Patch, "The Legend of Compulsory Unification," 860.

81. Jakob Kaiser, "Mehr Zusammenarbeit," *Soziale Ordnung* 5, no. 6 (May 1951): 1–2; Höffner, "Die Sozialisierung der Grundstoffindustrien," 125; Wolfgang Schroeder, *Katholizismus und Einheitsgewerkschaft. Der Streit um den DGB und der Niedergang des Sozialkatholizismus in der Bundespreublik bis 1960* (Bonn: Dietz, 1992), 137–139.

82. Kurt L. Shell, *The Transformation of Austrian Socialism* (New York: SUNY Press, 1962), 217–218; Herrick Chapman, *State Capitalism and Working-Class Radicalism in the French Aircraft Industry* (Berkeley: University of California Press, 1991), 269.

83. Ludwig Erhard, *Wohlstand für Alle* (Düsseldorf: Econ-Verlag, 1957), 118.

84. The standard account remains Hans Gunter Hockerts, *Sozialpolitische Entscheidungen im Nachkriegsdeutschland. Allierte und deutsche Sozialversi-*

cherungspolitik 1945 bis 1957 (Stuttgart: Klett-Cotta, 1980). See also, more recently, Alfred C. Mierzejewski, "Social Security Reform the German Way: The West German Pension Reform of 1957," *Journal of the Historical Society* 6 (2006): 407–442.

85. Wilfrid Schreiber, *Existenzsicherheit in der industriellen Gesellschaft* (Cologne: Bachem, 1955) 45, 28, 22, 15. On the effect on women, see Robert Moeller, *Protecting Motherhood: Women and the Family in the Politics of Postwar West Germany* (Berkeley: University of California Press, 1993), 130–134. For Erhard's view, see Mierzejewski, "Social Security Reform the German Way."

86. *Mater et magistra,* secs. 55, 57, 99, 91–92, available at http://w2.vatican.va /content/john-xxiii/en/encyclicals/documents/hf_j-xxiii_enc_15051961_mater .html.

87. *Gaudium et spes,* especially sec. 68, available at http://www.vatican.va/archive /hist_councils/ii_vatican_council/documents/vat-ii_const_19651207 _gaudium-et-spes_en.html. The story of Höffner's intervention is told in Trippen, *Joseph Kardinal Höffner,* 2:43–44.

88. Pierre Haubtmann, "Simples réflexions sur les fondements de l'intervention de l'église dans le temporel," in *Construire l'homme* (Paris: Les éditions ouvrières, 1961), 9–38; Pierre Haubtmann, *Pierre-Joseph Proudhon. Sa vie et sa pensée* (Paris: Beauchesne, 1982) (thesis defended in 1961).

89. Compare Terence Renaud, "The Jewish Question in French Catholic Theology, 1944–1965," available at http://terencerenaud.com/writings/the-jewish-question /; Richard C. Vinen, "The End of an Ideology? Right-Wing Antisemitism in France, 1944–1970," *Historical Journal* 37 (1994): 365–388.

90. Gérard Cholvy et al., *La France religious, 1945–1975. Reconstruction et crises* (Paris: Editions Privat, 2002), 81; Maria Mitchell, *The Origins of Christian Democracy: Politics and Confession in Modern Germany* (Ann Arbor: University of Michigan Press, 2012), 199 (for Adenauer); Axel Schildt, *Zwischen Abendland und Amerika. Studien zur westdeutschen Ideen-landschaft der 50er Jahre* (Munich: Oldenbourg, 1999), quotation at 78, 68–82 on the collapse of the complex of West-defending organizations more broadly.

91. Étienne Gilson, "Hitler fera-t-il notre révolution?," *Temps Présent* 9, no. 21 (12 January 45): 1, 8. For CDU discourse on the schools, including parental rights, see Mitchell, *The Origins of Christian Democracy,* 110–115; for the legal situation, see Mark Ruff, *The Battle for the Catholic Past in Germany* (New York: Cambridge University Press, 2017), chap. 2 in general, 69 on Helmut Bojunga, 83 on Saxon concordat. For the French case, see Oliver Wykes, "The Decline of Secularism in France," *Journal of Religious History* 4 (1967): 218–232; Arthur Plaza, "Paix ou guerre scolaire? Les divisions du Mouvement republicain populaire (1945–1960)," in *Politiques de la laïcité au XXème siècle* (Paris: Presses universitaires de France,

2007), 481–504. For the Austrian, see Reinhold Wagnleiter, *Coca-Colonization and the Cold War: The Cultural Mission of the United States in Austria after the Second World War* (Chapel Hill: University of North Carolina Press, 1994), chap. 6.

92. M. M. Postan, *An Economic History of Western Europe, 1945–1964* (London: Methuen, 1967), chap. 2.

93. Matthias Schmelzer, *The Hegemony of Growth: The OECD and the Making of the Economic Growth Paradigm* (New York: Cambridge University Press, 2016).

94. Overall, see Jessica Pearson-Patel, "From the Civilizing Mission to International Development: France, the United Nations, and the Politics of Family Health in Postwar Africa, 1940–1960" (PhD diss., New York University, 2013). For the Catholic story, see Giuliana Chamedes, "The Catholic Origins of Economic Development after World War II," *French Politics, Culture and Society* 33 (2015): 55–75.

95. Information on Schmitz's life comes from Wolfgang Schmitz and Helmut Wohnout, "Meine Ideen waren durch das Denken in Ordnungen geprägt," in *Demokratie und Geschichte: Jahrbuch des Karl von Vogelsang-Instituts zur Eforschung der Geschichte der christlichen Demokratie in Österreich,* ed. Helmut Wohnout (Vienna: Böhlau, 1999), 63–95.

96. Hans Schmitz, *Die berufsständische Ordnung nach der 'Quadragesimo anno'* (Vienna: Schriftenreihe des Österreichesn Heimatdienstes, 1933), 5; Monika Löscher, '... *der gesunden Vernunft nicht zuwider ... ?' Katholische Eugenik in Österreich vor 1938* (Vienna: Studienverlag, 2009), 138.

97. Theodor Pütz, "Marktmechanismus, wirtschaftliche Macht und Wirtschaftsordnung," *Jahrbuch für Sozialwissenschaft* 2 (1951): 1–20.

98. On America as the new home of Weimar, see Udi Greenberg, *The Weimar Century: German Émigrés and the Ideological Foundations of the Cold War* (Princeton, NJ: Princeton University Press, 2014).

99. For biographical information on Kummer, see Erwin Bader, *Karl Kummer. Ein Leben für die Sozialpartnerschaft* (Vienna: Institut für Sozialpolitik und Sozialreform, 1993), esp. 31. For his dissertation, see Karl Kummer, "Die Kommanditgesellschaft auf Aktien und das Führerprinzip" (Jur. diss., Universität Erlangen, 1937). On Kummer as a social politician, see interview with Josef Taus in Jorg Mählich and Robert Schediwy, eds., *Zeitzeugen und Gestalter österreichischer Wirtschaftspolitik* (Vienna: Lit, 2008), 199–224, this quotation at 204.

100. August Knoll, *Das Kapitalismus-Problem in der modernen Soziologie* (Vienna: Herold, 1953), 20.

101. Wolfgang Schmitz, *Der Ausgleich der Familienlasten. Allgemeine Theorie und Praktische Vorschläge in Österreich* (Vienna: Ueberreuter, 1954), 5, 9, 46; Helmut

Schwab, "Warum Familienlastenausgleich?," in *Im Dienste der Sozialreform. Festschrift für Karl Kummer,* ed. Anton Burghardt et al. (Vienna: Reinhold, 1965), 493–502, at 496. For an overview, see Emmerich Tálos, *Staatliche Sozialpolitik in Österreich. Rekonstruktion und Analyse* (Vienna: Verlag für Gesellschaftskritik, 1981), 340–342.

102. Oliver Rathkolb, *The Paradoxical Republic: Austria 1945–2005* (New York: Berghahn, 2010), 103.

103. "Katholiken und ÖVP," *Die Furche* 15, no. 41 (10 October 1959): 1.

104. Wolfgang Schmitz, "Die österreichische Wirtschaft an der Schwelle zur Freihandelszone," *Österreichische Monatshefte* 13, no. 12 (December 1957): 8–10; Fritz Bock, "Die europäische Integration," *Österreichische Monatshefte* 15, no. 12 (December 1959): 1–4.

105. *Der Sozialhirtenbrief der österreichischen Bischöfe* (Innsbruck: Tyrolia, 1957), 9, 44, 24, 10, 20. The text was a corporate production of the Bishops' Conference and included an extensive commentary from Bishop Rusch.

106. Peter Van Kemseke, *Towards an Era of Development: The Globalization of Socialism and Christian Democracy, 1945–1965* (Leuven: Leuven University Press, 2006), 217–220.

107. "Was wir wollen" (1958 party platform), available at http://austria-forum.org /af/AEIOU/%C3%96sterreichische_Volkspartei,_%C3%96VP/Was_Wir _Wollen_1958.

108. Spicka, *Selling the Economic Miracle.*

109. François Perroux, *Le capitalisme* (Paris: Presses universitaires de France, 1960), 131–132; Perroux, *Les comptes de la nation,* 193. For Menthon, see Laurent Ducerf, "Les démocrates chrétiens face à l'économie: Du refus affirmé à l'acceptation tempérée du libéralisme économique (années 1930–années 1950)," in *Les 'chrétiens modérés' en France et en Europe, 1870–1960,* ed. Jacques Prévotat and Jean Vavasseur-Desperriers (Paris: Septentrion, 2013), 281–290 at 284; Gustave Thibon, "Christianity and Freedom," in *Christianity and Freedom: A Symposium* (London: Hollis & Carter, 1955), 1–17 at 11; *Mouvement républicain populaire. Comte-rendu sténographique des congrès national. 10e congrès national, Lille, 27–30 mai 1954* (Paris: Fondation nationale des sciences politiques, 1954), 149; Pierre Pflimlin, *Sortir de l'Ornière. Pour une politique nationale de productivité,* supplement to *Force nouvelles* 53 (January 1954); Charles Flory, "L'expansion économique, renouvellement des problèmes sociaux," in *Les exigences humaines de l'expansion économique* (Semaines Sociales de France) (Lyon: Chronique sociale de France, 1956), 15–32 at 19.

110. Hans Schmitz, "Der soziale Gedanke im österreichen Katholizismus," in *Die soziale Verantwortung des Christen in der modernen Gesellschaft,* ed. Matthias Glatzl (Vienna: Missionsdruckerei St. Gabriel, 1958), 13–26 at 24–25;

Walter Riener, "Die soziale Fragestellung der Gegenwart," in ibid., 26–39 at 26.

111. Wolfgang Schmitz, "Die Leistung in der Wirtschaft als sittliche Pflicht," in ibid., 40–46 at 41, 45, 43–44, 45.

112. Gerhard Steger, *Christ und gesellschaftliche Verantwortung. Am Beispiel der* ibid., 1984), 123–126.

113. Anton Burghardt, "Die soziale Frage—unlösbar!," *Die Furche* 14, no. 24 (14 June 1958): 20–21.

114. Walter Riener, *Soziales Handbuch. Katholische Soziallehre und soziale Gegenwart* (Vienna: Brüder Hollinke, 1956), 108–110.

115. Wolfgang Schmitz, *Die Österreichische Wirtschafts- und Sozialpolitik* (Vienna: Herder, 1961). On Riener's reaction, see Schmitz and Wohnout, "Meine Ideen waren durch das Denken in Ordnungen geprägt," 85.

116. Herbert Husinsky, "'Entideologisierung' oder klares Bekenntnis?," *Österreichische Monatshefte* 14, no. 1 (January 1958): 8–10 at 8; Schmitz, *Die Österreichische Wirtschafts- und Sozialpolitik*, 12–13; Wolfgang Schmitz, "Eine Theorie der gesellschaftspolitischen Zielsetzungen," *Wirktschafts-politische Blätter* 6 (1950): 266–268.

117. Wolfgang Schmitz, "Kirche und Wirtshcaft. Kopernikanische Wende im II. Vatikanum," *Europäische Rundschau* 14 (1986): 55–70.

118. *Mater et magistra*, sec. 73.

119. *Populorum progressio*, secs. 76, 48–49, available at http://w2.vatican.va/content /paul-vi/en/encyclicals/documents/hf_p-vi_enc_26031967_populorum .html.

120. Emmanuel Mounier, *Feu la chrétienté* (Paris: Seuil, 1950), 11–12.

6. The Return of Heresy in the Global 1960s

1. For a lively account, see Greil Marcus, *Lipstick Traces* (Cambridge, MA: Harvard University Press, 1989), 279–322.

2. Michel Mourré, *In Spite of Blasphemy*, trans. A. W. Fielding (London: John Lehmann, 1953), 89, 112, 208.

3. For a major exception, see Gerd-Rainer Horn, *The Spirit of '68: Rebellion in Western Europe and North America, 1956–1976* (New York: Oxford University Press, 2007).

4. For reflections on this process, see Ronald Granieri, "Politics in C Minor: The CDU/CSU between Germany and Europe since the Secular Sixties," *Central European History* 42 (2009): 1–32; Martin Conway, "The Age of Christian Democracy: The Frontiers of Success and Failure," in *European Christian Democracy: Historical Legacies and Comparative Perspectives*, ed. Thomas Kselman and

Joseph Buttigieg (Notre Dame, IN: University of Notre Dame Press, 2003), 43–67.

5. The literature on religion and the 1960s is growing enormously. This summary is based on Wilhelm Damberg, *Abschied vom Milieu? Katholizismus im Bistum Münster und in den Niederlanden, 1945–1980* (Paderborn: Schöningh, 1997), 173–222; Hugh McLeod, *Religious Crisis of the Sixties* (New York: Oxford University Press, 2007); Patrick Pasture, "Christendom and the Legacy of the Sixties: Between the Secular City and the Age of Aquarius," *Revue d'histoire ecclésiastique* 99 (2004): 88–116; Mark Ruff, *The Wayward Flock: Catholic Youth in Postwar West Germany, 1945–1965* (Chapel Hill: University of North Carolina Press, 2004); Denis Pelletier, *La crise catholique: religion, société, politique en France, 1965–1978* (Paris: Payot, 2002).

6. For a few examples of this burgeoning literature, see Justin Beaumont, ed., *Faith-Based Organisations and Exclusion in European Cities* (Bristol: Policy, 2012); José Casanova, *Public Religions in the Modern World* (Chicago: University of Chicago Press, 1994); Grace Davie, *Religion in Modern Europe: A Memory Mutates* (New York: Oxford University Press, 2000); Colin Roberts, "Secularisation and the (Re)formulation of French Catholic Identity," in *Catholicism, Politics and Society in Twentieth-Century France,* ed. Kay Chadwick (Liverpool: Liverpool University Press, 2000), 47–72 at 50–51.

7. For two recent and sophisticated historical accounts, see Camille Robcis, "Catholics, the 'Theory of Gender,' and the Turn to the Human in France: A New Dreyfus Affair?," *Journal of Modern History* 87 (2015): 892–923; Kimba Allie Tichenor, *Religious Crisis and Civic Transformation: How Conflicts over Gender and Sexuality Changed the West German Catholic Church* (Lebanon, NH: Brandeis University Press, 2016).

8. John M. Kramer, "The Vatican's 'Ostpolitik,'" *Review of Politics* 42 (1980): 283–308; Philippe Chenaux, *L'église catholique et le communisme en Europe (1917–89). De Lénine à Jean-Paul II* (Paris: Cerf, 2009), chap. 8.

9. Darcie Fontaine, *Decolonizing Christianity: Religion and the End of Empire in France and Algeria* (New York: Cambridge University Press, 2016).

10. Bernard Häring, *My Witness for the Church* (Mahwah, NJ: Paulist, 1992), 20–24.

11. This distinction is drawn in John L. Allen, *Pope Benedict XVI: A Biography of Joseph Ratzinger* (London: Continuum, 2005), 32–33.

12. Bernhard Häring, *The Law of Christ: Moral Theology for Priests and Laity,* trans. Edwin G. Kaiser (Westminster, MD: Newman, 1961), 1:1, ix, 46.

13. Ibid., 3:138, 514–534. For more on these themes, see Bernhard Häring, *Macht und Ohnmacht der Religion. Religionssoziologie als Anruf* (Salzburg: Otto Müller, 1956), chap. 2.

14. Bernhard Häring, *Road to Renewal: Perspectives of Vatican II* (Staten Island, NY: Alba House, 1966), 64.

15. Häring, *My Witness for the Church*, 15.

16. Lukas Rölli-Alkemper, *Familie im Wiederaufbau. Katholizismus und bürgerliches Familienideal in der Bundesrepublik Deutschland, 1945–1965* (Paderborn: Schöningh, 2000), chap. 2; Mark Ruff, "Catholic Elites, Gender, and Unintended Consequences in the 1950s: Towards a Reinterpretation of the Role of Conservatives in the Federal Republic," in *Conflict, Catastrophe and Continuity: Essays in Modern German History*, ed. Frank Biess, Mark Roseman, and Hannah Schissler (New York: Berghahn, 2007), 252–272.

17. Häring, *The Law of Christ*, 3:268–269, 346.

18. Ibid., 280, 283, 306.

19. John T. Noonan, *Contraception* (Cambridge, MA: Belknap, 1986), 474n; Häring, *Road to Renewal*, 167.

20. Häring, *Road to Renewal*, 74.

21. Robert McClory, *Turning Point: The Inside Story of the Papal Birth Commission* (New York: Crossroads, 1995), 177.

22. Ibid., 182.

23. Quoted in Martine Sevegrand, *L'affaire Humanae vitae. L'Église catholique et la contraception* (Paris: Karthala, 2008), 158.

24. Dagmar Herzog, *Sex after Fascism: Memory and Morality in Twentieth-Century Germany* (Princeton, NJ: Princeton University Press, 2005), chap. 4.

25. Gerhard Eberts, "Das Nein aus Rom," *Mann in der Zeit* 16 (August 1968): 3–4; Johannes Gründel, "Noch nicht das letzte Wort," *Mann in der Zeit* 16 (August 1968): 18; "Zum Wohle oder auf Kosten der Frau," *Mann in der Zeit* 17 (September 1968): 42–43; *Mitten in dieser Welt. 82. Deutscher Katholikentag* (Paderborn: Bonifacius-Druckerei, 1968), 283.

26. Bernhard Häring, *Free and Faithful: An Autobiography* (Ligouri, MS: Triumph, 1998), 81.

27. Bernhard Häring, "The Encyclical Crisis," in *The Debate on Birth Control*, ed. Andrew Bauer (New York: Hawthorn, 1969), 42–60 at 43, 59.

28. "Das Konzil ist tot," *Kritischer Katholizismus* 2 (6 September 1968): 3.

29. For an overview, see McLeod, *Religious Crisis of the Sixties*, chap. 7.

30. Christian Schmidtmann, *Katholische Studierende 1945–1973. Ein Beitrag zur Kultur- und Sozialgeschichte der Bundesrepublik Deutschland* (Paderborn: Schöningh, 2005).

31. Florian Bock, *Der Fall 'Publik'. Katholische Presse in der Bundesrepublik Deutschland um 1968* (Paderborn: Schöningh, 2015).

32. Bernard Häring, *A Theology of Protest* (New York: Farrar, Straus and Giroux, 1970).

33. Dietmar Mieth, "Eine durchwachsene Bilanz. Die 'Kölner Erklärung' von 1989 und ihre Wirkungen," *Herder Korrespondenz* 63 (2009): 65–70. For an account of Catholic peace activists, see Daniel Gerster, *Friedensdialoge im kalten Krieg. Eine Geschichte der Katholiken in der Bundesrepublik 1957–1983* (New York: Campus, 2012).

34. Marie-Dominique Chenu, *La doctrine sociale de l'Église comme idéologie* (Paris: Cerf, 1979); Gundlach quoted in Benjamin Ziemann, *Encounters with Modernity: The Catholic Church in West Germany, 1945–1975* (New York: Berghahn, 2014), 80; Nell-Breuning quoted in Norbert Blüm, *Reaktion oder Reform. Wohin geht die CDU?* (Reinbek: Rohwolt, 1972), 100; Claire Toupin-Guyot, "Les Semaines Sociales et le 'Troisième home' (1962–1977)," in *Les semaines sociales de France. Cent ans d'engagement social des catholiques français, 1904–2004*, ed. Jean-Dominique Durand (Paris: Paroles et Silences, 2006), 75–88 at 78. For more on this theme, see Jean-Yves Calvet, "'L'enseignement social de l'église' en France après Vatican II," in *Le mouvement social catholique en France au XXème siècle*, ed. Denis Maugenest (Paris: Cerf, 1990), 167–188.

35. Joseph Pinard, "Paul Vignaux dans la vie syndical et politique française," in *Paul Vignaux, Citoyen et philosophe (1904–1987)*, ed. Olivier Boulnois (Turnhout: Brepols, 2013), 27–50 at 30; Jacques Maritain, *Oeuvres complètes*, ed. Cercle d'études Jacques et Raïssa Maritain (Paris: Éditions Saint-Paul, 1982–2007), 6:347–348.

36. Paul Vignaux, *De la CFTC à la CFDT* (Paris: Les Editions Ouvrières, 1980), 127; *L'Express* quoted in Arthur Plaza, "From Christian Militants to Republican Renovators: The Third Ralliement of Catholics in Postwar France, 1944–1965" (PhD diss., New York University, 2008), 203.

37. "A propos d'un discours M.R.P.," *Reconstruction* 60 (January 1953): 2–6.

38. Paul Vignaux, *Philosophy in the Middle Ages: An Introduction*, trans. E. C. Hall (New York: Meridian, 1959).

39. Georgette Berault [Vignaux], "Conscience politique et conscience religieuse," *Reconstruction* 43 (April 1957): 17–24 at 18.

40. Paul Vignaux, "Ne pas oublier la Hongrie," *Cahiers Reconstruction* 41 (February 1957): 3–7 at 5, 6. See also Madeleine Singer, *Histoire du S.G.E.N. 1937–1970. Le Syndicat général de l'Education Nationale* (Lille: Presses universitaires de Lille, 1987), 261.

41. Paul Vignaux, "Pour comprendre la CFTC" (January 1955), Archives CFDT, fonds Paul Vignaux, CP / 14, p. 6.

42. "Problèmes d'orientation de la CFTC," Archives CFDT, CP / 14 / 4, p. 12.

43. "CFTC—Dossier Évolution," CFDT Archives, Paris, CP / 14 / 4, annexe 2.

44. Quoted in Frank Georgi, *L'invention de la CFDT 1957–1970* (Paris: Les Éditions de l'Atelier, 1995), 215.

45. Eugène Decamps interviewed in *La CFDT* (Paris: Seuil, 1971), 156 (he also cited Mounier and Maritain).

46. *Gaz Elecriticté* 140 (May 1964): 4–5; Everett M. Kassalow, "The Transformation of Christian Trade Unionism in France," *Journal of Economic Issues* 8 (1974): 1–39 at 5.

47. Georgi, *L'invention de la CFDT*; Kassalow, "The Transformation of Christian Trade Unionism in France," 7–9.

48. For these quotations, see Georgi, *L'invention de la CFDT*, 491–492. For a full examination of the CFDT and 1968, see ibid., chaps. 9–10.

49. "Communique de l'Action Catholique Ouvrière," KADOC, Leuven, Archief Mouvement Mondial des Travailleurs Chrétiens (MMTC), 6.4.5 / 3.

50. "Notre Actions dans l'année écoulée 1968," Archief MMTC, 6.4.5 / 2. For the general story, see Grégory Barrau, *Le Mai 68 des catholiques* (Paris: Éditions de l'Atelier, 1998).

51. Georgi, *L'invention de la CFDT*, 452.

52. Jean Raguènes, *De mai 68 à LIP—Un dominicain au cœur des luttes* (Paris: Karthala, 2008).

53. Paul Vignaux, "Unité d'action," *Syndicalisme universitaire* 440 (12 October 1967): 3; Charles Pietri and Paul Vignaux, "13 Mai 1968," *Syndicalisme universitaire* 463 (16 May 1968): 3; "Propositions du S.G.E.N.," *Syndicalisme universitaire* 464 (13 June 1968): 19–20 at 20; Paul Vignaux, "Négocier, voter," *Syndicalisme universitaire* 465 (20 June 1968): 3. On Vignaux, *autogestion*, and 1968, see Georgi, *L'invention de la CFDT*, 491; Paul Vignaux, "La CFDT," *Contrepoint* 20 (1976): 195–205 at 203–205; Singer, *Histoire du S.G.E.N*, chap. 10.

54. R. W. Johnson, *The Long March of the French Left* (London: Macmillan, 1981), 109.

55. Jacques Julliard, *Le choix de Pascal. Entretiens avec Benoît Chantre* (Paris: Declee de Brouwer, 2003), 77–86.

56. Pierre Rosanvallon, *Democracy Past and Future,* ed. Samuel Moyn (New York: Columbia University Press, 2006), 31; Pierre Rosanvallon, *The Demands of Liberty: Civil Society in France since the Revolution,* trans. Arthur Goldhammer (Cambridge, MA: Harvard University Press, 2007).

57. Paul Vignaux, "Propos d'un catholique libéral sur la crise de l'église," *Contrepoint* 6 (1972): 95–103.

58. Gustavo Gutiérrez, *A Theology of Liberation,* trans. John Eagleson and Caridad Inda (Maryknoll, NY: Orbis Books, 1988).

59. Johannes B. Metz, *Theology of the World,* trans. William Glen-Doepel (New York: Herder and Herder, 1968); Johannes B. Metz, *Faith in History and Society: Toward a Practical Fundamental Theology,* trans. David Smith (New York: Seabury, 1980).

60. Anton Pelinka, "Friedrich Heer. Die zentrale Figure des intellektuellen Lebens der Zweiten Republik Österreich," in *Die geistige Welt des Friedrich Heer,* ed. Richard Faber and Sigurd Scheichl (Vienna: Böhlau, 2008), 11–22.

61. Friedrich Heer, "Die Wiedergeburt des katholischen Gehorsams," *Hochland* 47 (1954–1955): 497–512 at 498.

62. Friedrich Heer, "Inwieweit kann Teilhard de Chardin den christlichen Erneuerungskräften zugerechnet werden?," in *Ein neues Menschenbild?* (Munich: Rex, 1963), 41–48 at 42, 45.

63. Friedrich Heer, "Atheisten und Christen in einer Welt," in *Kirche und Zukunft*, ed. Wilfried Daim, Friedrich Heer, and August M. Knoll (Vienna: Europa-Verlag, 1963), 41–70 at 53; M. D. Chenu and Friedrich Heer, "Is the Modern World Atheist?," *Cross Currents* 11 (1961): 5–24 at 22.

64. Friedrich Heer, "Christentum ohne Anziehungskraft," in *Kritik an der Kirche*, ed. Hans Jürgen Schultz (Stuttgart: Kreuz, 1958), 34–51 at 37; Friedrich Heer, "Europas Zukunft," *Hochland* 52 (1959–1960): 482–486 at 482, 484, 485, 482.

65. Friedrich Heer, *Der Glaube des Adolf Hitler. Anatomie einer politischen Religiosität* (Munich: Bechtle, 1968), 523.

66. Friedrich Heer, *God's First Love*, trans. Geoffrey Skelton (New York: Weybright and Talley, 1970), 402.

67. Heer, "Christentum ohne Anziehungskraft," 35.

68. Friedrich Heer, "Der 30. Jänner," *Die Furche* 14, no. 5 (1 February 1958): 1–2 at 1; Evelyn Adunka, *Friedrich Heer (1916–1983). Eine intellektuelle Biographie* (Vienna: Tyrolia, 1995), 207; Anonymous [almost certainly Friedrich Heer], "Algier und Wir," *Die Furche* 16, no. 6 (6 February 1960): 1.

69. Wilfried Daim, *Der Mann der Hitler die Ideen gab* (Munich: Isar, 1958); Günther Nenning, *Anschluß an die Zukunft* (Vienna: Europa-Verlag, 1963), 135–140.

70. Mark Ruff, *The Battle for the Catholic Past in Germany, 1945–1975* (New York: Cambridge University Press, 2017), chap. 5.

71. John Connelly, *From Enemy to Brother: The Revolution in Catholic Teaching on the Jews* (Cambridge, MA: Harvard University Press, 2012).

72. Franz König, "Zusammenarbeit der Weltreligionen," in *Kardinal Franz König. Worte zur Zeit* (Vienna: Herder, 1968), 119–131; Franz König, "Islam und Christentum—Heute," in ibid., 132–151.

73. Friedrich Heer, "The Need for Confession," in *The Storm over the Deputy*, ed. Eric Bentley (New York: Grove, 1964), 166–172 at 169.

74. Friedrich Heer, "Eichmann: Gestern-heute," *Die Furche* 17, no. 50 (16 December 1961): 1.

75. Heer, *God's First Love*, 362, 392. Nenning and Daim had similar theories, but while they focused specifically on a small number of Austrian Catholic racists, Heer indicted the Church and its culture as a whole.

76. Heer, *Der Glaube des Adolf Hitler*, 12, 495.

77. Heer, *God's First Love*, 398.

78. Heer, "Die Wiedergeburt des katholischen Gehorsams," 501.

79. Chenu and Heer, "Is the Modern World Atheist?," 22.

80. Heer, *God's First Love,* 393, 394, 404.

81. Chenu and Heer, "Is the Modern World Atheist?," 15; Heer, "Atheisten und Christen in einer Welt," 61.

82. Heer, *Der Glaube des Adolf Hitler,* 599.

83. Some of these are chronicled in Massimo Faggioli, *The Rising Laity: Ecclesial Movements since Vatican II* (Mahwah, NJ: Paulist, 2016).

84. Antonio Spadaro, S.J., "A Big Heart Open to God: An Interview with Pope Francis," available at https://www.americamagazine.org/faith/2013/09/30/big -heart-open-god-interview-pope-francis; *Laudato si',* secs. 15, 162, 232, available at http://w2.vatican.va/content/francesco/en/encyclicals/documents/papa -francesco_20150524_enciclica-laudato-si.html.

Acknowledgments

The writing of a book, especially a first book, is a longer and more complicated process than most people probably imagine. This book was written over many years in many cities. Parts were written in cramped bus seats, others were mangled in the haze of the first year of parenting. And it was not written alone. Books emerge from life, and living is a communal enterprise. Despite the fiction of my lonely name on the cover, this book was only possible because, over those years, so many people granted me such an inestimable amount of intellectual and personal charity. I am happy to acknowledge at least some of them here.

The first steps toward this project took place at Haverford College, where I had the pleasure of working, above all, with Linda Gerstein. It was her tutelage, her endless knowledge, and her zest for argument that first attracted me to history. Jane Caplan and Paul Jefferson were inspiring teachers, as well. At Columbia University, I had the privilege of studying with an extraordinary group of historians. Volker Berghahn introduced me to European historiography, Mark Mazower showed me how to properly read, and Carol Gluck nursed me through a crisis of confidence. Pierre Force got me thinking about political economy and urged patience with primary sources. Victoria de Grazia and Harry Harootunian convinced me that good history can have a political conscience. The Mellon Interdisciplinary Graduate Fellows Program, despite lacking windows, provided me with unforgettable intellectual community and free printing. William McAllister has been, for so many of us, the Virgil guiding us toward a fulfilling academic and personal life. I was lucky enough to have an exceptional team of advisers, as well. Paul Hanebrink has been a model of support and friendship ever since we first met for coffee over Chesterton. Susan Pedersen, with her indefatigable intellectual energy, provides a lodestar for me and many of her other students. Her indelible example has shown me the frisson of dense archival work and institutional awareness. Above all, Samuel Moyn has been an unflagging champion of this project. He has the great gift of asking the right question: the question that seems simple but, upon reflection, is devastating (usually in a good way).

Beyond Columbia, I have been blessed to work at generous and welcoming institutions. The Society of Fellows at the University of Chicago was a model of intellectual honesty and seriousness. At Duke University, I have had the privilege of joining an intellectually adventurous department—one that gave me the energy and space I needed to complete this book. Dirk Bönker, Malachi Hacohen, Anna Krylova, Martin Miller, Simon Partner, and Susan Thorne, above all, have shared their time and expertise with me. Claudia Koonz was kind enough to stuff my mailbox with fascinating finds from her own past projects. John Martin and Sumathi Ramaswamy have been exemplary chairs, while Edward Balleisen, Sally Deutsch, Bruce Hall, Reeve Huston, and Phil Stern especially have made me feel welcome. I have had numerous opportunities to present portions of this work in the Triangle: at the Triangle Intellectual History Seminar, the North Carolina German Studies Seminar, and a Franklin Humanities Institute Book Workshop. Through these venues, I received excellent advice from Luke Bretherton, Karen Hagemann, Konrad Jarausch, Anthony LaVopa, Emily Levine, Sylvia Miller, William Reddy, K. Steven Vincent, and others. My writing group has been a constant source of insight and support, so I am grateful to Nicole Barnes, Eli Meyerhoff, Jecca Namakkal, Gabe Rosenberg, and Matt Whitt.

The arguments in this book gestated slowly over the years, thanks to the colleagues mentioned and the ones I met in the many other venues in which this book was presented. The following individuals provided indispensable forums and commentary: Marco Duranti, Katherine Fleming, Stefanos Geroulanos, Peter Gordon, Jochen Hellbeck, Rajesh Heynickx, Nitzan Lebovic, Jan-Werner Müller, Philip Nord, Till van Rahden, Camille Robcis, Daniel Steinmetz-Jenkins, Todd Weir, and Larry Wolff. Martin Conway and William Patch generously agreed to attend my book workshop, and the comments they gave me then and in the years since have done a great deal to shape the book. Carlo Invernizzi Accetti, in his inimitable way, pushed me to recognize my own dogmatism. In the last stages of writing, a series of conversations with Elizabeth Shakman Hurd, Brannon Ingram, Mark Ruff, and Judith Surkis helped me to give the argument its final shape.

Writing a book is both a personal and an intellectual journey. I was lucky to undertake this project with a group of like-minded scholars working on similar topics. In addition to some of those already named, Rosario Forlenza, Denis Kitzinger, Aline-Florence Manent, Florian Michel, Sarah Shortall, and Borja Villalonga have provided constant insights, both through their own work and their commentary on my own. Giuliana Chamedes, Udi Greenberg, Piotr Kosicki, and Matthew Mesick read significant portions of the manuscript and gave crucial feedback. While they might not agree with everything that remains, the book is much better for it. Noah Strote and Stephen Milder have been sources of wit, fraternity, and intellectual exchange. In New York, in the perilous late stages of graduate education, I had the good fortune of living alongside Adam Bronson, Buyun Chen, Isabel Gabel, Eric Held, Andrew Liu, Mary Maddox, Matilda Mock, Olivia Moreton, Michael Neuss, Eileen Ryan, Alex Sears, Matthew Siblo, Simon Taylor, Cheyenna Weber, and Matthew Weinstein. My students at Columbia, the University of Chicago, and Duke pushed me to clarity and reminded me why I was drawn to academia in the first place. In Durham, I have found a community and a home, most crucially at the Durham Friends Meeting. I am grateful as well to Kayla Fuller, Jenn June, Patricia Roberts, Kathie Stephens, Courtney Steves, and Monica Turner. Felix Czmok, Jillian Slaight, and Victoria Zurita provided invaluable research assistance.

This book is a product of a great deal of institutional support. I have had a wonderful experience with Harvard University Press. Joyce Seltzer believed in this project and has done a great deal to shape the final product. Kathleen Drummy, Michael Higgins, Melody Negron, and Stephanie Vyce helped steer it to completion. I have also received research funding from the Franklin Humanities Institute, the New York Consortium for Intellectual and Cultural History, Columbia's Graduate School of Arts and Sciences, the Social Science Research Council, the American Theological Librarianship Society, the Council for European Studies, and the German Academic Exchange Service. Like any researcher, I am indebted to many librarians and archivists, some of whom I never met. I did intensive work on this project at the libraries of Columbia University, the University of Chicago, and Duke University, along with the Bayerische Staatsbibliothek and the Bibliothèque nationale de France. I also visited about twenty archives in six countries. In lieu of listing them all here, I will simply say that the archivists, like the librarians, were a constant source of friendly concern and intellectual probity. Books like this are only possible because so many people have made it their life's work to catalog and store the materials that provide their scaffolding. I have also been lucky to be aided by dedicated university staff, including Jamie Hardy, Cynthia Hoglen, Ruebe Holmes, Sharee Nash, and Beth Monique Perry.

This is largely a book about faith and family. However much I might wrestle with the former, the latter has been a constant source of stability and love. My grandparents have provided a sense of my own history—especially the original James Chappel, who also read and commented on this manuscript. My parents, Joanne and Gary Chappel, have supported me in more ways than I can know, as have Becky, Matt, Charlotte, Shannon, and Jon. My wife, Bethany, has been an editor and a confidante. I could not have written this without her. During the final stages of its writing, our son Oscar was born. While his intellectual contributions have been minimal, he has buoyed me with hope: the rarest of emotions, especially for academics and especially in 2017. If Christianity is right about anything, it is that a firstborn son can change the world. This book is for him.

Index